Grades K–3

Activity Math

Using
Manipulatives
in the
Classroom

Anne M. Bloomer
Phyllis A. T. Carlson

Addison-Wesley Publishing Company
Menlo Park, California • Reading, Massachusetts • New York
Don Mills, Ontario • Wokingham, England • Amsterdam • Bonn
Sydney • Singapore • Tokyo • Madrid • San Juan • Paris
Seoul, Korea • Milan • Mexico City • Taipei, Taiwan

This book is dedicated to all those students who inspired us to create these lessons and who helped us refine them. Without them, the book would never have been written! A special dedication to Mrs. B's fourth grade class, who wanted all their names listed, but said they would settle for one line.

A sincere thank you to Roger Carlson and Joseph Bloomer, who gave us continuous encouragement and help. Thanks to Steven Carlson, who contributed art ideas. We are grateful to the entire staff at Excelsior School, Minnesota, who have been a constant source of support. Our thanks also go to Stuart Brewster, Michael Kane, and Mali Apple of Addison-Wesley Innovative Division for their expertise and belief in the project.

We appreciate the assistance of the following teachers who critiqued and piloted lessons: Jan Birkholz, Mark Broten, Kris Grimstad, Sara Lovelace, Nancy Maas, Pam Orr, Eileen Poul, Joan Rogers, and Sharon Thompson.

Managing Editor: Michael Kane
Project Editor: Mali Apple
Production: Karen Edmonds
Design: Vicki Philp
Cover Art: Rachel Gage

ISBN 0-201-45505-6

4 5 6 7 8 9 10- ML-97 96 95 94 93

Contents

Symbol Key

■   Manipulative introduction of a key skill or subskill.

☐   Procedure includes writing. Reinforcement of a concept at a connecting or more abstract level.

Introduction

The National Council of Teachers of Mathematics (NCTM) made specific recommendations in the *Curriculum and Evaluation Stantards for School Mathematics*. One recommendation was to increase the use of manipulative materials.

The use of manipulatives enhances concept formation when both the concrete and connecting stages are fully understood before moving to the abstract. This way of instructing students promotes understanding of the "why" as well as the "how" of mathematics. The fundamental concepts developed in this way enable the student to build on "old" knowledge and adapt it to new tasks and situations.

Although many books about using manipulatives have been written, most cover one particular material and its uses. Teachers, however, need to teach the skills covered in their texts, and it is often too time-consuming to check each book to see which might apply to the current skill.

We therefore developed skill-based lessons that include several kinds of appropriate manipulatives for each skill and that are easily adaptable to any text. Since activities are for both concrete and connecting levels, these lessons provide ample opportunity for students to see relationships and to develop understanding, along with a high level of confidence. This multi-sensory way of instruction is ideal for students of all abilities. Cooperative learning is also a key element.

Lessons cover most skills. Some skills and materials, however, such as calculators, that are usually covered adequately in regular textbooks are not treated in this book, as it is intended to be supplemental to a basal math program.

Lessons are divided into the following strands:

1. Number Skills
2. Place Value
3. Addition
4. Subtraction
5. Multiplication
6. Division
7. Fractions
8. Decimals
9. Geometry
10. Measurement

Book features include

1. Scope and Sequence with sub-skills and appropriate grade levels listed
2. Lessons correlated with NCTM Standards
3. Section on making and using manipulatives
4. Materials needed listed by grade level
5. Reproducible pages
6. Lessons organized by strands—specific lessons easily found

7. Perforated pages, punched for a binder
8. Labels for strand and chapter dividers

Lessons are written in a step-by-step way to make the teacher's initial job easier. Features include

1. Skill, boxed near the top of the page
2. Key sub-skills identified
3. Approximate time
4. Materials, listed and explained
5. Anticipatory Set—motivating introductory activities
6. At least two manipulatives for each skill
7. Identification of, and procedures for, both concrete and connecting stages
8. Practice and Extension—activities tying skills to problem solving and real-life uses.

Rationale for Using Manipulatives

Putting Theory into Practice

Children construct, test, and change ideas as they integrate them into their structure of understanding. As they explore and interact with their environment, they build understanding at the concrete, then the semiconcrete or representational level, and finally at the abstract level. Appropriate experiences need to be provided to facilitate each stage of this process. Merely providing blocks to work with—the concrete level—will not necessarily ensure that a student will be able to multiply a 3-digit number by a 1-digit number on paper.

Doris H. Gluck (*Arithmetic Teacher*, vol. 138, no. 7 [March, 1991], p. 13) offers the following paradigm for helping students make connections between the concrete and the abstract:

> Blocks
> Blocks and teacher writes
> Blocks and student partner writes
> Blocks and write
> Writing only
> Repeat with another physical model

We urge you never to shorten the connecting stage of both using materials and writing the process at the same time. Otherwise, many students will never make the connection between the concrete and abstract. They will have built few bridges. Even if they have learned the sequence of steps in an algorithm, they may not be able to use this knowledge in a meaningful way.

The use of manipulatives not only aids with specific skills, but helps students discover the connections between operations and different areas of mathematics. We have included such connections in our lessons, tying new skills to previously experienced ones. Students who have made these connections using manipulatives, especially when these are presented in a problem-solving or real-life format, will know better which operation to use in solving a new problem. They can often work out an answer even if their paper-and-pencil skills are still at a lower level.

Communication

Because of students' natural interest in using materials and discovering new ideas, working with manipulatives leads to discussion, whether you want it or not! Since communication about math is important as students construct, evaluate, and integrate their ideas, each lesson includes opportunities for discussion. You can guide students toward fuller understanding by using such questions as the following reprinted with permission from *Professional Standards for Teaching Mathematics*, copyright 1991 by the National Council of Teachers of Mathematics.

- Helping students work together to make sense of mathematics

  "What do others think about what Janine said?"
  "Do you agree? Disagree?"
  "Does anyone else have the same answer but a different way to explain it?"
  "Would you ask the rest of the class that question?"
  "Do you understand what they are saying?"
  "Can you convince the rest of us that that makes sense?"

- Helping students to rely more on themselves to determine whether something is mathematically correct

  "Why do you think that?"
  "Why is that true?"
  "How did you reach that conclusion?"
  "Does that make sense?"
  "Can you make a model to show that?"

- Helping students learn to reason mathematically

  "Does that always work?"
  "Is that true for all cases?"
  "Can you think of a counterexample?"
  "How could you prove that?"
  "What assumptions are you making?"

- Helping students learn to conjecture, invent, and solve problems

  "What would happen if . . . ? What if not?"
  "Do you see a pattern?"
  "What are some possibilities here?"
  "Can you predict the next one? What about the last one?"
  "How did you think about the problem?"
  "What decision do you think he should make?"
  "What is alike and what is different about your method of solution and hers?"

- Helping students to connect mathematics, its ideas, and its applications

  "How does this relate to . . . ?"
  "What ideas that we have learned before were useful in solving this problem?"
  "Have we ever solved a problem like this one before?"
  "What uses of mathematics did you find in the newspaper last night?"
  "Can you give me an example of . . . ?"

Students also need to communicate about math in writing. Journals are a good way to do this, helping students integrate their knowledge and you to assess their understanding. Some possible topics for journal entries:

- what I learned in class today
- what helped me understand it
- why would it be important to know it

Even just asking "Why?" after student responses is a good way to begin to improve communication. Eliciting answers and conjectures from the class, instead of giving them yourself, guides you in assessing understanding, increases students' confidence, and helps students think of themselves as sources of knowledge. Be prepared for new directions and ideas!

Assessment

We as teachers want to prepare students to reason, problem solve, make connections, and communicate about mathematics, yet we must also prepare them for standardized tests consisting mostly of computation, with one or two word problems. We are often held accountable for those test results.

We also assess students and ourselves daily in order to create tasks, guide students' thinking, pace the lessons, and evaluate the day's procedures. We give tests, assign written work, observe small groups, interview students one on one, watch them work, ask questions, and evaluate class discussion.

Some concerns have arisen that students taught from a manipulative base do not test well. Our students have been very successful on standardized tests. We teach from a manipulative base and use the basal for worksheets, assignments, and tests. Often, we do not assign anything until students have worked with the manipulatives for several days and have connected writing with the concrete activities. It is a mistake to go to the abstract, written-only problems too soon.

If you have taught all three steps, students will have an appropriate knowledge of the abstract symbols and how they connect to the concrete. They also will have more tools for problem solving.

When students work with manipulatives, daily assessment of their progress is made easier. You can quickly see whose blocks are not positioned correctly and who is slow at starting. Students can see what others are doing and by comparison evaluate their own activities and understanding.

Because you can see students' mistakes, they can be caught early, and you can guide students' exploration or to use questions to suggest a different tack. Thus, the chance is less that a student will do every homework problem wrong. In going over written work, ask what would be happening with the blocks. Often students will catch their own errors, since the written algorithm closely corresponds to the concrete.

Staff Development

Most elementary teachers have heard about the above-mentioned Standards and wish to improve their teaching but are unsure how to do so. Pre-service teachers also need to know the best methods of presentation.

Standard 4: Knowing Mathematical Pedagogy

The pre-service and continuing education of teachers of mathematics should develop teachers' knowledge of and ability to use and evaluate—

- instructional materials and resources, including technology;
- ways to represent mathematics concepts and procedures;
- instructional strategies and classroom organizational models;
- ways to promote discourse and foster a sense of mathematical community;
- means for assessing student understanding of mathematics.

(Reprinted with permission from *Professional Standards for Teaching Mathematics*, copyright 1991 by the National Council of Teachers of Mathematics.)

Teachers need to focus on creating learning environments that encourage students' questions and deliberations—environments in which the students and teacher are engaged with one another's thinking and function as members of a mathematical community. In such a community, the teacher-student and student-student interaction provides teachers with opportunities for diagnosis and guidance and for modeling mathematical thinking, while, at the same time, it provides students with opportunities to challenge and defend their constructions. (Reprinted with permission from *Professional Standards for Teaching Mathematics*.)

Teachers have to develop a structure to identify, assess, and use appropriate mathematical instructional materials. This structure should be developed from the teacher's knowledge of basic mathematical concepts, a recognition of what information is necessary for each specific skill, as well as an understanding of the connections between concrete, visual, graphical, and symbolic representations of those skills. It should include the knowledge of different ways to present these representations for each mathematical skill and

task. This book provides some ways to help teachers with their development of this internal structure; it is aimed at helping teachers learn about a variety of concrete materials and a range of ways to use them to explain different mathematical concepts. The book also focuses on how to make the connections between the concrete and more abstract representations understandable for the students.

Because this book is tied to the Standards, it makes an ideal basis for in-service or pre-service presentations. Teachers involved in hands-on doing of the lessons become more confident in using the materials and instructional techniques. By working through several skills within a strand and its related strands, they can see both the abstract and concrete connections between operations.

Practicing teachers are bound by the curriculum of their district and by the time constraints inherent in their work. Consequently, although they want to leave a workshop or class with ideas leading to improved instruction, they also want those ideas to translate easily into improved, usable lessons.

Group activities promote communication and even greater understanding. Having groups of teachers solve or propose problems, find more tie-ins to real-life math or extensions to other curricular areas, can help them develop practical ideas. They can write notes within each lesson, thereby making it more probable that what is learned in in-service training will affect what is taught to the students.

How to Use This Book

Don't Panic—Start Here

For many of us teachers the Standards are exciting yet overwhelming. How can we balance the desire to implement a new approach with the need to cover the growing curriculum, assess with prescribed tests, stay within a tight schedule, write meaningful comments on student papers, and all the rest? We need support, time, and the kind of knowledge that easily translates into actual lessons.

By no means does this book explain completely how to teach mathematics well. It focuses on the use of manipulatives as one tool for helping students construct meaningful understandings of mathematics. It offers a start—a way for teachers to become comfortable with new ways of presenting material.

Time is short. Manipulative and inquiry lessons take longer, both initially and because you need to include the connecting stage. You may fear you will never cover the curriculum or that students will not have the written skills to pass the required tests. Halfway through the year, you may start to get that familiar feeling of panic. We know it happens because we've been there.

An interesting thing happens, however, as the skills become more difficult. Because of the groundwork done earlier in the year, students often see new skills as a "free ride" (Bohan, Harry, "Mathematical Connections: Free Rides for Kids," *Arithmetic Teacher*, vol. 38, no. 3 [November, 1990], pp. 10-14.), something they can figure out because they already know how a particular operation works. Because they often see advanced lessons as requiring not new skills but logical extensions of what they have already learned, they begin to grasp concepts more quickly. Therefore, subsequent skill acquisition occurs at a much faster pace.

Using Lessons

Pick what looks interesting to you. Geometry and measurement are easy areas to begin with, using selected lessons. If, however, you begin to teach an operation such as subtraction using manipulatives, students will do better if you teach all subtraction that way. This helps the students draw the necessary connections. Manipulating place value blocks for 1 hour during the year won't be very effective in helping students understand subtraction problems.

You also need to keep to the sequence of skills within a strand. Keeping to the sequence gives students the steps of understanding they will need to construct a coherent whole. The Scope and Sequence section lists sub-skills for each lesson, and these are also identified within lessons by the symbol ■.

We also often extend skills as we are teaching them. If students have learned to add 2-digit numbers, they are delighted to find they can add numbers in the millions the same way, especially if they do it in the hallway on large sheets of paper taped to the walls. They are proud that they can do this feat.

Students need to see math both as something that works in the real world and as an abstractness. They need to know that 2 + 3 equals 5 not just with buttons, but also with fingers, etc. The symbols stand for the buttons and the ideas. We allow students to use physical materials for as long as they want. As connections are made, students come to see that it is easier and faster to work with just the symbols and that the symbols can then be used to solve problems it would be difficult to set up physically. The procedures that include activities at the connecting level are marked with the symbol □.

We have tied the written algorithms directly to the manipulation of the materials since math language only represents what happens in the real world. Consequently, look carefully at the illustrations showing the written algorithm in each lesson. Changes are suggested to assist students in making this connection. Division, especially, is a change, but students learn it more quickly and are more adept at error analysis since they can tie it to what was happening with the blocks.

The lessons are more directed than perhaps is desirable; the eventual goal is an inquiry-type lesson. Again, we offer a start. For those teachers accustomed to teaching from a manual, for new or pre-service teachers, the script is there. You may feel just as comfortable reading through it ahead of time and presenting it on your own. You know best what kinds of problems and scenarios appeal to your students. It may be that dividing sheep just doesn't engage them as much as anteaters dividing up an ant nest, or aliens dividing their toes to fit into shoes before they land.

As you use each lesson, we suggest that you mark it with the chapter and page numbers of the corresponding section of your textbook, and that you file the lessons by chapters. For a new basal, you can easily refile the lessons. Earlier lessons, good to use as antecedent skills, can be placed at the beginning of the appropriate chapter. Resource room teachers may prefer to keep the lessons organized by strands since they usually teach more than one grade level.

Parent Involvement

Parents are interested in helping their children succeed in school, but many have their own anxieties about assisting with written math homework. Try sending students home with materials, such as laminated place value mats, and the assignment to teach their parents how it is done at school. One student taught multiplication with peas and french fries! Whole families have become involved in finding hundred board patterns. Some parents say they have understood written multiplication and division for the first time.

The Practice and Extension section in each lesson offers games, activities, challenges, and tie-ins with real-life uses of math. These also are good ways to have students and parents work together. You might suggest some of the activities if you send newsletters home with your students. Another good resource is *Family Math* (Jean Kerr Stenmark, Virginia Thompson, and Ruth Cossey, the Regents, University of California, Berkeley, California, 1986).

Parents often are willing to donate materials such as frozen dinner plasticware, buttons, and items for treasure boxes. They also can be asked to help make place value mats of file folders or to cut bills for students use. Reproducibles have directions for both of these.

Other materials to cut out or make are number lines to have on hand, pattern blocks, geoboards, fraction bars, bills, decimal bars, and coins. See the Manipulative Information section for directions on making these and more.

Reproducibles good to send home include

counter-trading boards:
    play games with materials found at home

blank matrix:
    fill in to 100, or to 1000 by 10s and look for patterns

matrix for facts:
    fill in facts for fact practice
    look for patterns

addition/subtraction table or multiplication/division table:
- patterns
- fact practice
- multiples and skip counting

pattern block sheets:
- fraction practice and games
- geometry—angles, polygons
- patterns

Multiplication Clue Rhymes:
- practice facts, students and parents can invent more

Multiplication Aids 1 and 2:
- finger math for multiplication

Number Find Samples 1 and 2:
- use also for addition and subtraction by covering every third line of numbers

bills (imitation paper money):
- make change
- games with dice for skill practice

decimal bars example sheet:
- color in decimal amounts and play matching or other games

geoboard paper:
- laminate and send home with markers for multiplication, fractions, and geometry

The benefits to this kind of homework are more than skill reinforcement. Students learn as they teach and are proud to show off their skills. Parents feel more comfortable helping with math and are pleased to be offered a low-stress way to become involved with their children's education.

Working with Manipulatives

General

Read the Manipulative Information section for ideas on specific materials; you will find that many are available in your school or classroom already.

Set up general rules for using manipulatives with the class at the beginning of the year. Each time a new material is introduced, discuss its safe use and where it will be kept in the classroom. Allow students time to play with any new manipulative. In their play, they will learn some of its properties.

Materials are manageable! Be aware that it is initially more time consuming to teach using manipulatives. It may seem to take twice as long to teach a lesson, and you may feel you will be unable to cover the year's objectives. But, you *can* cover the objectives, and you will be pleased with the final results.

Plan to use more than one manipulative to teach and practice each skill. Students are at different stages in constructing their understanding of mathematics. The use of a new tool will help them re-evaluate this understanding and will often provide some connections for those students whose grasp of skills is tenuous.

A final word about manipulatives and math anxiety. We don't allow students to say "I don't get it," but have them say, "I don't *quite* get it *yet*." This creates an expectation and trust in the students that they *will* understand the material. They know

- it will be presented in several ways, with several different manipulatives;
- it's all right if they don't understand well at first;
- they can use the manipulatives for as long as they feel a need to; and
- they have a teacher, each other, and their previous experience to draw on for help.

Their comfort and confidence levels increase, and the amount of math anxiety decreases.

Storage and Day-to-Day Use

Collections of materials are used more often if they are accessible. Use permanent storage containers for each type of manipulative, with both lid and container marked to indicate the contents. Try

- coffee cans
- envelopes in a shoe box
- ice-cream buckets with lids
- margarine tubs with lids
- frozen dinner plasticware
- cardboard pencil boxes
- plastic and cardboard sweater and shoe boxes

For day-to-day use, have enough microwave or other plasticware trays or tubs for each child. Materials can be counted out just once into the trays. The filled trays can be stacked for easy distribution and collection each day. Materials are then also available if students want to use them at other times.

When students have to share, keep materials for each group in reclosable freezer bags. Use a holepunch to punch a hole in the bags so that the bags will lie flat. Label with a permanent marker, or include an inventory list in each bag to help keep materials in place.

Using the Overhead Projector and Transparencies

Commercial manipulative sets for the overhead are available, although most manipulatives silhouette nicely. When color is important or the real materials are larger than you wish, use the reproducibles, either as-is or reduced in size, to make heavyweight transparencies. Draw others by hand on heavy acetate, color with a permanent marker, and cut out.

Buy colored transparency pens and a spray bottle. Write on transparencies or the glass itself, spray with water, and wipe off with paper towels. You can mark patterns in different colors, write numbers beside manipulatives, etc. Three-hole punch your transparencies, and keep them in a three-ring notebook with a punched sheet of plain paper behind each one. Use dividers to sort by categories to help you quickly find what you want.

Choose the reproducibles appropriate for your grade level. The following are useful as transparencies: blank matrix, counter-trading boards, geoboard paper, graph paper, hundred boards, matrix for facts, number lines, moon stations, and place value mats.

Manipulative Information

What is it? What can I use in its place? How can I make it?

In this section are listed descriptions, alternatives, and directions for making the materials used in the lessons. See the grade level charts for lists of materials you will need and the strands in which they are used. Plan to have enough for at least every two students. Some commercial sources are listed at the end of the section.

Not everyone can afford to buy commercial materials. Try garage sales, thrift stores, and asking for donations from parents and commercial businesses. Ask parents to help make materials. If you do make your own, use sturdy materials. It is relatively inexpensive to have a printer run off your master patterns on card stock, which comes in bright colors. For laminating, try using clear self-adhesive paper. If you chill it in the freezer before using, it is easier to work with. The Education Center, Inc., offers a non-heat laminating dispenser and film that work very well and give a nicer result than obtained with self-adhesive paper.

Attribute blocks

Sets for the primary level vary in shape, color, and size: triangles, rectangles, circles, squares, and sometimes hexagons, each in several colors and a variety of sizes. Loops or circles are available to aid in sorting by attribute. Traditional, more advanced sets vary in shape, color, size, and thickness. Links are also available that vary in shape, size, and color. To make your own attribute sets, see "Paper shapes."

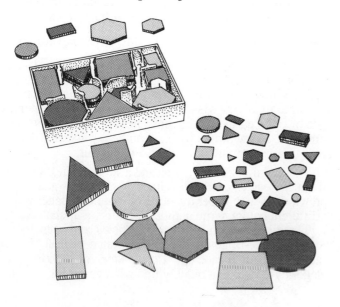

Chalkboards, individual

Available commercially. Use dark-colored poster board or railroad board cut to approximately 9" × 12". Use old cotton socks for erasing. Store socks in coffee cans or shoe boxes, with a piece of chalk in each sock.

Containers

The best ones stack for easy storage. Many are available commercially.

> bowls
> egg cartons
> frozen dinner, microwave plasticware
> juice cans
> half-pint milk cartons from school lunches
> margarine tubs

Counters

Commercial ones are available in all shapes, sizes, and colors. Some are one color on one side and another on the second. Transparent ones may also be used on the overhead.

If you get different colors, you can use them as counter-trading materials. You can spray-paint your own materials.

> beads
> beans
> buttons
> construction paper—small squares
> craft sticks
> paper clips
> poker chips
> washers

Counter-trading materials

A place value board with places marked with colors instead of values so that it can be adapted to various bases. Available commercially as chip-trading materials. Use with chips or counters (see above) to match the colors. See Reproducibles for boards.

Cubes, non interlocking

Commercially available in various sizes, in one color or many. Some 1 cm cubes have a mass of exactly 1 g, which is nice for measurement. See "Interlocking cubes and things" for cubes that snap together.

Cuisenaire® rods

Ten different-colored proportional lengths, representing 1 through 10. The one cube is a cubic centimeter. You could also use strips of colored graph paper.

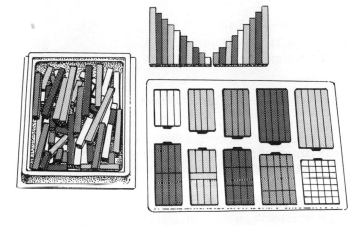

Decimals

We do not advise revaluing the place value materials for decimals. If a one is made the size of a hundred flat, many students will not understand the relationship of a tenth to one. Available commercially are decimal stamps and Decimal Squares, which are cards marked with a variety of decimals amounts.

Decimal bars

See Reproducibles for these bars, which are marked with decimal divisions and match paper money bills in size. Duplicate 25 of each per student in the same color as the U.S. paper money. You can also fill in various amounts with a marker, duplicate, and laminate. Make a transparency, and color it in with pen. See Reproducibles for file-folder place value mats with decimal extensions.

Decimals—graph paper

Cut ½" graph paper into 10 × 10 squares and label: 1. Cut 1 × 10 strips and label: ¹/₁₀ = 0.1. Cut 1 × 1 squares and label: ¹/₁₀₀ = 0.01. A sheet and a half of paper will make 3 ones, 23 tenths, and over 20 hundredths; laminate first to make a permanent set. Use grains of rice for thousandths—about ten cover a hundredth square, thereby preserving the size relationships. Store in envelopes.

Dice

Available in several sizes and colors, blank or with numbers. Mark blank dice with a marker or with stick-on dots. Try the fuzzy ones intended to be hung in cars.

Foam rubber dice: Use a long, narrow strip of foam rubber as wide as it is thick—1" to 3". Cut it into cubes with a single-edge razor blade, and mark dots or numbers with a permanent marker. Sponge dice: Use dense sponges. Cut with a knife, and mark with a permanent marker.

Fractions

Many kinds are available: bars, circles, squares, ones that stack, cards, and tiles.

> Cuisenaire® rods
> felt fraction bars
> paper fraction bars (see below)
> paper plate fraction circles

Fraction bars—paper

Use 3" × 18" strips of construction paper: red, blue, orange, green, and yellow, one of each color per student. The red piece is left as the whole unit. Have students fold the blue strip in half, crease the fold well, and cut on the line to make two halves. The orange strip makes fourths: first fold and cut into halves, then fold and cut each half to make fourths. Continue in the same way, making the green strip into eighths and the yellow into sixteenths. Store in a business-size envelope, folding the red strip to fit. For a set extending to eighths or less, 3" × 12" strips can be used. Use as above for fractions wanted.

Geoboards

Available in 8" or 10" sizes, with a 5 × 5 pin arrangement. Rubber bands in different colors fit around the pins. Some can be used side by side for a larger number of pins, and some have pins in a circle on the back. See Reproducibles for geoboard paper, which can be substituted. If paper is laminated, students can use markers.

To make your own boards, which can be grouped together, use rubber cement to temporarily attach graph paper of appropriate size (see Reproducibles for 1" graph paper) to boards for marking nail arrangement. Pound in 25 finishing or round-top nails for each board at the marked points. Try to have all nails extending to the same height.

> 5" board: nails 1" apart, ½" margins
> 7½" boards: nails 1½" apart, ¾" margins
> 10" board: nails 2" apart, 1" margins
> circles: mark center and every 30° or less around the circle

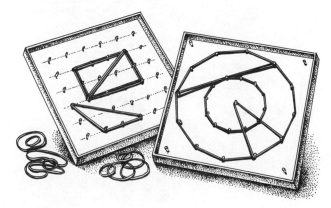

Geometric solids

Sets are available in wood, foam, or plastic, with varying pieces per set. Also available are plastic shapes that link together to construct both polyhedra and two-dimensional shapes.

cones—ice-cream cones, thread cones (available at some fabric stores)

cylinders—toilet paper rolls, oatmeal boxes

triangular prisms—put three sharp creases in a toilet paper roll; some candies are triangular prisms

rectangular prisms—cereal boxes, etc.

sphere—marbles, balls, oranges, shapes made from clay, paper mâché, etc.

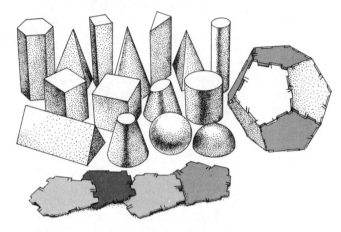

Interlocking cubes and things

Interlocking cubes snap together and are available in many colors and in sizes starting at 1 cm. Larger sizes are better for primary grades. Unifix® cubes join in a straight line; Multilinks™ connect on all six sides. The cubes can be formed into rods or sticks. Some sets include interlocking prisms, which are good for teaching spatial awareness. Shapes other than cubes (e.g., plastic links, 1 ½" pliable links) can link together to make chains.

paper clips (largest size available)

tiles or colored graph paper squares, laid end to end

Measurement—materials to measure

Water is messy but interesting, because 1 L of water has a mass of 1 kg. Students enjoy discovering that fact. Provide towels or rags.

beans
O-shaped cereal
pasta, especially the colored kind
popcorn, popped and unpopped
rice

Measurement—sets of containers

Have some containers that are of glass or clear plastic. You at least need clear measuring cups. Canning or jelly jars are alternatives. Use a permanent pen to make a line all the way around the containers to mark the desired capacities. You will need identical containers for demonstrating relationships among units.

Cup measures:

½-pint milk cartons with tops cut off
8-oz paper cups

Pint measures:

pint half-and-half cartons with tops cut off
pint jars

Quart measures:

quart milk cartons
plastic soda bottles with tops cut off and edges taped
quart jars

Gallon measures:

pails
two ½-gallon cartons taped together
gallon milk containers

Money—bills

Play money is available. See Reproducibles for our bills, $1 to $100,000. Run off back-to-back for two-sided bills. Use different colors for different denominations, starting with green for $1. Bills fit on file-folder place value mats (see Reproducibles) and work also with decimal bars (see Reproducibles).

Money—coins

Available as coins and stamps. Use coin stamps on tag board, then cut the board first into squares.

counters—designate colors as amounts
washers—spray-paint them

Number cards

Use blank index cards to make 2" × 3" (cut 4" × 6" cards) cards with numbers on them. Use for number identification, 1-to-1 correspondence, problem solving, and working with equations.

Number-and-dot cards

Use blank 4" × 6" index cards to make a teacher set. Students write numbers 1 to 9 with a marker of one color on 3" × 5" or 4" × 3" (cut 4" × 6" cards) cards. Students make dots on the cards with a marker of another, dark color.

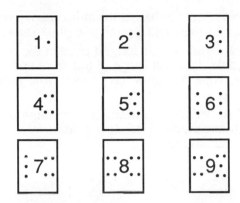

Number line on the floor

Commercial ones have numbers on squares about 6" to 8" on each side.

> floor tiles—write numbers with markers
> carpet squares—pin or tape on numbers

Number line—Secret Code

A long banner 6"–9" wide, divided into squares numbered 1–100, one number per square. Put high on the wall or cut into groups of ten squares and use as a large hundred board. It's a good idea to make this and put it up before the first day of school.

> bulletin board or chart paper cut and colored
> computer banners, colored with markers
> large number cards, colored with markers

Numbers are coded:

> multiples of 2: red heart, upper left corner
> multiples of 5: blue square lower right corner
> multiples of 10: green diagonal line
> odd numbers: brown
> even numbers: black

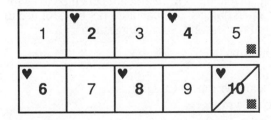

Paper shapes

Use construction paper or colored card stock. Cut triangles, circles, and squares in three or four sizes, each in three or four colors. Laminate first for permanence.

Pattern blocks

Very useful sets of six different-shaped blocks that relate to each other; e.g., six triangles cover a hexagon. See Reproducibles for full-size patterns and color descriptions. If you must substitute, reproduce on the heaviest paper possible, print on colored card stock, or use as templates to cut out cardboard ones. A paper cutter works well. Hope for a parent with a jigsaw who will cut some from thin wood painted the appropriate colors!

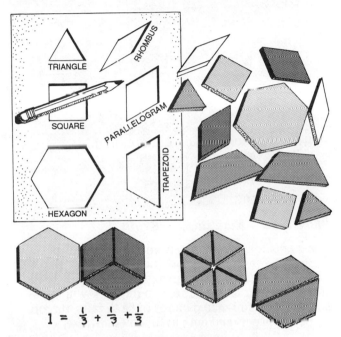

$$1 = \frac{1}{3} + \frac{1}{3} + \frac{1}{3}$$

Place value and base ten materials

Place value materials are extremely useful, and we suggest you have a small set available for the overhead as well. Commercial block sets are three-dimensional, based on a cubic centimeter one cube. Ten rods are marked to show the divisions into cubes. Hundred flats are marked as well. Hollow, cardboard thousands cubes that hold ten hundred flats each are less expensive than wood or plastic. Some sets link together so that students can build larger amounts. Sticks are for bundling into tens and hundreds. See illustration on the following page.

If you make your own place value sets from paper, laminating the paper before cutting it is a good idea. Counters can be used to represent 1000s. Allow 20–25 ones and tens, and 10–12 hundreds per student set.

> buttons or beans for 1s, craft sticks for 10s
> computer paper borders—for 1s, 10s
> counter-trading materials—see Counter-trading
> Cuisenaire® rods for 1s and 10s
> interlocking cubes—for 1s, 10s
> masking tape folded back on itself—cut squares for 1s, rectangles for 10s
> milk carton, ½ gallon—slice off the top, turn upside down for 1000s cube

Place value—bean sticks and rafts

Use beans for ones. Use ten small lima beans per craft stick for tens. Glue on, then cover with glue. For a 100-bean raft to use as an example, glue ten bean sticks together and reinforce on the back with cross sticks. Draw full-size pictures of bean rafts, run off on heavy paper, and cut out for students' use.

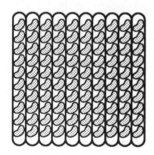

Place value—graph paper

Follow cutting directions for "Decimals—graph paper." Label 10 × 10 square as 100; 1 × 10 bar as 10; and 1 × 1 square as 1. Store in envelopes.

Plastic links: see "Interlocking cubes and things"

Tangrams

A seven-piece puzzle set that fits together to make a large square. To make your own, start with a 5" × 5" square of construction paper. Fold from corner to corner into a triangle shape. Lick the fold and tear. You now have triangle A and triangle B.

Triangle A: fold and tear into two smaller triangles. Set aside. These are the large triangles.

Triangle B: fold the top point down to the midpoint of the base. Check that you have a triangle and a trapezoid. Lick and tear. Set triangle aside. This is the medium triangle.

Trapezoid: fold in half, a vertical fold from midpoint of base to midpoint of top. You now have smaller trapezoids C and D.

Trapezoid C: fold in half at the midpoint of the base. You have a square and a small triangle. Lick and tear.

Small trapezoid D: with longest point of the base to the left, fold right-hand edge of trapezoid up to lie along top edge. You now have a small triangle and a parallelogram. Lick and tear.

Total: 1 square, 2 small triangles, 1 medium triangle, 2 large triangles, and 1 parallelogram.

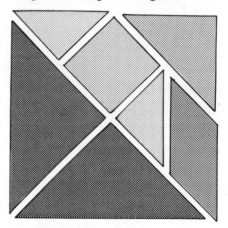

Tiles

Available in wood or plastic in various colors. To make your own from paper, color if necessary, laminate, and cut with a paper cutter.

1" × 1" ceramic tiles left over from tile stores
1" × 1" construction paper, tag board, or card stock squares
1" × 1" graph paper squares (see Reproducibles)

Treasure boxes

Collections of many small objects that are in the same category but have differences can be assembled. Send notes to parents early in the fall, asking them to help collect such items. Fill cardboard pencil boxes with these small objects, one category per box, for use in many of the lessons. Some suggestions:

buttons
keys
candy wrappers (at Halloween)
gum wrappers
shells
beans—various kinds
old jewelry
business cards
pasta—various kinds

Where can I find it?

Catalogs are numerous. Listed are some we have found particularly useful. Teacher stores are another source and often have their own catalogs, which may be quite complete.

Creative Publications. Many materials and resources. Separate catalog of primary-level material as well.

> 5040 West 111th Street
> Oak Lawn, IL 60453-9941
> 1-800-624-0822

Cuisenaire Company of America, Inc. Many resources and materials, some with free teacher guides.

> 12 Church St., Box D
> New Rochelle, NY 10802
> (914) 235-0900
> 1-800-237-3142

Dale Seymour Publications. Materials, many teacher resources, and posters.

> P.O. Box 10888
> Palo Alto, CA 94303-0879
> outside California: 1-800-USA-1100
> in California: 1-800-ABC-0766

Delta Education, Inc. Many manipulatives and teacher guides.

> P.O. Box 915
> Hudson, NH 03051-0915
> outside New Hampshire: 1-800-258-1302
> in New Hampshire: call collect 889-8899

Didax, Inc. Materials, games, and resources.

> One Centennial Drive
> Peabody, MA 01960
> (508) 532-9060
> 1-800-458-0024

The Education Center, Inc. Non-heat laminating dispenser and film for do-it-yourself laminating. Construction materials, games.

> 1607 Battleground Ave.
> P.O. Box 9753
> Greensboro, NC 27429
> 1-800-334-0298

Educational Teaching Aids (ETA). Many different manipulatives.

> 620 Lakeview Parkway
> Vernon Hills, IL 60061
> (708) 816-5050
> 1-800-445-5985

Lakeshore Learning Materials. Infant through elementary. Manipulatives, some resources.

> 2695 Dominguez St.
> P.O. Box 6261
> Carson, CA 90749
> (213) 537-8600
> 1-800-421-5354

Summit Learning, Inc. Materials and resources.

> P.O. Box 493
> Ft. Collins, CO 80522
> 1-800-777-8817

Reprinted with permission from *Curriculum and Evaluation Standards for School Mathematics*, copyright 1989 by the National Council of Teachers of Mathematics.

Standard 1: Mathematics as Problem Solving

In grades K–4, the study of mathematics should emphasize problem solving so that students can:

- use problem-solving approaches to investigate and understand mathematical content;
- formulate problems from everyday and mathematical situations;
- develop and apply strategies to solve a wide variety of problems;
- verify and interpret results with respect to the original problem;
- acquire confidence in using mathematics meaningfully.

Standard 2: Mathematics as Communication

In grades K–4, the study of mathematics should include numerous opportunities for communication so that students can:

- relate physical materials, pictures, and diagrams to mathematical ideas;
- reflect on and clarify their thinking about mathematical ideas and situations;
- relate their everyday language to mathematical language and symbols;
- realize that representing, discussing, reading, writing, and listening to mathematics are a vital part of learning and using mathematics.

Standard 3: Mathematics as Reasoning

In grades K–4, the study of mathematics should emphasize reasoning so that students can:

- draw logical conclusions about mathematics;
- use models, known facts, properties, and relationships to explain their thinking;
- justify their answers and solution processes;
- use patterns and relationships to analyze mathematical situations;
- believe that mathematics makes sense.

Standard 4: Mathematical Connections

In grades K–4, the study of mathematics should include opportunities to make connections so that students can:

- link conceptual and procedural knowledge;
- relate various representations of concepts or procedures to one another;
- recognize relationships among different topics in mathematics;
- use mathematics in other curriculum areas;
- use mathematics in their daily lives.

Standard 5: Estimation

In grades K–4, the curriculum should include estimations so that students can:

- explore estimation strategies;
- recognize when an estimate is appropriate;
- determine the reasonableness of results;
- apply estimation in working with quantities, measurement, computation, and problem solving.

Standard 6: Number Sense and Numeration

In grades K–4, the mathematics curriculum should include whole number concepts and skills so that students can:

- construct number meanings through real-world experiences and the use of physical materials;
- understand our numeration system by relating counting, grouping, and place-value concepts;
- develop number sense;
- interpret the multiple uses of numbers encountered in the real world.

Standard 7: Concepts of Whole Number Operations

In grades K–4, the mathematics curriculum should include concepts of addition, subtraction, multiplication, and division of whole numbers so that students can:

- develop meaning for the operations by modeling and discussing a rich variety of problem situations;
- relate the mathematical language and symbolism of operations to problem situations and informal language;
- recognize that a wide variety of problem structures can be represented by a single operation;
- develop operation sense.

Standard 8: Whole Number Computation

In grades K–4, the mathematics curriculum should develop whole number computation so that students can:

- model, explain, and develop reasonable proficiency with basic facts and algorithms;
- use a variety of mental computation and estimation techniques;

- use calculators in appropriate computational situations;
- select and use computation techniques appropriate to specific problems and determine whether results are reasonable.

Standard 9: Geometry and Spatial Sense

In grades K–4, the mathematics curriculum should include two- and three-dimensional geometry so that students can:

- describe, model, draw, and classify shapes;
- investigate and predict the results of combining, subdividing, and changing shapes;
- develop spatial sense;
- relate geometric ideas to number and measurement ideas;
- recognize and appreciate geometry in their world.

Standard 10: Measurement

In grades K–4, the mathematics curriculum should include measurement so that students can:

- understand the attributes of length, capacity, weight, area, volume, mass, time, temperature, and angle;
- develop the process of measuring and concepts related to units of measurement;
- make and use estimates of measurement;
- make and use measurements in problem and everyday situations.

Standard 11: Statistics and Probability

In grades K–4, the mathematics curriculum should include experiences with data analysis and probability so that students can:

- collect, organize, and describe data;
- construct, read, and interpret displays of data;
- formulate and solve problems that involve collecting and analyzing data;
- explore concepts of chance.

Standard 12: Fractions and Decimals

In grades K–4, the mathematics curriculum should include fractions and decimals so that students can:

- develop concepts of fractions, mixed numbers, and decimals;
- develop number sense for fractions and decimals;
- use models to relate fractions to decimals and to find equivalent fractions;
- use models to explore operations on fractions and decimals;
- apply fractions and decimals to problem situations.

Standard 13: Patterns and Relationships

In grades K–4, the mathematics curriculum should include the study of patterns and relationships so that students can:

- recognize, describe, extend, and create a wide variety of patterns;
- represent and describe mathematical relationships;
- explore the use of variables and open sentences to express relationships.

Scope and Sequence

Number Skills

	K	1	2	3

1. Establish number sequence
    to 10
    to 20
    to 50
    to 100
	•	•	•	

2. Classify by likenesses or differences	•	•		
3. Classify by position and positional relationships		•	•	

4. Classify by shape and size
    by shape
    by size
	•	•	•	

5. Classify by kind and use
    by kind
    by use
	•	•	•	

6. 1-to-1 correspondence
    to 10
    to 20
	•	•	•	

7. Patterns in objects: shape, size, color, position
    one attribute
    two attributes
    positional changes
	•	•	•	•

8. Identify numbers missing from a sequence: after, between, before
    after, between
    before
    skip counting
		•	•	

9. Ordinal numbers through 30th
    to 5th
    to 10th
    to 20th
    to 30th
	•	•	•	

10. One more and one less
    one more
    one less
	•	•	•	

11. Compare numbers through 10
    understand <, >, ≠
    number sentences
	•	•	•	

12. Count by 10s
    to 100
    estimate by 10s
		•	•	•

13. Count by 5s
    to 25
    to 50
    to 100
	•	•	•	

14. Count by 2s
    to 40
    to 100
	•	•	•	

15. Count by 100s				•

	K	1	2	3
16. Odd and even numbers		•	•	•

17. Patterns in number sequence: addition or subtraction in the rule
    addition in the rule
    subtraction in the rule
    graphing sequences
			•	•

18. Patterns in number sequence: multiplication or division in the rule
    multiplication in the rule
    division in the rule
    graphing sequences
				•

Place Value

	K	1	2	3

1. Place value through 19
    to 10
    to 19
	•	•	•	

2. Place value through 99
    regrouping
    expanded notation
		•	•	•

3. Compare numbers through 99		•	•	•
4. Place value through 999			•	•
5. Compare numbers through 999				•

6. Place value through 9,999
    regrouping and expanded notation
    compare numbers through 9,999
				•

7. Place value through 99,999				•
8. Round to the nearest 10 and $10				•
9. Round to the nearest 100 and $100				•
Note: Round to the nearest $1; see Decimals Skill #5.				

Addition

	K	1	2	3

1. Concrete addition: understand the symbols + and =
    symbol meaning
    count to reach a sum
	•	•	•	

2. Addition facts and fact families to 9 (horizontal form)		•	•	

3. Add zero
    understand zero
    use zero
		•	•	

4. Addition facts to 9 (vertical form)		•	•	

5. Addition facts to 18
    horizontal form
    vertical form
		•	•	•

	K	1	2	3

6. Addition facts: doubles and near doubles
    doubles
    doubles +1
    doubles −1
		•	•	•

7. Addition facts: missing addends
    recognize missing numbers
    count up to find missing numbers
    use subtraction to find missing numbers
		•	•	•

8. Sums to 18: more than two addends		•	•	•
9. Add tens		•	•	•
10. Add 2-digit numbers: sums to 99		•	•	•
11. Add 2-digit numbers: sums above 99			•	•
12. Add 2-digit numbers: more than two addends			•	•

13. Add 3-digit numbers
    with regrouping, no zeros
    with regrouping, with zeros
    mixed digit addends
			•	•

Note: Add with money; see Decimals Skills #3 and #4.				

Subtraction

	K	1	2	3
1. Concrete subtraction: understand the symbol −	•	•	•	

2. Count backward and identify one less
    count backward
    one less
	•	•	•	

3. Subtraction facts
    from 9 or less
    from 12 or less
    from 18 or less
		•	•	•

4. Fact families
    to 6 or less
    to 18 or less
    number sentences
    check subtraction with addition
		•	•	•

5. Subtraction facts: doubles and near doubles
    doubles
    doubles +1
    doubles −1
		•	•	•

6. Subtraction facts: missing numbers		•	•	•

7. Subtract tens
    from 10s
    from 2-digit numbers
		•	•	•

8. Subtract 2-digit numbers and check with addition
    no regrouping
    with regrouping
    1 digit subtrahends
		•	•	•

ACTIVITY MATH

	K	1	2	3
9. Subtract 3-digit numbers: no zeros, check with addition			•	•
10. Subtract 3-digit and larger numbers: regroup both 10s and 100s across zero			•	•

11. Subtract from 3-digit numbers: 1- or 2-digit subtrahends
    no regrouping, no zeros
    with regrouping, with zeros
				•

Note: Subtract with money; see Decimals Skills #3 and #4.				

Multiplication

	K	1	2	3
1. Concept of multiplication using serial addition			•	•
2. Multiplication facts: products to 12			•	•
3. Multiplication facts: products to 25				•

4. Commutative property of multiplication
    multiplication chart
    fact families
    prove equalities
				•

5. Multiplication facts: products to 81				•

6. Relationship of multiplication to division
    recognize relationship
    missing factors
				•

7. Multiples of 10: multiply 10s by 1-digit numbers
    multiples of 10
    multiply 10 by 1-digit numbers
    multiply multiples of 10 by 1-digit numbers, no regrouping
    multiply multiples of 10 by 1-digit numbers, with regrouping
    traditional algorithm
				•

8. Multiply with more than two factors				•

9. Multiply 2-digit numbers by 1-digit numbers
    partial products
    traditional algorithm
				•

10. Multiply 100s by 1-digit numbers
    partial products
    traditional algorithm
				•

11. Multiply 3-digit numbers by 1-digit numbers
    partial products
    traditional algorithm
				•

Division

	K	1	2	3
1. Division concepts: sharing and repeated subtraction				•

2. Division facts
    divide with two kinds of objects, no regrouping
    divide with two kinds of objects, with regrouping
    divide with base ten materials
				•

3. Multiplication and division fact families: relate division to multiplication				•

	K	1	2	3

4. Divide a number by itself, divide by 1, and divide zero
    divide a number by itself
    divide by 1
    divide zero
				•

5. Use multiplication to check division				•

6. Missing dividends and divisors
    missing dividends
    missing divisors
				•

7. Divide 2-digit numbers by 1-digit numbers
    no regrouping
    with regrouping, 2-digit quotients
    with regrouping, 1-digit quotients
    zeros in the quotient
				•

Fractions

	K	1	2	3

1. Understand halves, thirds, and fourths
    equal parts
    written form
    relate size of the whole to size of the fraction
	•	•	•	•

2. Understand and write fractions
    identify fractions
    different fractions of a whole
    fractions equal to 1 and 0
    find a fraction of a number
		•	•	•

3. Compare fractions
    like denominators, same-size whole
    like denominators, different-size wholes
    unlike denominators
				•

4. Find equivalent fractions
    use equivalency chart
    use multiplication
				•

5. Order fractions
    like denominators
    unlike denominators
				•

6. Add and subtract fractions: like denominators				•
Note: Relate fractions to decimals; see Decimals Skill #1.				

Decimals

	K	1	2	3

1. Relate fractions to decimals: recognize and order tenths
    relate fraction tenths to decimal tenths and place value
    relate decimals to fractions equivalent to tenths
    order tenths
    order fractions and decimal tenths
				•

2. Add and subtract tenths
    add tenths
    subtract tenths
				•

	K	1	2	3

3. Add and subtract money: amounts to $1.00
    recognize coins and values; make equivalent amounts
    add money using place value
    subtract money using place value
	•	•	•	•

4. Add and subtract money: amounts above $1.00
    add money
    subtract money
			•	•

5. Round decimals to the nearest whole number
    round tenths
    round to the nearest $1.00
				•

Geometry

	K	1	2	3

1. Patterns in geometric shapes: two and three dimensions
    attribute patterns
    positional change patterns
    building-on patterns
    relate numbers to patterns
    three-dimensional patterns
				•

2. Understand and classify angles
    understand angles
    90°
    30° and 45°
				•

3. Understand and find perimeter
    understand perimeter
    relate perimeter and area
    find formula for the perimeter of rectangles
		•	•	•

4. Define polygons				•

5. Find lines of symmetry
    understand symmetry
    multiple lines of symmetry
		•	•	•

6. Understand and find area
    area with whole units
    area with half units
				•

7. Find area: rectangles
    find formula for the area of rectangles
    area of squares
    area of shapes of more than one rectangle
				•

8. Classify solid figures
    understand face, edge, and vertex
    classify solid figures
    three-dimensional spatial visualization
				•

9. Understand congruence and similarity
    congruence
    similarity
    scale
				•

Note: Volume; see Measurement Skill #11.				

Measurement

	K	1	2	3

1. Pre-skills for measurement: length, weight, and capacity
  length
  weight
  capacity
	•	•	•	•

2. Measure length by inches, feet, and yards
  inches
  measure to the nearest inch
  feet
  yards
		•	•	•

3. Change one unit of length to another: inches, feet, and yards
  change larger to smaller units
  change smaller to larger units
  compute using mixed measurements
				•

4. Measure length by centimeters and meters
  centimeters
  meters
		•	•	•

5. Change one unit of length to another: centimeters and meters
  change larger to smaller units
  change smaller to larger units
  compute using mixed measurements
				•

6. Understand capacity: cups, pints, quarts, and gallons
  cups, pints, quarts, and gallons
  change one unit to another
  compute using mixed capacities
		•	•	•

7. Understand capacity: liters and milliliters
  liters
  milliliters
  change one unit to another
  compute using mixed capacities
		•	•	•

8. Measure temperature and read thermometers
  measure temperature
  find changes in temperature
		•	•	•

9. Understand pounds and ounces
  pounds
  ounces
  change one unit to another
  compute using mixed weights
		•	•	•

10. Understand kilograms and grams
  kilograms
  grams
  change one unit to another
  compute using mixed masses
		•	•	•

11. Measure volume
  understand volume
  measure volume
  find formula for the volume of a rectangular prism
				•

Note: Area and perimeter measurement; see Geometry Skills #3, #6, and #7.				

	1	2	3	4	5	6	7	8	9	10	11	12	13
Number Skills 1		•	•	•		•							•
Number Skills 2		•	•						•		•		•
Number Skills 3	•	•	•	•		•			•		•		•
Number Skills 4	•		•						•		•		•
Number Skills 5	•		•			•					•		•
Number Skills 6	•	•	•	•	•	•					•		•
Number Skills 7	•		•						•				•
Number Skills 8	•	•	•	•		•							•
Number Skills 9		•		•		•							•
Number Skills 10	•	•	•	•		•	•	•					•
Number Skills 11	•	•	•	•		•	•						•
Number Skills 12	•	•	•	•	•	•	•	•	•				•
Number Skills 13	•	•	•	•		•	•	•	•		•		•
Number Skills 14	•	•	•	•		•	•	•	•		•		•
Number Skills 15	•	•	•	•		•	•	•	•				•
Number Skills 16	•	•	•	•		•		•			•		•
Number Skills 17	•	•	•	•		•	•	•	•		•		•
Number Skills 18	•	•	•	•		•	•	•	•		•		•
Place Value 1	•	•	•			•							
Place Value 2		•	•			•							•
Place Value 3	•	•	•	•		•							•
Place Value 4		•	•	•		•		•					•
Place Value 5		•	•	•		•							•
Place Value 6	•	•	•	•		•	•				•		•
Place Value 7		•	•			•							•
Place Value 8	•	•		•	•	•		•					•
Place Value 9	•	•		•	•	•		•					•
Addition 1		•	•	•		•	•	•					•
Addition 2	•	•	•	•		•	•	•					•
Addition 3	•	•	•	•		•	•	•			•		•
Addition 4	•	•	•	•		•	•	•					•
Addition 5		•	•	•		•	•	•					•

	1	2	3	4	5	6	7	8	9	10	11	12	13
Addition 6	•	•	•	•		•	•	•					•
Addition 7	•	•	•	•		•	•	•					•
Addition 8	•	•	•	•	•	•	•	•					
Addition 9	•	•	•	•		•	•	•					•
Addition 10	•	•	•	•	•	•	•	•					•
Addition 11	•	•	•	•	•	•	•	•					•
Addition 12	•	•	•	•	•	•	•	•					•
Addition 13	•	•	•	•	•	•	•	•					•
Subtraction 1	•	•	•	•		•	•	•					•
Subtraction 2		•	•	•		•	•	•					•
Subtraction 3	•	•	•	•		•	•	•					•
Subtraction 4	•	•	•	•		•	•	•					•
Subtraction 5		•	•	•	•	•	•	•					•
Subtraction 6	•	•	•	•		•	•	•					•
Subtraction 7	•	•	•	•		•	•	•					•
Subtraction 8	•	•	•	•	•	•	•	•					•
Subtraction 9		•	•	•		•	•	•					•
Subtraction 10	•	•	•	•		•	•	•					•
Subtraction 11		•	•	•		•	•	•					•
Multiplication 1	•	•	•	•		•	•	•					•
Multiplication 2		•	•	•		•	•	•					•
Multiplication 3	•	•	•	•		•	•	•					•
Multiplication 4		•	•	•		•	•	•	•		•		•
Multiplication 5		•	•	•		•	•	•	•				•
Multiplication 6	•	•	•	•	•	•	•	•	•		•		•
Multiplication 7	•	•	•	•	•	•	•	•					•
Multiplication 8	•	•	•	•		•	•	•	•				
Multiplication 9	•	•	•	•	•	•	•	•					
Multiplication 10	•	•	•	•	•	•	•	•					
Multiplication 11	•	•	•	•	•	•	•	•					
Division 1	•	•	•	•		•	•	•	•		•		•
Division 2	•	•	•	•		•	•	•			•		•
Division 3		•	•	•		•	•	•	•		•		•
Division 4	•	•	•	•		•	•	•					•

	1	2	3	4	5	6	7	8	9	10	11	12	13
Division 5	•	•	•	•		•	•	•	•				•
Division 6	•	•	•	•	•	•	•	•	•				•
Division 7	•	•	•	•		•	•	•			•		•
Fractions 1	•	•	•	•					•			•	
Fractions 2	•	•	•	•					•		•	•	•
Fractions 3		•	•	•					•		•	•	•
Fractions 4		•	•	•					•		•	•	•
Fractions 5	•	•	•	•							•	•	•
Fractions 6	•	•	•	•					•			•	•
Decimals 1	•	•	•	•					•			•	•
Decimals 2	•	•	•	•						•	•	•	
Decimals 3	•	•	•	•	•							•	
Decimals 4	•	•	•	•	•							•	
Decimals 5	•	•	•	•	•							•	
Geometry 1	•	•	•	•		•		•	•		•		•
Geometry 2		•	•	•				•	•	•			
Geometry 3	•	•	•	•		•		•	•	•	•		•
Geometry 4	•	•	•						•		•		•
Geometry 5	•	•	•						•				•
Geometry 6	•	•	•	•	•	•	•	•	•	•	•	•	•
Geometry 7	•	•	•	•		•		•	•	•	•		•
Geometry 8	•	•	•	•					•		•		•
Geometry 9	•		•					•	•	•		•	•
Measurement 1		•	•		•	•				•	•		
Measurement 2		•	•	•	•	•		•	•	•	•		
Measurement 3	•	•	•	•	•	•		•		•	•		•
Measurement 4		•	•	•	•	•		•	•	•	•		
Measurement 5	•	•	•	•	•	•		•		•	•		•
Measurement 6	•	•	•	•	•	•		•		•	•		•
Measurement 7	•	•	•	•	•	•		•		•	•		•
Measurement 8		•	•	•	•	•		•		•	•		
Measurement 9		•	•	•	•	•		•		•	•		•
Measurement 10		•	•	•	•	•		•		•	•		•
Measurement 11	•	•	•	•	•	•		•	•	•	•		•

Many materials may be purchased through catalogs and at teacher stores. You will need at least enough for student pairs; catalogs will have guidelines for sets. We have also listed many alternatives in the Manipulative Information section. Many materials, such as cards, dice, and counters, also can be used for the Practice and Extension activities in a variety of strands.

R: a Reproducible for this

R/lam: a Reproducible for this; we suggest laminating it back to back with another Reproducible for permanence.

S: student-made materials, generally from Reproducibles

Kindergarten

	Number Skills	Place Value	Addition	Subtraction	Multiplication	Division	Fractions	Decimals	Geometry	Measurement
attribute blocks	•									
balance scale—1 or more										•
beads and string	•			•						
coins—1¢, 5¢, 10¢	•	•						•		
containers—small, for general use	•			•						•
counters, various colors—20 or more/student	•			•						
craft sticks on which beans have been glued	•									
cubes—1 cm (good to have larger sizes as well); 20 or more/student	•									
Cuisenaire® rods	•									•
decks of cards—1/pair; at least 1 teacher deck	•									
dice—1 set/pair	•							•		
dot-to-dot pictures for reproducing	•									
geoboards—1/student or pair							•			
graph paper—½" or larger (1"— R)	•						•			
index cards—1 package for teacher	•		•							
interlocking cubes	•			•			•			•
number cards, or number-and-dot cards—large teacher set	•		•	•						
objects—small, collections of various kinds, some similar (e.g., buttons, beans, tiles); 20 or more/student	•		•	•					•	•
other place value materials—(see Manip. Info. section for suggestions) 1 set/student or pair		•								
paper shapes—(see Manip. Info. section) 1 set/pair or group	•									
pattern blocks	•									
place value materials to 10s—1 set/student or pair	•	•								
plastic links	•									
scales—a variety of types										•

	Number Skills	Place Value	Addition	Subtraction	Multiplication	Division	Fractions	Decimals	Geometry	Measurement
Secret Code number line—(see Manip. Info. section)	•									
symbol cards—large teacher set	•				•			•		
treasure boxes—(see Manip. Info. section) 1/group	•		•	•						•
S—number-and-dot cards made from index cards; 10/student	•		•	•						
S—symbol cards made from index cards; 10/student	•			•				•		
R/lam—hundred boards; 1/student	•									

Grade 1

	Number Skills	Place Value	Addition	Subtraction	Multiplication	Division	Fractions	Decimals	Geometry	Measurement
attribute blocks	•									
balance scale—1 or more										•
beads and string	•			•						
blank dice—2 pairs				•						
coins—all values	•	•		•				•		
containers—small, for general use	•		•	•				•		•
counters, various colors—20 or more/student	•	•	•	•			•	•		•
counter-trading materials to 100s—1 set/student or pair			•	•						
craft sticks on which beans have been glued	•									
cubes—1 cm (good to have larger sizes as well); 20 or more/student	•		•	•						
Cuisenaire® rods	•									•
decks of cards—1/pair; at least 1 teacher deck	•	•	•							
dice—1 set/pair	•	•	•	•				•		
dominoes—1 set/group	•									
dot-to-dot pictures for reproducing	•									
egg cartons—1/student				•						
geoboards—1/student or pair							•		•	
graph paper—¼", ½", 1"—R; 1 cm—R	•	•	•	•			•		•	•
index cards—1 package for teacher	•	•	•							
interlocking cubes	•		•	•			•			•
letter cards—large teacher set	•									
measurement sets for capacity, weight—1 or more										•
number cards, or number-and-dot cards—large teacher set	•		•	•						

	Number Skills	Place Value	Addition	Subtraction	Multiplication	Division	Fractions	Decimals	Geometry	Measurement
objects—small, collections of various kinds, some similar (e.g., buttons, beans, tiles); 20 or more/student	•		•	•			•	•		•
other place value materials—see (Manip. Info. section for suggestions) 1 set/student or pair		•	•	•						
paper shapes—(see Manip. Info. section) 1 set/pair or group	•									
pattern blocks	•						•		•	
place value materials to 100s—1 set/student or pair	•	•	•	•						•
plastic links	•			•						
scales—a variety of types										•
Secret Code number line—(see Manip. Info. section)	•									
symbol cards—large teacher set	•		•	•				•		
tangrams—1 set/student or pair									•	
thermometer—1/pair or group										•
tiles—20 or more/student									•	
tracing paper—2 or more pads	•									
treasure boxes—(see Manip. Info. section) 1/group	•		•	•						•
S—bills to $10 (see Manip. Info. section for amounts)		•						•		
S—fraction bars; 1 set/student							•			
S—number-and-dot cards made from index cards; 10/student	•		•	•						
S—symbol cards made from index cards; 5/student	•		•	•				•		
R/lam—counter-trading boards to 1000s; 1/student or pair			•	•						
R/lam—hundred boards; 1/student	•		•	•						
R/lam—place value mats to 100s; 1/student or pair	•	•	•	•				•		

Grade 2

	Number Skills	Place Value	Addition	Subtraction	Multiplication	Division	Fractions	Decimals	Geometry	Measurement
adding-machine tape—1 roll		•			•					
attribute blocks	•									
balance scale—1 or more										•
beads and string	•			•	•					
blank dice—2 pairs				•						
coins—all values	•	•		•				•		
containers—small, for general use	•		•	•				•		•

	Number Skills	Place Value	Addition	Subtraction	Multiplication	Division	Fractions	Decimals	Geometry	Measurement
counters, various colors—20 or more/student	•	•	•	•			•	•		•
counter-trading materials to 1000s—1 set/student or pair		•	•							
craft sticks on which beans have been glued	•									
cubes—1 cm (good to have larger sizes as well); 20 or more/student	•		•	•						
Cuisenaire® rods	•									•
decks of cards—1/pair; at least 1 teacher deck	•	•	•							
dice—1 set/pair	•	•	•	•				•		
dominoes—1 set/group	•									
dot-to-dot pictures for reproducing	•									
egg cartons—1/student					•	•				
geoboards—1/student or pair						•	•		•	
graph paper—½", 1"—R; 1 cm—R	•	•	•	•	•		•		•	•
index cards—1 package for teacher	•	•	•							
interlocking cubes	•		•	•	•		•			•
letter cards—large teacher set	•									
measurement sets for capacity, weight—1 or more										•
number cards, or number-and dot cards—large teacher set	•		•	•						
objects—small, collections of various kinds, some similar (e.g., buttons, beans, tiles); 20 or more/student	•		•	•	•		•	•		•
other place value materials—(see Manip. Info. section for suggestions) 1 set/student or pair		•	•	•						
paper shapes—(see Manip. Info. section) 1 set/pair or group	•									
pattern blocks	•						•		•	
place value materials to 1000s—1 set/student or pair	•	•	•	•						•
plastic links	•			•						
scales—a variety of types										•
Secret Code number line—(see Manip. Info. section)	•					•				
symbol cards—large teacher set	•		•	•				•		
tangrams—1 set/student or pair									•	
thermometer—1/pair or group										•
tiles—20 or more/student	•				•				•	
tracing paper—2 or more pads	•									

	Number Skills	Place Value	Addition	Subtraction	Multiplication	Division	Fractions	Decimals	Geometry	Measurement
treasure boxes—(see Manip. Info. section) 1/group	•		•	•	•					•
S—bills to $100 (see Manip. Info. section for quantities)		•		•				•		
S—file-folder place value mats to 1000s; 1 file folder/student			•					•		
S—fraction bars; 1 set/student							•			
S—number-and-dot cards made from index cards; 10/student	•		•	•						
S—number squares, 1" × 1"—10/student				•						
S—symbol cards made from index cards; 5/student	•		•	•				•		
R/lam—counter-trading boards to 1000s; 1/student or pair			•	•						
R/lam—hundred boards; 1/student	•		•	•	•					
R/lam—place value mats to 100s; 1/student or pair	•	•	•	•				•		

Grade 3

	Number Skills	Place Value	Addition	Subtraction	Multiplication	Division	Fractions	Decimals	Geometry	Measurement
adding-machine tape—1 roll		•			•					
attribute blocks	•								•	
balance scale—1 or more										•
beads and string	•			•	•					
blank dice—2 pairs				•	•					
coins—all values	•	•		•				•		
containers—small, for general use			•	•		•		•		•
counters, various colors—20 or more/student	•	•	•	•	•	•	•	•		•
counter-trading materials to 100,000s—1 set/student or pair		•	•	•	•					
cubes—1 cm (large sizes are nice to have as well); 20+/student	•		•	•	•	•			•	•
Cuisenaire® rods						•	•			
decks of cards—1/pair; at least 1 teacher deck		•	•	•						
dice—1 set/pair		•	•	•		•		•		
dot-to-dot pictures for reproducing	•									
egg cartons—1/student				•	•					
geoboards—1/student or pair					•		•		•	
graph paper—½", 1"—R; 1 cm—R	•	•	•	•	•	•	•	•	•	•
index cards—1 package for teacher		•			•					
interlocking cubes	•		•	•	•	•	•		•	•

	Number Skills	Place Value	Addition	Subtraction	Multiplication	Division	Fractions	Decimals	Geometry	Measurement
measurement sets for capacity, weight—1 or more										•
number cards—large teacher set		•	•	•						
objects—small, collections of various kinds, some similar (e.g., buttons, beans, tiles); 20 or more/student	•		•	•	•	•	•	•		•
other place value materials—(see Manip. Info. section for suggestions) 1 set/student or pair			•	•						
paper shapes—(see Manip. Info. section) 1 set/pair or group	•								•	
pattern blocks					•		•		•	
place value materials to 1000s—1 set/student or pair	•	•	•	•	•	•		•		•
plastic links	•			•						
protractors—1/student or pair									•	
scales—a variety of types										•
Secret Code number line—(see Manip. Info. section)	•				•					
solid geometry sets—1 or more									•	
symbol cards—large teacher set			•	•				•		
tangrams—1 set/student or pair									•	
thermometer—1/pair or group										•
tiles—20 or more/student	•				•	•			•	
toothpicks—1 package							•			
treasure boxes—(see Manip. Info. section) 1/group	•		•	•	•					•
S—bills to $100,000 (see Manip. Info. section for quantities)	•	•	•	•	•	•	•	•		
S—decimal bars to ¹/₁₀ (see Manip. Info. section for quantities)								•		
S—decimal extensions for file-folder place value mats; 1/student								•		
S—file-folder place value mats to 100,000s; 1 file folder/student		•	•	•	•	•		•		
S—fraction bars; 1 set/student							•			
S—number cards made from index cards; 10/student		•	•	•						
S—number squares, 1" × 1"; 10/student					•					
S—symbol cards made from index cards; 5/student			•	•				•		
R/lam—counter-trading boards to 100,000s; 1/student or pair		•	•	•						
R/lam—hundred boards; 1/student	•		•	•	•	•				
R/lam—moon stations; 1/student							•			
R/lam—place value mats to 1000s; 1/student or pair	•	•	•	•	•	•		•		

Labels for File Folders, Dividers, or Book Sections

Each teacher has his or her preferred method of organizing materials. If you like organization, photocopy these labels onto heavier paper. If you do not like organization, skip this page. Here are some ways you might use these labels.

If you file materials for each textbook chapter in a separate file folder:

Use the "Chap.____" labels for file folders keyed to textbook chapters. Tear out the lessons you need, and file them in the appropriate folders.

If you use loose-leaf notebooks:

Tear out and file the whole book by strand using the strand labels with purchased notebook dividers.

Or, use the "Chap.____" labels and notebook dividers. Tear out the lessons you need, and file by textbook chapter.

Or file the whole book by strands, but have dividers for textbook chapters as well. File the lessons you actually use by chapter.

If you like to keep your books intact:

Use the strand labels and tape to the edge of the first lesson in each strand to facilitate finding the desired lessons.

Front Pages	Multiplication	Measurement	Chap. _____	Chap. _____
Number Skills	Division	Reproducibles	Chap. _____	Chap. _____
Place Value	Fractions	Chap. _____	Chap. _____	Chap. _____
Addition	Decimals	Chap. _____	Chap. _____	Chap. _____
Subtraction	Geometry	Chap. _____	Chap. _____	Chap. _____

Number Skills 1

Skill: To establish number sequence

Time: Varies with readiness level

Materials:

interlocking cubes: 10 of 1 color per student

number cards: large teacher set and 1 set per student pair

Cuisenaire® rods: 1 set and 10 extra 1s per student

coins: pennies; 10 per pair

number dot-to-dot pictures: commercial, with numbers to 10, 25, or more

counters: 10 or more per student

graph paper: ½" squares or larger

teacher-made dot-to-dot pictures: if desired

See Reproducibles for: number lines to 25 (taped together), hundred boards

Anticipatory Set

Use *interlocking cubes, 10 per pair.*

Have students work in pairs and make designs with the cubes, allowing some time to play. Now have students make a design that looks like steps. (They should lay the design flat on their desks.)

Discuss designs and what names could be given to each of the steps. Help students "see" number names by counting and by pointing out that each step is one larger than the preceding one. Leave steps in place.

Procedure 1

To establish and practice number sequence to 10

Kindergarten:

Have students practice number form by drawing pictures using each numeral.

Hang the pictures in the room for students to use as reference when working with this number sequence. Example pictures:

All grade levels:

Use *number cards, Cuisenaire® rods, pennies,* and *interlocking cubes left in position from Anticipatory Set.*

Students push steps to the top of their desks.

Hand out number cards to the pairs of students.

Sequence the large number cards in the chalk tray.

Students rote count with you and then order their numbers to look like the ones on the chalk tray.

Students mix up their cards and repeat the ordering process.

Remove the cards from the chalk tray and check to see that each pair is able to order the numbers from 1 to 10.

Have students look at the steps on their desks. Ask: Which step could be number one?

Students respond: The first step.

Have students separate their steps so that they look like columns, and place card number 1 under the first step.

Students place cards and count their steps with their partners.

Now have students work in groups to combine their cubes to make more steps.

Students work together to complete task, order these steps from 5 to 10, and read the numbers to each other.

Give student groups Cuisenaire® rods with which to make steps, flat on their desks. Have them cover the top of each rod in turn with one rods, thereby proving that each larger rod is the given number.

As students are finishing, allow time to play with the rods, to experiment, to see other relationships.

Encourage discussion among the groups and move around the room to monitor and observe.

Students who are fluent with the number sequence can use pennies to help other students who are unsure of the counting order.

Procedure 2

To establish and practice number sequence to 20

Use *dot-to-dot pictures, number lines, pennies,* and *1 counter per pair of students.*

Give each student a taped-together number line. Draw a number line on the board and show the students where and how to place numbers on the line.

Students copy as you write numbers on the board. They complete the number line all the way to 25.

Check to see that the number lines are correct and have the students place them at the top of their desks for future use. Tape the lines down so they will stay in place.

Have students combine their pennies so that each pair has 20.

Students take turns counting the pennies aloud while their partners check the number line by moving the counter along it. Now they are ready to move on to the next part of the procedure.

Have students work in pairs to complete dot-to-dots.

Students take turns; one draws the lines and the other moves the counter along the number line, checking to see what the next number should be. Allow students to complete several pictures to develop knowledge of number sequence and to enjoy working with numbers.

Procedure 3 □■

To establish and practice number sequence to 50

Use *interlocking cubes, hundred boards, counters,* and *dot-to-dot pictures.*

Work in groups of five and have each student build a train that is ten cubes long. Then members of each group join their trains.

Students complete task, and all count with you: One, two . . . fifty.

Instruct students to now orally count in their groups. One person places counters on the hundred board, while others say the number.

When students have completed that task, they form pairs and work on dot-to-dot pictures that use numbers between 25 and 50. They take turns showing the next number on the hundred board and making the lines.

Have students make up stories in which they need to count pennies; they use the counters as pennies. The number needing to be counted can be between 10 and 50. Students share stories with the class.

Procedure 4 □■

To establish and practice number sequence to 100

Use *hundred boards, counters, graph paper,* and *dot-to-dot pictures.*

Have students read all the numbers on the hundred boards, placing a counter on the board as they say a number.

Students now copy the numbers in order onto the graph paper. They check each other's work and take turns reading the numbers to peers.

Next have students individually complete dot-to-dot pictures, checking with the hundred board if they are unsure of the next number. Monitor as the students are working.

Practice and Extension

Extend the counting activity to 100 by making a class number line from 1 to 100 on wide *adding-machine tape*. The number should be at least 3 inches high so that they can be easily read by the students, if need be. Post the large number line around the room, maybe above the bulletin boards.

Place *tracing paper* over a *simple line drawing*. One student helps hold the tracing paper in place while another student puts dots on any corner, point, or turn in the outline of the drawing. Together they number the dots in order as they would be connected to make the drawing. Tracing paper dot-to-dots are then exchanged with another pair of students who will try to complete the drawing. Be careful to use very simple drawings or shapes.

Make a number line on the floor, numbering tiles, etc.

Have the class estimate how many steps must be taken to go to the music room, the gym, the lunchroom, etc. Then have them count the steps. Do they become more accurate with practice? What strategies are they using? Make a class chart of the number of steps to each place.

Number Skills 2

Skill: To classify by likenesses and differences

12" ×18" paper: 1 per group
treasure box or other objects
attribute blocks: 1 set per group

Time: 2 periods

Materials:

paper shapes: circles, squares, triangles, rectangles;
several colors each—1 set per group

Anticipatory Set

Ask all students wearing something blue to stand. Discuss what is the same about these students. How many ways are the students all alike? Discuss how the students standing are different. See how many differences you can elicit from the class. Discuss the meanings of *alike*, *same*, and *different*, to insure that students understand these words and their usage before you begin to work on classification.

Procedure 1

To develop the concept of *classification by likenesses and differences*

Use *paper shapes*.

Make a grid on the board two squares wide and several squares down. Say: We will be looking at how groups of things are alike and different.

Divide students into groups of three. Distribute sets of colored cut-out shapes to the groups. Have students in each group find three things that are alike in some way.

Students from each group hold up their three things. They explain how their things are alike.

On the board or overhead, label the left column with "A" or "Alike":

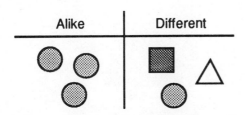

Alike	Different

In the top left square of the grid, draw a representation of one way the members of a group are alike. Continue around the class collecting data on likenesses and charting these on the left side of the grid. Now have the student groups find three things that are different.

Students from each group hold up their three things.

Label the right-hand column with "D" or "Different." Ask students how their things are different.

Students explain how their three things are different. Let them help each other in describing differences.

Draw a representation of all the differences on the right side of the grid.

Procedure 2

To classify objects by either likenesses or differences

Use *objects* and *12" × 18" paper*.

Students work in groups. Have students fold paper in half vertically, and label sides "Alike" and "Different."

Students follow directions and are ready to classify objects.

Hand out a variety of the objects to each group. Each group should appoint a recorder, who will chart the likenesses and differences.

Students sort objects, and recorder represents the likenesses on the left side of the paper.

After students have sorted and recorded one way, have them put objects back together and sort again according to another way in which the objects are alike.

Students continue finding and charting likenesses for about five minutes. They discuss their findings.

Students re-sort their objects and concentrate on how the groups are different. Recorder charts all the differences on the right side of the paper.

After students have found several ways to sort their objects, discuss each group's rules. Groups can now shift tables and try to guess the rules of the other groups.

Make a class chart of several different kinds of likenesses and differences.

Continue until students are aware of many different ways of looking at common objects.

Procedure 3

☐

To practice classifying by likenesses and differences

Use *attribute blocks*.

Have students work in groups to classify and record attribute blocks by various likenesses and differences.

They follow the same procedures as in Procedure 2.

In pairs, students take turns placing blocks in a one-difference train, so that each block differs from adjacent blocks in just one way. They explain their reasoning to their partners.

Students make a picture record of their one-difference trains.

Extend this activity by having students make two-difference trains and record the differences with pictures.

Practice and Extension

Have students work in pairs, making drawings to show likenesses and differences of a new group of objects. They chart them with the likenesses in one column and differences in the other column.

Have students work in pairs, making drawings to show likenesses and differences of objects in a given real-life category, such as trees. They chart them with the likenesses in one column and differences in the other column.

Have students discuss the likenesses and differences of items in *catalogs* or *animal books*.

Number Skills 3

Skill: To classify by position and positional relationships

Time: At least 2–3 periods

Materials:

2" paper circles: several colors; about 12 per group

12" × 18" paper: 1 per group

dominoes: 1 set per group

number cards: 1 to 9; large teacher set and 1 set per student

scissors

crayons

26 large alphabet cards: lowercase letters

1 die

See Reproducibles for: place value (pv) mats to 100s, graph paper with 1" squares

Anticipatory Set

Use *objects*.

Check and monitor understanding of *above, below, beside, left, right, under, on, etc.* by placing objects in different positions around the room. For example, put a book on the top of a table, a ruler under a table, or a chair beside a table on the left.

Students take turns telling where objects in the room are located. After a correct answer, the student can place the object in another position. The purpose is to demonstrate that the students know the meaning of the positional words. This prior knowledge is necessary before the students can begin classifying.

Procedure 1

To classify by positional placement

Use *paper circles* and *12" × 18" paper*.

Have students work in groups of three or four. Give directions for placement of the circles, such as: place a green circle in the top left corner of the large paper.

Monitor completion to make sure all students understand the directions.

Continue with directions until all the position words previously introduced have been used.

Students who consistently respond correctly may take turns giving the placement directions.

Procedure 2

To develop placement awareness of left and right

Use *dominoes*.

Have students work in groups of three or four and give each group a set of dominoes. Tell them the rule: the touching sides of two dominoes must both have the same number of dots.

Discuss whether they can use the middle position.

Ask students to describe where they are placing each domino; for example, is the new domino to the left or to the right of one already on the desk? In order to be accurate, all students playing together must be on the same side of the desk.

(If students are having problems, they can learn the hand clue and use the hidden 'L.')

Procedure 3

To develop understanding of positional relationships using 2-digit numbers

Use *number cards* and *pv mats*.

In groups, have students combine their cards.

Draw a card whose number the students place in the ones column of the pv mat. Discuss that the next number will be in the tens column. Ask: Is the tens column to the left or right of the ones column?

Students respond: Left.

Now draw a card whose number will go in the tens column, and then repeat questions.

Students place cards and tell you what positional relationships they see.

Discuss the fact that they also have been using the base ten positions as they placed the numbers. This is the numbering system that we use to solve mathematical problems.

This system causes numbers to have a different value depending on their placement. Discuss this with students.

Remind students that just as objects can be above or below other objects, numbers can be placed on a paper mat above or below other numbers. Draw another card, and tell them to place that card below the number card in the ones column.

Continue with the tens place on the place value chart. Repeat questions and encourage discussion.

Students now have two 2-digit numbers on their mats.

Continue procedure until students are aware of the importance of position when dealing with numbers.

Procedure 4

To develop and practice the concept of *classifying by position,* using objects

Use *objects, graph paper, scissors,* and *crayons.*

Have students work in small groups. Using two sheets of graph paper, they label and outline with crayons as shown in 1a. They turn the second sheet sideways, fold vertically, and label as in 1b.

1a

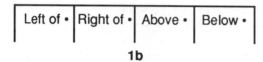

1b

Have students place objects on the large numbered squares. Recorder for the group writes the numbers and draws a picture of the objects in the appropriate column on the charts.

Students discuss charts, placements, and positions. They explain where each of their objects is. Each group member should give a part of the explanation to the class. Students then display charts.

Procedure 5

To develop and practice the concept of *classifying by position,* using letters

Use *letter cards, graph paper,* and *crayons.*

Place the alphabet cards where all the students can see them.

In groups, have students use graph paper to make the following chart headed "Letters with Stems and Tails."

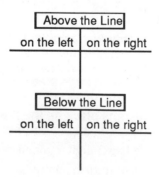

Groups decide where to write each letter of the alphabet that has a stem or tail.

Students work cooperatively to decide where to write each letter. Then the whole class discusses the placement.

Lead the discussion with questions such as: which position, left or right, has more stems? Which position has more tails? Which position has short stems? Where did the short tails occur? How many letters have no stems or tails at all?

Students discuss and then display their charted results.

Procedure 6

To write numbers using positional relationships; to relate to numbers up to 20

Use *graph paper, crayons, teacher set of number cards,* and *die.*

Have students work individually. Draw a card and have students write that number on their papers.

Now have them place a one to the left of the first number. Call on a student to read the new number.

Continue activity, telling them to place new numbers under the previous set. Discuss the value of each number.

Can students place and read numbers that have a 2 as the left-hand number, a 3, a 4?

Challenge students to write the original 1-digit number again, and place a number to its right. Can they read the resulting 2-digit number? Are they able to switch and place on the right correctly?

Toss the die twice, and change whether you tell them to place the number on the left, or the tens side, or on the right, the ones side.

Practice and Extension

Have students make up games to play in which they classify numbers.

Make a class display of the various completed charts.

Have students take turns explaining the skill of classifying to the class. How would this be useful in real life? (giving directions, making maps, etc.)

Number Skills 4

Skill: To classify by shape and size

Time: 2 periods

Materials:

12" × 18" sheets of drawing paper: 2 per student

crayons

pattern blocks

treasure box or other objects

paper shapes: three sizes of each shape desired; 1 set per group

attribute blocks: 1 set per group

Anticipatory Set

Use *drawing paper (1 per student)* and *crayons.*

Students divide paper into two pieces. On one piece, they draw and color a tree, of any kind. On the other piece, they draw and color a house, again any kind. (If students work slowly, they will finish only one picture while others finish two. This is not important.) Tell students to set the pictures aside. Later they will classify them.

Procedure 1

To develop the concept of *classification by shape*

Use *pattern blocks, objects, paper shapes,* and *12" × 18" paper.*

Set up stations around the room with boxes of items in shapes you wish to classify. Review the shapes the students are familiar with: circle, square, rectangle, triangle.

Demonstrate on an overhead, or hold up large shapes that the students might not yet know.

Students discuss shapes that are new to them, for example, oval, parallelogram, rhombus, diamond, octagon, pentagon, hexagon, or other polygons.

Have students take 12" × 18" paper and make columns with headings for the shapes that have been presented. Possible headings:

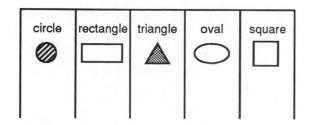

circle	rectangle	triangle	oval	square

Students move from station to station, in small groups. They look at each set of objects and draw a representation, or write the name, of objects that fit the columns. As they move about, monitor the discussions that the students have about each set of objects.

Have groups share lists with the class and discuss how they arrived at their choices. Were some objects hard to classify? Why or why not? Did the groups agree or disagree on the classifications?

Procedure 2

To classify common objects by their overall shapes

Use *pictures from the Anticipatory Set* and *chart from Procedure 1.*

Instruct students to look at the pictures they drew earlier. They are to decide the overall shapes in their pictures.

Students then take turns presenting their pictures to the class and explaining the overall shapes that they drew. Students discuss whether or not they agree with the presenter.

In groups, have students write down the names of objects in the room that fit each pattern on the Procedure 1 charts. After about 10 minutes, the class gathers together and the members discuss the classifications they have made, how they made their decisions, and how they classified objects that were of more than one shape.

Procedure 3

To develop the concept of *classification by size*

Use *attribute blocks* and *paper shapes.*

Discuss the meanings of *small* and *large*. Have students generate other words that describe size.

Have students line up according to height, and discuss these facets of size: tall, short, in between.

Now have students work in groups and make charts that are labeled with the size words that the class has chosen to use. They are to place the attribute blocks and paper shapes in the appropriate columns on their charts.

After completing task, the groups move about the room and see if the other students placed the objects in the same places. They discuss any discrepancies.

Discuss relative size and make sure all students understand that a large dog is not the same as a large car, which is different in size from a large building.

Procedure 4 □

To practice *classification by size*

Use *pattern blocks, objects, paper shapes,* and *classroom objects.*

Review the meanings of *small, large,* and *relative size.* Discuss measuring to find exact sizes.

Students work in groups and choose one of the manipulatives. Each group decides which members of the group are small, large, or belong in some other category the class has chosen to use.

After each group has completed its assignment, the members take turns presenting to the class. Each group must justify why it chose to describe a particular object as small or large.

As a culminating activity, have students chart some of the objects used earlier on charts that classify size, shape, and color of the objects. This can be done by pairs or individual students.

Practice and Extension

Leave the *objects* out for further exploration by the students on their own time.

Encourage students to draw more pictures, look for, and label the shapes.

Have students draw shapes and then make pictures from the shapes, joining art and math.

Have students write about a favorite toy, describing its relative shape and size; then read these sentences to the class, combining math and language activities.

Make a class chart of the *tree drawings,* sorted by height, width, and shape.

Make individual charts to display that use *catalog pictures,* and have them sorted by shapes or actual size.

Have students bring in *containers* (unbreakable) from home, and display them according to shape and/or size.

Students can use *interlocking cubes* to make patterns which they can discuss with the class, describing the resulting shapes. This can tie in with introductions of other math skills; e.g., addition and multiplication.

Have students collect *objects from outside* (such as leaves, twigs, etc.) and make charts labeling the shapes and sizes of the items.

Number Skills 5

Skill: To classify by kind and use

Time: Varies with readiness level

Materials:

pictures of people: from magazines

treasure box or other objects

place value (pv) materials to 10s

deck of cards: 1 per student pair

Anticipatory Set

Use *pictures from magazines*.

Hold up the pictures one at a time and discuss with the class what the various people's occupations are. Discuss that different people like to do different kinds of work, and that is what makes for a diverse world. Also discuss that there are people of all kinds, sizes, and colors in this world, and that each may choose his or her own role in life; choosing, within limits, his or her own usefulness to society.

Procedure 1

To develop the concept of *classification by kind*

Use *treasure box objects*.

Work with the class as a whole and discuss the different objects with regard to the general and specific categories each belongs to, what category each represents; e.g., toy dinosaurs represent the category animals, extinct animals, dinosaurs, and toy animals.

Ask questions that will require the students to develop the categories for each object. Help the students to understand that most objects can be classified in several different categories.

Procedure 2

To develop the concept of *classification by use*

Use *classroom objects*.

Follow the same format as in Procedure 1 and ask questions that will enable the students to develop several different categories for use of items; e.g., used to write with, used to gain information, used to write on, and used to sit on.

Encourage them to identify several categories for each object, then explain their ideas. Ask if all agree with the categories suggested.

Procedure 3

To classify by kind and/or use

Use *cards, pv materials, paper,* and *objects*.

Have students work in pairs to make charts of categories. They fold each paper in half vertically and label one side "Kind" and one side "Use."

Each pair takes a number of objects and decides how to categorize them.

Encourage students to classify by *both* kind and use if the objects are appropriate. For example, buttons and pins can be classified in kinds (e.g., round, square, two holes, fastener on back) and according to uses (e.g., to fasten, as decoration).

Students develop categories and classify objects, while you move around the room and monitor progress.

Next, students take a card from the deck and attempt to place it in one of their categories.

Were some of the student pairs able to do this? If so, discuss the types of categories they chose for their objects.

Have students discuss whether most object categories and number categories are the same. Why or why not?

As the class discusses the categories for the cards, help them come up with categories that include number sense; e.g., ones, tens.

After developing categories, student pairs chart some of the cards from their deck of cards. They pick the cards randomly, picking at least ten cards so they can see a pattern.

Now have students take some of the pv materials and classify them according to whether they represent tens or ones. Could they use some of the same categories they used for the cards? Why is this so?

This should relate to early learning of the base ten concept.

Practice and Extension

Have students cut pictures from *catalogs* and make *charts* with the pictures pasted under the appropriate category heading. Discuss the different charts, categories, and ways of placing objects in the various categories.

Extend the activity with *pv materials,* so that students get the chance to relate the several different *pv manipulatives* to our numbering system. Include using *number cards* and classifying these numbers as tens or ones.

Number Skills 6

Skill: To understand 1-to-1 correspondence

Time: Varies with grade level

Materials:

number line on the floor: to 20 (see Manipulative Information section)

clothespins: 10 per group

hangers: 1 per group

treasure box or other objects

container

number cards: large teacher set

cards with simple action words such as hop, jump, clap

bag of jelly beans

Cuisenaire® rods: 1 set per group

number-and-dot cards: 1 set per group (see Manipulative Information section)

craft sticks: with number on one side and the same number of beans glued to the other—1 set per group

See Reproducibles for: number lines to 25, graph paper with 1 cm squares

Anticipatory Set

All grade levels:

Use *number line on the floor*.

Have each student take a turn jumping the full length of the line, saying the numbers aloud as he or she jumps. After all have jumped, have the class count and clap from one to five. Repeat this with other short rhythms.

Kindergarten:

Use a *shorter number line* and a *picture line on the floor:*

Have one student stand at start of the number line. This student has taken no steps; place a 0 under the word start. Another student stands at start and takes one step. Where is he? (On the ball.) Mark that place 1. Next student starts at 0 and takes two steps; put a 2 under the ice-cream cone. Continue to develop the numbers.

Now play games that help with listening and following directions, as well as with grasping 1-to-1 correspondence of numbers and actions. Student stands at start. She jumps forward two jumps. Where does she land? (On the ice-cream cone.) Jump forward two jumps and backward one jump. Where does she land? (On the cherries.) Continue with these kinds of directions.

Later have students give a value to each of the pictures by counting the special things about that picture; e.g., there is one boat on the ball, two scoops of ice cream on the cone, three cherries on the stem.

Procedure 1

To count objects to 10

Use *clothespins, hangers, ten objects,* and *container*.

Have students count out loud as you drop 10 objects into the container.

Each group of students takes a hanger and more than 10 clothespins. Students take some of the clothespins and clip them onto the hanger without the others seeing. Students have a quick look at the hanger and then guess the number of clothespins used.

Students then count chorally the number of clothespins on the hanger. Were their estimates correct?

Have students rotate roles and repeat exercise. Walk around and monitor the processes. After several rotations, discuss whether or not their estimates have become more accurate. Why or why not?

Procedure 2

To count actions to 10

Use *number cards* and *cards with actions*.

Turn both piles of cards face down. Randomly select students and draw a card from each pile. Student is to hop two times if the cards *2* and *hop* are turned over. Continue the exercise, giving each student at least one chance to participate.

Vary this activity by having the students read the numbers and the action words.

Some of the number cards may be modified by printing the number words on them. This will help the students learn to read the number words.

Procedure 3

To count objects to 20

Use *classroom objects*.

Have students count chorally to 20 and clap their hands for each number. Divide the class into groups of three or four.

Groups count out loud to 20 while clapping their hands.

Assign different classroom objects to each group for counting. For example, blue books, books on the bottom shelf, pencils in a container.

After they have counted their assigned objects, each group reports to the class. For example, blue books: one, two, three.

Continue counting objects until all have the concept.

Procedure 4

To estimate and count objects

Use *bag of jelly beans* and *objects*.

Have students work in groups. Pass the unopened bag of jelly beans to each group. Each group guesses how many beans are in the bag. Record the guesses on a chart on the board. Ask: Are many guesses close to each other? Does any group want to change its guess?

Now open the bag and count chorally with students to find the exact number of beans.

Hand out some to each group. Have them estimate and then count how many they have.

Each group reports on its estimate and the actual number of beans it has, while a recorder writes all the numbers on the board. Now students can eat the jelly beans. (Be aware of any dietary concerns students may have.)

Add the amounts on the board and give students total numbers, both of the total estimates and the actual amounts. Were these estimates more accurate than the earlier ones? Discuss.

Now give each group varying amounts of objects (above 12). Have groups first estimate how many objects they have, then write that number down before counting aloud for the entire class. How accurate were their estimates?

Continue with different numbers of objects until all have grasped the concept.

Procedure 5

To relate the sequence of numbers to the number of objects

Use *individual number lines* and *small objects*.

Students work individually and make a group of objects below each number on the number line, so that they have a stair of objects on their desks. This is an excellent time to monitor and see that the notion of 1-to-1 correspondence has been fully developed.

Procedure 6

To relate the sequence of numbers to the number of objects, and draw the relationship

Use *Cuisenaire® rods, graph paper, number-and-dot cards, objects (buttons with differing numbers of holes can add an extra dimension), and craft sticks.*

Have students explain how Cuisenaire® rods relate to numbers.

Working in small groups, students take graph paper and color outlines of the rods in appropriate colors. They write the corresponding number on each drawing.

Have students place objects on cards having numerals on them; one object on card number one, four objects on card number four, etc. (If using buttons, have students place on the cards the corresponding number of buttons having the corresponding number of holes; e.g., two buttons, with two holes each, on card number two.) Students can then draw the numbers and the buttons.

Students use the craft sticks by looking at the number side, drawing that many beans, then looking at the bean side. They use the sticks in sequence.

Students complete activities, and each student should have three different representations of 1-to-1 correspondence on the graph paper.

Practice and Extension

Use *paper, stamp pad,* and *stamps* and let students make counting sheets. They fold the paper to mark off four rectangles on each page. They stamp various amounts in each rectangle. Use pages to practice counting. Students give oral responses, working in pairs. Exchange pages for more practice.

Students play Number Match in pairs. They use a *deck of cards (ace through six)* and one *die. Each* player gets five cards, and the rest are put in the middle as a draw pile. Player One throws the die and removes from his hand the card with the number shown on the die, if he has it. He then replenishes his hand from the draw pile. Player Two does the same. After using all the cards in the draw pile, they go through the cards remaining in their hands. The first one out of cards is the winner.

Students make *number cards* and attach *paper clip* chains to the cards using the appropriate number of clips.

Students make a chart by gluing *beans* or *peas* to *craft sticks* to show each number from 1 to 10 or 20.

Number Skills 7

Skill: To identify patterns in objects: shapes, sizes, color, position

attribute blocks: 1 set per student pair
cubes: any size; several colors
crayons

Time: 3 periods

Materials:

counters, beads, tiles, or identical objects: different colors

paper shapes: 3 shapes, 3 sizes of each shape, 3 colors of each shape and size; 1 teacher set and 1 set per student or student pair

Note: The students need to know these sorting skills in the following order. If they do not, space this practice over several days.

a) by color
b) by shape
c) by size
d) by color and shape, etc.

Procedures progress from easier to more difficult. After identifying the desired level of difficulty, use a previous Procedure as an Anticipatory Set.

Anticipatory Set

Use *counters, beads, tiles,* or *identical objects*.

Have students sort objects by color. Have students group objects of same color into piles of two. Next have students make groups of two items of different colors. Ask students what other combinations they can find to make. Students can work in pairs and copy each other's groupings.

Procedure 1

To use one attribute

Use *paper shapes, counters, cubes, or attribute blocks*, and *crayons*.

Make single line patterns and have students copy. Vary only one attribute each time: colors only, using small squares; size only, using red squares; shape only, using small red shapes. Ask what variation will come next.

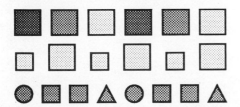

Students copy pattern. They predict the next item and continue the pattern.

Have students make their own pattern, using red squares, etc.

Students work in groups and devise individual patterns. They copy and describe one another's pattern, predict the next one, and continue the pattern.

Introduce patterns using combinations such as: all small squares—one blue, a red and blue touching, one blue, etc. Have students copy, predict, and continue the patterns, working in groups.

As students work, move from group to group monitoring. Have students describe patterns orally. Ask questions such as: how many shapes, or blocks, are in the sequence before it repeats? What categories, such as size or shape, are in the pattern?

When students are competent, have them individually draw patterns, exchange papers, and continue the other student's pattern.

Procedure 2

To use two attributes

Use *paper shapes* or *attribute blocks*.

Make single line patterns and have students copy. Use patterns which vary in two attributes: all squares varying in color and size, all large shapes varying in color and shape, etc. Ask what will come next. See example illustration next page.

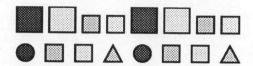

Students copy the pattern. They predict the next item and continue the pattern.

Students next work in pairs to devise their own patterns. One pair copies another's pattern, predicts the next element, and continues the pattern.

Introduce patterns using combinations varying in two attributes: all squares—one small blue, a large red and large blue touching, one small blue, a large red and large blue touching, etc. Have students copy, predict, and continue the patterns, working in pairs as before.

Monitor as before, asking for descriptions and categories.

When students are competent, have them draw their patterns; the partners check drawings for accuracy.

Have students solve patterns in which the middle of the sequence is missing.

Use *treasure boxes* and have groups create a series. Then each group moves to the neighboring group's series and tries to figure out the rules for it. Repeat movement of groups.

Have students use *paper shapes, attribute blocks,* or *pattern blocks* to explore tiling patterns made up of two or more shapes, which fit together in a pattern that completely covers a space. Students can copy the patterns onto *graph paper,* and color them.

Procedure 3

To understand positional changes

Use *paper shapes, counters, cubes,* or *attribute blocks.*

Start by varying only one attribute: using paired items, reverse which one is above and which is below, or which is left and which is right.

Example: Using small squares, make a pattern of one blue, a red above a blue, one blue, a blue above a red.

When students can copy, predict, and continue the patterns, they then work in pairs as before.

Next vary two attributes. Example: Using only squares, make a pattern of small red ones paired with large blue ones, large red ones paired with medium blue ones.

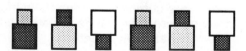

When students can copy, predict, and continue the patterns, they then work in pairs as before, to make, extend, and draw patterns.

Practice and Extension

As students become adept, suggest they try the next level of difficulty. Can they make patterns using a *different manipulative?* Can they devise patterns using *shoes or students?* An example might be: boy, girl, girl.

Number Skills 8

Skill: To identify numbers missing from a sequence: after, between, before

pattern blocks: 1 set per student
interlocking cubes: 2 colors; 10 per group
counters: 10 per group
See Reproducibles for: hundred boards

Time: Varies with readiness level

Materials:

index cards for number dots: 10 per student
crayons: 1 per student

Anticipatory Set

Use *index cards* and *crayons*.

Have students write numbers on a set of blank index cards, one per card. They then put the corresponding number of dots on the flip side of the card. Students then sequence the cards on their desks.

Have a general discussion of the meanings of *before*, *after*, and *between*, to identify the level of students' understanding.

Procedure 1

To develop the concepts of *after* and *between*, using patterns

Use *pattern blocks*.

Demonstrate a pattern, using the blocks and have the students predict what the next block will be. For example:

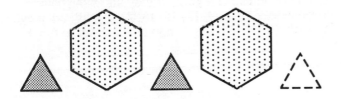

Students discuss the *after* block and explain why they chose the one they did.

Would any other block fit the pattern? Why not?

Demonstrate another pattern with a missing block in the middle of the sequence. Again have students discuss and explain their reasoning.

Students work in groups to sequence the blocks. They take turns making patterns and predicting what the next block should be.

Now have students work with patterns that have a block missing from the middle of the sequence.

Be sure that each student has a chance to complete this task, finding the *between* block, and understands the pattern sequencing. Ask students to describe their patterns.

Procedure 2

To develop the concept of *before*, using patterns

Use *interlocking cubes*.

Demonstrate a pattern using the blocks and have the students predict what the first block should be:

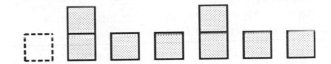

Students discuss the *before* block and explain why they chose the one they did.

Would any other block fit the pattern? Why not?

Students now work in groups and complete the same type of activity as in Procedure 1. As an alternative, have them make secret sequences, copy them with crayons, but leave off the first figure. Students can then exchange the drawings and complete the sequences.

Procedure 3

To identify numbers missing from a sequence

Use *number cards from Anticipatory Set.*

Have students work in pairs and take turns setting up number sequences with missing numbers before, after, or between other numbers. The student who sets up the pattern must say whether the missing number is before, after, or between; then the other student must identify the missing number. They can use the dots on the back of the cards to check their correctness.

Tell students to create a story to go with their sequences; e.g., runners in a race with numbers on their shirts. Which one is missing?

Students work together and complete task, as you move about the room to check on understanding.

After a set amount of time has elapsed, let each pair explain one of the sequences they used.

Procedure 4

To identify missing numbers, using skip-counting sequences

This procedure can be used to reinforce skip-counting after it has been introduced.

Use *hundred boards* and *counters.*

Have students count chorally by 10s to 100. Divide class into groups and give each group 1 hundred board and 10 counters. Have students lay counters on 10, 20, 30. Ask what number should next be covered with a counter.

Students respond: 40.

Continue with sequencing, having whole class respond to the questions.

Have students place counters on 20, 30, 50. Ask: What number is missing from the sequence?

Students respond: 40.

Continue with these types of sequences until entire class is responding correctly.

Have students place counters on 37, 47, 57, 77. What number is missing from this sequence?

Students respond: 67.

Continue with these types of sequences, omitting numbers before, after, and between members of the sequence given.

Give each group another hundred board and instruct them to add a 0 to each number.

Repeat activities above, with sequences of 100, 200, 300 and ending with sequences like 340, 440, 540.

Continue with similar activities and use sequences such as 2, 4, __ , 8; 3, 6, 9, __ ; __ , 10, 15.

Monitor students to make sure that they understand the concept and that it can be used with different number sequences.

Procedure 5

To practice writing sequences

Use *interlocking cubes.*

Give a sequence of numbers with one missing.

Students write the sequence and put a __ where the missing number belongs. For each number, they put together the corresponding number of cubes, and place each cube stick above the written number:

They ascertain whether the missing number is before, between, or after. Then they write the missing number on its line. The class discusses the sequence.

Continue to present sequences of numbers to the class for them to write, putting in the missing number where it is needed. Have the class discuss responses.

Practice and Extension

Number *craft sticks,* putting one number on each stick. Set up a station with sets of sequences. In their spare time, the students can try to solve as many of the sequences as possible. They can make a chart of the sequences they are able to solve. At the end of the week, have them share their charts with the class.

Give students *number cards* to hold in front of themselves. Have students work in groups to decide which numbers will stay seated. The rest of the group stands in front of the class in a sequenced line. Class has to identify which numbers are missing. When their number is called, those group members join the line.

Have students make up everyday problems dealing with times when they would want to know the relationship between sequences of numbers. For example, Daryl buys tickets to the ball game for his Scout troop. The ticket numbers are Row C, seats 24, 25, 26, 27, and Row D, seats 19, 20, 21, 22. Are these seats close together? How do you know?

Students write a sentence or paragraph about how the knowledge of patterns and number sequencing can help them solve problems. For example, number sequences help them to know if answers to multiplication problems are logical. If they know the pattern or sequence of 3, 6, 9, 12, 15, 18, 21, 24, 27, 30, they know that 17 would not be a logical answer to 6×3.

Number Skills 9

Skill: To understand the ordinal numbers through 30th

Time: 2 periods
Materials:

crayons

drawing paper: 3 per student (kindergarten and grade 1)

index cards: for number-and-word cards, already made for lower grades—1 set per student for numbers desired

calendars: several months per group (for numbers through 30th)

counters: 10 per group

large rubber ball: marked with permanent marker; see illustration in Procedure 1

12" × 18" drawing paper: grade 2 only; 1 per group

plastic links: 20 per group

interlocking cubes: 45 per group

Anticipatory Set for kindergarten and grade 1

Use *crayons* and *drawing paper.*

Have each student make three pictures of trees, one without leaves, one with green leaves, and one with yellow or red leaves. Talk with the class about the fact that when we start a new calendar year, the trees do not have leaves. Students show you this tree. That is the first picture. Continue with the trees for summer and fall. Students save their pictures for later use, after writing a 1, 2, and 3 on the backs of the appropriate pictures.

Anticipatory Set for grade 2

Use *blank cards* and *crayons.*

Have students make number-and-word cards for first through tenth. Use the words on one side and the symbols *1st, 2nd,* etc. on the other side.

Have ten students stand in a line ordered from shortest to tallest. Number them off one through ten and have each student display the appropriate card. Introduce this as the skill that is in the lesson for today.

Procedure 1 □ ■

To develop the concept of *first through tenth* (for kindergarten, *first through fifth*)

Use *number-and-word cards, calendars, counters,* and *rubber ball;* for grade 2 only, use *12" × 18" paper.*

Have ten students stand up in front of the class. Order the students from shortest to tallest. The class decides which number place each student has. Other students hand out cards to the ordered students, so each of these has a number name. Repeat with another group of students.

The entire class chorally counts the students, first one through ten, and then first through tenth.

Have a large calendar that all can see and discuss which week of the month is the first, the second, etc.

Relate the days of the week to their positions; which day is the first, the second, etc.

Give each group of four students ten counters. As a group they are to line up the counters and place the word cards under the correct counter.

Monitor group activities to be sure the students are comprehending the concept.

Kindergarten and grade 1:

Have students take their pictures of trees and label them as first, second, third.

Grade 2:

Working in groups, have students take the drawing paper and divide it into 10 sections. They choose an activity, like getting ready for school, baking cookies, or washing the family car. They draw pictures representing parts of the activity and label those pictures first through tenth.

Students do this and make a chart they can present to the class. The class discusses whether or not they think the pictures are correctly labeled.

All grades:

As an ending activity for this procedure, show the class a ball marked as in the illustration below. Review *1st, 2nd,* etc.

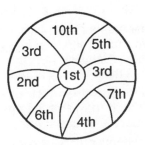

Students form a circle and bounce the ball from one to another. A student catches the ball, reads the position word that is under the right thumb, and then bounces the ball that many times. The ball is tossed to another student who repeats the activity. This can be done as a playground or recess activity.

Procedure 2 □■

To develop the concept of *first through twentieth*

Use *plastic links, interlocking cubes, number-and-word cards to 10th,* and *blank cards for completing series.*

Have students work in groups and complete the number card sets to 20th.

Give each group 45 interlocking cubes. The students are to take the interlocking cubes and build nine towers, each one with one more story than the preceding one.

Students complete task and mark the buildings as first, second, etc., using their cards.

Discuss the buildings. If the third building is placed on top of the ninth building, how many stories are there now? (12) If you rode an elevator to the top, what place number would the top floor be? (12th)

Continue with similar questions and activities.

Students rebuild buildings and show the corresponding card in response to the questions.

Collect the cubes and hand out 20 links. These are to be placed in a long line. Call out places in random order and have students show the link and the correct card for that position. Continue until all the links have been named.

Procedure 3 □■

To develop the concept of *first through thirtieth*

Use *calendars, counters, number-and-word cards to 20th,* and *blank cards for the remaining numbers.*

Have students work in groups and complete the number card sets to 30th.

Give each group a calendar, or part of a calendar that has several months on it, and several counters. Call out a number, e.g., 14.

Students find that number and place a counter on it. One person from each group then gives a statement about the date, e.g., "January 14 is the second Monday," or "It is the 14th day of the month."

Be sure to include months of 31 as well as 30 days. At this time, it may also be appropriate to introduce February's unusual number of days.

Each group of students orders its cards and takes turns reading them from first to thirtieth. Then they mark their calendars with 1st through 30th.

Older students may now write on paper the cardinal numbers as numerals, the ordinal abbreviations, and the ordinal numbers as spelled words; e.g., 20—20th—twentieth.

Practice and Extension

Have students practice at home rote counting from first through forty-ninth.

Students write a simple paragraph, or series of sentences, describing a common activity using ordinal words to show sequence of steps; e.g., *How to Jump Rope: First, get a length of rope twice as long as you are tall. Second, take each end of the rope in a hand. Third, swing the rope with both hands so it goes over your head.*

Students play Calendar Toss by taking turns tossing a *bean bag* at a large `calendar` on the floor. Students must correctly read the number the bean bag lands on, saying the day of the week, the name of the month, and the day's ordinal name; e.g., "The bag is on Tuesday, March 12th." Student with the most correct responses after five minutes is declared winner.

When students have lined up to leave the room, ask questions like "Megan is fourth in line. Who is third? What position is Aron in?"

Have students use a *number line* and write 1 to 25 above the line, and 1st to 25th below the line.

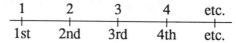

Have stations of differing patterns around the room, e.g., a pattern of *squares, circles,* and *triangles.* If one square is first in line, where are two more squares? If a circle is fourth, where is another circle? What positions are the triangles in? Make other patterns, using *treasure box objects, colored counters,* and other *objects.*

Number Skills 10

Skill: To develop the concepts of *one more* and *one less*

Time: 2 periods

Materials:

interlocking cubes: 10 per student

treasure box or other objects

beads and string

calendar

counters

graph paper: ¹/₂" squares or larger

scissors

crayons

See Reproducibles for: number lines to 25 (taped together) 1 per student pair

Anticipatory Set

Use *interlocking cubes (5 per student)*.

Have students first do a forward-counting activity such as rote counting while clapping, orally counting each student, counting desks or books, etc. Review knowledge of number sequence.

Now have each student make a small train with four cubes. Instruct them to remove two of those cubes. How many are left in the trains? Students discuss.

Now have students take their two joined cubes and add three more cubes to the trains. Discuss how long the trains are now. Move on to Procedure 1.

Procedure 1

To develop the concept of *one more*

Use *fingers, interlocking cubes,* and *objects*.

First have students hold up three fingers. Tell students in row one to hold up one more finger.

Students tell you that those in row one are holding up four fingers.

Continue briefly until students grasp the idea that they already know "one more" because they know the basic number sequence for lower numbers.

Have students move into small groups and hand out about 15 interlocking cubes and 15 objects to each group.

Call out a number and tell the students to take one group of the manipulatives and build a parade that number of objects long.

Tell them to use the other group of manipulatives to build another parade that is one longer than the first.

Students discuss in groups how to make a parade that is one longer than the first, while you move about the room and monitor their progress. One group presents its parades, and the other students discuss whether or not they agree with the group's work.

Continue the procedure, changing groups if necessary, until all students understand the concept of parades that are one more.

Procedure 2

To develop the concept of *one less*

Usc *interlocking cubes, number lines,* and *beads and string*.

First, have students work in small groups. They take the cubes and build trains of a specified length.

Now call out a number that is one less than that given previously and have the students build another train of that length.

Students complete tasks and discuss what they observe about the trains.

Have students work in pairs. First, they complete the number lines. Next, one student uses beads and string, and the other student uses the interlocking cubes. Call out a number and have the first student string that many beads on the string.

One of the students places beads on the string.

Now call out the number that is one less than the previously given number. The other student builds a train of that many cubes. Is the train of cubes longer than the string of beads?

Students respond either yes or no, depending on the size of their beads. Most will say yes.

Discuss the number of beads on the string and the number of cubes in the train.

Have students take their number lines and place a bead on the number that corresponds to the number of beads on the string. Now place an interlocking cube on the number that the train represents.

Students do as requested and see that there is one less cube than beads; that the number of the train's parts is in fact smaller than the number of beads on the string.

Repeat the activity, using other numbers. Help the students understand that the length of the object constructed will vary according to how large the individual parts are, even though the relationships of the numbers remain constant.

Procedure 3

To practice counting for one more and one less

Use *calendar*, *counters*, and *number lines*.

Have students count the calendar days until they reach today's date. Point to today's date. Tomorrow is one number more. It will be ___? Yesterday was one number less. It was ___?

Students respond with the numbers.

Use other days of the month and have the students find the day, respond with the day that is one more, and the day that is one less.

Students work in pairs and place a counter on the number 5 on the number line. Have them put a finger on the number that is one more. Say, "One more than 5 is . . ." (Wait for response.) Continue all the way up the number line to 25.

Students complete oral activity with you, moving their counter, pointing to the next higher number, and saying that number in response to your question.

Now have students place a counter on the number 25 on the number line and put their fingers on the number 24. One less than 25 is . . .

Students respond: One less than 25 is 24. Students complete oral activity, continuing all the way down the number line to 0.

Procedure 4

To write the process of one more and one less as addition and subtraction problems

Use *graph paper*, *scissors*, and *crayons*.

Each student works independently. Call out a randomly selected number such as 7, and have students color in that many squares on the graph paper.

After coloring squares, students write the number that tells how many are colored, under the colored squares.

Have students chorally count the number as you write it on the board.

Now tell students to color in one more square. On the board write 7 + 1 = ___.

Tell students the language of math just explains what they can do with objects. The language for the activity they just completed is on the board, but one number is missing. What should that number be?

Students respond with the correct number and discuss what they have been doing.

Continue with some plus-one numbers until all are able to write down on the graph paper what they have done.

Now students cut out their lines of colored graph paper. They take a designated set and cut off one square. As they complete the activity, they discuss how many squares are still in the line.

Relate the activity and its result to simple subtraction by writing 9 − 1 = 8 on the board. Again discuss with students that this is math language. It tells what we do when we cut off or take away a part of something.

Students write on paper what you have written on the board.

Allow students to "teach" the concept by taking turns showing a line, cutting off one of its units, and writing in math language on the board what they have done.

Practice and Extension

Leave out *plastic links* and encourage students to make necklaces, first of one length, and then with one link more or one less. They should write on paper how long the first necklace was, whether they added or took away one, and how long the second necklace was.

Have students play *games* in which *dice* are used to set the number of spaces to be moved. The first time through the game, they move one more space than the number shown on the dice. The second time, they move one less space than the number shown.

Give the students a number; e.g., 7. Ask them what they can say about this number. (It is one more than 6. It is one less than 8.) Repeat with other numbers.

Have students make up word problems like: "Bobby has one more cookie than Yvonne. Yvonne has two cookies. How many does Bobby have?"

Number Skills 11

Skill: To compare numbers through 10

Time: 2 periods

Materials:

Cuisenaire® rods

number-and-dot cards plus an extra card marked with the number 10: 1 set per student

number cards: large teacher set

symbol cards with >, <, =, *and* ≠ *on them:* 1 set per student

counters: 10 per student

plastic links

beads (or O shaped cereals) and string

dice: 1 pair

See Reproducibles for: number lines to 25 (taped together)

Anticipatory Set

Use *Cuisenaire® rods*.

Hand out materials and have students work in groups of three or four. Let them have time to play with the materials and encourage them to build with the rods. After a few minutes of play, ask students if they have discovered anything about the small cubes and the longer rods. Lead them to realize that ten of the small cubes are the same length as one rod.

Discuss the concepts of *greater than* and *less than*; have students demonstrate with the rods. Relate this to *one more* and *one less*, from previous lessons.

Divide the students into four unequal groups. Tell all the students to hold up ten fingers. They then compare and see which group has the most fingers raised. Which group has the fewest raised fingers?

What else could they compare? Have students decide other ways to compare numbers of fingers.

Procedure 1

To compare numbers with regard to size

Use *Cuisenaire® rods, teacher number cards,* and *number-and-dot cards*.

Make sure the students understand that each rod represents a different number. Go over the values of each, and place colors and corresponding numbers on the board for the students to use as a reference, if one is needed.

Give each group three rods of various lengths. Tell students to place the shortest rod on the left side of the desk. Place the longest rod on the right side of the desk. Place the in-between rod in the middle. Now under each rod place the correct number card.

Students place rods as instructed, and read their numbers in order.

Discuss with students that the rods and the numbers go from smallest to largest, or least to greatest.

Groups exchange rods and repeat activity. Some of the groups should present their sequences to the entire class.

Review *shortest to tallest* and have students line up according to height.

Students then relate their position in line by giving the regular number and the ordinal number for it.

Have four students step in front of the line and change places. The rest of the class has to decide what the new values should be for these students.

Procedure 2

To understand the meaning of the symbols: ≠, <, >

Use *counters, symbol cards,* and *number-and-dot cards*.

Have students place three counters on one side of their desks, and one counter on the other.

To convey meanings of < and >, discuss with students such ideas as: which end of an ice-cream cone holds the most, or the open mouth of an alligator, or that a dinosaur eats a smaller animal.

Students discuss that the largest amount goes in the opening. They then place appropriate symbol card (< or >) between their counters.

Repeat with other number pairs. Monitor student activities and responses.

Discuss previous lessons in which the students learned about the symbol = . Show the symbol for "does not equal" (≠) and discuss.

Have students place three counters on each side of their desks. Ask which symbol should go between this number pair.

Students respond: The equal sign. They place this symbol between the two groups of counters, and discuss both symbols and what each means.

Repeat exercises like those above with the counters and the symbols = and ≠.

Now have students take their number cards and set up number relationships, one that uses < , one that uses > , and one that uses ≠ .

Students set up their number pairs and then check to see if those around them have displayed correct sequences.

Procedure 3

To develop comparison of numbers using objects

Use *plastic links, beads and string, dice,* and *number-and-dot cards.*

Have the students work in groups. Have each student use one of the sets of manipulatives. Roll the dice and announce the number shown by the two dice. (If their total is more than 10, call out the number 10.)

One student makes a chain of that number of items and places the correct number card next to it. Throw dice again, and ask a second student to make a chain. Continue until each student has made a chain.

After students have made chains, they discuss with each other which is longer, shorter; whether any are equal to others. They display the chains on their desks with symbol cards showing relationships between them.

They check other groups' relationships. Groups then report to the class which is their longest chain, shortest chain, and whether or not they had any that were equal in length.

Repeat the activity several times.

Procedure 4

To practice comparing numbers

Use *counters, beads, number-and-dot cards, symbol cards,* and *number lines.*

Have students work in pairs. Each takes a handful of beads and estimates their number. They then count them and find the appropriate number card.

Students complete task and place counters on the appropriate spots on the number line.

Next, students use symbol cards and number cards to lay out a relationship between their numbers. They write this relationship on a chart.

Have pairs join to form groups of four and repeat the procedure. What problems did they have in setting up relationship lines? When might they need to know if an amount was larger or smaller?

Practice and Extension

Have students use a *deck of cards* and play the game War.

Have students take *old game boards* and make up games that use *symbol cards* and *number-and-dot cards,* 1 through 10.

Have students individually color two rows of *graph paper* one color; then color two more rows another color. They cut the rows of one color into separate squares. Discuss the fact that when put in a line, the cut squares are the same length as the uncut rows.

Discuss the values of *dimes, pennies,* and *nickels.* Encourage students to make up real-life situations or problems to solve with the coins, which take into account their different values.

Number Skills 12

Skill: To count by tens

Time: 2 periods

Materials:

Secret Code number line (see Manipulative Information section)

simple line drawings from children's coloring books, or commercial dot-to-dots

tracing paper

coins: dimes; 10 per pair

counters: enough to cover ½ sheet of paper per group (approx. 40 one-inch counters)

paper: ½ sheet per group

See Reproducibles for: hundred boards—1 per pair, number lines to 100—1 per group

Anticipatory Set

Use *Secret Code number line, coloring book pictures,* and *tracing paper.*

Give each student a picture and a piece of tracing paper. They are to make dots on the outline of the picture, so that they end up with a picture that is like a dot-to-dot. When students finish, they set aside the pictures. Now call their attention to the green diagonal line on the Secret Code number line. Today they are going to find out why certain numbers have this line. Move on to Procedure 1.

Procedure 1 ■

To develop the sequence of tens to 100

Use *hundred boards, dimes, counters, and dot pictures from Anticipatory Set.*

Have students work in pairs and give each pair a hundred board, dimes, ten counters, and their own dot pictures.

Chorally count from 1 to 10, placing a counter on each number. Ask what value a dime has.

Students respond: 10 cents.

Place a dime on 10 and remove counters. Now count from 1 to 10 again, this time placing counters on 11 to 20. Repeat question and place a dime on 20. First dime is 10; add 10 more for 20.

Students follow directions and then report they have two dimes on their boards. They count 10, 20.

Continue until end of board has been reached, and a dime is on each multiple of 10. Ask students if they see any pattern to the numbers that are covered by dimes.

Students respond: They all end in zeros.

Now, chorally count with students: "One dime— 10; two dimes—20; etc."

After all students have responded correctly, have them look at their dot pictures and place a dime on each dot. Have them write numbers beside each dot (dime).

Students complete task and write 10, 20, 30, etc. on their dot pictures.

Have students exchange pictures and complete the partner's drawing.

Procedure 2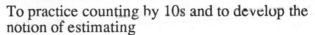

To practice counting by 10s and to develop the notion of estimating

Use *number lines to 100, fingers, counters,* and *half sheets of paper.*

Groups first number the number lines from 10 to 100. Monitor for accuracy.

Have students stand up, hold up their fingers and count off by tens. Students can use their fingers to go by ones to the next ten if needed. Other students check the completed number lines to see if the response is accurate. As each student counts, echo the correct response, sometimes going all the way back to ten to reinforce the sequence.

Students count off by tens until they reach one hundred.

Discuss the term *multiple* with students. They have been counting the multiples of 10.

After all students have responded to the count-by-tens exercise, ask why they think it may be important to be able to count by tens.

Hand each group a large, randomly chosen number of counters. Without counting, groups decide how many they have.

Students guess and write that number down on paper.

Now students separate the counters into groups of ten. Students discover they can group by tens and count the total by counting by tens. They compare their total with the earlier estimate.

Students can now expand on the earlier discussion. They will probably realize that in counting dimes it would be easier if they could count by tens; and that it is easier to group objects in tens, and then count groups by tens to arrive at a total. Some students may also see how the skill could help in estimating.

Lead the discussion to estimating the amount of money needed to buy a group of items that cost around ten cents each; to being able to estimate how much they are going to spend before they check out at a store's cash register; and to estimating other items in multiples of ten.

Groups now take half sheets of paper and counters. After estimating the number of counters needed to cover the sheet, they put the counters on the paper in groups of ten.

After every ten counters, they change colors. When they have finished, they count the number of groups by 10s. They write the tens as they count. Any leftovers are added to arrive at the final total.

Were they close to being correct in their estimates? Did they use an even number of tens to cover the paper?

Working in groups, students make up a real-life situation where they could use estimating by tens, and then counting by tens to find the answer.

Each group uses its number line to prove the answer. After a set amount of time, each group presents its situation and answer to the class for discussion.

Practice and Extension

Have students take *graph paper* and color rectangles that are 10 squares wide with *crayons*. Each rectangle should be a different number of squares tall. Beside each rectangle, they write the number of squares in that rectangle; e.g., 40 beside a rectangle 4 by 10. (They can add the four lines of squares, if necessary, to find the total number.) They write down how many tens it took to equal that amount. Four 10s = 40. This is a pre-multiplication skill.

Put a number of *plastic links* in a large *container* and have the students estimate their number. After each student has guessed, count the links out in groups of ten, and then count the groups by tens, adding any leftovers, to arrive at the final answer.

Set out *counters, counter-trading boards,* and *dice.* The students can play counter-trading games, trading for a ten counter each time they arrive at a group of ten ones. Emphasize that this skill will help them in other math activities.

Have students count by tens, instead of by ones, as they *jump rope* on the playground. Can they make up a rhyme to use when jumping and counting by tens? One example:

10 . . . 20 . . . 30 . . . 40
50 . . . 60 . . . up I go
Now count backward; please go slow.
40 . . . 30 . . . 20 . . . 10
Jump once more, and out again!

(This rhyme has four beats per line.)

Number Skills 13

Skill: To count by fives

Time: 3 periods

Materials:

Secret Code number line (see Manipulative Information section)

plastic links: 5 of the same color per student

markers

coins: nickels; 10 per student

simple line drawings from children's coloring books

tracing paper

counters: 5 per student pair

graph paper: of any size

scissors

beads and string

number line on floor (see Manipulative Information section for suggestions)

See Reproducibles for: number lines to 100 (taped together) 1 per student group, hundred boards—1 per student pair, blank matrices—1 per student pair

Anticipatory Set

Use *Secret Code number line.*

Encourage students to notice the blue squares and discuss what they think the squares might show them. Remind students of the green diagonal line that they discussed when counting by tens.

Have students hold up their right hands. Count the right hand fingers in each row by ones. Ask: How would it be easier to count? Answer: by fives. Now count the fingers in each row by fives. Go on to Procedure 1.

Procedure 1

To develop the sequence of fives to 25

Use *plastic links.*

Have students make a chain of the five links. Ask how many links are in the chain. (5) Each student then joins his or her chain to the differently colored chain of another student. Ask: How long is the chain now?

Students respond: 10 links.

Students join more chains, each of a different color, and respond to questions until each chain is 25 links long. Each chain now belongs to five students who will work as a group.

Students take turns in their groups counting the sections of 5 links. Monitor to ascertain that each student has grasped the pattern: 5 . . . 10 . . . 15 . . . 20 . . . 25.

Have students list these numbers vertically. Do they see any patterns? In previous lessons, we discussed multiples of 10. What might these numbers be called?

Students respond: Multiples of 5. They discuss the patterns they see in these numbers, and they guess that the next multiple of 5 would be 30.

Procedure 2

To develop the sequence of fives to 50

Use *number lines, markers, nickels, coloring book pictures,* and *tracing paper.*

Working in groups, have students number all long tic marks on a number line by 10s to 50; i.e., 10, 20, etc.

Give each group several pictures and tracing paper. They are to make outlines of the main part of the pictures, using about 10 dots spaced as in dot-to-dot pictures.

Students complete the number line as instructed. They make several pictures and set them aside.

Chorally count the smaller tic marks 1, 2, 3, etc., to 50. As the class counts, the students write in the numbers.

Now have students place a nickel on all the numbers ending in five. Ask how many lines are between those numbers. (9) Would we be counting by fives if we only used those numbers? (No.)

Students discuss and decide that in order to count by fives, a nickel must be placed on every fifth number.

Groups now decide where to place the other nickels on the number line. Monitor to see that all are correctly placed.

Now chorally count with students: "1 nickel—5; 2 nickels—10; etc."

After students have responded, have them look at their dot pictures and place a nickel on each dot.

Now they write numbers beside each dot and nickel. Ask: What will be the first dot number? (5) What will be the second dot number? (10)

Students number the pictures. They monitor each other and after numbering correctly, they exchange pictures and complete the line drawings with markers.

Procedure 3 ◻◼

To develop the sequence of fives to 100

Use *hundred boards*, *blank matrices*, *markers*, *nickels*, and *counters*.

Students work in pairs; each pair has a hundred board, 20 nickels, and 5 counters. Count chorally from 1 to 5, placing a counter on each number. Ask what value a nickel has.

Students respond: 5 cents.

Place a nickel on 5 and remove counters. Students then write the numbers 1, 2, 3, and 4 on the blank matrix with one color and 5 in the second color.

Now count from 1 to 5 again, placing counters on 6 to 10. Repeat question and place a nickel on 10.

Students follow directions and report that they have two nickels on their boards. They have covered numbers 5 and 10. They write the numbers 6 through 10 on the matrix, using the two colors as before.

Continue until both boards have been completed and a nickel is on each multiple of 5. Ask students if they see any pattern to the numbers covered by nickels.

Students respond: They all end in fives or zeros. They form two straight lines on the hundred board. The pattern on the matrix is the same.

Students chorally read the numbers that are covered by nickels.

Procedure 4 ◻

To write multiples of 5 to 100

Use *graph paper*, *scissors*, *number line on the floor*, and *beads and string*.

Students work in large groups. Have each student place five beads on a string. They count the total number of beads by fives and report to the class how many beads they have used.

Students do this as a review of counting by fives. They record the numbers on a sheet of paper labeled "Multiples of Five."

Students now work independently. Each cuts from a piece of graph paper rectangles that are 5 squares wide. Each rectangle should be a different number of squares high.

Have students count the lines by fives and put the correct total number on the rectangle, also listing how many lines of five are in each rectangle.

Explain that the math language way of writing that 2 rows of 5 squares are 10 squares is 2 × 5 = 10, or 2 fives = 10.

Students cut rectangles and label each; e.g., 6 fives = 30. They save these for a class chart.

As students finish that activity, have them line up and take turns "jumping" or "stepping" the number line, orally counting by fives.

Students return to their desks and write the multiples of 5 to 100 on paper. After they finish activities, they are ready to put together the class chart of the rectangles, from 1 five = 5 to 20 fives = 100. If you prefer, use the form: 1 × 5 = 5 to 20 × 5 = 100.

Practice and Extension

Have students count by fives as they *jump rope* on the playground. Can they make up a rhyme to use when jumping and counting by fives? Example:

> 5 . . . 10 . . . 15 . . . 20
> I sure have jumped a plenty
> Now say only 5 and 10
> Jump once more and out again!

(The rhyme has four beats per line.)

Students use *beads and string* to make necklaces that are 50 beads long, with every fifth bead a specified color.

Have students make up real-life situations in which they earn *nickels* and have to count them to see how many they have. They then go to the store and spend a specified number of the nickels. Count by fives to see how much money was spent. Count by fives to see how much money they have left.

Students pick up handfuls of *counters*, estimate how many there are, group them by fives, and then count the groups.

Students can fill *box lids* with *counters*, changing colors every five counters. They then count the total by fives, using the differing colors.

Play Five Down. Have students stand and number off. After all the students have done so, the first student continues with the next number. Each student whose number is a multiple of five sits down. How far will they have to count before all are seated? When only a few students are still standing, can they predict who will be the last to sit?

Number Skills 14

Skill: To count by twos

Time: 3 periods

Materials:

Secret Code number line (see Manipulative Information section)

scissors

tape

interlocking cubes: 6 each of 2 colors per student pair

calendar

beads and string

dot-to-dot pictures: 1 per student

markers

tracing paper

place value (pv) materials to 100

plastic links

graph paper: of any size; 1 sheet per student

See Reproducibles for: number lines to 100—1 per student pair, pv mats to 100s—1 per student pair, hundred boards—1 per student pair

Anticipatory Set

Use *Secret Code number line.*

Students discuss what they can buy in or by twos at the store. What word is often used to describe things we buy by twos? (pair) Discuss what constitutes a pair.

Why do you suppose we say a pair of jeans? Discuss. Now have students push their desks together and discuss that the class is now arranged in pairs of students. How many students are in a pair? (2)

Challenge students to discover how today's math activities are related to the Secret Code number line.

Procedure 1

To develop the sequence of twos to 40 or less

Use *number lines, scissors, tape,* and *interlocking cubes.*

Students work in pairs. Have students tape together number lines and chorally count the tic marks. As they count, they number the marks to 40, or as far as desired.

Students count tic marks and number them.

Give each pair of students 12 interlocking cubes. They build a tower two stories high, alternating colors.

Touch the first cube and whisper "one," and then say in a normal voice "two," while touching the second cube.

Students follow your example.

Have students build another two-cube tower on top of the first. As they touch the blocks, they whisper "three" and say "four" in a full voice.

Continue the process until tower is 12 stories high. What pattern do they see in the towers?

Count with students by having them touch the first two cubes, think "one," and say "two."

Continue the process up to the number 12.

Student pairs check each other as they count by twos.

Now have students take the number line and circle each number they spoke out loud.

Can they see a pattern on the number line?

Students should see that every other number is circled.

Have student extend the pattern as far as desired, while monitoring their progress. Then have students chorally read all the circled numbers.

Procedure 2

To practice the sequence of twos to 40 or less

Use *calendar, beads and string, dot-to-dot pictures, markers,* and *tracing paper.*

Take the calendar and have students tell which days are on multiples of two. Can they extend this to the next month?

If the month has 31 days, can they realize they have to start at one and skip a day in their count? For example, if Monday is the thirtieth, the next even number is in the next month; it is Thursday the second.

Give each pair beads and string. Count the days again. For every day that is a multiple of two, they put two beads on the string. How many beads are on the string when they finish the month?

Students work in pairs, check each other as to the next correct day, add two beads to the string, and then count by twos to see how many beads they have.

Discuss this process so students can see the relationships.

Give each student a dot-to-dot picture and tracing paper. They are to reproduce the dots, but not the numbers, on the tracing paper. Students now number their dot-to-dot tracings using only multiples of two.

Students then exchange their pictures with partners to see if their pictures can be completed as numbered.

Procedure 3 □■

To develop the sequence of twos to 100

Use *pv mats, pv materials, hundred boards, markers, plastic links,* and *paper.*

Working in pairs and using pv mats and materials, students build numbers by twos. Have one partner exchange roles with the other whenever a ten is reached. One builds a number; the other records the number.

Monitor progress to see that all are building and recording numbers correctly.

Student pairs work at their own pace. If a pair finishes ahead of the others, they can use the time to write down what they believe is occurring.

As they are finishing, give each pair of students a handful of plastic links. They are to guess how many there are and then count by twos to see what the actual number is.

Students complete assignment. They discuss how accurate their estimates were.

Now have each pair take a hundred board and place a link on each of the first five numbers they said when counting by twos. When links are correctly placed, they color the numbers with markers. What numbers do the students think will be colored on the *second* line?

Students respond: 12, 14, 16, 18, and 20. They color those numbers on the hundred boards. If they do not see that or understand the pattern, let them place links on every other number prior to coloring the numbers.

What kind of pattern do the students see beginning? Will this continue? Discuss responses. Have students finish the hundred-board patterns and then discuss again. Were they correct? What do they think would happen if the pattern were continued?

Students complete the pattern and discuss their findings.

Procedure 4 □

To write the sequence of counting by twos

Use *completed hundred boards, graph paper, scissors, markers,* and *Secret Code number line.*

Working individually, students use graph paper to outline rectangles that are 2 squares wide and differing number of squares high. They mark on the rectangles their size; i.e., the number of squares inside the rectangle. They cut out the rectangles and order them by size on a chart. Students present their charts to the class.

Discuss with students that they now know some skills that will be useful when they come to the math skill of multiplication. Show students how to write the relationships using math language.

Now students each write down the sequence of counting by twos. They use the completed hundred board to check their accuracy.

Call their attention to the Secret Code number line. Ask: What is the code for multiples of two?

Students discuss. Next they write, and exchange story problems that can be solved by knowing multiples of two.

Practice and Extension

Students can *jump rope*, using a skip-counting rhyme:

> 2 . . . 4 . . . 6 . . . 8
> Susie ate a piece of cake
> 2 . . . 4 . . . 6–8 . . . 10
> Jump once more and out again!

Have students make up their own rhymes.

Students list all the multiples of 2 that are between the two numbers of a pair like 28 and 35.

Students play the game Two Down. Students number off, and every one whose number is a multiple of two sits down. When only a few students are left, see if the class can predict which will be the last one to sit.

Have students jump the *number line on the floor* (see Manipulative Information section) while counting by twos.

Number Skills 15

Skill: To count by hundreds

Time: 1 period

Materials:

place value (pv) materials to 100: use counters as 1000s if necessary

coins: pennies; 100 per group

calendar: one 12-month, one-page

collections of 100 things: students each bring one collection

See Reproducibles for: number lines to 1000 (taped together) 1 per group, pv mats to 1000s—1 per group, blank matrices—1 per student, bills—100s only; 10 per group

Note: This lesson is a good one to have as a Hundredth Day Activity. If your students have been keeping track of the number of days of school, you can build on their desire to count hundreds of different things.

Anticipatory Set

Use *fingers* and *number lines to 1000 (1 per group).*

Have students stand up, hold up their fingers, and count off by tens. Students can use their fingers to go by ones to the next 10 if needed. Students count off by tens until they reach 100, or farther if so desired.

Working in small groups, students then number the number line by tens, writing on the small tic marks. Have them go only to the first long tic mark, to 100.

Discuss the fact that counting by tens and counting by hundreds is similar. Allow students to explore why they think this may be true. Go on to Procedure 1.

Procedure 1

To develop the sequence from 100 to 1000

Use *pv materials, pv mats,* and *number lines from Anticipatory Set.*

Have students work in small groups and place the number 100 on their pv mats.

Students do task and chorally read: Zero ones, zero tens, one hundred.

Now have students place another 100 on their mats. How many do they have now? (200) They are to chorally read and then have one group member mark the large tic marks on the number line.

Students chorally read: Zero ones, zero tens, and two hundreds. One of the group writes 200 on the number line in the appropriate place.

Continue activity until the pv mats show 1000 and the number line reads 100 to 1000.

Ask students to discuss patterns they can observe in the number line and on the mats.

Students should respond: There are two zeros on each number in the hundreds place. They discuss any other patterns they see.

Procedure 2

To practice counting objects by hundreds

Use *pennies, calendar, collections,* and *completed number lines*

Work in groups and have each group count their pennies to verify that they have 100. If we now want to find out how many pennies the entire class has, do we need to count out each penny?

Students discuss possible ways to count the pennies. They may suggest counting by tens as well as hundreds.

Post the calendar and discuss with students the number of days on the calendar. Count off 100 days and make a slash mark. Count off another 100 days and make another slash. Continue.

Call attention to the fact that these 100 days are different ones than the first 100 school days that were counted earlier, if they were.

Students take turns presenting their collections of 100 things to the class. They discuss how many items in all they have in the classroom. They also discuss the number of similar objects they have; e.g., someone brought 100 grains of popcorn, and someone else brought 100 grains of rice; these 200 objects are foods and similar in form.

Continue to discuss and group the collections as students practice counting by hundreds.

Students use the number line to check accuracy of counting, if needed.

Chorally read through the numbers on the number line. As a final part of this procedure, have students make a graph showing the amounts of similar objects they have in their hundred collections.

Students may also want to display their collections for the entire school to view.

Procedure 3

To write the sequence of hundreds to 1000.

Use *pv mats, bills,* and *blank matrices.*

Randomly call out multiples of 100 for students to represent with the bills on their pv mats.

Working in groups, students make numbers on their pv mats using the bills, and record the numbers in order. Monitor progress as students are working.

Remind students of the matrices they used earlier that went from 1 to 100. Have students work individually and fill in the blank matrix from 100 to 1000. Ask them to look for patterns and similarities as they fill in these matrices according to the numbers they put on the number line earlier.

Students discuss patterns and then story problem situations that could be solved using multiples of 100.

Have students brainstorm to find other times when it would be useful to be able to count by hundreds.

Practice and Extension

Put a number of *pop-can flip-tops* in a large *container* and have the students estimate the number. After each student has guessed, count the tops out in groups of ten and then count the groups of tens by hundreds. Donate these to the local McDonald's for the Ronald McDonald House, or to some other charity that collects pop-can flip-tops. The entire school can join the collection activity.

Set out *counters, counter-trading boards,* and *dice.* The students can play counter-trading games, trading for a ten counter each time they arrive at a group of 10 ones, and trading for a hundred counter each time they arrive at a group of 10 tens. After a set amount of time, the student with the most hundred counters wins. Stress that this skill will help them in other math activities.

Have students build rectangles that are 10×10 squares, using *1 cm graph paper.* They can build designs and count the 100s in the designs. Save the squares to use as extra 100 flats in later lessons.

Students can make a 1000 board, using a *blank matrix.*

Number Skills 16

Skill: To understand odd and even numbers

Time: 2 periods

Materials:

Secret Code number line (see Manipulative Information section)

calendar

dot-to-dots: teacher-adapted to even numbers only

interlocking cubes: red and blue; 10 per student pair

crayons: in colors to match interlocking cubes

place value (pv) materials to 100

simple line drawings from coloring books

tracing paper

See Reproducibles for: pv mats to 100s—1 per student, hundred boards—1 per student, number lines to 100 (taped together) 1 per student pair, blank matrices—1 per student, graph paper with 1" squares—1 sheet per student

Anticipatory Set

Use *Secret Code number line.*

Draw on the board or overhead a strange-looking creature with three eyes, three ears, five arms, three fingers on each hand, five legs with seven toes on each foot. Discuss why this creature looks odd. Name the creature and suggest that students can later make their own "odd" creatures, name them, and write a descriptive paragraph about them. Discuss that many of our body parts come in pairs, and that for that reason our bodies look symmetrical.

Call attention to the Secret Code number line. Today they will discover the final code.

Procedure 1

To develop the concepts of *odd* and *even*

Use *calendar, dot-to-dots, interlocking cubes,* and *crayons.*

Mark off the days of the month to the present date. Use one color for the even dates and another color for the odd dates. Ask students what they notice about the calendar dates. Discuss patterns.

Students discuss. They should see the similarities to the code.

Have student pairs complete the dot-to-dots. Did the sequence of numbers remind them of anything else they have studied in math?

Students complete dot-to-dots, and discuss the fact that even numbers remind them of multiples of, or skip counting by, twos.

Tell students to work in pairs and build towers of interlocking cubes, alternating colors. If using red and blue, start with red. We will discuss patterns and relationships of all the patterns after completing the towers. Name the blue cubes "even" and the red cubes "odd."

Students complete towers and discuss relationships.

Then have students dismantle the towers and share the cubes with each other, one student taking the blue and the other the red. Remind them of the concept of *pairs* talked about in the Anticipatory Set. Did each student receive the same number of cubes? (yes) If the cubes could be shared with two people as pairs, is the number of cubes even? (yes)

Students discuss relationships until they understand that *even* means being a multiple of two.

Using paper and two colors of crayons, student pairs now count and record until they reach their total number of cubes. They count blue 1, and write 1 in blue, red 2 and write 2 in red, etc.

Monitor their progress. Continue procedure until all have grasped the concept of odd and even numbers.

Procedure 2

To practice with even numbers

Use *pv mats, pv materials, hundred boards,* and *crayons.*

Call out numbers at random. Students use the pv materials to make the numbers on their pv mats.

Students complete task. As each number is built, they discuss whether the number is odd or even.

Continue to give numbers, mostly even, for the students to place and decide upon.

Now refer students to the hundred board. Have students color in all the multiples of two on the hundred boards. These numbers and any other number that is divisible by two are even numbers.

Students complete task. If they ask about divisibility by two, discuss with them the concept of *pair* covered earlier, and also the sharing method they used to find out if a number is odd or even.

Discuss how many even numbers are on the hundred board. Could they guess without counting? How many even numbers are between 25 and 50? What would help them guess an accurate number? Did they remember divisibility or sharing?

Procedure 3 ☐

To practice the concepts of *odd* and *even*, stressing odd numbers

Use *line drawings, tracing paper, number lines,* and *completed hundred boards.*

Have students work in pairs. Have them write the numbers not colored on the hundred board on their number line. They now have a skip-counting sequence of twos starting with one. These are the odd numbers. It is odd or hard to count by twos, starting with one instead of two.

As students complete the tasks, they read the sequence of odd numbers to each other.

Now give each pair a simple line drawing and tracing paper. They are to place the paper over the drawing and make a dot-to-dot, which they will exchange with another pair of students.

After numbering the dot-to-dot with sequential odd numbers, beginning with one, students exchange pictures for completion.

Discuss with students the same kind of questions that were used earlier. How can you find the number of odd numbers between 30 and 50? How many are there? How can you figure it out without counting? Are there the same number of even numbers? How about between 39 and 50?

Procedure 4 ☐

To complete additional practice of the concepts of *odd* and *even*

Use *blank matrices* and *graph paper.*

Have students work individually, placing the numbers from one to one hundred on the matrix, then labeling the numbers with an "e" or an "o" for *even* or *odd.*

Students take a sheet of graph paper and make a checkerboard pattern which corresponds to an odd-and-even pattern.

Have students write a description of a game they could play on their checkerboard that would use some part of the concept of odd/even. They share games which then are left out for free time activities.

Practice and Extension

Have students take a handful of small *objects.* They count the objects by two and record the number as odd or even on a chart.

Students *jump rope* to the following chant:

2 . . . 4 . . . 6 . . . 8
Even numbers to the gate.
1 . . . 3 . . . 5 . . . 7
Can I jump to eleven?
Count odd numbers; let me know:
Just how many steps to go!
1 . . . 3 . . . 5, . . . etc. (students continue counting by odd numbers until they miss)

Students have a *shoe box* with two colors of *counters* in it. Students reach in the box and draw out counters two at a time. If both are of the same color, they record "even" on a chart; one of each color is recorded "odd." How many would they have to draw to be sure of having two of the same color?

Have students make "odd creatures" suggested in Anticipatory Set.

Students play *games* left out from Procedure 4.

Number Skills 17

Skill: To find patterns in number sequences: addition or subtraction in the rule

Secret Code number line (see Manipulative Information section)

graph paper: of any size

markers

Time: 2+ periods

Materials:

1 cm cubes or tiles

rulers: 1 per student

Anticipatory Set

Write the following number sequence on the board: 31–34–37–35–38–41–39. Ask what number comes next. (42) Students probably will not see that the pattern is +3 +3 –2 +3 +3 –2. Leave the sequence on the board for later solving. Do not tell students what the next number is.

Procedure 1

To find patterns: addition in the rule

Use *cubes or tiles, ruler, plain paper,* and the *Secret Code number line.*

Have students draw a horizontal line across their paper halfway down. This will be the base line. Instruct students to place one cube on the line. To the right of that, they place another cube. A second cube goes directly above it on the paper. Finally, they place three cubes. Do they see a pattern?

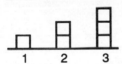

Students respond: The lines of cubes get bigger by one each time. They write the numbers 1, 2, 3 in a horizontal line, about 1/2 inch apart, on the bottom half of their paper.

Have students lay a ruler along the tops of the cubes. What do they notice? (the top cubes all touch the ruler along a diagonal)

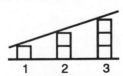

This is a regular pattern; the number of cubes increases by the same amount each time. How did we get from the 1 to the 3? (added 1 each time) We

can see they increase by one when we look at the cubes. What other way can we find the increase from one number to the next?

Students respond: Subtract the smaller from the larger.

What would be the next number? (4) We can find the difference between numbers by looking at the cubes or by subtracting. If you write how you got from one number to the next, it will help you see a pattern and you can predict the following number:

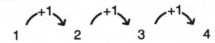

Students next place cubes for the sequence 2–3–5–6–8 on their papers. They also write this, as before.

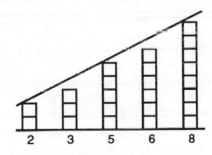

Have students lay their rulers along the tops of the cubes. What do they notice? (Not all the top cubes touch the ruler) The columns of cubes will touch the ruler if they form a regular series. Which columns do touch? (every other one) Every other time the same amount is being added. What would the next number of cubes be?

Students count cubes to see how much is added each time. They write +1 +2 +1 +2 above and between their numbers in the form shown above. They find the next number is 9.

What two ways could you find the pattern? (from the blocks and by subtracting)

Circle the following numbers on the Secret Code number line for students to solve: 0–1–3–6–10–15. (+1, +2, +3, +4, +5)

Procedure 2 　　　　　□■

To find patterns: subtraction in the rule

Use *cubes or tiles, rulers, plain paper,* and the *Secret Code number line.*

Repeat the procedure, using subtraction sequences. Use: 6–5–4–3; 7–6–4–3–1. Students should note that the direction of the ruler is reversed in subtraction. The numbers used to solve the sequence will be negative, as the numbers are decreasing.

Use the Secret Code number line as before. Circle: 35–34–31–30–27. Tell students the series is read on the number line from right to left this time, and challenge them to solve it. (–1, –3, –1, –3) Students should realize that they also could solve the series starting with 27 and adding numbers.

Procedure 3 　　　　　□■

To graph sequences

Use *graph paper, markers,* and *rulers.*

Have students draw a horizontal line across their paper six squares down from the top as a base line. Have them start at the base line and color a vertical column of squares for each number. Dictate the following series: 1–2–3–2–3–4–3–4.

Students color squares for the sequence and use their rulers to help show patterns. They write the series below the base line.

Have students put a dot at the midpoint of the top of each column. They use a ruler to draw a line connecting the dots. Ask: What does the graph tell us?

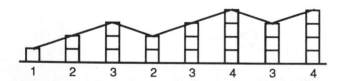

| 1 | 2 | 3 | 2 | 3 | 4 | 3 | 4 |

From the directions the line takes, students should see that they have both subtraction and addition. There is a regular series. The next number would be five.

Remind students that we can subtract to get the difference between numbers. Have students write +1 +1 between 1 and 2, and 2 and 3. What is the difference between the 3 and the next number, 2? (1) Will this be a +1 or a –1?

Students respond: Minus 1; the number is getting smaller. They finish writing the numbers.

Dictate sequences which include both addition and subtraction until students are competent in them.

Have them solve the problem from the Anticipatory Set. Then have them predict what the next three numbers would be.

Practice and Extension

Have students create sequences on the back of *graph paper.* Then turn the paper over and color in the sequence. Remind them that they must repeat the sequence for the pattern to become clear. Have them write a story problem to go with the sequence. Now they can exchange and try to solve each other's problems. Students may enjoy posting the more interesting designs made by the sequences.

Number Skills 18

Skill: To find patterns in number sequences: multiplication or division in the rule

Time: 1–2 periods

Materials:

cubes or tiles: about 20 per student

rulers: 1 per student

graph paper: of any size

markers

Anticipatory Set

Write the following sequence on the board: 1–2–6–12–36. Ask what number comes next. (72) Students probably will not see that the pattern is ×2 ×3 ×2 ×3. Leave sequence on the board for later solving.

Procedure 1

To find patterns: multiplication in the rule

Use *cubes or tiles, rulers,* and *plain paper.*

Have students draw a horizontal line across their paper halfway down. This will be the baseline. Write 1–2–4–8 on the board. Instruct students to place one block on the line, then two blocks, then four blocks, then eight blocks. Be sure blocks make flat vertical lines on the paper.

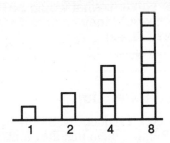

Students write the numbers in a horizontal line on the bottom half of their paper. Do they see a pattern?

Have students try to lay a ruler across the tops of the blocks:

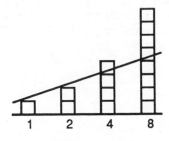

Students discover that this sequence is not formed by repeatedly adding the same numbers, for if it were the ruler would touch the tops of all the columns.

The numbers get large very quickly, which is a clue to remember. Ask: How can we get from the first number to the second? (add 1) How can we find how much to add?

Students respond: Subtract to find the difference between each number and the next.

On the board write +1 above and between the 1 and 2. Find the amounts to be added and mark them on your written sequence. Can you predict the next number?

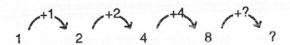

What have you discovered?

Students may notice that the same number is not added each time, and that each new number added is the same as the preceding number in the sequence.

Addition didn't help us here. The ruler showed us that. Is there another way to get from 1 to 2?

Students respond: Multiply by 2.

Write ×2 above the +1 in the sequence. Try to get from one number to the next by multiplication. What do you discover when you do that?

Students write ×2 above their addition numbers, in the form shown above. They discover a regular sequence.

What are the differences between sequences made by addition and those made by multiplication?

Students respond: The numbers get bigger more quickly with multiplication; the tops of the columns don't line up in a straight line as they do with addition.

Repeat this exercise with several other multiplication sequences.

Procedure 2

To find patterns: division in the rule

Use *cubes or tiles, rulers,* and *plain paper.*

Write: 9–3–1 on the board.

Students place blocks, write the sequence, and check with rulers.

The ruler slants downward to the right. Ask: What kind of sequence have you had before that gave the ruler a similar slant? (subtraction) Why does the ruler slant this way?

Students respond: The numbers are getting smaller.

But, does the ruler show that this sequence is made by subtraction?

Students respond: No, the ruler does not touch the tops of all the columns.

What do you notice about the size of the numbers? (they get smaller very quickly) How else could you get from 9 to 3? (divide by 3)

Students write ÷3 above their numbers.

What do you notice about both multiplication and division sequences? (the numbers go up and down quickly, and the columns don't line up with the ruler)

Provide students with more sequences to practice with. Ask them to first make predictions of what operations will be found in the rule.

Procedure 3

To graph curves of multiplication and division sequences

Use *graph paper, markers,* and *rulers.*

Have students draw a horizontal line across their paper near the bottom as a baseline. Have them start at the baseline and color a vertical column of blocks for each number. Dictate the following sequence: 3–6–12–24.

Students color blocks for the sequence and use their rulers to help themselves see patterns. They write the sequence to the side. They should recognize it as a multiplication sequence and be able to write ×2 above the numbers. If not, instruct them to write *all* ways to get from each number to the next.

Have students draw a line connecting the midpoints of the top blocks of the columns. Point out to them that they can smooth out their line to make a curve. (see illustration)

What pattern do they see? Where would the line go for the next number?

Students can see that the line is not straight and would rise even more quickly as the sequence progresses.

Sequences made by addition and subtraction give straight lines and sequences made by multiplication and division give curves on a graph.

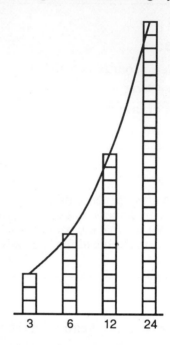

| 3 | 6 | 12 | 24 |

Write: 2–4–8–16–8–4–2.

Students color numbers and write the sequence to the side. They write ×2 ×2 ×2 ÷2 ÷2 ÷2 between the numbers and graph the tops of the columns.

If necessary, give students more sequences until they are competent.

Have them solve the problem from the Anticipatory Set. After solving, what would be the next number? What would they have to do to reverse the sequence? (÷3, ÷2)

Practice and Extension

Have students create sequences for others to solve on *graph paper.* Remind them that they must repeat the sequence for the pattern to become clear. Have students create a story problem to go with each sequence. They then exchange papers and see if they can solve each other's patterns.

Tell students they have worked hard at a job. Their boss says he will double their salary each month. Have students start with a salary of one dollar, chart several months' numbers, and make predictions about their future earnings.

Place Value 1

Skill: To understand place value through 19: counting and comparing

graph paper: ½" squares; cut into 1 × 10 rows—4 per student

crayons: 2 of different colors per student

scissors

Time: 4+ periods

Materials:

place value (pv) materials to 10s: any two kinds

coins: pennies and dimes

Anticipatory Set

Use *plain paper* and *pv materials*

Hand out materials and have students work in small groups of three or four. Let them have some time to play with the materials and encourage them to build with the blocks or sticks.

After a few minutes of play, ask students if they have discovered anything about the small blocks and the longer rods.

Lead them to realize ten of the small blocks are the same length as one rod. (If using craft sticks, they should see that ten sticks are the same as one bundle.)

Have students take paper, draw a line down the center, and label the right side "Ones" and the left side "Tens."

Procedure 1

To develop the concept of place value to 10

Use *paper from Anticipatory Set* and *pv materials*.

Tell students to work individually and to place a one cube on the right side of the paper, in the column labeled "Ones."

Have them place another cube in the ones column. Ask: How many cubes are on the paper?

Students respond: Two.

Continue procedure until you have nine cubes in the ones column.

Hold up another one cube and have students place one on their papers.

Ask them if they could substitute anything else for the 10 one cubes. Help them see that 10 ones is the same as 1 ten.

Repeat procedure until the class has grasped the notion that 10 ones are the same as 1 ten, and that in our numbering system whenever we reach ten we change the ones into a ten.

Students continue placing and counting one cubes up to ten, and then trading them for a ten rod or bundle.

They put this on the left side of the paper, labeled "Tens." They report how many they have by saying, "I have __ ones and __tens."

Ask the class if they can think of any times in our lives when this is useful. Discuss responses, encouraging comparisons of the pv materials with money.

Repeat the procedure with second place value material.

Procedure 2

To work with place value to 10

Use *prepared paper* and *coins*.

Follow Procedure 1, using paper and coins. Encourage students to make up real-life situations or problems to work on with the coins.

Procedure 3

To practice place value to 10

Use *fingers* and *prepared papers*.

Divide the students into four unequal groups. Tell all the students in each group to hold up ten fingers.

Students hold up the stated number of fingers. They then compare and see which group of students has the most fingers, and which group has the fewest fingers raised.

Have students think of other ways to compare numbers of fingers.

Now have students write numbers in the correct places on their paper mats. They can work in pairs and give each other randomly chosen numbers, or you can give randomly chosen numbers to the whole class.

Students check their own work by comparing it with that of others.

Procedure 4 ◻▪

To understand place value through 19

Use *graph paper rows, crayons, scissors, plain paper*, and *pv materials*.

Have students, working independently, color two of the rows one color. Have them color the other two rows another color.

Students should now cut both rows of one color into ten one squares each. Discuss that together ten squares are the same length as the longer ten-square rows.

Have students fold a plain piece of paper vertically dividing the paper into two long halves.

Have students use the crayon the color of their one squares to write "Ones" at the top of the right-hand column.

They use the other crayon to write "Tens" at the top of the left-hand column.

Have students place one of the squares in the ones column on their paper, and say "one." Have them add another one square and say "two." Continue until they are at the number nine.

Ask: How many numbers can we have in the ones place? (9) Have them add one more square to the ones column.

They now have too many numbers in the column. What can they do? (trade for a ten) Make sure that they all trade the ten one squares for one ten-square row.

Now have students write the number 10 on the paper, being sure they put the 1 in the tens column and the 0 in the ones column.

Students do as instructed, and each reads the number to another student.

Instruct the students to build the number 11 by placing a one square in the ones column.

They write the number and read it chorally.

Follow the same procedure with 12.

Then introduce the "Crazy Teenagers." These are the only numbers for which the ones number is read first. Other numbers are easier to read because the tens number is read first; e.g., 34 is "thirty-four."

Students discuss and practice saying the teens.

Now have them build the number 13 with the manipulatives, and write the number on the paper. Chorally read the number. Have each student read the number to another.

Continue with the other numbers through 19.

Give students the pv materials and more of the vertically halved paper.

Students should follow the previous activity with the different materials and demonstrate understanding of the concept.

Caution: After they have mastered the "Crazy Teenagers," be sure students are not reading 21 instead of 12.

Procedure 5 ◻

To write numbers through 19

Use *coins* and *vertically halved plain paper*.

Hand out materials, and call out numbers for students to place, read, and write.

Working in pairs, students make numbers on the paper with the dimes and pennies. After making a number with the manipulatives, they write the number at the bottom of the paper below the coins.

After each has checked with another student, they clear off the paper and are ready for the next number you call.

Students continue to make numbers with the coins, write the numbers on paper, and read the numbers until all are responding correctly.

Practice and Extension

Have students play counter-trading games in groups of three or four, using *paper, 1 die*, and *counters*. One student shakes a die and calls out the number of counters to be placed in the ones column. The first student to remember to trade for a ten calls out "ten" and wins that round. Students can then trade positions.

Allow the students to play more advanced forms of counter-trading as they become capable.

Use strips of *graph paper* cut into ten rods and one squares, and *19 blank index cards*. Working in groups, students write numbers 1 to 19 on cards and turn them over. Each draws a number and uses rods and squares to show value. Other students check.

Students play Show Me, a game in which one student rolls a die and calls out a number, using the die number as either the ones or tens digit. The other students must show the number correctly on a *pv chart*, using *any manipulative*. A right answer is worth a point. The first student to score five points wins.

Place Value 2

Skill: To understand place value through 99: regrouping and expanded notation

dice

place value (pv) materials to 10s

See Reproducibles for: pv mats to 100s, bills to 10s—in different colors

Time: 1+ period

Materials:

counters: two different colors; 12 of each per student

markers or crayons: same colors as counters

Anticipatory Set

Use *pv mats, crayons or markers,* and *counters.*

Hand out the counters to each student. Instruct students to color rectangles at the top of the pv mat to correspond to the counter colors. Have all use the same color for the ones and the other color for the tens place. Leave hundreds white at this point.

Have students place one counters on their mats and count them. Ask if anyone remembers what happens when we have gathered ten ones. Students should remember to trade them for a ten counter.

Set counters aside until Procedure 3.

Procedure 1

To understand regrouping; only using manipulatives

Use *bills, completed pv mats from Anticipatory Set,* and *dice.*

Hand out 10 one-dollar bills and 10 ten-dollar bills to each student. Roll one die and have students place that number of bills in the ones place and count chorally to the number as they do so.

Students place bills and chorally count to the number.

Roll the die again and have students add that many $1 bills to their mats, counting chorally as they do. After they have made several tens trades successfully, begin rolling two dice and have them place the larger number in the ones place and the smaller number in the tens place.

Discuss that after they have the placed numbers, the smaller digit has a greater value than the larger digit.

Students chorally count as they add bills to their mats, trade up as needed, and chorally read the number.

Continue until students have mastered the process.

Students monitor each other and check for accuracy, while you move about and also monitor.

Procedure 2

To practice regrouping and writing numbers

Use *pv materials, completed pv mats from Anticipatory Set, dice, paper,* and *pencils.*

Use same procedure as in Procedure 1, but add paper-and-pencil work. Explain that after choral reading of the number shown with the pv materials, each student is to write it.

Students chorally count, trade up as needed, chorally read the number, and write the number on their papers.

Continue until you have reached the number 99.

Procedure 3

To understand expanded notation

Use *counters, pv mats from Anticipatory Set, dice, paper,* and *pencils.*

Hand out counters and pv mats. Ask students to place four one counters on their mats. Have them choral read the number as "0 tens, 4 ones."

Students place counters and give desired response.

Roll two dice and have students place that amount of counters on their mats. Instruct them to trade up if needed.

Students place counters, trade up if needed, and chorally read number "__tens and __ones."

Have students write on their papers the number they have just read. Continue to 99, with students placing counters, trading, reading, and writing.

After reaching the number 99, ask what would happen if one more counter were added. What do we need to have to prove this with our counters?

Students discover they must trade 10 ones for a ten. Now they have 10 tens and these need to be traded for something.

Either hand out a different color counter or have students trade them all in and write the number 100 on their papers.

Practice and Extension

Use *pv mats, counters,* and *quiet dice* (large foam squares made into dice). Play in pairs or groups of three. Roll the dice and place counters. The first one to reach 99 wins.

Use *number lines to 100.* Students each write down six 2-digit numbers. They work in pairs and write their numbers on the number lines in the correct order.

Place Value 3

Skill: To compare numbers through 99

Time: 1 period

Materials:

counters

crayons

blank index cards: 10 per student

deck of playing cards: ace through nine only

place value (pv) materials to 10s

See Reproducibles for: pv mats to 100s, number lines to 100—have these already numbered to 100 by tens for first graders; 1 per student

Anticipatory Set

Use *pv mats, counters, crayons,* and *blank index cards.*

Students color the pv mats to correspond to the selected value of each color counter. For example, if the ones place is to be shown with red counters, color the word "Ones" red.

Students work in pairs. Each student makes number cards for zero through nine. They shuffle both sets of cards together, and turn them face down.

Each student draws two cards from the pile. They choose which card will be the ones number and which the tens number. One student places counters on the pv mat to represent the number he or she has chosen. The other student reads the number.

They reverse roles. Continue for about five minutes, with each student getting several chances to draw and choose numbers, as well as chances to read numbers. Save cards for Procedure 2.

Procedure 1

To develop the concept of comparing numbers through 99

Use *pv mats, pv materials,* and the *deck of cards.*

Discuss with the students how the value of a number depends on its place within a larger number.

Shuffle cards; then draw two. Ask students which is the larger number. Instruct students to place one cubes representing this number in the ones place on their mats.

Students place cubes. They orally read the number.

Now instruct students to place ten rods to represent the smaller number in the tens place on their mats.

Students complete activity and read the number.

Now which number is larger?

Students respond: The number in the tens place.

Why?

Students respond: We have that many tens instead of ones.

Tell students to make the largest number possible with the two numbers that were drawn.

Students place materials then read the resulting 2-digit number.

Continue with other pairs of numbers, having students represent both the smallest and largest numbers they can make using the two numbers.

Now draw four numbers. Students make two 2-digit numbers using the smaller numbers in the ones place, the larger numbers in the tens place.

Have students cover up the ten rods and compare only the ones. Which is bigger?

Next have them cover the ones and compare only the tens. Which is bigger?

Now compare both entire numbers. Which is bigger? Why?

Students respond: The number with the most in the tens place. Tens are worth more than ones.

Repeat until students can correctly predict which will be the larger number before checking with materials.

Procedure 2

To compare numbers using a number line

Use *number lines* and *index cards from Anticipatory Set.*

Instruct students to number the line to 100 by tens.

Have students work in pairs. Each pair shuffles two sets of index cards together. One student draws two cards and makes the largest number possible using those two numbers. The partner checks, and if in agreement, places the number in the correct place on the number line.

Have students then take the same two numbers and make the smallest number possible. They place this new number on the number line.

Students then reverse roles and repeat the activity.

After five turns in each role, students exchange number lines with another pair of students. Do these students agree with the placement of numbers on the number line?

Have the students switch partners and repeat the activity until they have understood the concept.

Procedure 3 ☐

To compare numbers using place value

Use *pv mats, counters,* and the *deck of cards.*

Shuffle cards; then draw two. Ask students which is the larger number. Instruct students to place counters representing this number in the ones place on their mats.

After placing the counters, students orally read the number.

Now instruct students to place counters representing the smaller number in the tens place on their mats.

Now which number is larger? (tens number) Why?

Students respond: The place dictates the value of the number.

Tell students to make the largest number possible with the two numbers that were drawn.

Students place counters and then read the resulting 2-digit number.

Continue with other pairs of numbers, having students represent both the smallest and largest numbers they can make using the two numbers.

Have students write the numbers on paper each time, first the smallest, then the largest. Students check correctness of each other's answers.

Practice and Extension

Have paired students play Megachallenge, using *cards.* First student draws two cards and makes the largest possible number. Second student does the same. The larger of the two numbers wins, and the student making it gets one point. First student to ten points wins the game.

Students can also play Minichallenge, making the smallest possible number.

Have students make up problem situations or games for which they need to know which number is bigger. For example, the group that has sold the most tickets will have the best seats at the All Star Baseball Game; who gets the best seats, the group that sold 56 or the group that sold 61?

Place Value 4

Skill: To understand place value through 999: regrouping and expanded notation

Time: 2 periods

Materials:

counters

crayons to match colors of counters

place value (pv) materials to 100s

adding-machine tape

3 dice

See Reproducibles for: pv mats to 100s (later you can use pv mats to 1000s), number lines to 1000

Anticipatory Set

Use *pv mats, counters,* and *crayons.*

Students color the pv mats to correspond to the selected value of each color of the counters. For example, if the ones place is to be shown with red counters, color the top of that column red.

Call out a number from zero to nine. Each student decides in which column to place that number. They place the counters on their mats.

Call out another number, and the students place that number. The third number called is placed in the remaining space.

Students compare numbers to see who has the largest number. How many different numbers did the class make?

Procedure 1

To develop the concept of place value through 999

Use *pv mats from Anticipatory Set* and *pv materials.*

Instruct students to place five cubes in the ones place. Have them chorally read "zero hundreds, zero tens, and five ones."

Now have them place four rods in the tens place and four more cubes in the ones place. Ask them to chorally read the number.

Students respond: Zero hundreds, four tens, and nine ones.

Ask: What will happen if you add one more cube to the ones place?

Students respond: We will need to trade for another ten.

Now have students place five rods in the tens place and one more cube in the ones place. Tell them to be ready to chorally read after trading up as needed.

Students respond: One hundred, zero tens, zero ones.

Continue with the exercise until you have added blocks and read up to the number 999.

Ask what will happen if we now add one more cube to the ones place. Discuss the need to have another place in order to create the number 1,000.

Procedure 2

To practice regrouping and expanded notation

Use *mats from Anticipatory Set, counters, adding-machine tape,* and *dice.*

Roll dice and have students add the numbers together. Students place counters on their mats representing the total. Tell them to chorally read the number.

Students respond: Zero hundreds, ___ tens, and ___ ones.

Each group assigns to one student the responsibility of writing the number on their adding-machine tape.

Roll the dice again and follow the same procedure, reminding the students to trade up as needed and to be ready to chorally read the resulting number.

Students do the assigned task and chorally read the resulting numbers. The assigned student writes this number on the adding-machine tape, making a number line.

Students are not all writing but are adding with you as an activity of the entire class, while the assigned students write on the adding-machine tape.

Continue with this procedure until you reach a number above 900. If desired, continue until 999, being careful not to go over 999.

Have class orally read the numbers from the tape in unison, starting at the smallest and reading up to the final, or largest, number.

Discuss the difference between reading chorally ___hundreds, ___tens, and ___ones, and reading the numbers in the usual way.

Procedure 3

To write numbers through 999

Use *number lines* and *dice*.

Have students take the number lines and number from 100 to 1,000 on the long tic marks.

Roll the dice and read the numbers shown as a 3-digit number. Students write this number on the number line.

Continue until there are at least ten different numbers on the number line. Have a student read the numbers on the line from least to greatest. Do the other students agree with the order in which the numbers were read? Another student can read the numbers in expanded form.

After doing these activities, students discuss what they have learned about place value.

Discuss with students the kind of math they used to do the regrouping. How do they think these activities are connected?

Practice and Extension

Have students make up games to play in groups of two or three using *pv mats to 1000s, cards with numbers zero to nine written on them,* and *counters.* They may need to color-code these mats as they did the earlier mats. These games can be left out to be used in free time to build competence. Some game ideas are Play to 1,000, Highest Number Wins, and Lowest Number Wins.

Have students display the *adding-machine-tape number lines from Procedure 2* around the school. Have students post a sheet under each line headed with a type of object such as paper clips. Other students can write problem situations on the paper, using the objects and one of the numbers shown. For example, how much would 742 paper clips weigh? How long would 321 paper clips be? Students can then estimate and measure.

Place Value 5

Skill: To compare numbers through 999

Time: 1 period

Materials:

deck of cards

paper: cut into small slips

counters: color-coded to represent numbers to 100s

dice: 1 per group of three students

See Reproducibles for: place value (pv) mats to 100s or 1000s, number lines to 100—1 per student, bills to 100s—in different colors

Anticipatory Set

Use *bills, pv mats,* and *cards.*

Draw a card and have students place that amount in the ones place. The next number is placed in the tens place; the third in the hundreds place.

How many $1 bills does each $100 bill stand for? (100) How many $1 bills does each $10 bill stand for? (10) Review reading numbers. Repeat until students can place and read numbers easily.

In their responses, students should give examples of items that might cost the different amounts of money. Students write the different amounts of money on slips of paper, one number per slip.

Repeat with two new sets of three cards. Students place, then write their number, then order and write the numbers in their group. When they feel ready, they may write first, then check with the bills.

Have students take number lines and place the numbers in order on the line in the correct sequence.

Procedure 1 □■

To develop the concept of comparing numbers through 999

Use *bills, pv mats, number lines, cards,* and *paper slips.*

Draw a set of three cards and have students place and read the number as in the Anticipatory Set.

Students leave this number on their mats.

Rearrange the digits and have students place this number below the first.

Which number do they think is larger? Why is one number bigger, even through they both have the same three digits?

Students discuss that the value of a number depends on its place.

Repeat with three new cards.

Ask students to name a rule for comparing numbers.

Students state that you start with the largest place and compare those numbers.

Next draw two sets of three cards and turn them over. Have half of the students arrange bills for one of the sets *in any order* on their pv mats. The other half does the same for the second set.

Students complete the activity. They should have many different amounts of bills on their mats.

Discuss which amount of money is the greatest. The least? If they had items costing these various amounts of money, which would be the least expensive? Why? The most expensive?

Procedure 2 □

To compare numbers using addition and regrouping

Use *cards, pv mats,* and *counters.*

If students have not yet colored the top section of their pv mats, have them do so now. Be sure the colors used correspond to the colors of the counters, and that all students represent the same place with the same color.

Take the deck of cards, shuffle it, draw three cards, and call out the numbers, giving the face cards the value of zero. If a ten is drawn, ask students what they will need to do during that turn. (regroup)

Students place counters on their mats with the number of the largest numerical value being placed in the ones place and the next largest in the tens place. The number having the smallest numerical value should be put in the hundreds place.

Write the number on the board and ask for two other numbers that could be made using these digits.

Which is the least? The greatest? Can students order the numbers?

Continue, adding the new number onto the number on the mat until you reach a number in the 900s.

Repeat, having students write the numbers in order after placing counters to represent them. Continue having students both place counters and write numbers until they are competent.

Procedure 3 □

To practice comparing numbers

Use *dice, pv mats,* and *counters.*

Students work in groups of three. One student rolls a die. The other two students place that many counters on pv mats in whichever place they choose, and write their numbers. Counters *cannot be repositioned.* After three rolls, students read numbers; the student with the largest number wins that round.

Students continue the activity for about 10 minutes, rotating roles. At the end of about 5 minutes, change the rule so that the student with the smallest number wins the round.

Have students discuss how their strategies changed when the rule was changed.

Practice and Extension

Students use the *slips of paper with money amounts from Procedure 1.* They shuffle the slips of paper and order them from least to greatest. Another student can check. Have students make up problems listing objects that might cost these amounts of money. They then can order the items from most to least expensive.

Students continue the *game from Procedure 3.* They can play with a *timer* and change the rules every three minutes.

Place Value 6

Skill: To understand place value through 9,999: regrouping, expanded notation, and comparing

Time: 2+ periods

Materials:

blank file folders, or tag board: 1 per student

rulers

scissors

1 die

counter-trading materials to 1000s

deck of cards: 1 for the teacher

See Reproducibles for: bills to 1000s—run off in different colors, directions for file-folder place value (pv) mats to 1000s; 1 per group, counter-trading boards to 1000s

Anticipatory Set (do this a day ahead)

Use *bills, pv mat directions, file folders, rulers,* and *scissors.*

Working in groups of four, students cut bills apart.

Hand out folders, directions, and rulers to each group. Each student will make one pv mat using the rulers to make each section equal. Have groups work with the sheet of directions to complete making file-folder pv mats to 1,000.

If folders are laminated, they will last the year and students can write directly on them with markers.

Procedure 1

To understand thousands: regrouping and expanded notation

Use *bills* and *pv mats.*

Give students some numbers to 999, and review reading of the expanded form, saying: __hundreds, __tens, __ones.

Have students place bills for the number 4,856 onto pv mats and read with you: four thousands, eight hundreds, five tens, and six ones.

Hold up a $1, and have them "add one."

Students place bills and read chorally: Four thousands, eight hundreds, five tens, and seven ones.

Continue adding $1 bills and reading until you have 10 $1 bills. Ask: What happens next?

Students respond: Regroup. They trade 10 $1s for a $10 and read chorally the expanded form for 4,860.

Hold up $10, and add tens until you reach 4,890. Add one more $10. Ask what happens next.

Students place bills and respond: Regroup for 100. They read the new amount.

Ask: What do you notice about the thousands?

Students respond: It's like the smaller numbers.

Now hold up combinations of bills, for example, one $100, five $10s, and four $1s.

Students place this amount on their pv mats below the 4,900, add, and regroup as needed.

Ask: What number do we have now?

Students respond: Five thousands, zero hundreds, five tens, and four ones.

Continue the procedure, giving amounts up to $9,999 that need more than one regrouping.

Procedure 2

To write numbers to 9,999

Use *die, bills,* and *pv mats.*

Divide the class in half, and play Money Madness to see which half finishes with the greatest amount.

Generate numbers for each side in turn by throwing the die. Make up stories to go with the numbers, such as inheriting $3,612. Have students place bills on their mats in the places dictated.

After placing a 4-digit number, students write the number on paper. Members of the group check each other. They add subsequent numbers, keeping a running total.

It is important for students to understand that the written form is just a description of what is actually happening. Students need much practice at this step.

After students become confident about the process, they can move to writing the problem first, and then checking with bills.

Procedure 3

To compare numbers to 9,999

Use *counter-trading boards* and *counter-trading materials.*

Have students place a colored counter over the labels on their mats if their mats are not color-coded.

Have students work in groups and place 1,111 on the mats. Ask: Are these ones all the same? (no)

How many ones to make one ten? (10) To make one hundred? (100) A thousand? (1,000)

Have students add one counter to a place of their choice. Who has the largest number?

Students place materials and discuss. They see that students who placed the counter in the thousands column have the largest number.

Write 2,111 on the board. Who has the next smaller number?

Students with 1,211 respond.

Discuss that the value of a number depends on its place. Repeat for 1,121 and 1,112.

Have students remove all but 1,111. This time have them add one additional block to *two* places of their choice.

What place should we look at first to find the largest number? (thousands) Why?

Repeat for other places.

Could we make a chart to be sure we have listed all the numbers in order? The biggest number will have what in thousands? (2) And in hundreds? (2) Repeat questions for rest of numbers so that the chart reads:

> 2,211
> 2,121
> 2,112
> 1,221
> 1,212
> 1,122

Repeat the procedure with other numbers to give students as much practice as is necessary.

Students write all possible numbers and then order them on paper after comparing them to their materials.

Later, have students write numbers in order and then check with materials. Students need much practice at the stage of both writing and using manipulatives.

Procedure 4 □

To practice comparing and writing numbers through 9,999

Use *pv mats, bills,* and the *deck of cards.*

Draw five cards; face cards are zeros. Have students decide where to put each digit on their pv mats. The object is to get the largest (or smallest) number.

Students must place each bill before the next card is drawn. They are allowed to ignore one number but must decide before the next number is drawn.

See who has the most thousands on their mat, then the most hundreds, and so on.

Students read each number in their group and write them in order.

Practice and Extension

Hand out *number lines,* and have students use *one color crayon or marker* to number to 1,000 by tens. Use *another color* to mark the hundreds. Using a *third color* and *another number line,* number by thousands to 10,000. Post the lines by thousands vertically. Place the lines by tens horizontally between thousands to give a visual representation of value.

Have students say address numbers. Have them become aware that certain numbers are *not* said as thousands, such as phone numbers, house numbers, sometimes years. Students compare their house numbers and the last four digits of their phone numbers. They work in groups and order the numbers from least to greatest.

Ask what would happen if we added *$1* more to the *bills* in Procedure 1; or one more *counter* to 9,999 *counters?* Let students experiment and discover the need to trade up to a larger number than they have a place for on their *mats.* Explain that this number is the ten thousands place number.

Use *dice* and generate four numbers. Have students write the largest or smallest number possible using those four digits. Have students explain why the number they wrote is the largest or smallest possible; make sure their explanations include the idea that the value of a number depends on its place. How many numbers can be made from the numbers shown on the dice? How did the students know if they had found them all? Did they look for patterns to help them? Does it make a difference if some of the dice-generated numbers are the same?

Place Value 7

Skill: To compare numbers through 99,999

Time: 2 periods

Materials:

letter-size envelopes: 1 per student

place value (pv) materials to 10,000s: use counters as 1000s and 10,000s

blank file folders: 1 per group

rulers

crayons or markers

10 index cards with numbers: 1 digit per card

5 index cards with pv place names: 1 name per card

See Reproducibles for: bills to 10,000s—in different colors, number lines to 1000—2 per student, pv mats to 1000s—1 per group, directions for file-folder pv mats to 100,000s—1 per group

Anticipatory Set

Use *bills, envelopes, number lines, pv mats,* and *pv materials.*

Assign a day in advance. Students cut apart bills, place them in envelopes, and set them aside.

On the day of the lesson, distribute the number lines and have students start labeling tic marks by 100s to 1,000 on the first. On the second number line, they begin labeling tics by 1000s to 100,000. Assign the completion of the job as homework. The number lines will be used tomorrow in Procedure 3.

Students work in groups. Give each group a pv mat. Review reading numbers to 9,999 and regrouping. Write a number to 9,999 on the board and have students display it on their pv mats with pv materials. Then dictate other numbers and have students display and write them.

Procedure 1

To develop the concept of comparing numbers through 99,999

Use *directions for file-folder pv mats, file folders, rulers, crayons or markers, bills,* and *envelopes.*

Have groups make one pv mat per group on file folders as shown in illustration. Do not have them write words yet.

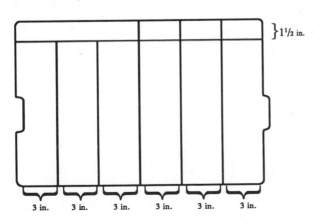

Draw a pv chart on the board, and write a number to 99,999 Draw a roof over the thousands places:

Thousands			Hundreds	Tens	Ones
Hundreds	Tens	Ones			

Students draw roofs on their pv mats.

Remind the students that they are familiar with having to bundle, trade, or regroup to get to the next place where there's more room.

When a number contains a thousand place, all those numbers above 999 live in a big house called thousand. Point out that the places are still called ones and tens, but now they are in the thousands' house and thousand is part of their name.

Write 87,654 on the board, and label places from right to left: Ones, Tens, and Hundreds, Ones, Tens. Draw a roof over the thousands, and write in the word "Thousands" in large letters.

Emphasize reading all the numbers in the house and then saying the house name. Compare to a family whose members all have the same last name.

Students label their pv mats as shown.

Have students take out the envelopes containing their bills. Dictate some numbers to 99,999.

Each group pools their bills to put the quantities dictated onto their pv mats. Students read the value of all the quantities in the thousands house before saying the house name. *The comma is the clue to say the house name.* Students check each other's accuracy.

Procedure 2

To practice comparing numbers

Use *file-folder pv mats, pv materials, crayons or markers,* and *index cards with digits and pv names.*

Students color-code thousand places on their pv mats to correspond with colors of available counters.

Dictate the number 8,888.

Students place pv materials on their mats corresponding to the number.

Read chorally: 8 thousands, 8 hundreds, 8 tens, and 8 ones. Draw a place value card and a number card. Have students read the number chorally. Make sure to include "zero___" for all places to the right of the one drawn.

Students place that number below the first one on their mats, then add and regroup as necessary. The group checks itself and reads the sum chorally.

Repeat activity until students become adept; then have them write down each number after it is placed. When they are comfortable doing that, they can first write the number, then check with the pv materials.

Challenge them by drawing more than one pv card and number. Students should become comfortable with a variety of possible place changes. Students should now be reading the number in the usual manner, not using expanded form.

need a place for 1,000 dots or numbers at about two-inch intervals, so there is space to write numbers. Groups can take a range of numbers to complete.

Post the completed number line in the hallway and encourage students to post statements on the number line, such as, "My house number is 5528." That statement would be posted between 5500 and 5600.

Use *file-folder pv mats to 100,000s* and *bills to 100,000s*. Have students play Millionaire, a game that expands their knowledge of place value to one million. Students begin with $100 on their mats, and use *three or four dice* to generate amounts of money to add to their existing amount. Students make up situations such as, "I earned $5,321 painting houses," to go with the numbers shown on the dice. The first student who needs to trade for a $1,000,000 bill is the winner. (You can create your own one-of-a-kind bill to use as the $1,000,000 bill.)

Procedure 3

To compare numbers through 99,999

Use *number lines from Anticipatory Set* and *markers*.

Have student groups take their two number lines from the Anticipatory Set, and write their address numbers in the appropriate places on one of the number lines.

Groups present their number lines to the class. They check to see if other students agree with their placements.

Each student takes an individual number line, writes on it the last five digits of his or her phone number in the appropriate position, and then writes the 5-digit numbers of all the group members on his or her individual number line.

Groups present these numbers to the class.

Were these numbers grouped closer together or farther part than the address numbers? Why? What would happen if the students used the first five digits of their phone numbers?

Students discuss that ordering and comparing ten thousands is like earlier skills.

Practice and Extension

Students use *place value name and number cards* and take turns, one saying place value and number, and the other writing numbers on a *paper pv mat*.

Use *adding-machine tape* and make a classroom number line marked in hundreds to 100,000. You

Place Value 8

Skill: To round numbers to the nearest 10 and $10

Time: 2+ periods

Materials:

clear tape

scissors

crayons or markers in two colors

file-folder or other place value (pv) mats to 100s or 1000s

pv materials to 100s

counters (any color): 1 per student

See Reproducibles for: number lines to 100—1 per student, Rounding Rhyme—1 copy per student, directions for file-folder pv mats to 1000s, or use pv mats to 100s, bills to 100s—in different colors

Anticipatory Set

Use *number lines, clear tape, scissors,* and *crayons or markers.*

Have students cut apart and tape strips into one long line, and label each longer mark by tens. They use a different color to label all numbers ending in five.

Discuss that we don't always need to know exact numbers. Sometimes we can estimate.

Procedure 1 ■

To round numbers from 1 to 99

Use *number lines from Anticipatory Set, copies of the Rounding Rhyme,* and *blank sheets of paper.*

Have students count on the number line, tapping each tick mark and emphasizing the multiples of ten. Explain that rounding is a way of estimating, or making a good guess. Ask: What on the number line looks the most round?

Students identify zero.

Tell students that a round number must end with a zero or more than one zero.

Have them look at the number line and put their finger on the mark for 14. Put another finger on the nearest number that ends in zero. What is it? (10)

Emphasize that sometimes it's more and sometimes it's less than the number we started with.

Students repeat procedure as you give: 7, 23, 18, 46, 12.

Have students write 16, 23, 18, 46, 62, and 35 on their paper.

Since we are rounding to the nearest 10, they should underline each digit in the tens place as a reminder.

Pass out the Rounding Rhyme and read with the class, using a rap rhythm:

> **Mark the place,**
> **Look to the right.**
> **Four or less are out of sight!**

> **Five and up**
> **Will buy one more,**
> **Before they, too, are out the door.**

> **In those empty**
> **Right-hand spaces,**
> **Zeros keep the proper places.**

Have students check the underlined number in 16. Is the space to the right five or up? (yes)

What does the rhyme say to do? (buy one more)

Have students write 2 over the 1 in the number 16. Because rounded numbers end in zero, what should we put in place of the 6?

Students respond: A zero. They write a zero over the 6.

Have students check their answer on the number line. Is 20 the closest 10 to 16?

Continue the procedure with 23. What does the rhyme say to do to the number 3?

Students respond: It's out of sight. They write a zero over the 3 and leave the 2 alone. They check the answer on their number lines.

Repeat with 18, 46, 62, and 35.

Point out that the rhyme tells us that we can buy one more with 5. Even though it's not closer to either the higher or the lower ten, it's halfway, so we can keep on going up.

Continue rounding practice with many numbers, especially ones ending in 5.

Students say the rhyme, write the numbers, cross out and replace, and then check on the number line.

Discuss when rounding is useful.

Procedure 2 ■

To round money amounts above and below $99

Use *pv mats, number lines from Anticipatory Set, bills, counters,* and *Rounding Rhyme.*

Dictate $53 to the students and have them place the bills on their mats. They may use a counter under the number in the 10s place to mark the place to which they're rounding.

Tell students: We're rounding to the nearest ten, or $10. Remember that sometimes we'll end up with more money, sometimes less.

On your number lines, we rounded higher at the halfway mark. How many dollars is halfway to $10?

Students respond: $5.

If we have $5 or more, we can regroup or "buy" a $10 bill. What will we do with less than $5?

Students discuss that rounded numbers end in zero. They will have to get rid of amounts under $5.

We have $53. Is $3 enough to buy $10? (no) What do we do? (get rid of it)

Students remove the $3. They check with both the number line and Rounding Rhyme to reinforce the concept.

Repeat with other 2-digit amounts, including $99.

Students place the bills, write the number, round the bills, then round the number.

Discuss with students how being able to round dollar amounts might help when grocery shopping. Where else would the skill be useful?

Students discuss other situations. They also compare this skill to other estimating skills they have learned.

Dictate a 3-digit number which the students place on their mats. Point out that they are still rounding to the nearest 10, not 100.

Students practice rounding with money, writing the numbers as well. They check with the number line and Rounding Rhyme.

As students' grasp of the concept improves, give numbers with 9 in the tens place and numbers above 5 in the ones place. Such numbers will force regrouping and change the hundreds number.

When students are competent, have them round numbers on paper first, then check each one with bills and the number line. They can also use the Rounding Rhyme to check their results.

Procedure 3 ☐

To practice rounding to the nearest 10

Use *pv mats, pv materials, number lines from Anticipatory Set,* and *Rounding Rhyme.*

Follow Procedure 2, using place value materials.

Students should both manipulate the materials and write their numbers. They should use the number line and the Rounding Rhyme as aids.

Remind the students that "buying one more" really means "trading up" on the pv mats. How can they prove this?

When they are comfortable with rounding, ask more abstract questions. What is the highest number that rounds to 90? (94) The lowest one? (85) The highest that rounds to 230? (234) What does 999 round to? (1,000)

Practice and Extension

Estimate sums of two 2-digit numbers by rounding both numbers and adding them.

Have students round the number of students in each classroom and add the rounded numbers to arrive at an approximate school size. Have them compare this number to the answer they get when they add the actual numbers. When might they choose one procedure over another?

Have pairs of students use *cards* in turn to generate large numbers. They round the numbers, keeping a running total. After so many turns, the winner is the student with the higher total.

Place Value 9

Skill: To round numbers to the nearest 100 and $100

Time: 2+ periods

Materials:

place value (pv) materials to 1000s: use counters as 1000s

file-folder or other pv mats to 1000s

counters: different color from above-listed; 1 per student

See Reproducibles for: directions for file-folder pv mats, if needed; or other pv mats to 1000s, Rounding Rhyme, number lines to 1000—1 per student, bills to 1000s—in different colors

Anticipatory Set

Use *pv materials, pv mats,* and *copies of the Rounding Rhyme.*

Write 10 different 3-digit numbers on the board. Have students choose one of the numbers and represent it with counters on their place value chart. Review rules for rounding to nearest 10 and have them round their numbers to the nearest 10. Read all rounded numbers. What do the students anticipate will be the rule for rounding to the nearest 100?

Pass out the *Rounding Rhyme* and review with the class using a rap rhythm.

> Mark the place,
> Look to the right.
> Four or less are out of sight!
>
> Five and up
> Will buy one more,
> Before they, too, are out the door.
>
> In those empty
> Right-hand spaces,
> Zeros keep the proper places.

Procedure 1 ☐■

To round 3-digit numbers

Use *number lines, copies of the Rounding Rhyme,* and *paper.*

Have students mark the number lines from 0 to 1000 by hundreds. Then have them count, tapping each tick mark and emphasizing the multiples of 100.

Review that rounding is a way of estimating, or making a good guess.

Have them look at the number line and put their finger on the mark where 134 would be. Put another finger on the nearest hundred. What is it? Emphasize that sometimes it's more and sometimes it's less than the number we started with.

Students respond: The nearest 100 is 100. They check with fingers on the number line and respond to questions as you give numbers over 100 for them to round.

Have students write: 476, 223, 598, 746, and 351 on their paper.

Since we are rounding to the nearest 100, they should underline the digit in the hundreds place as a reminder. Ask: What does the rhyme say to do for 476?

Students respond: We can buy one more.

Have students write 5 over the 4 in the number 476. Tell students that when rounding to the hundreds place, we ignore the ones place. The only number to the right that we look at is the one in the tens place. Because rounded numbers end in zero, what should we do to the 7 and 6?

Students respond: The right-hand spaces are zeros. They write zeros over the other two numbers, and then they write the rounded number.

Have students check their answers on the number line. Is 500 the closest 100 to 476? Ask what the rhyme tells us to do with 223.

Students respond: The 2 and 3 are out of sight. They write a zero over the 2 and 3, leaving the 2 hundred number unchanged. They check the answer on their number lines.

Repeat with the other numbers. Point out that for 351, we follow the rhyme, even though 50 is not closer to either hundred on their number line.

When students become adept at rounding numbers above 100, introduce numbers below 100. Have students round numbers over 51, under 49, then 50. Discuss which is closer to 50, 0 or 100. Remind them, that halfway buys the next number when rounding.

Practice with many 3-digit numbers.

Discuss when rounding to nearest 100 is useful.

Procedure 2 ☐■

To round 4-digit and larger numbers

Use *pv mats, bills, number lines, copies of the Rounding Rhyme,* and *counters.*

Dictate $563 to the students and have them place bills and round the amount to the nearest 100. They may use a counter under the number in the hundreds place to mark that place. Have students check their answers on the number line.

Repeat with other 3-digit numbers, including 999.

Students place the bills, write the number, round the bills, then write the rounded number.

Introduce a 4-digit number for the students to place on their mats. Point out that they are still rounding to the nearest 100. Ask: How could you use the number line to check? Does the rounding change the number in the thousands place? (not usually)

Students practice rounding with money, writing the numbers, and checking with the number line.

Students will need a lot of practice when the number rounded is in the middle of the original number.

Students round first with money, check with the number line, and then write the number.

When students have mastered working with 4-digit numbers, introduce larger numbers.

As students become competent, they can round on paper first, then check with the bills or the number line.

Procedure 3 ☐

To practice rounding numbers to the nearest 100

Use *pv mats, pv materials, number lines,* and *the Rounding Rhyme.*

Follow Procedure 2, using pv materials.

Students should both manipulate the materials and write their numbers. They should use the number line and Rounding Rhyme as aids.

Remind the students that "buying one more" really means "trading up" on the pv mats. How can they prove this?

Have them round 4,990. What other numbers would force regrouping?

Students round and regroup 4,990 to 5,000. They brainstorm for other numbers that would require regrouping thousands.

When they are comfortable with rounding, ask more abstract questions. What is the highest number that rounds to 900? The lowest one? The highest that rounds to 1,200? What about 9,999?

Practice and Extension

Estimate sums or differences of two 3-digit numbers: round both numbers and add or subtract. Have them then do the problems with actual numbers.

Have students round 3-digit numbers to the nearest 10. When would this skill be useful? Students should realize that sometimes it would be very useful when working mentally with money problems. It would help with estimating skills.

Have students write down their phone number and house number and underline the digits in the hundreds place. If they were to write the numbers to the nearest 100, what would they be? Have them orally read the rounded numbers.

Addition 1

Skill: To understand concrete addition: the symbols + and =

Time: 2–3 periods

Materials:

paper plates or 6" paper circles: 1 per student

"cookies": 1" to 2" paper circles; 9 per student

8" × 10" tag board with symbols + and =, one per side

treasure box or other objects

number-and-dot cards (see Manipulative Information section): 1 teacher set

blank index cards: for making number-and-dot cards and symbol cards; 11 per student

markers or crayons

Anticipatory Set

Use *paper plates* and *"cookies."*

Give each student a paper plate and several "cookies." Ask each student to count his or her cookies. They then work with partners and see how many cookies they have together. Discuss with the class the counting of total numbers of cookies. Students change partners and do the same activity again.

Procedure 1

To understand the meaning of the symbols + and =

Use *tag board*, *paper plates*, and *"cookies."*

Have students place two cookies on their plates. If two students each have two cookies, how many do they have all together? (4) Hold up symbol card, showing +, and tell students this symbol means to join groups together or to add them. When we add, we are actually joining groups of items together so we can find a total number.

Turn the card around so the sign = shows. Tell students that this sign means "equals." When we say an addition sentence, we are saying what is the total number of items in the groups. Now have the students place more cookies on their plates.

Students place cookies, and each tells you how many are on his or her plate now. They count the cookies to do this.

Hold up the + sign. Ask: What did this tell us to do? (add or join) Tell students to join their cookies with their partners. Hold up the = sign. What did this tell us? (equal or total amount) Have the pairs of students count their total number of cookies. What is the total amount that each pair has?

After all students have responded, continue the procedure. Students work with different partners and different amounts of cookies until they understand the concrete process, and all can tell you the meaning of the symbols.

Procedure 2

To review on the following day

Use *objects* and *tag board.*

Repeat Procedure 1, using this manipulative.

Procedure 3

To count to reach a sum

Use *number-and-dot cards, blank index cards, markers,* and *objects.*

Review with students the meanings of + and = signs.

Hand out the blank index cards to each student. On one of them they are to place a + sign and on another an = sign. Now instruct them to choose a marker and with it to write a large number on each of the other cards, as you have done on your cards. Display the teacher's set for the students to copy. Tell them to first copy only the numbers.

Students copy the numbers onto their cards, using the same marker to make all the numbers.

Tell the students that learning to tap numbers can be a way to speed up their counting. They are to mark dots with another color.

As you show the teacher set, or demonstrate on the board, students mark each number card with the correct number of dots. Begin with number one.

Students choose one color and mark the number one as you have marked it on the board. As they place the dot, they say "one."

Continue with the other numbers, telling the students to stay with the same color marker that they chose to mark the dot on the first number.

Students continue to mark their numbers until all are completed.

As a fun activity and to help students remember, have each repeat his or her name while tapping a number; e.g., Sue would say "Sue, Sue, Sue, Sue," while she tapped the dots on the number four. Make sure all students get a chance to tap a number and say their name. Have them imagine that the dots on the numbers make pictures to help them remember the counting-dot positions.

Hand out objects to student pairs. Tell them to take card 1 and card 5. Demonstrate how they are to add these two numbers together, saying the numbers as they count.

Students tap the five, saying "one, two, three, four, five." As they tap the one, they say "six."

Now they are to check with the objects. If they put one object on the counting dot of the 1 card and place five on the dots on the 5 card, do they have six objects in all? (yes)

Students continue activity with other numbers, one counting and the other checking by means of the objects.

Have students place their + card between the two numbers that they are joining together. They practice with numbers and objects until they are comfortable with the process.

Procedure 4 □

To learn the written form of addition

Use *student sets of number-and-dot cards and symbol cards* and *objects*.

Review the meanings of the symbols + and =.

Give each student up to nine objects and have each separate out two objects and three objects. How many objects in all? (5) Write on the board 2 + 3 = 5. Tell students this is the written form for the process that they have been doing. This is the math language for joining or adding groups together. It says what we can do with the objects.

Students complete task and see they have five objects.

Next, students take out the cards with the numbers 2 and 3. Between these two, they place the + card, and

after the 3 they place the = card. They move their objects so that two objects are on the 2 card and three objects are on the 3. After counting, they move the objects to the end of the row so they have 2 + 3 = five objects.

Instruct students to lay out cards 3 and 5. The fastest way of joining these two groups is to say the largest number, five, and then count from there, using the counting dots on the three.

Students orally respond: Five, six, seven, eight. They discover they have eight counting dots.

Write 3 + 5 = 8 on the board. Have students place the signs with their numbers as before, showing the answer with the objects.

Continue with numbers of which the sum is nine or less, and have the students count, check with objects, and then see if the number sentence on the board shows the same answer.

Students continue the guided practice.

Now you can move to the stage where students write as well as use manipulatives. As students do each step with numbers and objects, they write the corresponding step on their paper. It is important for students to understand that the written form is just a description of what is actually happening. Students need much practice at this step.

Practice and Extension

Students make up games to play with their *number-and-dot cards*.

Students practice counting the dots shown on *dice*. They roll dice and count the dots. The first one to record all numbers from 2 to 12 is the winner.

Addition 2

Skill: To understand addition facts and fact families to 9: the horizontal form of addition

small containers: 2 per student

cubes: any size; 9 per student

cards bearing the symbols + and =: 1 set per student

number-and-dot cards from Addition 1: 1 set per student

Time: 2 periods

Materials:

treasure box or other objects: 9 per student

counters: 9 per student

Anticipatory Set

Use *objects*.

Hand out nine objects to each student. Ask them to count how many they have.

How could they separate the objects into groups?

Allow about five minutes for students to play with the objects, moving them into and out of several different groupings.

Procedure 1 ▪

To develop the concept of *joining groups*

Use *objects*.

Have students lay out two objects on their desks.

Ask: If two students join their groups, how many will they have together?

Working in pairs, students join their groups. They count their objects and see that they have four.

Students then each lay out three objects. They join their two groups of objects and find that together they have six.

Have students continue working in pairs, all with the same number. Then tell student A to lay out three objects and student B to lay out two objects.

Students join their groups and see that together they have five objects.

Continue with this part of the exercise.

Tell students that the mathematical name for this kind of joining is addition.

Procedure 2 ◻▪

To recognize the horizontally written form of addition

Use *counters* and *containers*.

Give each student two containers and nine counters. Tell them to place the containers side by side. In one

container they are to place three counters. In the other container they are to place four counters. Ask students how many they have all together.

Students count their counters and respond: 7.

Write on the board 3 + 4 = 7. Say: This is one way we write a description of what we have done with the counters. It is called an equation and both sides of the equation must match. Are three pieces of candy plus four pieces of candy the same amount as seven pieces of candy? (yes)

Continue with all the combinations to nine. Introduce the word *fact*. An addition fact consists of two numbers that together equal another number, a term that will be used throughout their work with mathematics.

Students combine the counters and say the answer, while you record their responses on the board, using the horizontal form of addition.

Procedure 3 ◻▪

To discover fact families

Use *cubes, counters,* and the *symbol cards*.

Have students lay out five cubes and four cubes. They should place the symbol + between the groups, and the = sign after the cubes. They should place the answer in counters after the equal sign. Ask: How many cubes do you have?

Students respond: 9.

Tell them to switch their groups to show four cubes plus five cubes. Now how many are there?

Students respond: There are still 9.

On the board write 4 + 5 = 9 and 5 + 4 = 9.

Explain that, just like people, numbers also have families. The two facts on the board are called a "fact family." Can you see any patterns to these equations?

Students discuss how these equations are related.

Ask the students to make another set of equations that would make a fact family.

Working in pairs, students try to make fact families. They share the facts with the class.

Record the fact families on the board as they are discovered. Continue until all the facts to nine have been reported and recorded on the board.

Procedure 4 □

To write the facts

Use *number-and-dot cards, counters,* and the *symbol cards.*

Have students lay out the cards on their desks. They place cards as you give them the numbers; e.g., you say, "Place a three card and a two card."

Students lay out the 3 and the 2.

Tell students: Between these two cards place the plus symbol, which means to add. Place the equal card after the numbers.

Students do as instructed and tell you the total is five. They place five counters after the cards on their desks.

Check to see that all have the correct form on their desks. Instruct students to take a piece of paper and write the same set of numbers on it.

Emphasize that this is just a description of what was done earlier with the counters and objects.

Continue until students have written all the addition combinations to nine on their papers.

Practice and Extension

Have students make up story problems with the number questions written in horizontal form. They exchange their problems with one another and solve the problems they have received.

Discuss how an equation could be compared to a seesaw.

Make *construction paper* balance beams with the problem on one end and the answer "balancing" it on the other end.

Use *balance scales* to show groups of objects on the left and the same number of objects in one stack on the right. Help students to see how these two sides balance when the numbers are equal.

Addition 3

Skill: To add zero

Time: 1 period
Materials:

paper plates or 6" paper circles: 1 per student
"cookies": 1" to 2" paper circles; 10 per student pair

number-and-dot cards: large teacher set
number-and-dot cards plus a zero card: 1 set per student
small containers
counters
cards marked with symbols + and =: 1 set per student
treasure box or other objects

Anticipatory Set

Use *paper plates, "cookies,"* and the *teacher set of number-and-dot cards.*

If students have not already made number-and-dot cards, have them put the numbers 0 to 9 on *blank index cards,* one number per card (see Addition 1). If they already have cards, they need to make only a 0 card.

Give each student a paper plate and several cookies. Shuffle the number-and-dot cards and draw one. Students place that number of cookies on their paper plates. Do several times, checking to see that each student has the correct number of cookies on his or her plate. Go on to Procedure 1.

Procedure 1

To understand the meaning of zero

Use *paper plates, "cookies,"* and *number-and-dot cards.*

Students work in pairs; each pair has two plates. Tell them: We are going to have a party and one plate will have four cookies on it. The other will have no cookies on it. How many cookies do you have in all?

Students place cookies and respond: 4.

Repeat, using other numbers.

Now have students lay the 5 card beside one plate and the 0 card beside the other. They are to place on each plate the number of cookies represented by the card next to it. Ask: How many cookies will go on the plates?

Students place cookies and respond: 5 and 0.

A zero is a round space with nothing inside it. It represents an amount of nothing. Discuss.

Continue activity until all students are putting the correct number of cookies on each plate and are able to tell you that the zero amount next to a plate means that there is nothing on that plate.

Procedure 2

To add the number zero to other amounts

Use *small containers, counters, symbol cards,* and *number-and-dot cards.*

Have students work in small groups, each group having two containers. Draw number cards at random; students place in the containers the number of counters shown on the number cards you have drawn. When you draw the zero card for a container, do they remember not to put counters in that container?

Students place counters in the containers as you say the numbers and write the problem on the board.

Have students count the number of counters in each of the two containers.

Students add the two amounts together to reach a total.

Finish the equation on the board, and have students empty their containers.

Continue exercise until students understand that zero added to a number totals the same value as the original number.

Now students also place symbol cards as you call out numbers. For example, you say: Place four counters in the first container and put a + card beside the container. Now place zero counters in the second container. Place the = card after the second container.

After students have placed counters and symbol cards, you ask: How many counters do you have? (4) Place a 4 card after the = card.

Students now place the number-and-dot cards.

You now have an addition problem like those we have done before. The problem reads 4 + 0 = 4.

Students continue to do the exercise until they are competent.

Procedure 3

To practice using zeros

Use *objects, paper,* and *pencils.*

Have students work in groups and sort their objects into alike groups; e.g., all toy animals, all screws.

After sorting the objects, the students make a group of five objects that are alike. Now they make another group of zero objects. How many objects do they have altogether?

Students sort objects and make the groups as requested. They respond: 5.

Tell them: Separate the group of five objects into two groups: one group has two objects, the second group has three objects. The third group still has no objects.

After the students have completed the task, ask how many objects they have altogether. (5)

This exercise helps establish that they can add several groups of objects, but that if one of the groups has no objects in it, the sum of the others will not change when that group is added to the others.

Students should now use paper and pencil to write the description of what they have shown with their manipulatives; i.e., $5 + 0 = 5$ and $2 + 3 + 0 = 5$.

Practice and Extension

Have students make a *chart* ordering the numbers 0 to 9. Have them also draw a picture representing each number; e.g., 0 balls, 1 ball, two balls, etc.

Have students make up problem stories in which one of the amounts is zero. They present the problems to the class to solve. For example: Tom has two red balloons and no blue balloons; how many balloons does he have?

Addition 4

Skill: To understand addition facts to 9: the vertical form of addition

Time: 1 period

Materials:

treasure box or other objects: 9 per student

counters: 9 per student

small containers: 2 per student

two cards, one showing the symbol +, the other a line to go under vertical form of addition: 1 set per student

number-and-dot cards from Addition 1: 1 set per student

Anticipatory Set

Use *treasure box objects*.

Hand out nine objects to each student. Ask them to count to see how many they have.

Then ask students to lay out two objects on their desks.

Students count out two objects and display them. Pairs of students join their objects and see that together they have a total of four objects.

Now students each lay out three objects. They join their groups as before to find that they have six objects all together.

Students continue working in pairs, at first both having the same number. Then tell student A to lay out three objects and student B to lay out two objects. Now how many do they have all together?

Students join their groups and see that they have five objects.

Allow about five minutes for students to work with the objects, moving them into and out of several different groupings.

Remind students that the mathematical name for this kind of joining is addition.

Procedure 1 □■

To recognize the vertically written form of addition

Use *counters* and *containers*.

Give students two containers and nine counters each. Tell them to put one container at the top of their desk and the other below it. In one container they are to place three counters. In the other container they are to place four counters. Ask students how many they have all together.

Students count their counters and respond: 7.

Write in vertical form on the board 3 + 4 = 7 (i.e., drawing a line beneath the two numbers to be added). This is one way we write a description of what we have done with the counters.

Continue with all the combinations to nine.

Students combine the counters and tell the answer, while you record the responses on the board, using the vertical form.

Procedure 2 □■

To review fact families

Use *objects, counters,* and *symbol cards.*

First review with students the meaning of the = sign. In the vertical form they have just watched you write on the board, what was used in place of this sign?

Students should be able to realize that a line under the problem has the same meaning as an equal sign.

Now have students lay out five objects and four objects, one group above the other. They should place the symbol + to the left of the set of objects, and the __ sign under the objects. Count the objects, how many are there? (9) They should place the answer in counters underneath two groups of objects.

Students do as instructed and tell you that five objects plus four objects equals nine.

Tell them to switch their groups so that they show four objects + five objects. Now how many are there?

Students respond: 9.

On the board write 4 + 5 = 9 and 5 + 4 = 9, using the vertical form.

Remind them that numbers also have families, and that the two facts on the board make a fact family. Can the students make another fact family?

Working in pairs, students make two related sets of facts.

They share their facts with the class, and you record the fact families on the board as they are reported, using the vertical form.

Is this similar to an activity we have done before? Discuss students' response and emphasize that addition can be written two ways, but the answer is the same.

Procedure 3

To write the facts

Use *number-and-dot cards, counters,* and *symbol cards.*

Have students lay out the cards on their desks. They place cards vertically as you give them numbers; for example, you say, "Place a three card with a two card under it, in the vertical form."

To the left of these two cards, place the plus symbol, which means to add. Then place the ___ card under the numbers and add them.

Students do as instructed and tell you the answer is five. They place five counters under the cards on their desks.

Check to see that all have the correct form on their desks. Students write the same set of numbers on a piece of paper. Emphasize that this is just a description of what was done earlier with the counters and objects.

Students write all the addition combinations to nine on their papers, using the vertical form.

Practice and Extension

Have students make up story problems with the number questions written in the horizontal form of addition. They exchange with one another and solve the problems they have received. Make sure the students change the horizontal form into the vertical form when solving the problems.

Make *construction paper* balance beams with the problem written vertically on one end and the answer "balancing" it on the other end.

Make *fact cards* with the problem on one side and the answer on the other for students to use in playing the game Concentration.

Encourage students to take their *flash cards* home to study the facts.

Let students make up games to play with their fact cards.

Addition 5

Skill: To understand addition facts to 18

Time: 3 periods

Materials:

treasure box or other objects: 18 per student

small containers: 2 per student

counters: 18 per student

symbol cards showing +, =, and __, the line used in vertical addition: 1 set per student

interlocking cubes: 18 per student

cards numbered 0 to 18: 1 set per student; students can make number cards for 10–18 and use number-and-dot cards for 0–9

Anticipatory Set

Use *treasure box objects* and *containers*.

Working independently, students separate their objects into two groups. The groups do not have to be equal. They place one group into one container and the other group into the second container. Now have the students count and tell you how many they have in each container and how many they have in all. Students take turns describing their objects and containers to the class, saying how many are in each group and how many they have in all.

Procedure 1

To discover fact families to 18 using the horizontal form of addition

Use *objects, counters,* and *symbol cards.*

Have students lay out one group of seven objects and another of four objects. They place the symbol + between the groups, and the = sign after the objects. They also place the answer in counters after the equal sign. How many are there? (11)

Tell them to switch their groups so the objects show four objects + seven objects. Now how many are there?

Students respond: There are still 11.

On the board write 7 + 4 = 11 and 4 + 7 = 11.

Remind students that numbers have families.

Working in pairs, students try to make two related facts. They share the facts with the class, and you record the fact families on the board as they are discovered.

Continue until all facts to 18 have been discovered.

Procedure 2

To develop fact families using the vertical form of addition

Use *interlocking cubes, counters,* and *symbol cards.*

First review with students the meaning of the equal sign. In the vertical form they have made before, what did they use in place of this sign?

Students should be able to realize that a line under the problem means the same as an equal sign.

Now have students lay out six cubes and four cubes, one group below the other. They should place the symbol + to the left of the two groups of cubes and the __ sign under them.

Tell them to count the cubes. Ask: How many are there? (10) They are to place the answer in counters below the groups of cubes.

Students tell you that six cubes plus four cubes equal ten cubes.

Tell them to switch their groups to show four cubes plus six cubes. Now how many are there?

Students respond: There are still 10.

On the board write 6 + 4 = 10 and 4 + 6 = 10. Use the vertical form.

Students tell you these two facts are a fact family.

Students now work in pairs and try to make several sets of related facts.

They share the facts with the class, and you record the fact families on the board as they are reported. Continue until all facts to 18 have been recorded.

Procedure 3

To write fact families to 18, both horizontally and vertically

Use *number cards, counters,* and *symbol cards.*

Remind students that addition facts can be written two ways, but the answer remains the same, as they have proven by finding facts both ways.

Have students work in pairs and lay out the cards on their desks as you give them numbers. For example, you say, "Place a three card and an eight card."

Tell student A to use the vertical form and the line, and student B to use the horizontal form and the equal sign.

Students then place the + card in the appropriate position and the line card or the = card in the correct place and show their answers with counters.

Students tell you the answer is 11, and they have 11 counters on their desks.

Check to see that all have the correct form of addition on their desks.

Instruct students to write the same set of numbers on a piece of paper. Emphasize that this is just a description of what they have done with the counters and objects.

Have students show the related fact on their desks by reversing the order of the number cards.

Check to see that all have the correct sequence, and then have them write that fact on their papers under the previous one.

Discuss that this set of numbers shows the fact family of 3 + 8 = 11 and 8 + 3 = 11, both vertically and horizontally.

Continue until students have written all the addition combinations to 18 on their papers.

Procedure 4 ☐

To practice using zeros

Use *objects, paper,* and *pencils.*

Have students work in groups and sort their objects into like groups; e.g., all toy animals, all screws.

After they have sorted the objects, have the students make, first, a group of 12 objects that are alike and then another group of zero objects. Ask how many objects they have altogether. (12)

Now have the students separate their groups of 12 objects into two groups, one group having 5 objects, the second group having 7 objects. The third group still has no objects. Ask how many they have altogether.

Students respond: There are still only 12 objects.

This exercise helps students to grasp that they can add several groups of objects, but that if one of the groups has no objects in it, the total number will not change when that group is added to the others.

Students should now begin to write on paper the description of what they have shown with their manipulatives; e.g., $12 + 0 = 12$, and $5 + 7 + 0 = 12$.

Continue to practice with other numbers until students are comfortable with the concept that 0 added to any number does not change the value of the number.

Practice and Extension

Using *index cards,* students make fact cards to use in the game of Concentration.

Students make *flash cards* for studying at home the addition facts to 18.

Make a class *chart* of the fact families to 18, writing them both vertically and horizontally.

Play Bingo by having students write the following problems in randomly chosen squares on a *5 × 5 piece of paper* marked off in squares:

9+9; 9+8; 9+7; 9+6; 9+5; 9+4; 9+3; 9+2
8+8; 8+7; 8+6; 8+5; 8+4; 8+3; 8+2
7+7; 7+6; 7+5; 7+4; 7+3
6+6; 6+5; 6+4; and 6+3.

The central square is a free space, and students label or mark it as such. You draw problems from a set of the *fact cards.* When a student gets "Bingo," he or she reads the problems and says the answers.

An alternative way to play is to cover the boards with possible answers. Students cover the correct answer when the problem is called.

Addition 6

Skill: To understand addition facts to 18: doubles and near doubles

Time: 3–4 periods

Materials:

dice: 1 die per group

number-and-dot cards from Addition 1: 1 set per group

counters: 2 colors; 18 of each color per student

small containers: 2 per student

interlocking cubes: 2 colors; 18 of each color per student

treasure box or other objects: 18 per pair

graph paper strips: 2 cm × 20 cm; 1 per student

1 cm cubes: 18 per student

markers, or crayons

paste, tape, or glue sticks

See Reproducibles for: graph paper with 1 cm squares, number lines to 25—1 per student

Anticipatory Set

Use *dice, number-and-dot cards,* and *18 counters.*

Divide the class into groups of three students. One student will use the die, another the cards, and the third the counters. The first student rolls the die; the second places on the desk a card with the same number as that shown on the die.

The third student places under both the die and the number-and-dot card, counters representing the sum of the two numbers shown on the die and the card. The group then reports to the class the numbers they "joined together" and the number of counters they used to represent the joined numbers.

Explain the meaning of the word *doubles* to the class after all have reported their results.

Procedure 1

To discover sets of doubles

Use *containers* and *counters.*

Have students place two counters of one color in one container and two counters of the other color in the second container. Ask how many counters they have used in all.

Students respond: 4.

Write the equation 2 + 2 = 4 on the board.

Now continue having students place equal numbers of counters in each container. Each time a new double is placed, you ask the same question.

Continue this exercise until students have completed addition of doubles through nine plus nine. As each question is answered, you write the corresponding equation on the board.

Procedure 2

To practice with doubles

Use *interlocking cubes* and *regular paper.*

Have students build trains of each color, beginning with two trains of two cubes each.

Have students then answer the following questions: Are the two trains the same length? (yes) What did we call two numbers that were the same? (a double)

Now have students join their two trains to make one long train. How long is the new train?

Students respond: 4 cubes.

Tell students to write the fact they demonstrated by joining the two trains into one longer train.

Students write 2 + 2 = 4 on their papers.

Have students continue with trains of other lengths until they have built two trains of nine cubes each.

Students build trains, discuss the resulting totals, and write the facts on their papers.

Procedure 3

To learn about plus-one near doubles

Use *containers* and *objects.*

Have students work in pairs to place five similar objects into each container. Ask whether they remember how many five plus five are.

Students respond: 10.

Now have students put one more object into one of the containers. How many are there in all now?

Students respond: 11.

Explain that a near double is one less or one more than a double and that you are going to look at those that are one more; doubles plus one.

We have discovered that the double of five plus five has a near double: five plus six.

Challenge students to make another double and to find a near double that relates to it.

Continue to work with objects until all the doubles from one plus one to nine plus nine have been covered and the plus-one near doubles have been established.

Procedure 4

To learn about minus-one near doubles

Use *containers* and *objects*.

Have students work in pairs to place four similar objects into each container. Ask whether they remember how many four plus four are.

Students respond: 8.

Remind students that a near double is one less or one more than a double.

Since we are now looking at the minus-one or one-less near double, remove one object from one of the containers. Ask: How many is one less than eight?

Students complete task and respond: 7.

We have discovered that the double four plus four has a near double: four plus three.

Challenge students to make another double and to find a near double that relates to it as a one-less double.

Continue to work with objects until all the doubles from one plus one to nine plus nine have been covered and the one-less near doubles have all been established.

Procedure 5

To work with doubles and near doubles

Use *2 cm × 20 cm strips of graph paper* and *cubes*.

Have students take the strips of graph paper and number the bottom row of squares from 1 to 20.

Students will place pairs of trains made of one cubes on the top row of squares. The trains will first be of equal length. For example, the trains of the first pair are one cube each.

Ask: How long is the train that is made when the two trains are joined together?

Students respond: 2 centimeters.

Have students then clear their strips.

The trains of the second pair are each two cubes long. How long is the train made by joining these two trains?

Students make the longer train, place it on the centimeter strip, and tell you that this train is 4 centimeters long.

Ask students to find the near double of the train that is plus one. How long would this train be? (5 centimeters)

Continue as above until you have completed all the doubles.

When the students made the last pair of trains, each nine cubes long, they found that 9 + 9 = 18 centimeters. Have them remove a cube from one of their nine-centimeter trains, and ask how long the total train is now.

Students respond: 17 centimeters.

Review that this is a near double, a double minus one. Continue this process until you have gone back to two trains of only one cube each.

Review the equations and the answers. Write one set of three equations on the board; e.g., 2 + 3 = 5 (double plus one), 2 + 2 = 4 (double), and 2 + 1 = 3 (double minus one).

Challenge students to make a different double and to find two near doubles that relate to it.

Students do as requested and report to the class.

As each pair of students reports, you record their responses on the board in sets of three equations.

Students now make three columns on a sheet of regular paper. They label columns "Doubles plus one," "Doubles," and "Doubles minus one."

Present the following problems to the students: ? + ? = 12; ? + ? = 14; ? + ? = 17; ? + ? = 18; ? + ? = 13. Ask: Which of these problems cannot be solved with doubles? How do you know? Could the answer to them be near doubles?

Students discuss. They copy the sets of equations from the board onto their papers. They now have a personal chart of all the doubles and near doubles whose sums are 18 or less.

Procedure 6

To relate the awareness of near doubles to problem solving

Use *number lines, markers or crayons, glue sticks,* and *counters (one color).*

Discuss how knowing the doubles and their near doubles could make problem solving faster as the students begin to learn other mathematical processes.

Have students number the tick marks on the number line from 1 to 24.

Students paste lines together and number as requested.

Now have students color-code the doubles as jumps, placing + numbers as shown.

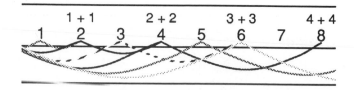

Students complete the task and are ready to solve problems.

Pose the problem of discovering the number of maple trees in a yard. If 5 trees are in front and 4 trees are in back, how could you use the knowledge of near doubles to quickly discover the answer?

Students discuss that they could use the near double four plus one or the near double five minus one.

Have students place a counter on the double answer for fives on their number line, and ask: One number less is what number?

Students place the counter and respond: 9.

Now have students move the counter to the answer for the double of four. One number more is what number?

Students move the counter and respond: 9.

Continue with other similar problems, and have the students place counters on both doubles that they could use.

Now you can move to the stage where students write, as well as use manipulatives. It is important for students to understand that the written form is just math language for the work they do with manipulatives.

Use many examples, as the concept of relationship of numbers is important to the full development of this concept.

Discuss the two near doubles that they have been working with and why they may choose one over the other. Do they prefer to add one or take away one? Discuss that either way is acceptable for doing mental math.

Practice and Extension

Have students make up problems that use doubles and near doubles. See whether they can verbally give the problems to each other and whether the other student can answer using mental math.

Make a class *chart* of doubles and near doubles to hang up in the room.

Addition 7

Skill: To use addition facts: missing addends

Time: 2–3 periods

Materials:

interlocking cubes: 2 colors; 9 per student

small containers: 3 per group

treasure box or other objects: 36 per group

markers or crayons

paste, tape, or glue sticks

scissors

counters

1 cm cubes: 18 per student

graph paper strips: 2 cm × 20 cm; 1 per student

See Reproducibles for: number lines to 25—1 per student, graph paper with 1 cm squares

Anticipatory Set

Use *interlocking cubes.*

Have students build trains of varying lengths, using interlocking cubes of one color only. Students work in pairs and join their trains to form an addition fact. Discuss the different facts that they have formed, the problems and the answers.

Review all the addition fact families that the students have learned previously, and explain that now they are going to look at them a different way.

Procedure 1

To develop recognition of the missing number

Use *containers* and *objects.*

Have students work in groups. Give groups three containers, and have them set two close together as "problem" containers; the other goes to the right and is designated as the "answer" container.

Instruct students to place 16 objects into the answer container. Then they should take 7 of the other objects and place them into one of the problem containers. Ask how many they need to place in the other problem container so that they will have a total of 16 in the problem containers.

Students place objects and respond: 9.

Relate this to the fact 9 + 7 = 16. Remind students of fact families, and place the following equation on the board: 7 + ? = 16. Ask: What number should be in the place of the question mark?

Students respond: 9.

Have students now empty all containers, and then place 18 of the objects into the answer container. Tell them to take some of the other objects and to place them into a problem container. What problem question have they created?

Students discuss the various problems they have created.

Place these problems on the board, with question marks in the places indicated. Have the students complete the problems and tell the class the numbers that should replace the question marks. Discuss responses, and place the completed equations on the board.

Procedure 2

To count up to find a missing number

Use *number lines, markers, glue sticks, scissors,* and *counters.*

Have students cut out and glue together the number lines. Have them use markers to number from 1 to 25.

Use story problems such as: I want to plant 12 rosebushes. I can plant 5 in the front yard. The rest will go in the back yard. On the board write 5 + ? = 12. Have students place counters up to 12, as below.

Students place a red counter on the number 5. They place yellow counters on 6, 7, 8, 9, 10, 11, and 12.

Ask: How many yellow counters did you use? (7) How many rosebushes will I plant in the back yard?

Students respond: 7.

Continue with other story problems. Write the equations on the board, and have students place counters as before to arrive at an answer.

Procedure 3

To develop the concept of using subtraction to find the missing number

Use *number lines from Procedure 2* and *counters.*

Discuss the relationship between addition and subtraction; the students will be using this skill. Tell students to place a counter on the number 12. This will be another way to discover how many rosebushes should be planted in the back yard.

They are going to plant 5 in the front yard and have a total of 12 rosebushes. Can they count 5 numbers back from 12 and arrive at a subtraction answer? Where did they place their last counter?

Students respond: 7.

Emphasize fact families, and write 5 + ? = 12 on the board, telling students that the equation they just solved looks like this. What number do they think they would land on if they started at 12 and counted back seven numbers?

Students respond 5, and then they do the counting to see whether they are correct.

Write that equation on the board, too.

Continue with all the fact families to 18, emphasizing the relationship to subtraction.

Procedure 4

To write the equations

Use *cubes, 2 cm × 20 cm graph paper strips, paper,* and *pencils.*

First have students number the cm strips, one number per square, from 1 to 20. Write equations on the board with question marks instead of one of the addends.

Have students copy the equations on their papers and then lay out cubes on their centimeter strips. For example, you tell them to place cubes for the equation ? + 7 = 13.

Students write the equation; they then look at the strip and, starting at the number 13, they cover seven squares—*counting backward.* The numbers 13, 12, 11, 10, 9, 8, 7 are covered.

Ask: What is the next number?

Students report that the next number is 6.

That is the number that replaces the question mark in the equation on the board. Now write 6 + 7 = 13, and have students copy this under the equation containing the question mark.

Introduce the form students will see in many textbooks: [ ] + 7 = 13. Discuss that the box could be replaced with a question mark.

Students need to know how to read these types of equations to ensure that they are able to understand what question is being asked.

Continue the process until students have written all the combinations whose sums are 18 or less.

Challenge students to create word problems with answers of 19 and 20; e.g., ? + 12 apples = 20 apples.

Students make up problems to exchange, and they discuss the relationship of subtraction and addition as it relates to missing addends.

Practice and Extension

Challenge students to create story problems. An example: I have 18 marbles, and 12 of them are blue. How many are not blue? Students start at the number 12 and use *counters* to represent marbles. They count up to 18 from 12 and see that they used 6 counters; so 6 of the marbles are not blue. Have students work together to make up problems, which they exchange with another pair of students, solving the problems they receive.

Use worksheets from the text that students have solved in earlier processes. Punch out or cover one number, and have them discover what that number was.

Have students take *15 counters* and make as many missing-number problems as they can, using only that many counters. Each problem must be presented as a situation.

Addition 8

Skill: To find sums to 18: more than two addends

Time: 1–2 periods

Materials:

treasure box or other objects: 18 per group

deck of cards

small containers: 3 per group

counters: 3 colors; 16 each per group

interlocking cubes: 3 colors; 16 each per group

number-and-dot cards 0 to 9: 1 set per student

blank index cards: for numbers 10 to 18; 1 set per group

1 cm cubes: 18 per student

graph paper strips: 2 cm × 18 cm; 1 per student

See Reproducibles for: graph paper with 1 cm squares

Anticipatory Set

Use *objects, paper,* and *pencils.*

Have students work in groups to sort their objects into alike groups; e.g., all toy animals, all screws.

After they have sorted the objects, have them make a group of five objects that are alike. Now they make another group of zero objects. How many objects do they have altogether? (5)

Have them separate their group of five objects into two groups. Now they have three groups: one group has two objects; the second group has three objects; and the third group has no objects.

How many objects do they have altogether? (5) This exercise helps establish that they can add several groups of objects. Write on the board the description of what they have shown with their manipulatives: 5 + 0 = 5, and 2 + 3 + 0 = 5.

Procedure 1

To add groups of objects

Use the *deck of cards, containers,* and *counters.*

Have students work in groups. You shuffle the cards and draw one.

Students place that number of red counters in one of the containers.

Draw another card.

Students place that number of blue counters in the second container.

Now select a third card, *making sure the total of the three numbers is not more than 18.*

Students place that many yellow counters in the third container.

Write the equation on the board, both vertically and horizontally, while the students count to reach a total.

Write the answers to both problems on the board in the correct places.

Students empty their containers.

Continue the procedure. Now include zero among the numbers by having jokers or face cards count as zero.

Procedure 2

To add groups of cubes

Use *interlocking cubes* and the *deck of cards.*

Follow the same steps as in Procedure 1, with students working in groups of three. Each student takes one color of the interlocking cubes and builds "trains" as you draw cards for the numbers.

Have the students combine their trains and arrive at a total number of interlocking cubes used. The problems should again be written on the board, either vertically or horizontally.

Procedure 3

To develop written forms

Use *1 cm cubes, containers, number-and-dot cards, counters,* and the *deck of cards.*

Divide the class into groups of four or five.

Draw three cards from the deck. For example, you draw a 5, a 3, and a 4.

One student places the cubes in containers to represent each number.

Another student lays a number-and-dot card beside each container.

A third student lays out counters to represent the total, placing them under the containers of cubes, as in the illustration on the next page.

The others record the problem in numbers.

Continue the exercise until the groups of students are competent in this skill.

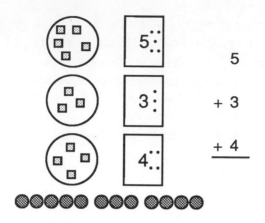

$$\begin{array}{r} 5 \\ 3 \\ + 4 \\ \hline \end{array}$$

Vary the exercise by having the groups estimate an answer before counting and placing the counters. What estimates may be too large? Too small? Why? Do students become more accurate with practice?

number line. After another number is given, the second student uses a different color to extend the first line that many spaces. The line will end at the number which is the total of the two numbers given. Students take turns giving numbers and marking the number lines.

Have students, divided into groups, each take a handful of *objects* and sort them into kinds. They combine the kinds to arrive at a total number of objects.

Have groups construct problem situations in which they have to add several numbers, such as buying items at a store. How many items did they buy? They can use *counters* to represent the items.

Challenge students to add long columns of numbers and to show with *manipulatives* that they have arrived at the correct answer.

Procedure 4

To practice the written form individually

Use *2 cm × 18 cm strips of graph paper* and *1 cm cubes*.

Have students place the centimeter strips on their desks, along with a separate sheet of paper. Tell students to number the bottom row of squares, one number per square.

Call out three numbers at random.

For each number, students place that many cubes on the strip, filling in squares from left to right. As they place the cubes, they also write the numbers vertically on their sheet of paper.

After they have placed cubes for all three numbers, they can read the answer from the strip.

After placing the cubes, students record the answer on their paper.

Continue to call out numbers at random, challenging students by sometimes having two addends, sometimes three, and sometimes four or more.

Be sure to keep the totals at 18 or less so that students can work with the manipulatives before recording the answers.

Students continue to complete problems in this manner until all have demonstrated competency with this concept.

Practice and Extension

Have each student use a *number line to 25*, taped together and numbered, and *two colors of markers*. As one student gives a number, the other student draws a line from zero to the given number, along the

Addition 9

Skill: To add tens

Time: 1 period

Materials:

counters: 18 per student

place value (pv) materials: 10s, 100s; blocks and one other type

1 die

See Reproducibles for: hundred boards—1 per student, pv mats to 100s—1 per student

Anticipatory Set

Use *counters.*

Give each student 18 counters. Have each make a group of two counters and a group of three counters. Ask how many they have in all. (5)

Now have them make groups of other amounts and discuss the resulting totals. Continue until you have reviewed most of the equations that add to 18 or less.

Tell them that since they know how to add ones, they are going to find it easy to add groups of even tens.

Procedure 1

To discover the sequence of tens

Use *hundred boards* and *counters.*

Have students take their hundred boards and place a counter on the first 10. How many does the counter represent? (10)

Now have them place a counter on the next number that ends in zero. What number did they cover? (20) How many counters have they used? (2)

Students continue to place counters on the next number ending in zero and respond with that number and the total number of counters used.

Ask: What skill does this remind you of?

Students respond: Counting by tens.

When you reached the number 90, how many counters had you used? (9)

Now have students take the counters off the hundred boards and place the counters on tens numbers as you call out numbers. For example, you tell them to place four counters and three counters.

Students do so and tell you that four ten counters and three ten counters equal seven ten counters.

Continue until students have clearly understood that adding groups of even tens is similar to adding single numbers.

Procedure 2

To practice adding groups of tens

Use *pv mats, ten rods,* and *hundred flats.*

Have students place, first, one ten rod on their mats, then three more rods. How many have they placed in all? (4 ten rods)

What number does that represent? (40)

Continue this exercise without going over 90 until students are comfortable with it.

Ask: What happens in our numbering system when we reach ten?

Students respond: We have to regroup.

Now give the students the problem of adding two tens and nine tens.

Students place rods and respond: We need to regroup to a hundred flat. They regroup and tell you that 2 tens and 9 tens equal 11 tens or 1 hundred and 1 ten.

Write on the board 20 + 90 = 110. Use the vertical form in a drawn pv chart.

Continue giving students numbers of tens to add.

Students place rods, give a total number of tens, and then regroup. They then give a final answer.

Write the problems on the board pv chart.

Procedure 3

To practice the concept of adding tens

Use the *other type of pv materials* and a *die.*

Have students work in groups. With a die you generate the number of materials to place in the ones column. The students add the next amount to the first and regroup as needed. When they get to ten, they exchange the ones materials for a ten. Now the numbers you generate will represent tens.

When the students reach 100, they trade a group of 10 tens for 1 hundred.

They should now have one piece of pv material representing 100 and possibly some pieces representing tens left. They leave these in place.

Begin at the ones place, and repeat the procedure. When the students reach the tens place, they add to the tens already there. Have them continue to add tens until they reach 200 and regroup.

Repeat the activity until 900 is reached.

Students discuss what this activity has shown them about adding tens.

Give students tens numbers to represent on their mats. This time, the numbers will be randomly chosen pairs of numbers, such as 30 + 40.

Students now write the addition on paper, after they have shown it show with manipulatives.

Practice and Extension

Have students make up problems that use adding even tens as part of their solutions. Then have them exchange their problems with one another and solve the problems they have received.

Make a class *chart* of adding tens.

Have students write down estimates, using even tens, of common school objects, activities, or places; e.g., the number of books on one set of library shelves, the number of steps to the office, or the number of trees on the playground. They then count to find out the actual amounts.

Addition 10

Skill: To add 2-digit numbers: sums to 99

counter-trading materials to 100s

graph paper: ¹/₂" squares; several sheets per student

See Reproducibles for: pv mats to 100s, counter-trading boards to 1000s, or use color-coded pv mats to 100s

Time: 2 periods

Materials:

place value (pv) materials to 100s

dice: 1 per student

Anticipatory Set

Use *pv mats* and *pv materials—1s and 10s*.

First, quickly review addition facts to 18. Then have students lay out on their mats a group of materials in the ones place and another in the tens place. Make sure the number of materials in each place is not greater than nine; e.g., six tens and three ones. Next, have them place two tens and five ones. Discuss the total. Continue for about 5 minutes.

Procedure 1

To add with regrouping

Use *pv mats, pv materials,* and *dice*.

Draw a pv chart on the board or overhead.

Demonstrate how to generate an addition problem by throwing the dice to get a ones number. Show this many ones materials on the chart. If you get a 10, 11, or 12, throw the dice again.

Use a die to get the number of tens for the first addend.

Students place ones and tens on their mats representing this number and then chorally read this number with you.

Generate the second addend the same way.

Students place the new materials below and separate from the first set, then chorally read the second number.

Check to see that all materials have been put into the correct place. Ask: How could you add the two numbers together?

Students should suggest counting how many ones, etc.

Tell students to draw a line below all the materials and to push all the materials below the line.

Pushing all the materials down at once is not what students are used to, but they will more clearly see the need to regroup.

Ask them to look at the ones and give a total. Do they have to regroup?

Students regroup the ones if necessary and then add that amount to the tens. Students can now read the total chorally.

The illustration shows 29 + 12 = 41.

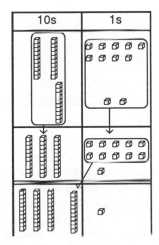

Point out that this regrouping is sometimes called "carrying."

Repeat the procedure until the students are competent in this part of the skill.

Students can now work in pairs and generate their own addition problems and solve them using this procedure. They are not doing any recording yet, but are using manipulatives and responding orally.

Have students practice with materials only until they are comfortable with the process.

Procedure 2

To practice adding with regrouping

Use *counter-trading materials, counter-trading boards, dice,* and *graph paper*.

Review the value of the counters and regrouping. Ask: Are the rules the same as they were for the other materials? (yes) If students need practice in counter trading, have them "add one," "add four," or "add ten" and read their results chorally.

Students make a recording paper labeled with color names or colors, instead of numbers. See Illustration 2a. They use dice to generate 2-digit numbers of counters to add, and they record the total.

When students are comfortable with this procedure, have them work with partners and compete to be the first to get to 99.

In the first turn, students generate two addends, record them, add them, and record the sum. They should push these counters to the top of the board. This sum will be the first addend for the second round.

When recording second and later turns, students write the new dice number below the previous total. Students who finish after two or three rounds may play again to see who has the *least* after a set number of turns.

Procedure 3

To write addition problems

Use *counters, counter-trading boards or color-coded pv mats, dice,* and *recording papers from Procedure 2.*

Tell students that you now want them to record all the regroupings they do.

Then tell them: Put two groups of counters on your chart that are large enough to need regrouping, and record them as before.

Then have the students push down the counters representing ones and record the total *even if it needs regrouping.* Repeat with the counters representing tens (Illustration 2a).

After the students have completed these tasks, tell them to start with the ones counters and regroup if necessary, and then to cross out the original number of ones on their recording sheets.

Then they are to write the remaining number of ones below and add any necessary to the tens, as shown in Illustration 2b.

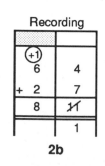
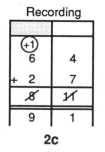

| 2a | 2b | 2c |

Add all tens as shown in Illustration 2c.

Continue step-by-step with students through similar problems.

Students generate numbers and work some addition

problems using this method. They record each separate step after doing it with materials.

When students are comfortable with this procedure, have them record and add their numbers on paper first, then check their answers with the counters.

When they can do this easily, you can introduce the shortcut recording method of "carrying."

Students should be allowed to check with materials and write the complete recording procedure until they are comfortable without it.

Have students practice the method of writing down the problem and recording the regroupings. Make sure they understand that this is just a description of what they have been doing with the manipulatives.

Practice and Extension

Have students use *pv mats, pv materials,* and *dice.* They generate one number and write it down. Then they generate a second addend and mentally add it to the first, writing down a total. They can check with materials or use paper-and-pencil addition.

Have students first do *problems from their textbook* on paper. They then round each number mentally and add them to get an estimated sum. Have them use this to find out whether their actual sum is probably right.

Challenge students to follow the same procedures to practice adding 2-digit numbers with more than two addends

Have students make up story problems that have 2-digit numbers. They share them with one another, taking turns trying to solve each other's problems.

Addition 11

Skill: To add 2-digit numbers: sums above 99

Time: 3+ periods

Materials:

graph paper: ¹/₂" squares; several sheets per student

scissors

clear tape

file-folder or other place value (pv) mats to 1000s

pv materials to 100s

counter-trading materials to 100s

dice: 1 per student

See Reproducibles for: directions for file folder pv mats to 1000s, pv mats to 100s, counter-trading boards to 1000s, or color-coded pv mats to 100s

Anticipatory Set

Use *graph paper, scissors,* and *clear tape.*

Have students make a recording strip by cutting their graph paper into long strips, three squares wide, and then taping the ends together. They then label the three squares at the top end of the recording strip: "100s," "10s," and "1s." Review the place names.

Give students take *file folders* with which to make the *file-folder pv mats,* if you wish to use them and they are not already made.

Procedure 1

To regroup to hundreds

Use *pv mats, pv materials,* and *recording strips from Anticipatory Set.*

Divided into groups, students read chorally the number of materials they have on their pv mats. zero hundreds, zero tens, zero ones.

They write 000 across their recording strips.

Have them add a one cube to their mat and read: zero hundreds, zero tens, one one.

They record 001.

Have students continue adding one, counting, and recording sums until they have reached ten and regrouped. Ask them: How many ones does it take to make a ten rod? (10) They should read the number 010 on their strips.

Have them continue adding one, counting, and recording sums until reaching 20 or so. Have them look for any patterns on their recording strips.

Students discuss any patterns they can find.

Tell students to turn the strips over, start with 60 on the mats, and add 10 at a time to 100. Ask how many ones are in each ten rod; how many ten rods in each hundred flat.

Students check their sheets for patterns.

Have students continue adding 10 at a time until they have 9 hundred flats, or until they have grasped regrouping ones and tens.

Students place pv materials and record sums. They discuss patterns found.

Procedure 2

To add with regrouping

Use *dice, pv mats,* and *pv materials.*

Draw a pv chart on the overhead or on the board.

Generate an addition problem by throwing a die to get the ones number. Show this many one cubes on the chart. Make another throw to get the number of tens for the first addend.

Students read this number chorally with you.

Generate the second addend the same way. Place the new materials below, and separate them from the first set. Read chorally. Ask: How could you add the two numbers?

Students should suggest counting how many ones, etc.

Draw a line below all the materials, and push all of them below the line. Have students read chorally the total. Pushing all the materials down at once is not what students are used to, but if it is done, they will more clearly see whether there is a need to regroup.

Students start with the ones and regroup as necessary.

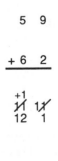

Students then regroup tens and read the total.

100s	10s	1s

	5	9
	+ 6	2
	12	1
+1	1̸2̸	1
	2	
	1 2	1

Give more sets of numbers, making sure you have made some regrouping necessary.

Students follow the same procedure with each new set of numbers that you dictate.

They can now use dice to generate their own addition problems and solve them using this procedure. They are not doing any recording yet.

Have students practice with materials until they are comfortable with the process.

Procedure 3

To practice adding with regrouping

Use *counter-trading materials, counter-trading boards, dice, graph paper, scissors,* and *clear tape.*

Review the value of the counters and regrouping. Ask: Are the rules the same as they were for the other materials? (yes) If students need practice with counter trading, have them "add one," "add four," or "add ten" and read their results chorally.

Students make a recording paper labeled with color names or colors instead of numbers. They use dice to generate a 2-digit number to show with counters. For example, if the numbers on the dice are 4 and 6, the student records either 46 or 64. They throw the dice again to generate another number.

Students record the numbers, show them with counters, combine the counters, and record the total.

When students are comfortable with this procedure, have them work with partners and compete to be the first to get to the hundred counter.

In the first turn, students generate two 2-digit addends, record them, add them, and record the sum. They should push the regrouped counters to the top of the board. This sum will be the first addend for the second round. When recording the second turn, students write the new dice number below the previous total.

How many students had to trade for a hundred counter on this turn? They can repeat the game while other pairs of students take a third turn.

Allow students to complete this exercise several times to build confidence in their grasp of the procedure.

Procedure 4

To write addition problems

Use *counter-trading materials, counter-trading boards, dice,* and *recording strips from Procedure 3.*

Tell students that you now want to see recorded all the regroupings they do.

Tell them: Put two groups of counters on your chart that are large enough to need regrouping and record them as before.

Push down all the counters representing ones and record the total, even if it needs regrouping. Do the same with the counters representing tens.

Recording Sheet

100s	10s	1s
	6	4
	+ 5	7
	11	11

3a

Recording Sheet

100s	10s	1s
	⊕+1 6	4
	+ 5	7
	11	1̸1̸
		1

3b

Start with the ones, and regroup if necessary.

Cross out the original number of ones on your recording sheet. Write the new number of ones below the original number and add to the tens as necessary (Illustration 3b). If this form of recording has not been put on the board or overhead, you may want to demonstrate at this time.

Recording Sheet

100s	10s	1s
	⊕+1 6	4
	+ 5	7
	1̸1̸	1̸1̸
	12	
	2	1

4a

Recording Sheet

100s	10s	1s
⊕+1	⊕+1 6	4
	+ 5	7
	1̸1̸	1̸1̸
	1̸2̸	
1	2	1

4b

Have them add all tens as shown in 4a, and regroup tens as shown in 4b.

Continue step-by-step with students through the problem.

It is important for students to understand that the written form is just a description of what is happening. Students need much practice at this step.

Pose the following problem: Rae Jean went to the library to do research, and she took out 15 books. She also photocopied 16 magazine articles. How many sources of material did Rae Jean have for her paper?

Students use counters to represent books and articles and then work out the problem.

Now encourage students to give a problem orally for the entire class to solve. Can they think of situations that would use higher numbers? Can someone make up a problem that uses 99 as one of the numbers?

Students should be allowed to check with materials as they solve the problems. They should write the complete recording procedure.

Continue until all students are comfortable with the process.

Practice and Extension

Have students use *pv mats, pv materials,* and *dice.* They generate one number and write it down. Then they generate a second addend and mentally add it to the first, writing down a total. They can check with materials or use paper-and-pencil addition.

Have students first do *problems from their textbook* on paper. They then round each number mentally and add them to get an estimated sum. Have them use this to check whether their actual sum is reasonable.

Have students make up story problems that have 2-digit numbers. They share with one another, taking turns trying to solve each other's problems.

How many different combinations can the students think of that total 99? 88? See how many different combinations they can devise for other selected numbers.

Challenge students to follow the same procedures and practice adding 2-digit numbers, using more than two addends.

Use *pv mats to 1000,* and extend the procedures to adding 3-digit numbers. For most this is a "free ride." They already know the skill.

Introduce a *thousand block* and challenge students to add *counters* and play the counter-trading game from Procedure 3 until one of them reaches a thousand block.

Note: The last three exercises build an awareness that can be used in a later skill.

Addition 12

Skill: To add 2-digit numbers: more than two addends

Time: 1 period

Materials:

deck of cards

containers: 3 per group

counters: 3 colors; 9 of each color per student

interlocking cubes: 2 colors; at least 9 each per student

file-folder or other place value (pv) mats to 100s

pv materials to 100s

number-and-dot cards 0 to 9: 1 set per student

dice: 1 per group

counter-trading materials to 100s

See Reproducibles for: directions for file folder pv mats to 1000s, pv mats to 100s—1 per student, counter-trading boards to 1000s—1 per group

Anticipatory Set

Use *deck of cards, containers,* and *counters.*

Have students work in groups. Shuffle cards and draw one. Students place that many red counters in one of the containers. Draw another card; that many blue counters go in the second container. Select a third card; the students place that many yellow counters in the third container.

Write the numbers on the board. The students count to reach a total. Continue the exercise.

Change the activity to adding two 2-digit numbers whose sums are under 99. Have students place two groups of counters on their desks, with one color for ones, another for tens. Each number should have two sets of counters. Students combine counters and tell you how many they have in all.

Procedure 1

To add groups of materials

Use *interlocking cubes, pv mats,* and the *deck of cards.*

Have students work in groups of three. As you randomly select numbers using the deck of cards, each student builds two "trains," using two colors of interlocking blocks. One color should represent the tens and the other the ones.

If you draw a 2-digit number, use that number; if you draw a 1-digit number, then you must draw a second card to create the 2-digit number that the students need for building trains.

Student groups combine their trains and arrive at a total number of interlocking cubes used. First, they combine the cube trains that are in the ones place on their mats. Then they combine the trains in the tens place, after trading any ones that need to be traded.

The problems should be written on the board.

After a few exercises, give students three numbers in the teens. Ask: Will the answer will be larger than 30? How do you know that? Have students estimate answers before counting the cubes.

Procedure 2

To demonstrate the written form

Use *pv mats, pv materials, number-and-dot cards,* and *1 die.*

Draw a pv chart on the board or overhead. Demonstrate how to generate an addition problem by throwing the die to get a ones number. Write this many ones on the chart.

Students place the cubes and read the number.

Use another throw to get the number of tens for the first addend. Write this on the chart.

Students place materials and chorally read the completed number with you.

Generate the second and third addends the same way. Have students place the materials for the second addend below and separate from the first set, then place the materials for the third addend below and separate from the second set.

Students place materials for the second and third addends and chorally read these numbers.

Ask: How could you add the three numbers together?

Students should suggest counting how many ones, etc.

Have students push all the materials below the line and chorally read each total: __ones, __tens, __hundreds. They regroup the ones and tens as needed.

Students do exercises and demonstrate knowledge of concept.

Now have students also lay a number-and-dot card beside the materials as they place materials on the mats; e.g., the number for the first addend is six tens and four ones.

They lay out the four one cubes and six ten rods. Next to the one cubes, they place the number card 4 and beside the ten rods they place the number card 6.

Students continue the exercise, using both the manipulatives and the number cards.

Procedure 3 □

To practice adding more than two addends

Use *counter-trading materials, counter-trading boards,* and *dice.*

Show how to generate a 2-digit number by throwing a die for the ones digit and throwing again for the tens.

Working in groups, students generate three 2-digit numbers. They place the counters on their boards and add to find the total amount. After all regroupings are done, the number left on the board is the first number of the next three.

Generate two more numbers and continue the exercise. Do this for about 5 minutes and then move on to the next procedure. Suggest to students that they try this game later to reinforce their skills. They can play to see who can reach 100 first.

Procedure 4 □

To develop the written form

Use *pv mats, pv materials,* and *paper to record problems.*

Have students work individually. Each student makes a recording sheet showing 100s, 10s, and 1s. Relate this to the number cards they used earlier, only this time they will be writing the numbers on their papers.

Make sure that they use spaces about ¹/₂-inch wide so that the problems look like those they will encounter in later math exercises. Several problems can thus be done on each paper.

Give them numbers to place as materials on their mats. Present the numbers in story problems, such as: Randy's Ice Cream Parlor had 13 new flavors of ice cream in June. It had 19 new flavors in July and 17 new flavors in August. How many new flavors were introduced in the ice cream shop all summer?

After they have placed materials and recorded numbers, have students look in the column for patterns of ten. Ask: How could this help you in estimating?

Continue the exercise, using story problems, until students are competent in this skill. Include some numbers for which they can find patterns of ten in either or both the ones and tens places. Learning this pattern will help build estimating skills.

Challenge students by sometimes having two addends, sometimes three, and sometimes four or more.

Students continue to complete problems in this manner until all have demonstrated competency.

Make sure students understand that the written form is only a description of what they are doing with the manipulatives.

Practice and Extension

Use *counter-trading boards* and *counters* to play the game of Trade Up. Students take turns using a die to generate 2-digit numbers to add. They follow Procedure 3. The one who reaches 500 first wins the game.

Students make up story problems to exchange with each other for solving.

Students use a *deck of cards* to play a game with more than two addends. Each student first draws two cards and then chooses where to place each number. (For example, a 2 and a 5 could be 25 or 52.) Then they repeat the procedure for addends number two and three. The student who has the closest total to 100, *without going over,* wins.

Addition 13

Skill: To add 3-digit numbers and mixed-digit numbers

Time: 1+ periods

Materials:

graph paper: ½" squares; 1 sheet per student

scissors

file-folder or other place value (pv) mats to 1000s

pv materials to 1000s, use counters as 1000s

dice: 1 per group

crayons or markers

counter-trading materials to 1000s

See Reproducibles for: directions for file-folder pv mats to 1000s, pv mats to 1000s, counter-trading boards to 1000s, or use color-coded pv mats to 1000s

Anticipatory Set

Use *graph paper* and *scissors*.

Have the class make recording strips by cutting graph paper into strips, four squares wide. Label the top squares: "1000s," "100s," "10s," and "1s." Review the place names, and introduce a thousand cube.

Review 2-digit addition problems.

Procedure 1

To add with regrouping; no zeros

Use *pv mats, pv materials,* and *recording strips from Anticipatory Set.*

Draw a pv chart on the board or overhead. Introduce this story: Liam kept a diary but only remembered to write in it on 129 days the first year. The second year, he wrote in it on 213 days. On how many days did he write in the diary?

Students place materials and chorally read the numbers. Then they draw a line below the materials and push all below the line. See the illustration. They start with the ones and regroup as needed. They read the sum chorally.

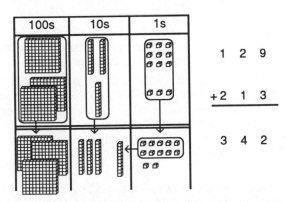

100s	10s	1s

	1	2	9
+	2	1	3
	3	4	2

Now have student groups generate their own addition problems, creating story situations that have 3-digit numbers in them. They should be recording, as well as working out the problems with materials.

Groups present problems and answers to the class.

Procedure 2

To add with regrouping; including zeros

Use *pv mats, pv materials, dice,* and *recording strips from Anticipatory Set.*

Use a die to generate a 3-digit number: ones, tens, then hundreds. Have students place materials and record on their recording strip as you write the number.

Tell students: The second number is tricky. You may use only numbers that are 4, 5, or 6.

Have each group throw a die to obtain the second addend. What should happen for those who didn't get an allowed number? (Use a zero.)

Emphasize this is a place holder, and make sure all zeros are recorded. Students *cannot use a zero in the hundreds place* but must continue to throw dice until they have an allowed number.

Students throw dice, place materials, record numbers, add materials, and record total.

Continue the procedure until students are competent in the skill.

Procedure 3

To practice writing addition problems

Use *counter-trading materials, counter-trading boards, crayons or markers, dice,* and *recording strips from Anticipatory Set.*

Students need to understand that the written form is just a description of what is actually happening with their materials. They need much practice at this step.

Students color-code their recording strips.

Copy Illustration 2a, found on the following page, onto the board. Use this to demonstrate the form for students as you work through the procedure.

Students use dice to generate numbers, put two groups of counters on the mat, and record as before. They push down all the counters representing ones, and then the tens and hundreds, recording the total number in *each* column (Illustration 2a).

Say: Start with the ones counters, and regroup if necessary. Cross out the original number of ones on your recording sheet. Write the new number of ones below, and show any necessary regrouping in the tens column. Circle the regrouped number (Illustration 2b).

Recording Sheet

1000s	100s	10s	1s
	1	6	4
	+ 2	5	7
	3	11	11

2a

Recording Sheet

1000s	100s	10s	1s
	1	⊕1 6	4
	+ 2	5	7
	3	11	11̸
			1

2b

Demonstrate Illustration 3a and say: Add all tens and record them like this. Continue to illustrate as in 3b and have students regroup tens as shown.

Recording Sheet

1000s	100s	10s	1s
	1	⊕1 6	4
	+ 2	5	7
	3	1̸1̸	1̸1̸
		12	1

3a

Recording Sheet

1000s	100s	10s	1s
	⊕1 1	⊕1 6	4
	+ 2	5	7
	3	1̸1̸	1̸1̸
		1̸2̸	
	4	2	1

3b

Continue step-by-step with students through the problem.

Students generate, work, and record some addition problems using this recording method. They record each separate step after doing it with the blocks.

When students are comfortable with the process, have them do problems on paper first and then check with the counters.

When they can do this easily, introduce the shortcut method of recording regrouping in which intermediate totals are not recorded. Remind them to continue circling the regrouped number.

Students check with blocks and write the complete recording procedure until they are comfortable with the shortcut method.

Procedure 4

To add mixed digit numbers

Use *counter-trading boards, crayons or markers, colored counters,* and *graph paper.*

Students use graph paper to make recording charts, and label them with colors or color names instead of numbers.

Present a story problem for students to place, record, and solve. Example: Lucy's Lamp Shop sold 374 table lamps and 26 floor lamps last month. How many total lamps were sold?

Before solving, have students look for patterns adding to 10. Remind them of rounding for estimating, and have them estimate an answer.

After placing materials, recording, and estimating, students solve problems for an exact total.

Have students now take turns giving uneven-digit problems for the whole class to estimate and then solve.

Students move to doing problems without manipulatives when they are comfortable with the process.

Practice and Extension

Use the *same materials as in Procedure 3.* Have students write down their first number, generate the second, and try to add them mentally. They write down their answer and check with the counters.

Have students use their *textbooks,* round the numbers, and add to get an estimate before doing the final addition. Have them check the two results to see whether their final sum is reasonable.

Extend the process to include 4- and 5-digit numbers. Set out problem situations for students to solve. Example: First Elementary School has 1,842 students. Second Elementary School has 964 students. How many elementary students are in the district? (Use look for tens and estimating before solving problems.)

Have students bring in *pictures of catalog items* costing amounts over and under $100. Students play in pairs using *pv mats* and *bills.* Students turn over two items and add amounts both with bills and on paper, ignoring any decimal amounts. The winner is the student who spent the most/least after three turns.

Have students extend practice to adding 3-digit numbers, using more than two addends. Use *pv mats,* place, record, and total. (356 + 178 +101) They may use *any of the manipulatives* to check.

Subtraction 1

Skill: To learn concrete subtraction: to understand the symbol –

Time: 1 period

Materials:

number-and-dot cards from Addition 1, or blank index cards for making them: 10 per student

cards with symbol –: 1 per student

2" paper circle "cookies" : 10 per student pair

paper plates or 6" paper circles: 1 per student pair

treasure box or other objects: at least 15 objects per student pair

counters: 10 per group

containers: 2 per group

interlocking cubes: 9 per student

Anticipatory Set

Use *blank index cards* if making number-and-dot cards.

Have students make number-and-dot cards as in the illustration if *not* using the ones from Addition 1.

Have students clap together in rhythm, first counting forward and then rote-counting backward.

Have each row of students count forward while standing next to their desks. Then have them count in reverse order while they sit back down in their seats.

Have students take turns in counting off the blast-off of a rocket: ten, nine, etc.

After using several of these activities, tell the students they may use counting backward to find how many less. The mathematical term for finding how many less is *subtraction*.

Procedure 1

To develop understanding of concrete subtraction and the symbol –

Use *number-and-dot cards, symbol cards, "cookies,"* and *paper plates.*

Have students work in pairs and use one paper plate and ten "cookies" per pair. Introduce a problem such as: I put 9 cookies on my plate.

Along came my big dog, who ate 5 of the cookies before I could stop him. How many cookies do I have left?

Have the student pairs place nine cookies on their plate. One of the students takes the part of the dog and "eats" five of the cookies. The other then counts to see how many are left.

Students do as requested and discover that they can take away items and arrive at the answer to a problem.

Remind students of earlier activities in which they "joined" two sets of numbers and called the process *addition*. This activity just completed was one of separating out a small set from a larger one. This process is called *subtraction*.

Students discuss the two related concepts of "joining" and "separating" sets of numbers.

Continue with this type activity until students are comfortable with the process.

Now introduce the symbol – card, and tell students to place that card beside their paper plate. This symbol means "to take away." It is similar to the addition symbol in appearance, but we have taken away one of the lines; this symbol then means "to take away, or minus."

Students place the symbol next to the paper plate and complete more problems using the symbol card to state "take away or minus" when they discuss the problems.

Continue with this kind of activity until students feel comfortable with the concept.

Procedure 2

To practice concrete subtraction

Use *objects* and *number-and-dot cards.*

Have students work in pairs. They are to make a parade of their objects. Encourage them to use several different kinds of objects.

Now instruct students to take their number-and-dot cards to show the number that they have in their parade.

Each pair of students should now decide what kind of objects they will separate out from their parade. They should set these aside and report to the class.

Students separate objects and report to the class how many were in their parade, how many they separated out, and how many were left in their parade at the end.

Have groups change partners several times and repeat the activity.

Procedure 3

To demonstrate knowledge of the subtraction symbol

Use *counters, containers, number-and-dot cards,* and *symbol cards.*

Have students work in groups. As you call out a number, the students place that number of counters in the first container. They then place the symbol card between the two containers. As you call out a second smaller number, the students place a card with that number on it in the second container.

Students place the counters and cards as shown.

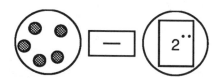

They remove the correct number of counters from the first container and place them into the second container, counting backward for each counter removed.

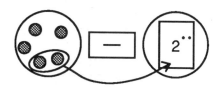

Ask: How many are left in the first container?

Students discuss and make up stories to fit the numbers.

Repeat the procedure several times, until students are familiar with the process of subtraction.

Now have students place a number-and-dot card with the counters in the first container. After removing the correct number of counters from the first container, they place the remaining counters on an answer number-and-dot card.

Procedure 4

To practice subtraction individually

Use *interlocking cubes, paper,* and *pencils.*

Have each student make a small train with cubes. Now instruct them to take away or separate out two of those cubes. Ask: How many are left in the trains?

Students do as requested and discuss. The number of cubes left will vary.

After discussion, have students write down the problems they created, with the answers. Remind them to use the horizontal, or equation, format.

Repeat the activity, giving students individual practice with the concept of *subtraction.*

Practice and Extension

Have students use any of the *manipulatives* in the room to explore the concept singly or in pairs.

Have students play games in which they have to count backward to reach a score.

Have students take turns "teaching" the concept to the class.

Have students use exercises and *manipulatives* from Procedure 3, placing the *containers* and the written description in the vertical format.

Subtraction 2

Skill: To count backward and identify one less

Time: 1 period

Materials:

interlocking cubes: 9 per student

crayons

scissors

tape, or glue sticks

counters: 1 per student

beads and string: at least 9 per student pair

calendar

See Reproducibles for: number lines to 25—1 per student

Anticipatory Set

Use *interlocking cubes.*

Have students first do a forward counting activity such as rote counting while clapping, orally counting each student, counting desks or books, etc.

Review the concept of *addition.*

Now have each student make a small train with the cubes. Instruct them to take away or separate out two of those cubes. How many are left in the trains? Students discuss.

Repeat the activity, and tell students that this math activity is called *subtraction.*

Procedure 1

To count backward from 25

Use *number lines, crayons, scissors, tape,* and *counters.*

Hand out number lines, and have students cut out the number lines and tape or glue them together at the tabs.

Now have students number the tick marks from 1 to 25 with a crayon.

Hand out one counter to each student, and tell them to place the counter on number 19.

Students work in pairs and take turns placing the counter and reading the numbers backward, going down all the way to 0.

Repeat with other numbers for about 5 minutes.

Have students place a counter on the number 25 on the number line, and put their finger on the number 24.

Say: One less than 25 is. . . (wait for response). . . 24.

Continue all the way down the number line to 0.

Students complete the oral activity with you, moving their counter, pointing to the next lower number, and saying that number in response to your question.

Procedure 2

To develop the concept of one less

Use *beads and string, interlocking cubes,* and *completed number lines.*

Have students work in small groups. They build cube trains of a specified length. Now call out a number that is one less, and have the students build another train that length.

Students complete the tasks and discuss what they observe about the trains.

Repeat with other numbers.

Now have the students work in pairs. One student uses beads and string, the other student uses the interlocking cubes. Call out a number, and have them string that many beads on the string.

Now call out the number that is one less than the previous number. The students should build a train of that many cubes. Ask: Is the train of cubes more than the string of beads?

Students respond: Yes or no, depending on the size of their beads. Most will say yes.

Discuss the number of beads on the string and the number of cubes in the train.

On their number line, have students place a bead on the number that corresponds to the number of beads on the string. Next they place an interlocking cube on the number that the train represents.

Students do as requested and see that there is one less cube so that train is actually smaller in number than the string of beads.

Repeat the activity with other numbers that the students are familiar with. These will probably be the numbers to ten, as this is usually an early skill.

Help students understand that the length of the train or string of beads will vary according to how large the individual items are. The relationships of the numbers remain constant, however; e.g., 6 is always one larger than 5.

Procedure 3

□

To practice counting back one less

Use *calendar* and *number lines*.

Note: Do not do this activity on the first day of the month.

Have students count on the calendar until they reach today's date. Point to today's date. Yesterday was one number less. It was ___? (now move the pointer to yesterday)

Students respond with the number.

Now use the calendar and give students other dates. Point to the preceding day, and ask what the date for that day is.

Students respond with the correct dates.

Have students take their individual number lines and write down 24 is one less than 25, etc.

Students write as instructed and complete the sequence all the way to 0 is one less than 1.

Practice and Extension

Use activities for counting backward such as counting off students as they line up to leave the room, counting the days that have passed on the *calendar*, and counting blast-offs.

Have students take *treasure box objects* and make parades that are one less than another parade. Students make picture charts of the two parades.

Have students make up story situations such as: Juan has 3 packages of gum. Carlos has one less. How many packages does Carlos have?

Subtraction 3

Skill: To learn subtraction facts

Time: 4+ periods

Materials:

interlocking cubes: 6 per group

beads and string: 9 per student pair

counters: 18 per student pair

containers: 1 per student pair

markers

die

number-and-dot cards: 1 set per student (see Addition 1)

card with symbol –: 1 per student

graph paper: any size; 1 sheet per student

egg cartons: 1 per group

treasure box or other objects: 12 per group

place value (pv) materials to 10s

plastic links: 18 per student pair

See Reproducibles for: number lines to 25 (taped together)—1 per student, pv mats to 100s—1 per group

Anticipatory Set

Use *interlocking cubes.*

Have students work in groups and build trains six cubes long. Tell them to separate the trains into any two parts. Discuss how they separated the trains. What do they think they were doing?

Do they see any relationship in the different train lengths that the various students made? Do all students see they still have six cubes?

Have students share their results. Some will have trains of five and one, some three and three, some four and two.

Discuss these relationships as parts of the whole starting train.

Procedure 1

To develop knowledge of facts from nine or less

Use *beads and string* or *counters and containers.*

Have students work in pairs with the beads and string. Each pair will work with a second pair for comparison studies. Each pair of students places nine beads on a string.

Instruct Pair A to take off four beads and Pair B to take off five beads.

Ask: Can you see a relationship between the two strings of beads?

Students do the activity and discuss possible relationships.

Repeat with removing seven and two beads; and again with removing other amounts of beads.

Continue the process with fewer than nine beads as a starting point until students are competent in the concept.

Students complete the tasks and continue working with beads until they are competent in the concept.

Procedure 2

To use count back to develop subtraction facts from nine or less; subtract zero

Use *number lines, markers,* and *1 die.*

Have students line up and count off backward. Remind them that they have been perfecting this skill in earlier lessons.

Hand out number lines, and have students number from one to ten. Each student should place a dot at the number nine.

Throw a die, and have students count back to subtract the number thrown from the number nine.

Students respond by counting backward each time you give them a new number.

Now have students place a dot at the number six. When you throw a six on the die, introduce the element of subtracting zero. (Can they see that if they take away nothing they still have the original number left?)

Introduce the subtract zeros as subtraction facts, and establish these facts from nine or less.

Students save the number line for procedures developing facts from 9 to 18.

Procedure 3

To write the process from nine or less

Use *number-and-dot cards, symbol cards, paper, 1 die,* and *graph paper.*

Introduce the symbol card, and tell students they should place numbers as you throw a die. You will give them the top, or minuend, number; then you will throw a die for the subtrahend, or take away, number.

Students use their individual number-and-dot cards and their symbol cards to display the problems on their desks. They write the correct answer on a piece of paper as shown:

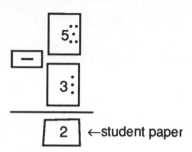

←student paper

They use the counting dots to count backward and should feel free to use manipulatives if they need to.

After students are comfortable with the process, have them take graph paper and write the problems and the fact families on their own.

Students write all the facts from nine or less, writing one number per square.

Procedure 4   ▢■

To develop facts from 12 or less

Use *egg cartons* and *counters or objects.*

Have students place 12 treasures in an egg carton, one in each section. Ask: If you take away one treasure, how many are left? (11)

Write 12 – 1 = 11 on the board. Have the students use paper to make a recording sheet, using the horizontal form.

Recording Sheet

Start	Take Away	Leaves	
12	1	11	12 – 1 = 11
12	2	10	12 – 2 = 10
12	3	9	12 – 3 = 9

Have students continue to remove treasures and count and record until all the facts from 12 are recorded. Now they place 11 treasures in the egg carton and repeat the procedure.

Continue until you have covered all the subtraction facts from 12 or less.

Procedure 5   ▢■

To develop facts using vertical form; from 18 or less

Use *pv mats, pv materials, markers,* and *plain paper.*

Have students place a ten rod and 8 one cubes to represent 18 on their mats. Ask them to separate out, or take away, 4 from the cubes. Ask: Is this possible? How many are left?

Students respond: Yes, 14 are left.

Now ask them to take away six of the cubes. Can they do this?

Students respond: No.

How can we get more ones?

Students discuss. *If needed, ask them whether we can regroup.*

Have students now regroup so that they have 14 cubes on their mats. They should tell you that they can now take away 6 of those cubes; 8 will be left.

Write on the board vertically, 18 – 4 = 14; and 14 – 6 = 8.

After developing all the facts and writing the problems on the board, have the students use a plain piece of paper to draw picture records of the facts as they discover them independently, using manipulatives:

10s	1s	
▭	⬭ ⬭ ⬭ ⬭	18
	⊠ ⊠ ⊠ ⊠	− 4
		14
▭	⬭ ⊠ ⊠ ⊠	14
		− 3
		11
	⊠ ⊠	12
▭	⊠ ⬭ ⬭ ⬭	− 3
	⬭ ⬭ ⬭ ⬭	9

Discuss the records they make of the activity.

After reviewing all the facts from 18 or less in the vertical format, have students practice the horizontal format.

Procedure 6   ▢■

To practice facts with problem solving; the concept of *dozen*

Use *egg cartons* and *plastic links.*

Have student groups pretend that they have to take a dozen cookies to the School Rally Day. They are to place one link— "cookie"—into each egg carton section. Discuss how many it takes to fill the egg carton.

Students discuss and realize that a dozen is 12.

Say: If only 7 of Bob's cookies were eaten, how many are left?

On the board write 12 – 7 = ? Have students make a recording sheet as in Procedure 4.

Students make a recording sheet. Then they each remove seven links. They record this, and then discuss the resulting answer.

Do more problems involving the concept of dozen until students will use *12* and *dozen* interchangeably.

After students are comfortable with the words, move onto other problem-solving situations.

Say: Tamara raises tulips for sale. Yesterday she picked 18 flowers and sold 8 of them. How many did she take home?

Have students work in pairs. One places 18 links (tulips) on a desk. Another student "buys" 8 tulips. The first student reports how many are left.

The student pairs work together and record with pictures what has happened.

Give problems for students to act out, solve, and record on paper. Record the horizontal form on the board. This form will translate to recognizing number sentences and thinking how to solve various kinds of subtraction questions later.

Procedure 7

To practice the written form from 18 or less; count to find answers

Use *number lines* and *counters*.

Have students take the number lines and place a counter on the number 18. On their papers they are to write 18, as you do it on the board.

Now they are to count back 7 spaces to the number 11, tapping each tic mark as they chorally read the numbers. On the board write –7 under the 18.

Students complete the task, copy the board onto their papers, and record the answer, 11.

After completing several count-backward examples, introduce the "count up" way of arriving at an answer. This is an easier way to count, especially if students do not have a number line at some later date.

Use 12 – 7 = 5 as the example. In this task the student places a finger on the number 7 and places counters on the numbers until the number 12 is covered. Ask: How many counters were placed? (5)

Students record on their papers, 12 – 7 = 5.

Remind students to count the numbers up, saying first the number where they placed their finger and then saying each of the other numbers aloud as they place the counters. Students will need a lot of practice with this part of the procedure.

This is a noisy activity, but the practice of saying the numbers aloud and counting to their partners is important in helping build fact knowledge, as well as the skill of counting mentally to find a subtraction fact answer.

Practice and Extension

Have students use *flash cards* and play games to increase speed and accuracy.

Make up sets of *mixed + and – flash cards* to increase awareness of signs and to practice facts.

Have students make up story problems, draw a diagram of the solution, and put the solution on the back. Then they can exchange for each other to solve.

Students make up games that use the *number-and-dot cards* or *number lines* to count backward.

Have students make up sets of *flash cards* to take home to practice the most difficult facts, *for them*.

Have students use the *addition/subtraction table* (see Reproducibles) to find answers and to practice facts. They can use these as answer checking for the games they create.

Subtraction 4

Skill: To understand fact families and to check subtraction with addition

Time: 4 periods

Materials:

2" paper circle "cookies": 12 per student

paper plates, or 6" paper circles: 2 per student

coins: pennies; 18 per group

narrow tag board strips: 2 per group

egg cartons: 1 per group

counters: at least two colors; 12 each per group

treasure box or other objects: 18 per group

graph paper: ¹/₂" squares or larger; 2 sheets per group

interlocking cubes, or beads and string: 18 per group

plastic links: 18 per student

See Reproducibles for: addition/subtraction tables—1 per group

Anticipatory Set

Have 10 students stand up in the front of the class. Ask the first 4 students to sit down. How many students are left standing? (6) What kind of math problem is this? (separating or taking away)

The 4 students come back up. How many are there now? (10) What are we doing? (joining or adding)

Have all the students in the first two rows stand. How many are there? What is this process? (adding) Have the students in the first row sit down. How many are left? What is this process? (subtracting)

Have the students in the first row stand again; is the number the same now as it was before? (yes) Tell the students that they are going to see how the relationship between adding and subtracting can help them know when an answer is correct.

Procedure 1

To develop the knowledge of subtraction fact families to 6 or less

Use *cookies* and *paper plates*.

Have students work independently. Give each student one paper plate and six cookies to place on the plate. Ask: If you went home and found six cookies on the kitchen table, how many would you eat?

Have each student remove the number of cookies that he or she would eat. Discuss how many are left on each student's plate.

Now give each student another paper plate and six more cookies, or have them work together in pairs.

This time, after placing six cookies on each plate, tell them to "eat" four cookies off one plate and two cookies off the other plate. Can they see any similarities to the numbers that they have on their plates?

Students discuss the paper plate cookies and see that the numbers for each set are related. That is, they see that 6 – 4 = 2 and 6 – 2 = 4.

Place both facts on the board, and introduce the students to fact families of subtraction. Remind them that they know about fact families from addition.

Continue until all the facts below 6 – 6 = 0 have been covered and all these fact families have been introduced.

Procedure 2

To develop the relationship between addition and subtraction in fact families to 18 or less

Use *pennies, addition/subtraction tables,* and *tag board strips.*

Instruct students to take their pennies and "act out" the following story.

Willie took 10 pennies out of his piggy bank. He found 2 more on the floor. Ask: How much money does he have now? (12¢)

Write 10¢ + 2¢ = 12¢ on the board.

Students now have 12 pennies on their desks.

He went to the store and bought a package of gum for 10¢. How much does he have left?

Students take out 10 pennies; Willie has 2 cents left.

Write 12¢ – 10¢ = 2¢.

He earned 10¢ by sweeping the front porch. How much does he have now?

As students complete this on their desks, write 2¢ + 10¢ = 12¢ on the board.

Students add back the 10 pennies and tell you he now has 12¢.

As he went inside, he accidentally dropped 2 pennies down the heat vent on the floor. How many pennies does he have left to put in his piggy bank? (10¢)

Write 12¢ – 2¢ = 10¢ on the board with the rest of the number sentences. Can students see a pattern?

Students discuss that all use the same numbers and that this looks similar to the fact families they learned about in addition.

Emphasize to students that a set of numbers like 2, 10, and 12 have both addition and subtraction sides to their fact families, just as people have two sides to their families.

Continue the exercise with stories about pennies from the piggy bank until all the fact families below 18 have been recorded on the board and discussed by the students.

Now introduce the addition/subtraction table, and show students how to use it to find subtraction answers, using tag board strips horizontally and vertically.

Students practice with the tables and strips to check the answers to various sets of numbers; e.g., 3, 6, and 9.

Procedure 3 □

To record fact families from 12 or less

Use *egg cartons* and *counters*.

Have students divide a paper in half and label each side with a color corresponding to a counter color; e.g., "Red" and "Blue."

Have each group discover and record how many different ways they can show the number 12.

Give an example: Place 2 blue and 10 red counters into the egg carton. Record 2 in the "Blue" column and 10 in the "Red" column, and then draw a line:

Red	Blue
10	2

Students work in groups to place counters and record different sets of numbers that equal 12.

When students have completed the task for 12, ask them to discuss what fact families they have found. Write on the board as the students discuss. Remind them to give four parts to each family.

As students discuss, have them notice that double numbers only have two parts to their fact families. Discuss why.

Continue the exercise for other numbers below 12 until students see the relationships and understand the process.

Procedure 4 □■

To develop the knowledge of number sentences

Use *objects, counters,* and *graph paper*.

Pick up a random number of treasure box objects, and hand some to a student. Show the class how many are left. Ask: How many did I start with?

Students discuss.

If you had picked up 11, given 6 to a student, and shown the class 5, you would write on the board the three numbers 5, 6, and 11.

Have the students take their counters and show one color group of 6 and another color group of 5. The number sentence that would show this is an addition sentence; 5 + 6 = 11.

On your desk, put the two color groups together so that you have 11 counters. Now take away the color group of 6 counters. How many are left? (5)

Say: I know the number started with, 11, and want to find out how many are left. This is a subtraction number sentence; 11 − 6 = 5. I can prove that this is correct by adding the two groups back together.

Students rejoin their two groups of counters and agree that they now have the same as before.

Have students work independently, drawing representations on graph paper and then writing the related facts:

$$11 - 5 = 6 \text{ left}$$

Continue until students see the direct relationship between addition and subtraction in fact families. As students draw the representations and write the facts, it is important for them to understand that the written form is just a description of what is happening.

Procedure 5 □■

To write problems; to check subtraction with addition

Use *interlocking cubes or beads and string* and *graph paper*.

Have students either build a train of 18 cubes or make a string of 18 beads. Ask them to separate out 9 of the materials. How many are left? (9) How could they prove that?

Students respond: They could put the two groups of beads back together and count them.

Students write the problem and its "checking partner" on their graph paper after using the manipulatives:

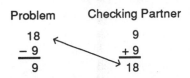

Problem	Checking Partner
18	9
− 9	+ 9
9	18

Continue until students are competent in the skill and can see that they can reverse the procedure to check an answer.

Procedure 6

To write number sentences to solve problems; to relate + and −

Note: This is a good way to introduce missing addends or missing numbers, as well as helping students see they can reverse the procedure to check problems.

Use *graph paper, plastic links, addition/subtraction table,* and *tag board strips.*

Write the fact family of 3, 4, and 7 on the board. Tell students to use links to represent the problem situation and then to write the numbers on the graph paper. They use the addition/subtraction table to find correct answers.

Students work the following problems, with you demonstrating on the board.

Help them see the relationship with number sentences and problem solving.

Say: Chris raises rabbits. Last night she fed her 3 rabbits. This morning she found 7 rabbits in the pen. How many rabbits were born last night?

Write 3 + [ ] = 7 on the board, or use an empty box instead of the brackets if your textbook uses a box to represent missing numbers. Relate to the illustration in Procedure 4.

The total number equals 7; take away the known number 3, and the number left is____? (4)

Explain that this is an addition equation, solved by subtraction and checked with addition.

Say: Mario raises dogs. This morning 4 puppies were born. He now has 7 dogs. How many did he have yesterday?

Follow the same procedure. ([ ] + 4 = 7; solved by subtraction; checked by addition)

Say: Mary Lou had 7 cookies. She gave Angelina 3 of them. How many does Mary Lou have left?

(7 − 3 = [ ]; subtract; check by addition)

Say: Jesse had 7 marbles. He lost 4 through a hole in his pocket. How many are still in his pocket?

(7 − 4 = [ ]; subtract; check by addition)

Say: Wesley had a bag of marbles. He lost 3 of them. He has 4 left. How many did he have in his bag before losing some?

([ ] − 3 = 4; solved by addition; checked by subtraction)

In this problem the unknown total equals the number taken away plus the number left. Students should discover this on their own during discussion.

Continue the activity with students giving you situations and then solving the problems with number sentences and links, writing the process on graph paper as they complete the problems.

Practice and Extension

Play the following on any *game board.* Write the numbers 7 through 12 on a *blank die.* Students first throw this die and get the minuend. They throw a *regular die* to get the subtrahend. Students are to move the number of spaces as shown by the difference.

Have students make + *and* − *flash cards* to practice with each other. They should shuffle the cards so that the facts are intermixed.

Students can play Subtraction Worms with *number lines* and one *die.* They roll the die and cross out two numbers that would give the answer. For example, if a student rolled a 5, he or she could cross out either 10 and 5, 11 and 6, etc. The student says "___ take away ___ = 5." The number sentence must be correct.

Play continues until the students can no longer cross out any numbers, or until the one who was able to cross off the most numbers after so many minutes or after a specific number of turns is pronounced the winner.

Subtraction 5

Skill: To learn subtraction facts: doubles and near doubles

Time: 3+ periods

Materials:

counters: 2 colors; at least 8 of each per student

scissors

crayons

clear tape

any or all of the following, students do not need identical materials: 18 per student pair

  treasure box or other objects

  plastic links

  beads and string

interlocking cubes: 2 colors; 18 per student pair

containers: 2 per student pair

1 cm cubes

2 cm × 18 cm strips of graph paper: 1 per student

See Reproducibles for: number lines to 25, graph paper with 1 cm squares

Anticipatory Set

Use *number lines, counters, scissors, tape,* and *crayons.*

Have students cut out the number lines, tape them together, and number the lines to 25. Present the following story, and have students place counters on the number line.

The ants and the grasshoppers had a picnic. The ants brought 3 lbs. of chicken. Students place 3 counters on the number line. They also brought 2 lbs. of potato salad, 2 lbs. of hamburgers, and 1 lb. of bread. Students place counters as you give the numbers. They should now have 8 counters on their lines.

Use the second color counter for the grasshoppers. They brought 2 lbs. of watermelon and 2 lbs. of chocolate cake.

Who brought the most food? (ants) How much more did they bring? (4 lbs.) How much food did they have altogether? (12 lbs. of food) They had 1 lb. of chicken, 1 lb. of potato salad, and 1 lb. of watermelon left after the picnic. How many pounds of food did they eat that day? (9 lbs.)

Briefly review addition and subtraction facts.

Procedure 1

To develop the concept of doubles

Use *treasure box objects, plastic links, beads and string,* and *interlocking cubes.*

Have students work in pairs and use one of the manipulatives to build a series of parades, chains, or trains by taking turns adding one at a time.

Have them keep track of how many each person adds to the total. When all are finished, ask whether any of them can tell you something interesting.

Students may tell you that they all put on the same number of items.

Now have students separate their manipulatives into two equal lengths by subtracting one at a time and rebuilding separate lengths.

Students complete the activity and tell you each length contains nine items.

Write 9 + 9 = 18 and 18 − 9 = 9 on the board.

Tell students now to build two eight-item constructions and to tell you what fact family they discover.

Students respond: 8 + 8 = 16 and 16 − 8 = 8.

Continue the activity.

Students complete the activity until they have covered all of the doubles below 9 + 9.

Have students exchange manipulatives and repeat if needed.

Procedure 2

To practice with doubles

Use *interlocking cubes* and *paper.*

Have student pairs build trains of each color; first, two trains of two cubes each.

Ask: Are the two trains the same length? (yes) What did we call two numbers that were the same?

Students respond: Doubles.

Now have students join their two trains to make one long train. How long is the total train?

Students respond: 4 cubes.

Have them separate the trains into two trains of one color each. How long is each train? (2 cubes)

Students build trains and record the numbers on paper in the same form that you wrote on the board in Procedure 1.

Have students continue with other train lengths until they have built two trains of nine cubes each.

Students discuss the resulting totals.

They now work backward on their own, taking away doubles and recording the results on paper, keeping the two parts of each double fact family together.

Monitor each pair's progress to be sure they understand the process.

Procedure 3　　　　　　　　　　　　　■

To develop the concept of near doubles; *doubles plus one*

Use *containers* and *treasure box objects*.

Have students work in pairs to place five similar objects into each container. Ask whether they remember how many five plus five are.

Students respond: 10.

Now have students add one more object to one of the containers. How many are there in all now?

Students respond: 11.

Say: A near double is one less or one more than a set of doubles. We are going to look at those that are one more, *doubles plus one.*

We have discovered that the double of five plus five has a near double; five plus six. In subtraction we say 10 − 5 = 5 is part of a double family. Its plus-one relative is 11 − 5 = 6.

Challenge students to make another set of doubles and to find a near double that relates to it.

Have students continue to work with objects until all the doubles, 2 − 1 = 1 to 18 − 9 = 9, have been covered and the doubles plus one have been established.

Procedure 4　　　　　　　　　　　　　■

To develop the meaning of near doubles; *doubles minus one*

Use *containers* and *treasure box objects*.

Have students work in pairs to place four similar objects into each container. Ask whether they remember how many four plus four are.

Students respond: 8.

Remind students that a near double is one less or one more than a set of doubles.

Say: Since we are now looking at the near double of minus one, or one less, remove one object from one of the containers.

Ask: How many would one less than eight be?

Students respond: 7.

We have discovered that the double of four plus four has a near double—four plus three. So the subtraction fact 8 − 4 = 4 has a near double of 7 − 4 = 3.

Challenge students to make another set of doubles and to find a near double that relates to it as a one-less double.

Continue to work with objects until all the doubles, 2 − 1 = 1 to 18 − 9 = 9, have been covered and the doubles minus one have all been established with the resulting subtraction facts shown.

Procedure 5　　　　　　　　　　　　　□

To work with doubles and near doubles

Use *1 cm cubes* and *2 cm × 18 cm graph paper strips*.

Have students number the centimeter strips from 1 to 18, one number per square. Have them place trains of cubes on the strip. Each train should be of equal length. For example, the first set of trains would be one cube each.

Ask: How long is the train when joined together?

Students respond: 2 centimeters.

The second set of trains would be two cubes each. How long is this train?

Students complete the trains, place them on the centimeter strips, and tell you that these trains are 4 centimeters long.

Ask students to find the near double that is plus one. How long would this train be? (5 cm)

Record on the board the subtraction and addition facts of the double shown, and the subtraction of the near double plus one; e.g., 2 + 2 = 4, 4 − 2 = 2, 5 − 2 = 3 and 5 − 3 = 2.

Have students continue with other trains until they have completed all the sets of doubles.

Now reverse the order, and have the students remove one of the cubes from one of their 9-centimeter trains. Now how long is the total train?

Students respond: 17 centimeters.

Write on the board: 9 + 9 = 18, 18 − 9 = 9, 17 − 9 = 8, and 17 − 8 = 9.

Review that this is a near double minus one. Continue the process until students have gone back to two trains of only one cube each.

Review the equations on the board.

Challenge students to make a train of equal numbers of cubes of two different colors, write the double family shown, find two near doubles that relate to it, and set up the corresponding subtraction facts.

Students do as requested and report their discoveries to the class. They discuss how they think this knowledge of near doubles might help in future math problems.

If students do not see that the knowledge of doubles and near doubles would help in estimating, pose the following problem situation.

Say: Maria had 7 granola bars and 8 apples for school snacks. How many days can she take snacks to school? Is it about 2 weeks or 3 weeks? How do you know?

Students discuss how near doubles could help in solving mental math problems and why they may choose one near double over the other.

Do they prefer to add one or take away one? Discuss that either way is acceptable for doing mental math.

Use many examples, as the relationship of numbers is important to the full development of this concept.

Students use manipulatives and write down the process to help them understand the relationships. They try to answer first using mental math.

Practice and Extension

Have students make up problems, solved with subtraction, that use doubles and near doubles. See whether they can verbally give the problems to each other and whether the other student can answer using mental math.

Make a class chart of doubles and near doubles to hang up in the room, or add the subtraction near doubles to a chart already made from addition lessons.

Subtraction 6

Skill: To use subtraction facts: missing numbers

Time: 3 periods

Materials:

interlocking cubes: 18 per student

containers: 3 per group

treasure box or other objects: 36 per group

markers

clear tape

scissors

counters: 1 of one color and 17 of another per student

narrow tag board strips: 2 per student

1 cm cubes: 20 per student

2 cm × 20 cm strips of graph paper: 1 per student

See Reproducibles for: number lines to 25—1 per student, addition/subtraction tables—1 per student, graph paper with 1 cm squares

Anticipatory Set

Use *interlocking cubes.*

Have students build trains of varying lengths, using two colors of the cubes. Discuss the addition and related subtraction facts they have formed.

Review all the subtraction fact families that the students have learned previously, and explain that now they are going to look at them a different way.

Procedure 1

To develop recognition of the missing number

Use *containers* and *objects.*

Give each group three containers. Have them set two close together as problem containers; the other goes to the right and is designated as the answer container.

Have students place 16 objects into the answer container. Then they should put 7 more objects into one of the problem containers.

Ask: How many objects do you need to place into the other problem container so that you will have 16 total?

Students respond: 9.

Relate this to the fact 9 + 7 = 16. Remind them of fact families, and place the following equation on the board: ? + 7 = 16.

Ask: What number should replace the question mark? How can you find the answer? What math process will you use?

Students respond: 9. We had to subtract to find the answer.

Have students now place 18 objects into the answer container. Say: Take some of the other objects and place them into a problem container. What problem questions have you created?

Students do as requested and discuss the various problems they have created.

Place the problems on the board, with question marks in the places stated.

Students discuss the numbers that should be in place of the question marks.

Discuss responses, and place the completed equations on the board.

Procedure 2

To count up to find a missing number

Use *number lines, markers, clear tape, scissors,* and *counters.*

Have students tape together the number lines and use markers to number from 1 to 25.

Use story problems such as: I want to plant a dozen rosebushes. I can plant 5 in the front yard. The rest will go in the back yard. On the board write 5 + ? = 12.

Have students place a red counter on the number 5 and yellow counters on 6, 7, 8, 9, 10, 11, and 12.

Ask: How many yellow counters did you use? (7) How many rosebushes will I plant in the back yard? (7)

Let a student write the subtraction solution of 12 − 5 = 7 on the board.

Continue with other story problems. Write the equations on the board, and have students place counters to arrive at an answer. Then write the addition fact that proves the subtraction fact is correct so that you have the two related facts on the board.

Procedure 3

To develop the concept of subtracting to find the missing number

Use *number lines from Procedure 2, counters, tag board strips,* and *addition/subtraction tables.*

Discuss the relationship between addition and subtraction.

Have students place a counter on the number 12. Say: This is another way to discover how many rosebushes should be planted in the back yard if we are going to plant 5 in the front and have 12 total rosebushes.

Students place counters and count back 5 numbers, using 12 as the first number, and arriving at a subtraction answer.

Ask: Where did you place your last counter? (on the 8) How many numbers don't have counters?

Students respond: 7.

Emphasize fact families, and tell students that the equation they just solved looks like this: Write 5 + ? = 12 on the board. Ask: What number do you think you would land on if you started at 12 and counted back 7 numbers?

Students respond: 6; 5 numbers would not have counters. They count to see whether they are correct.

Write the equation 12 – 7 = 5 on the board.

Now place the equation 12 – ? = 7 on the board. Ask: How do you think this kind of question should be answered? Can you locate the answer on the addition/subtraction table?

Students respond: Subtract 7 from 12. They place the strips on the table and read the answer. They tell you the equation should read 12 – 5 = 7.

Discuss that they take a known total and subtract a known amount to "find" the unknown number in an equation.

Continue working with facts below 18 until students are competent with the process.

Procedure 4 □

To write equations

Use *1 cm cubes* and *2 cm graph paper strips*.

Have students number the cm strips, one number per square, from 1 to 20.

Write equations on the board with question marks. Have students copy the equations onto paper and then lay cubes onto their centimeter strips. For example: ? + 7 = 13.

Have them look at the strip and, starting at the number 13, cover 7 squares—counting backward—13, 12, 11, 10, 9, 8, 7. Ask: What is the next number?

Students respond: 6.

That is the number that goes in the equation on the board; there are 6 numbers without cubes. Now write 6 + 7 = 13, and have students copy this under the equation with the question mark.

Introduce the form students will see in many texts of [ ] + 7 = 13. (Use an empty box instead of brackets if your textbook uses a box in place of missing numbers.) Discuss that the brackets (or box) could be replaced with a question mark. Students need to comprehend the reading of these types of equations to ensure that they are able to understand what question is being asked.

Students discuss that even though the equation is addition, the problem is actually solved with subtraction. They should see that the correct answer could then be proven by using the addition sentence originally given.

Continue the process until students have written all the combinations that total 18.

Be sure to include some questions that are subtraction, solved by subtraction, like 15 – ? = 8.

Challenge students to create problems with the answers of 19 and 20.

Discuss responses.

Practice and Extension

Expand the concept to include such equations as [ ] + 12 = 25, and 28 – [ ] = 16. Students should see that in order to answer the question, they need to subtract what is known to arrive at the unknown.

Challenge students to create story problems, such as: I have 18 marbles, and 12 of them are blue. How many are not blue? Students start at the number 12 and use *counters* to represent marbles. They count up to 18 from 12 and see that they used 6 counters; so 6 of the marbles are not blue.

Have students work together to make up problems and exchange with another pair of students to solve.

Use *worksheets* from the textbook that students have solved in earlier processes. Punch out or cover one number, and have them discover what that number is.

Subtraction 7

Skill: To subtract tens

Time: 1 period

Materials:

scissors

clear tape

markers

place value (pv) materials to 10s: two types

counters

die

counter-trading materials to 10s

See Reproducibles for: number lines to 100—1 per student, hundred boards—1 per student, pv mats to 100s—1 per student, counter-trading boards to 1000s, or color-coded pv mats—1 per student

Anticipatory Set

Use *number lines, scissors, tape, hundred boards,* and *markers.*

Have students count off by tens, first forward and then backward.

Have students make number lines and write the multiples of ten on them. Have them color in the multiples of ten on the hundred boards.

Discuss the patterns that they can see on their number lines and hundred boards.

Procedure 1

To subtract tens from tens

Use *pv mats, pv materials,* and *completed number lines.*

Have ten students hold up fingers as they count off by tens. Write the final number on the board. Now ask some of the students to put their hands down. Count by tens the fingers still showing. Write this new final number on the board. For example: 100 . . . 70 . . . .

Students discuss that they "took away" sets of ten fingers. When they did, they changed only the number in the tens place.

Repeat the exercise if needed, and then have students move on to the pv materials and pv mats.

Have students place five ten rods on their mats. Now tell them to remove two of those rods. Ask: How many are left? (3)

Place a copy of the illustration on the board:

10s	1s
5	0
−2	0
3	0

Continue giving students numbers of tens to subtract.

Students place rods, pull down the desired number, and then give a final answer.

Write the problems on the board pv chart. Continue giving numbers through the hundreds so that students can see the pattern.

Discuss that when subtracting tens from tens, they only have to take away or subtract the number in the tens column. Emphasize that they must remember to place zeros in the ones column as placeholders.

Students should be able to come up with reasons why this is so.

Discuss the patterns of the multiples of tens that they can see on the number lines and how that relates to the problems they have been doing on the place value chart.

Procedure 2

To explore patterns of subtracting tens from 2-digit numbers

Use *hundred boards, number lines,* and *counters.*

Have students work in pairs. Explain that one of them is to use the number line, the other is to use the hundred board, and both will use counters to show numbers.

Instruct students to place counters on the number 93. Now say: Count back and place a counter on the number that is ten less.

Students count back and place a counter on 83. They discuss what the two counters show.

Now tell students to place another counter on the number that is ten less than 83.

Students tell you that this counter is on 73.

Continue to number 53, having students discuss the patterns on both hundred boards and number lines.

Choose another starting number, and have students place counters as before.

Students complete the exercise and discuss that only the tens number changes when they subtract ten from 2-digit numbers. They discuss all the patterns they can see on their finished number lines and hundred boards.

Procedure 3

To subtract multiples of ten from 2-digit numbers

Use *other pv material, die,* and *pv mats*.

Have students work in groups. Use a die to generate a number for them to place in the ones column. Throw again for the number to place in the tens column. Have students chorally read the final number.

Tell students a number to place in the tens column to subtract. Remind them to place a zero in the ones column.

Students subtract and discuss what this activity has shown them about subtracting tens. They should see that working with tens is similar to working with ones.

Relate the activities to the patterns they were able to see in earlier procedures.

Procedure 4

To practice subtracting tens using story problems

Use *counter-trading boards* and *counters*.

Have students make up story problems in which ten or multiples of ten need to be subtracted from a number.

For example: Adelia took 32 oranges to school for her birthday treat. She dropped 10 of them on her way to the bus. How many did she have when she arrived at school?

Students place counters on their mats or boards to represent the numbers given in the problems. They then work with the manipulatives to discover the answer. As they do each step with materials, they write the process on paper.

Another example: Use counters to represent dimes. Jeff goes to the store with 9 dimes and spends 5 dimes for peanuts. How many dimes are left? How much money is that?

Students work in groups to make and exchange problems involving subtracting tens from 2-digit numbers. For extra practice they can exchange problems with another group and try to solve the new problem situations.

Procedure 5

To write problems

Use *pv materials* and *pv mats*.

Tell the students that they now should show in writing what the manipulatives have been showing as they worked out problems.

Students write the corresponding steps on paper, being sure to record the zeros where needed. They use the manipulatives as long as they feel the need.

Practice and Extension

Brainstorm with students how to subtract 10 from 100. From 120.

How about subtracting 30 from 140? 90 from 180?

Students use *dimes* to solve story problems about money. They take turns giving a partner a problem to act out. Some of the problems should use *counters* for pennies so that the numbers can be varied.

Subtraction 8

Skill: To subtract 2-digit numbers and check with addition

Time: 3+ periods

Materials:

place value (pv) materials to 10s

graph paper: ½" squares or larger; several sheets per student

special dice: one: 0 to 5, other: 4 to 9; 1 teacher set

counter-trading materials

washable markers

See Reproducibles for: pv mats to 100s—1 per student, counter-trading boards to 1000s, or color-coded pv mats

Anticipatory Set

Compare 2-digit numbers: Which is more, less? What is one less, one more, ten less, ten more, etc.?

Have each student take out any two books. Chorally count the books for the whole class by twos. Ask a student to remove all the math books. How many books are still out on desks? What would the number sentence be for this problem? Discuss responses.

Procedure 1

To develop the concept of 2-digit subtraction; no regrouping

Use *pv mats* and *pv materials.*

Have students place six ten rods and eight one cubes on their mats. Then have them pull down two ten rods and five one cubes (Illustration 1a).

Place Illustration 1b on a pv chart on the board:

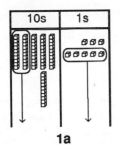

10s	1s
6	8
−2	5
4	3

1a   **1b**

Discuss the remaining materials. Students should see that when the numbers do not require regrouping, it is just as if there were two separate problems.

Continue the procedure until the students are competent in this part of the skill.

Procedure 2

To expand the concept of 2-digit subtraction; regrouping

Use *graph paper, pv mats, pv materials,* and *special dice.*

Draw a pv chart on the board or overhead.

Demonstrate how to generate a subtraction problem by throwing a die to get the ones number. Put this many one cubes on the chart.

Use one more throw to get the number of tens for the minuend. Introduce vocabulary if you have not already done so.

Students chorally read this number with you.

Generate the subtrahend in the same way. Use smaller numbered die for the tens number. Pull down materials representing the subtrahend, and separate them from the total set.

Students chorally read.

Ask: How many materials are now left at the top of the mat?

Students work with the materials as instructed and answer the question.

Push all the materials back together, and have students chorally read the total. This will help them see the relationship and understand the checking process.

Continue the procedure.

Have students practice with materials only until they are comfortable with the process.

Now you can move to the stage in which students write, as well as use manipulatives. Have them label graph paper:

T	O	
2	12	
8̸	2̸	
−1	6	
1	6	

As students do each step with materials, they write the corresponding step on their paper, being sure to write down the regrouped number in the appropriate position.

It is important for students to understand that the written form is just a description of what is actually happening. Students need much practice at this step.

Procedure 3

To develop a procedure for checking subtraction with addition

Use *pv materials*, *pv mats*, and *special dice*.

Draw a pv chart on the board. Students will place materials on their mats.

Say: A dairy farmer has 74 milk cows. He decides to let some have calves, and so for a short period of time 48 of them are "dry." How many cows did he have to milk during that time?

Students place rods and cubes on their mats representing the number 74. They regroup, pull down, and count what is left. (See Illustration 3a.)

Instruct students to push back together the two groups of pv materials and to tell you the resulting total.

Students respond: 74.

Write the form on the board as shown in Illustration 3b, circling regrouped numbers for addition.

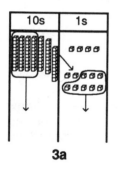

3a   3b

Continue the procedure, using the dice to generate the two numbers.

When students feel competent in the procedure, they should write the problems on paper after solving them with the manipulatives. Make sure they use the same form that you have shown on the board, as this short way of writing the checking process is more likely to be successfully completed by students in the future.

Procedure 4

To subtract 1-digit numbers from 2-digit numbers

Use *special dice, washable markers,* and *pv materials and pv mats,* or *counter-trading boards and counter-trading materials.*

Toss both special dice to arrive at the number for the minuend. Tell students to place rods and cubes on their mats to represent the number. Then tell them to use the washable marker to write the digits beside the manipulatives:

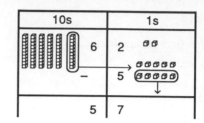

Now toss the dice with the higher numbers on it for the 1-digit subtrahend.

Students place materials and record as instructed. They pull down the number to subtract.

Ask: Do you need to regroup? How many ones are left? How many tens? Place the problem on the board with the answer as the students respond.

Continue the procedure until students are competent in the placement of the numbers, always remembering to place the 1-digit number in the ones column.

When students are competent, tell them to write each step on paper after doing it with materials. Make sure they still remember to keep the ones in line with each other.

Remind students to use the addition checking form taught earlier.

Procedure 5

To problem solve with number sentences; to write number sentences

Use *pv mats* and *pv materials*.

Include subtraction to solve addition problems, as well as story problems of subtraction. Remind students to use the other skill to check their answers.

Students place rods and cubes on the mats to represent the number of pigs in the following story.

Farmer Brown raises pigs. In January, she had 28 pigs. After some piglets were born in March, she had a total of 93 pigs. How many piglets were born in March?

Say: Since something was added, this is an addition sentence, 28 + [ ] = 93. We could count from 28 to 93 but that would take a long time, so we need to find the difference between the numbers. We subtract to find the answer, even though the number sentence is addition.

Students take the rods and cubes and "place" 93 pigs on the pv mat. They take away 28 of them.

Make sure the students "trade down" or regroup on their mats. Ask: How many are left?

Students respond: 65.

So how many piglets were born in March? (65)

Write the completed number sentence on the board: 28 + 65 = 93.

Explain that since this was solved by subtraction, the fulfilling of the original number sentence is the checking procedure.

Students do oral and manipulative work with similar problems, such as: David raises rabbits. Yesterday he bought 17 rabbits. He now has 46 rabbits. Assuming none were born during the week, how many did he have last week? (? + 17 = 46)

Encourage students to make up other examples. If none are forthcoming, give these to start:

(1) Rajiv collects pennies. He had 32 pennies this morning. At noon Markus traded him some. Rajiv now has 47 pennies. How many did he get from Markus?

(2) Zola raises chickens. She collected 23 eggs yesterday. After collecting eggs today, she had a total of 52 eggs. How many did she collect today?

(3) Zola took the 52 eggs to market but could only sell 36 of them. How many did she take back home?

After working orally and cooperatively, students can move to writing on paper and then checking with manipulatives.

Practice and Extension

Students write story problems to exchange with each other, writing the solution on the back for self-checking. They can estimate and then solve the problems. How close were their estimates?

Help students sharpen estimation skills by posting questions around the room; e.g., If you subtract 33 from 61, will your answer be above 40? Below 20? Near 30?

Make up games to solve with subtraction and to check with addition.

Expand the procedures to include many-digit problems. It is good for the students to see that the math process is the same no matter how many digits are involved. Students can use the *addition/subtraction table* to check accuracy.

Expand uneven-digit problems to be 3-digits minus two digits.

Students can use *pv mats* and *blocks* or *number lines* and *counters* to play Race to Zero. They play in pairs

or small groups and use a *pair of dice* to obtain the subtrahend. They either place blocks on the mat or counters on the number line to show the number 99. They throw the dice and take away the number shown. When they reach the number 11, they use only one die.

Subtraction 9

Skill: To subtract 3-digit numbers, no zeros, and check with addition

place value (pv) materials to 100s

See Reproducibles for: addition/subtraction tables: 1 per student, pv mats to 100s, bills to 100s—run off in different colors

Time: 2+ periods

Materials:

narrow tag board strips: 2 per student

graph paper: ½" squares; 1 sheet per student

Anticipatory Set

Use *addition/subtraction tables* and *tag board strips.*

Write on the board the numbers 8 and 7. Have students locate these numbers on the matrix. Have them place strips and tell you that the lines meet, or intersect, at the number 15. What number facts would be in the family of 7, 8, and 15? (8 + 7 = 15, 7 + 8 = 15, 15 − 7 = 8, and 15 − 8 = 7)

Review how to use the tables with other numbers. Have students give all the facts for each family.

Put 54 − 23 = 31 vertically on the board.

Ask if anyone has an idea how to prove your answer is correct. Encourage discussion.

Procedure 1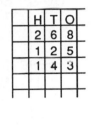

To develop the concept of subtracting 3-digit numbers; no regrouping; to check with addition

Use *pv mats, pv materials,* and *graph paper.*

Have students make individual place value recording strips to hundreds on graph paper, using one square per place.

Now have students work in groups to place blocks halfway down, in the correct columns of their pv mats to represent 125. Tell them to place the blocks for 143 below (Illustration 1a).

Have them write these two numbers on their graph paper, leaving a top set of squares blank (Illustration 1b).

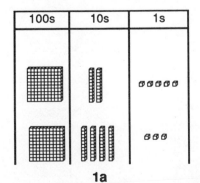

1a

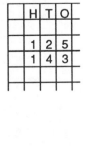

1b

Next have them add the numbers by pushing all blocks in each column to the *top* of their mat, to reach a total of 268 (Illustration 1c).

Have students chorally read the resulting number and write this total *above* the first two numbers on their graph paper chart (Illustration 1d).

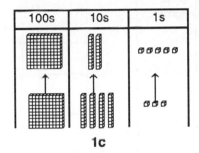

1c   1d

Ask: If 268 is the total, what would you have left if you took away 125?

Students show this with materials.

How could we show this on paper?

Students respond: Place a minus sign in front of the 125, and place a line below it.

What kind of problem did we start with? (addition: 125 + 143) What kind did we just do? (subtraction: 268 − 125) How are these two problems related to each other?

Students discuss the relationship.

Give students another subtraction problem to do with blocks and on paper.

Now have students take the blocks they subtracted and see whether they can prove their answer is correct.

Students discuss their regrouping, subtraction, answers, and possible ways to prove it is correct.

If they do not come up with addition as a way of checking, suggest you are looking for a way to check subtraction. It will have more meaning if they arrive at the conclusion for themselves.

Students practice several examples on their mats and graph paper.

Continue the procedure until the students are comfortable with the idea of subtracting and adding as related and reversible activities.

Procedure 2

To subtract 3-digit numbers; with regrouping

Use *pv mats, pv materials,* and *graph paper recording strips from Procedure 1.*

Have students place blocks halfway down, in the correct columns of their pv mats to represent 167. Then have them place the blocks for 576 below (illustration 2a). Have them write these two numbers on their graph paper, leaving a top set of squares blank (illustration 2b).

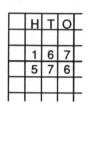

100s	10s	1s

H	T	O
1	6	7
5	7	6

2a   **2b**

Students push all the blocks to the top, regrouping as necessary to reach a total of 743. They write this total above the first two numbers on their graph paper chart.

Ask: If 743 is the total, what is left if we take away 167? How could we show this on paper?

Students show with blocks and respond: 576 is left. We show this on paper with a minus sign in front of the 167.

H	T	O
7	4	3
− 1	6	7
5	7	6

Ask the same type of questions as in Procedure 1. Have students discuss the relationship of addition to subtraction.

Have students practice several examples on their mats and graph paper, showing regrouping.

Procedure 3

To practice 3-digit subtraction

Use *pv mats, bills, addition/subtraction tables,* and *tag board strips.*

Repeat Procedure 2, using the mats and bills.

Relate the minuends to the amount of money they started with, the subtrahends to items purchased, and the difference to the amount they have left.

Tell them to return items and receive their money back. This amount added to what they had left should equal what they started with.

Encourage students to make up their own stories to go with the process.

Students should be practicing writing the problems, as well as using the manipulatives. When they feel confident, they can begin solving the problems on paper first and then checking with the manipulatives.

Make sure they understand that the written form is just the way of writing on paper what they can show and prove with manipulatives.

Students can use the addition/subtraction table and tag board strips to check their answers.

Practice and Extension

Challenge the students to write subtraction story problems using 3-digit numbers. A partner works the problem and checks the work with addition. The partner rewords the problem so that, using the same three numbers, it becomes an addition question.

Extend activities so that the students can see the same math procedure works for larger-digit numbers.

Subtraction 10

Skill: To subtract 3-digit and larger numbers: to regroup both tens and hundreds across zero

Time: 2 periods

Materials:

graph paper: ¹/₂" squares or larger; 2 sheets per student

place value (pv) materials to 100s

See Reproducibles for: pv mats to 100s, bills to 100s—run off in different colors

Anticipatory Set

Use *graph paper.*

Write ten 3-digit numbers (without zeros) on the board. Students copy the numbers onto graph paper, placing each separate digit in a separate square.

After copying, the students underline the five largest numbers and then rewrite those numbers on the graph paper. Underneath they write the five smallest numbers.

Students exchange papers and have 3 to 5 minutes to try to solve some or all of the problems.

Students should remember to check each subtraction with addition before moving on to the next problem. As a variety of problems are possible, share only some of the problems and answers; then move on.

Procedure 1

To extend the concept of regrouping

Use *pv mats, pv materials,* and *graph paper.*

Have the students work in small groups. Discuss with students whether they had to do any regrouping as they worked on the subtraction problems. Review both 2-digit problems with regrouping, and 3-digit problems.

Students discuss and review the regrouping skill.

Have students place materials on the pv mats to represent the number 550. Ask them to take away 135 blocks.

Encourage students to discuss the regrouping necessary. Have them show how they would regroup using the materials.

Students discuss and regroup as necessary, pull down materials to be subtracted, and discuss what they did.

Ask: What would happen if we wanted to take away 167?

Students discuss the additional borrowing needed.

Now have students clear their mats and place materials for 400. Ask: Will you need to regroup to subtract 136? (yes)

Students refer to the problem before and to previous subtraction experience to regroup the materials to show three hundreds, nine tens, and ten ones.

Stress that we can only regroup one place at a time.

Can you prove that the materials still total 400?

Students add and find the total value is still 400.

If you now take away 136, how many will you have left?

Continue the procedure until the students are comfortable with the regrouping process. Be sure to use numbers with zero in only the tens place, as well as those with two zeros.

Students should now copy new problems from the board onto graph paper, as they did in the anticipatory set.

Explain that you need to see regrouping on their papers. Example: 403 − 255. If we put these numbers onto a pv chart, do we have enough ones to take away five? (no) What do we need to do?

Students respond: We need to regroup. They place 403 with materials, then regroup: three hundreds and ten tens.

Now we can regroup the tens to have 9 tens and 13 ones.

Students complete this regrouping on their mats as you put the following illustration on the board.

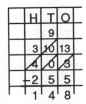

Cross out the original numbers showing each manipulation of the materials, and write the new numbers above.

Ask: Do we have the same total as before? (yes) Now can we take away five ones? (yes) Can we take away five tens?

Students respond: Yes. They do the subtracting and tell you they have eight ones and four tens left.

Can we take away two hundreds? (yes) What is the final answer? (148)

Students record each part of the process on their paper, after completing steps with the materials.

Continue the procedure until students demonstrate understanding.

Students write each step of the problem as they do it with materials. When they feel comfortable, they solve the problem first on paper and then check with materials.

Procedure 2

To practice subtracting 3-digit numbers; to check subtraction with addition

Use *pv mats, bills,* and *graph paper.*

Repeat Procedure 1 with mats and bills.

Tell students they have $500 to spend, which they should place on their mats. Tell them to choose items that will interest them, costing: $296; $94; $10, etc.

Because the placement of the zeros is varied, students will have to think about what they are doing, not just repeat the previous procedure.

Have students make a recording strip:

H	T	O		Check		
	9					
4	10	10		①	①	
$5	0	0		$2	0	4
-2	9	6		+2	9	6
2	0	4		$5	0	0

Students pull down the amounts to be subtracted and write each step as they do it with blocks. After doing the subtraction, they prove the addition check with blocks and then write it down.

After students are competent in the process, they can begin working and checking the problems first on paper and then proving them with the manipulatives.

Expand the checking part of the instructions so that the students are able to do it all on only one extra line. (See Illustrations 3a and 3b for procedures.)

Students need to show regroupings in the subtraction and circle the carried number in the checking part (Illustration 3b).

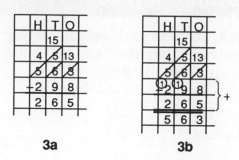

3a **3b**

Students need much practice with this kind of checking.

Practice and Extension

Have students use *number cards* to work on making subtraction problems that use all the digits from one to nine: one 3-digit number for the minuend, one for the subtrahend, and one for the difference. There are several possibilities; e.g., $954 - 683 = 271$.

Students can use *newspapers* for data and ideas to write word problems using 3-digit numbers; encourage them to use both addition and subtraction questions when writing the problems. Students exchange problems, estimate answers, and try to solve each other's problems.

Have students use a *deck of cards* to generate problems. The first three turned over are one number, the second three are another number. Face cards and tens are zeros. They subtract the smaller number from the larger, using the *manipulative of their choice.* Challenge teams to make up games to share.

Expand activities and the concept to include subtraction and checking of 4-digit numbers, 5-digit numbers, and larger numbers.

Subtraction 11

Skill: To subtract from 3-digit numbers: 1- or 2-digit subtrahends

Time: 1+ periods

Materials:

file-folder or other place value (pv) mats to 100s

pv materials to 100s

dice

decks of cards: 1 per group

graph paper: ½" squares or larger; 1 sheet per student

counter-trading materials to 100s

See Reproducibles for: directions for file folder pv mats to 1000s, pv mats to 100s, bills to 100s in different colors, counter-trading boards or color-coded pv mats

Anticipatory Set

Use *pv mats* and *pv materials.*

Have students place materials on their mats to represent the number 634.

Write the number 478 on the board, and instruct students to show what would be left if they took away that many materials. Discuss.

What do they think they would do if the number had only been 78? Ask them to think about which place value position the 8 occupies.

Procedure 1

To subtract 1- or 2-digit subtrahends; no regrouping; no zeros

Use *pv mats, pv materials,* and *dice.*

Have students place 888 on their mats.

Students place materials and chorally read: eight hundreds, eight tens, eight ones.

Say: We want to take 32 away. How many ones will we take away? (2) How many tens? (3) How many hundreds? (none)

Students remove 32 and have 856.

Repeat with other numbers (no regrouping). Emphasize the place value of digits in both minuend and subtrahend.

Write a pv chart on the board, and write 856 on it. We want to remove 32 again. What does the 3 stand for? (3 tens) Where shall I write it? (in the tens column)

What does the 2 stand for? (2 ones) Where shall I write it? (in the ones column)

Students subtract with the materials.

Throw the dice to generate a 2-digit number to take away. Ask the same kind of questions.

Students answer questions and subtract by removing the correct number of materials.

Repeat the procedure with several other problems, emphasizing place value of each number.

Ask what would happen if you did not pay attention to the place value.

Give problems for students to do with materials. Do the problems on the board as students report each step. Students are not writing yet.

Write some problems in a horizontal format for better monitoring of student competence.

Procedure 2

To regroup; to use zeros

Use *pv mats, bills, deck of cards,* and *graph paper.*

Have students label the graph paper "1s," "10s," and "100s" in squares at the top of the paper.

Have students place $436 on their mats. Then tell them to write the number on the graph paper, placing each digit under the correct place value heading.

Ask: What would happen if you wanted to take away a 2-digit number? A 1-digit number?

Students discuss that they will not be subtracting from the hundreds, and in the second case they would not subtract from the tens either.

Shuffle the deck and draw a card. Tell students that is the number they are to subtract (jacks are 11, queens are 22, and kings are 33).

Have students write down, chorally read, and then do the problem. As students do each step with bills, they should write the corresponding step on their graph paper, keeping their place value columns lined up correctly.

It is important for students to understand that the written form is just a description of what is actually happening. Students need much practice at this step.

You can make this concept more meaningful by having students make up a story problem to go with the exercise: amounts spent on a shopping trip, change received, etc.

After practicing with several problems, have the students discuss a problem like 305 − 53 with 0 in the tens place.

Have students chorally read both numbers, and then ask them to tell you how to regroup in order to subtract from zero.

Students complete the task and discuss regrouping over zero.

Provide more practice with subtracting with zeros.

Continue the exercise, using both pv mats and graph paper to help students line up their problems correctly.

Write some of the problems on the board in a horizontal format.

After students become confident about the process, they can move to doing the problem first on paper and then checking with bills.

Let a student try to teach a lesson on borrowing. Other students should pretend not to know how to borrow and should follow the "teacher" directions exactly.

Have students bring in *mail order catalogs* of expensive items. See who can start with $999 in *bills*, buy a variety of items, and come closest to spending all their money.

Expand money concepts to include subtracting *dimes* and *pennies*, as well as *dollars*. Does the basic concept change? (no)

Procedure 3 □

To practice regrouping with zeros

Use *decks of cards, graph paper, pv mats* and *pv materials*, or *counters* and *counter-trading boards*.

Repeat Procedure 2 with new materials. Have students use decks of cards to generate numbers for the problems.

Have students practice problems in their textbook or other materials using graph paper as an aid until they are very comfortable with the process.

When students begin using lined paper instead of graph paper, have them turn the paper sideways. This will help them keep the numbers in the correct place value column.

Practice and Extension

Expand the procedures to use larger minuends and a variety of subtrahends. Check to see that students remember to keep place value in mind when placing numbers.

Have students take turns using *dice* to generate problems. The first three throws give the minuend, the next two throws give the subtrahend. If they throw a one, make it a zero instead. See who has the most or least left after three turns.

Students race to "spend all their money" and get to a zero amount. Choose a starting amount of three or more digits. Then use *dice* to generate a 2- or 3-digit number to subtract. As they get closer to zero, they use fewer dice. Students make story problems, such as: "Now I am going to the store with $___ to buy a bike costing $___. My change will be $___." As an alternative if time is short, see who has the least (or most) amount after three to five turns.

Multiplication 1

Skill: To understand the concept of multiplication using serial addition

treasure box or other objects

geoboards and rubber bands

See Reproducibles for: geoboard paper—1 sheet per student, graph paper with 1" squares—1 sheet per group

Time: 1 period

Materials:

beads and string: 3 or 4 of each color available per student pair

Anticipatory Set

Use *beads and string.*

Have students work in pairs and sort out three groups of two beads each. How many groups do they have? (3) How many beads are in each group? (2)

Have them take three beads of each color and place them on their desks so that they can see them all. How many groups did they have? (Answers will depend on how many different colors were available.) How many beads were in each group? (3)

Next have students string necklaces of groups of beads, such as three red beads, three clear beads, three green beads, three blue beads, and three yellow beads. How many beads did it take to complete the necklace? (15) Encourage students to generate similar situations and arrive at total amounts.

Students continue to use the manipulatives to represent small groups of small numbers until they are familiar with the properties of serial addition problems.

Now give the students some examples of unequal groups. Example: donations of 5 bags of clothes; in one bag were 4 items, another had 6 items, and so on. What is the difference with this type of addition? (The numbers are not all the same.)

Students discuss the necessary properties for serial addition problems and practice with small groups of numbers until they are confident about the process.

Explain that when we add equal groups as we have been doing in serial addition, a shortcut called *multiplication* may be taken. That process is one we will begin to learn.

Procedure 1

To understand serial addition

Use *objects* or *beads and string.*

Have students work in pairs or groups of three or four. Make sure that each group has enough objects for some practice in serial addition. Have students set out four groups of three objects each. Then have them work together to arrive at a total. Did they count or add?

Students discuss their findings and make up situations in which they might use the idea of serial addition.

Have students take beads of different colors or objects of different kinds and place them into groups of two or three each. Ask: How many groups do you have? How many objects are in each group?

Students discuss what they did. They report how many groups of objects, how many were in each group, and how many total objects they had. They should become aware of adding groups to arrive at total amounts.

Give students many groups of equal numbers that they need to total; e.g., donations to the Goodwill of 6 bags of 7 shirts each; how many shirts in all?

Procedure 2

To develop the concept of multiplication as serial addition

Use *geoboards, rubber bands,* and *geoboard paper.*

Have students work in groups with one geoboard per group and one sheet of paper per student. They should take a rubber band and close off a figure that is one square by two squares, or two pins by three pins.

Have them enclose another figure of the same size and shape.

Students complete the task and copy the figures onto their geoboard paper.

Ask: How many squares were enclosed in all? (4) Did you add or count?

Put on the board 2 groups of 2 squares = 4 squares. This is the form for multiplication. Write 2 × 2 = 4. This is math language for this activity.

Have students enclose one more figure like the first. Now how many squares in all? (6) Put 3 × 2 = 6 on the board.

Students copy the third figure onto their geoboard paper.

Continue the procedure with other-size rectangles. Write each discovered fact on the board.

When students become comfortable with the process, you can move to the stage at which students write, as well as use manipulatives.

As students complete each figure on their geoboards or paper, have them copy the equation that you have written on the board onto their geoboard paper below the figure represented.

It is important that students understand that the written form is just a description of what is actually happening.

Have students work together to make other problems on the geoboards and copy onto their paper, counting to discover the multiplication sentence proven. They are not actually trying to solve problems but are writing down what their geoboards show.

Have each student write down a problem situation in which each of several people have the same number of some object. They exchange with a peer to solve and then post the completed problems as samples of serial addition.

Procedure 3

To practice serial addition

Use *any objects* and *graph paper*.

Have groups of three or four students use the objects on graph paper to show problems involving serial addition and place the serial addition solutions beside the objects.

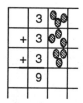

For example, this graph could show the situation of three students with three erasers each. How many erasers in all?

Students work in groups to make up similar situations, to display objects, and to write serial additions.

In the next stage, have students write and solve problems first, then check with manipulatives.

Continue until they grasp the concept of multiplication as serial addition and are ready to move on to some basic facts.

Practice and Extension

Students use *any of the objects* and write problems that can be solved with serial addition. They answer the problems on the back of the paper and then exchange papers with a partner.

Have students make up people problems and then act them out: If three pairs of students work together, how many students in all?

Multiplication 2

Skill: To learn multiplication facts: products to 12

Time: 2 periods

Materials:

adding-machine tape, widest possible markers or crayons

interlocking cubes or tiles: 12 per student

treasure box or other objects: 12 per student pair

egg cartons: 1 per student pair

Secret Code number line (see Manipulative Information section)

See Reproducibles for: number lines to 25 (taped together)—1 per student, hundred boards—1 per student

Anticipatory Set

Use *adding-machine tape* and *markers or crayons*.

Have students work in groups of four or five and mark off the tape into squares. Then have them number the squares from 1 to 12. If you cannot fasten the tape to the floor, have students hold the tape on the floor.

Other students should take turns jumping first by ones, then twos, threes, and fours. As they jump, they should keep an oral record; e.g., two jumps of two squares is four squares.

Have students discuss what they have just done. What mathematical process did they use when they added together the same-size jumps? (Students should arrive at the process of multiplication by discussing serial addition properties.)

Procedure 1

To develop the concept of rows of objects

Use *interlocking cubes* or *tiles*.

Have students lay out a row of four cubes or tiles. How many do they have in one row? (4)

Instruct students to place another row of four cubes under the first row. They have two rows of four cubes each. Ask: How many cubes are in both rows? (8)

Tell them to lay a third row of four cubes under the first two rows. How many in all? (12)

Tell students the rows are rows of students in a classroom. On the board draw three rows of four squares each as shown in the illustration.

If students stand on one side of the group, they can see three rows. Write 3 on the board next to the rows.

If they go around the room, they can see that four students are in each row. Now write the number 4 above the figure on the board.

Put a × at the corner. How many students in all? (12) Put this number beside the figure on the board.

Students discuss the fact shown and state it in the multiplication sentence equation form.

Now have the students build a row of five cubes, and under it another row of five cubes. Follow the same procedure as before.

Continue with other facts whose products are 12 or less. Students are not writing at this time.

Students should complete the exercises and display an understanding of the process before proceeding.

Procedure 2

To develop facts to 12

Use *objects* and *egg cartons*.

Have students work in pairs. Give each pair one carton and 12 objects. Tell them to set out three groups of 3 objects each.

Next have students count them by placing them in the egg carton, using only three spaces in the egg carton.

Students do as instructed. They tell you they have nine objects.

Write on the board $3 \times 3 = 9$. Tell students this number sentence represents their three groups of three objects.

Continue the practice with the objects and the egg cartons. Have students practice without writing down the multiplication facts. You continue to write the facts on the board as they practice. Develop all facts with answers of 12 or less.

Students should realize that the sentence you write on the board is only a representation of what is actually happening in the process. When competent in the concept, they may write down the facts as they discover them.

Procedure 3

To find patterns; to practice facts

Use *number lines, markers or crayons, hundred boards,* and the *Secret Code number line.*

Have students place the numbers from 1 to 25 on the tick marks of their number lines.

Each student works independently and completes the assignment.

Now have the students use crayons to mark off their number lines in "jumps" of different colors and different group lengths. For example, color jumps of two in red, jumps of three in green, etc.

Tell students to look for patterns and places where the jumps landed on the same number.

Students complete the task and discuss what their number lines show.

Now have students work on hundred boards and place a colored dot on the even numbers while counting by twos. They should color only to the number 20.

Students complete the task and then place a different color dot on multiples of three to 18. They repeat with different colors for fours to 20, and fives to 20.

Ask students what patterns they see. What do they predict would happen if they continued to color the board? Where do the numbers overlap?

Discuss with students all the conclusions they draw. Extend the activity to 100, and discuss the many patterns they can see.

Students copy the basic facts to 12 on paper after you correctly write them on the board.

Call attention to the Secret Code number line, and ask students whether any of the patterns they see are similar to the ones they just completed. Discuss responses.

Practice and Extension

Place the *adding-machine tape* on the floor, and have students practice the skip or jump counting.

Have students make *flash cards* and play the game of Concentration. Students can use cards and make up other games.

Place a *card with the number 12* on a table. Have students use *objects* to show the combinations of factors: one group of 12, two groups of 6, etc. Repeat for products from 1 to 11.

Have students color *graph paper* rectangles to show facts. Display as a bulletin board the facts they have learned. Relate this to the hundred board activity in Procedure 3.

Extend the *hundred board* activity to 100, if not done previously.

Multiplication 3

Skill: To learn multiplication facts: products to 25

Time: 2 or 3 periods

Materials:

pattern blocks: 5 of the same shape per student

graph paper: any size; about 3 sheets per student pair

scissors: 1 per student pair

geoboards and rubber bands: 1 per student pair

cubes: any size; 25 per group

number line on the floor (see Manipulative Information section)

Secret Code number line (see Manipulative Information section)

markers: 3 colors

counters

See Reproducibles for: geoboard paper—1 per student pair, number lines to 25—1 per student

Anticipatory Set

Use *pattern blocks*.

Give students five blocks each (same shape—either all triangles, rectangles, or squares). Tell each student to find out how many total sides are on their shapes. Did they multiply, add, or count to find the answer?

Hold up three pattern block hexagons. How many sides in all? How did they arrive at the answer?

Challenge students to combine their shapes into two figures. Now how many sides does each shape have? If they can make two identical shapes, how could they find the total number of sides? Review the concept of multiplication.

Procedure 1

To discover facts and the multiplication sentence form

Use *graph paper and scissors* or *geoboards and geoboard paper*.

Have students draw squares or rectangles on the graph paper or geoboard paper. Ask: How many different-size squares or rectangles can you make that cover 25 or fewer squares? Have each student make three or four shapes.

Students work in pairs and draw shapes. They cut them out if using graph paper, placing them onto a separate sheet of same-size graph paper. If using geoboards and dot paper, they copy the designs onto the geoboards.

Discuss with students that rows are the across lines, like rows of seats in an auditorium, and columns are down lines, like columns of a building.

Tell students that the number in each row is the same as the number of columns in the rectangles drawn. Have students discuss how many rows and columns are enclosed by the shapes they have drawn.

These two numbers can make up part of a multiplication sentence. (row × column; r × c) If students know

how many rows and how many columns, they can find out how many squares in all by doing serial addition or by multiplication.

Have students write down the numbers for one rectangle and then count the total number of squares enclosed.

This is the third number in the multiplication sentence, row × column = total. Make a chart on the board showing the formula, r × c = t.

Students write down the numbers and count the total number of squares for each of their rectangles. Each pair of students will have a different set of numbers.

Explain that they have been discovering multiplication facts. As students report the numbers, you write the discovered fact on the board or overhead chart.

Have students continue to make more figures while you record the multiplication facts that each figure represents.

Procedure 2

To develop facts

Use *cubes* and *regular paper*.

Have students work in groups of three or four and use 25 cubes to build rectangles.

After building several rectangles, the students discuss how many cubes they used to build each rectangle. They discuss how many rows were in each rectangle and how many cubes were in each row.

Remind students that these two numbers can make up part of a multiplication sentence. If they know how many rows and how many cubes are in each row, they can write a multiplication problem. They can find the answer by doing serial addition or by doing multiplication.

Continue the process until all facts below 26 have been developed. As students draw representations of the facts, tell them to write down the facts on their paper.

Procedure 3

To practice facts

Use a *number line on the floor*.

Have students jump by twos, threes, and fours, counting aloud as they jump. One jump times two is two, two jumps times two is four, etc.

Students take turns jumping on the number line and chanting the times facts as you monitor. Later students can do this on their own as practice.

Procedure 4

To develop story problems

Use *counters*.

Have students act out facts such as: 2 groups of 3 children is how many children?

Ask them to think of a problem that could be solved by using a multiplication fact and show it with counters. If necessary, start them out with a problem about a birthday party to which 5 children are invited and where each is to receive 2 balloons. How many balloons are needed?

Encourage them to develop their own story problems. Allow time for all students to participate in making up and answering problems.

Procedure 5

To discover patterns

Use *number lines*, *colored markers*, and the *Secret Code number line*.

Have students fill in their number lines and use different colored markers to make series of jumps by twos, threes, fours, and fives.

Ask: Did you see any patterns? Did you notice where jumps landed on the same number? Could you make any predictions about a longer line? What multiplication facts have you just shown on the number line? What similarities do you see on the Secret Code number line?

Procedure 6

To practice facts

Use *counters* and *cubes*.

Have students make groups of two (and later three, four, and five) with counters. Ask them to write down how many of each type group they could make with 25 counters.

Students group counters and write down the multiplication facts they are able to prove with the counters.

Now instruct students to find how many are in two groups of two.

Students make two groups of two and write down on paper the discovered fact.

Continue the procedure, covering all facts with products under 26.

Repeat by having students build groups of three threes, four twos, etc., using the cubes. Tell them to write down the multiplication fact as they display the array. Have students work in pairs and check each other's work for accuracy.

Practice and Extension

Use *Number Finds* (see Reproducibles), and have students circle any two adjacent numbers whose product is 25 or less. Later they can make their own number finds for others. Have students name their monsters and write a descriptive paragraph about them.

Have students make a *list of facts* with products of 25 or less. Who can write down the most facts in a certain amount of time?

Have students play Concentration with *index cards*. The fact is on one card and the answer is on another.

Have students make their own *flash cards of facts* (self-correcting answers on the back) to use in pairs or to make up games for other students to play.

Have students list ways that knowing multiplication facts can be useful to them when they go shopping.

Hand out *Multiplication Clue Rhymes* (see Reproducibles) for students to use at home.

Multiplication 4

Skill: To understand a multiplication chart and the commutative property of multiplication

Time: 1 period

Materials:

graph paper: ½" squares; several sheets per student

scissors

cubes: any size; 10 per student

narrow strips of tag board: 2 per student

light-colored markers: 1 per student

geoboards and rubber bands: 1 per student pair

See Reproducibles for: matrices for facts—1 per student, multiplication/division tables—1 per student, geoboard paper—1 sheet per student

Anticipatory Set

Use *graph paper, scissors,* and *cubes.*

Have each student cut a 5" × 5" square. Have students start in the upper left hand corner with 1 and number across to 10 and down the left side to 10, one number per square.

Using the leftover graph paper, have students cut out several smaller squares and rectangles and place these pieces on their 5" × 5" square lined up with the top left corner.

Review rows and columns. What multiplication facts using rows and columns do their rectangles show?

Have them use different corners of their rectangles for placing. Does this change the fact? The answer?

Have each student build a wall with some of the cubes. Choose some walls to describe to the class. How tall, and so on, are they? What would happen to the walls if the earth shifted and the walls fell down? Would the same amount of total materials still be there?

Tell students to find the product of 2 × 3 and then 3 × 2. What do they notice? (Answer is the same.)

Challenge students to explain how the strips could be used to find products.

Allow students to experiment with the strips; let a student who finds how to place them and read the answer, explain to the class.

Students complete their matrices, highlighting every other row and column (even numbers) with markers to aid in finding products.

Ask students to find patterns on their multiplication/division tables.

Students find and draw loops around patterns. They discuss the class's findings.

Have students practice finding facts using the table and tag board strips.

Cover matrices with clear self-adhesive paper or laminate them. This treatment will keep them useful for the entire year.

Procedure 1 ◻◼

To make multiplication charts

Use *matrices for facts, multiplication/division tables, tag board strips,* and *markers.*

Distribute the matrices and tables. Explain that the students will be charting all of the answers to multiplication facts.

Say: A times sign goes in the upper left-hand square.

Students fill in the products for rows 0 to 3 while you distribute tag board strips.

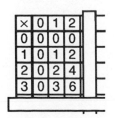
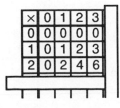

Alternate Procedure 1 ◻◼

To generate multiplication tables

Use *matrices for facts, cubes, markers,* and *tag board strips.*

Review that the numbers on the left are rows, and numbers on the top are columns. Have students put an × in the corner and label the top and side as shown in the illustration.

Say: We wish to fill in the total number of cubes in each square. Start with an array of one row, one column.

Students build that array, count the squares, and write 1 in the first blank matrix box. They continue to fill in numbers across, building the array first, counting the objects, and writing the number.

As the numbers get larger, students work in groups so that they have enough manipulatives.

Question students about possible uses of a matrix, and point out patterns as suggested earlier.

Students may take turns explaining different sets of multiplication facts.

Procedure 2 □■

To understand the commutative property of multiplication using fact families

Use *cubes, geoboards and bands,* and *geoboard paper.*

Have students work in pairs and build a row of five cubes. On top of this row they should build another row of five cubes, making a structure five cubes wide and two cubes high. Ask: How many cubes did you use? (10) This shows two groups of five.

Now have students place the structure vertically so that they have two columns of five rows. How many cubes? (10) This shows five groups of two. We call this the commutative property of multiplication.

Students discuss that the commutative property is similar to fact families that they have worked with before.

On the board write 5 × 2 = 10 and 2 × 5 = 10.

Repeat the procedure with 4 × 5, 3 × 5, and 6 × 2.

Students write the multiplication sentence shown by each set of problems.

Have students now work in pairs with geoboards and geoboard paper. One encloses a rectangle 3 by 4. How many squares are enclosed? (12) The other student encloses a square that is 4 by 3.

Ask: How many squares are enclosed? (12) Are these equal in size? (yes) What are the equations shown by these figures?

Students respond: 3 × 4 = 12 and 4 × 3 = 12. They continue to work with the geoboard, checking commutative properties of several sets of facts, copying the designs onto the geoboard paper, and writing the times facts shown.

Procedure 3 □

To prove equalities

Use *graph paper* and *scissors.*

Have students work in pairs. Have one partner cut out any size rectangle and label it with the fact it represents. Example: 7 × 6 = 42. Have the other partner cut out the commutative shape and label it.

Students cut and label the rectangles.

Have students lay rectangles on top of each other and count squares to prove they are equal. Encourage students to show higher multiplication facts.

Students continue to create buildings by cutting rectangular shapes; and the peer partners construct a same-size building using the commutative fact.

Make a class chart of all buildings, showing the two commutative facts together.

Practice and Extension

Use *flash cards* and play Concentration, finding the two commutative facts in order to win the round.

Give students several sets of facts to answer with their *multiplication/division tables.* As students find the answer to one fact, they are to write down the corresponding commutative fact and then check their table for accuracy.

Can students think of a way to prove whether the commutative property of multiplication would still be true for higher numbers, such as 12 × 36? Would using *graph paper* help?

Suggest that students keep their *matrices* out when doing multiplication problems so that lack of memorization of the facts will not prevent them from learning a new concept.

Have students add other patterns to show multiples to the classroom *Secret Code number line.* This line can be adapted to use for any set of multiples or prime numbers.

Multiplication 5

Skill: To learn multiplication facts: products to 81

Time: 3 or 4 periods

Materials:

place value (pv) materials to 10s

graph paper: ¹/₂" or larger; 3 sheets per student

scissors

washable markers

See Reproducibles for: pv mats to 100s—1 per student, and 1 per group, Multiplication Clue Rhymes—1 per student, Garden Glove Multiplication—1 per student, Finger Nines—1 per student

Note: If students learn their facts using place value materials, it will be much easier for them to learn to do 2-digit multiplication.

Anticipatory Set

Use *pv materials—ones only.*

Have groups make rectangular arrays in which the rows each have three cubes. How many multiplication facts can they discover?

Review with students that rows are the across lines and columns are the down lines. Compare them to rows of seats and columns of buildings.

Now have students try making arrays with more columns. What times facts do these show? Have students write the facts they have shown.

Procedure 1

To discover facts

Use *pv materials to tens* and *pv mats.*

Draw on the board or place on the overhead, five rows of six cubes in the ones place.

Students copy this with pv materials on the group mat and write the numbers on their individual pv mats.

Have the class chorally count the materials to get a total of 30.

Group Mat		Individual Mat	
10s	1s	10s	1s
			6
			6
			6
			6
			6
			30

Ask: Do the materials need to be regrouped? Why? How many digits can be written in one place? (The most is nine.) Our number system packages numbers by tens. Be sure students understand the place value system.

Students regroup and show 30 on group mats with rods. They write 3 in the tens column and 0 in the ones column.

Group Mat		Individual Mat	
10s	1s	10s	1s
			6
			6
			6
			6
			6
			3̶0̶
		3	0

Show students how to write this as multiplication:

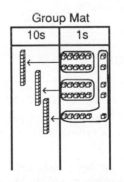

Group Mat		Individual Mat	
10s	1s	10s	1s
			6
			6
			6
			6
		×5	6
			3̶0̶
		3	0

Students copy this on their mats.

The circle around the × 5 indicates that these are "just the directions" for how many groups of six they take.

Continue the procedure, following these steps with students until all facts with answers 25 to 81 have been discovered.

Students demonstrate the numbers with materials, writing serial addition on small mats, regrouping as needed, and writing regrouping on paper. They then write the multiplication fact shown.

Procedure 2 ☐

To practice facts

Use *graph paper* and *scissors*.

Have students cut out rectangles and squares that use more than 25 graph squares but with sides that are 9 or fewer squares. Have them exchange cutouts and label the fact shown.

Procedure 3 ☐

To use additional methods of fact practice

Use *Multiplication Clue Rhymes, Garden Glove Multiplication, Finger Nines,* and *washable markers.*

Note: *This is best taught over 2 days.*

Hand out Garden Gloves sheets, and go over them with students. Tell them to use markers to write the numbers on their fingers. Students may also bring in clean, cotton garden gloves to mark.

Have them practice several facts until they are confident that they can do the procedure.

Hand out the Finger Nines sheet, and teach the trick of reading the answer to nines multiplication problems. Practice as a class until all are proficient.

Hand out the two pages of Multiplication Clue Rhymes, and read them together. Tell students to take them home and to practice until they remember the facts.

Practice and Extension

Have students make up games that use times facts. Check the accuracy of their answers on the *matrices.*

Have students make *cards* of the facts they think are the most difficult. They can use these for the game of Concentration.

Challenge students with a *Number Find* exercise. They can use the ones from the reproducibles or make their own and exchange with other students. Be sure students do the writing activities suggested on the Number Finds.

Have students use *counters* to make arrays. Tell them to draw a picture of the arrays and to label each one with the facts shown. Make sure students remember the lesson on commutative property of multiplication and label each array with two facts. Display these arrays on a class chart called Multiplication Arrays.

Have students practice *Garden Gloves* and *Finger Nines* until mastered. Each one of these activities takes many repetitions.

Multiplication 6

Skill: To understand the relationship of multiplication to division; missing factors in equations

Time: 2 periods

Materials:

1" tiles, or alternatives: about 24 per student pair

geoboards and colored rubber bands: 1 per student pair

counters: 20 per student

egg cartons: 1 per student pair

thin tag board strips: 1 per student

graph paper: any size; 1 sheet per student

See Reproducibles for: multiplication/division tables—1 per student

Anticipatory Set

Use *tiles* and *blank sheets of paper.*

Review that rows are across and columns are down. Compare them to rows of seats and columns of buildings. Review that the number of rows times the number in the row equals the product.

Students experiment with materials and find a way to show both multiplication and division facts. They compare what they discovered. How are facts alike?

Have students record their numbers with the appropriate signs on the paper. How would they find the answer for a fact they haven't learned?

Procedure 1

To discover relationships

Use *tiles* and *multiplication/division tables.*

Explain that the tiles are pigs in a pigpen. A farmer has divided them into four lines but needs to keep them from running into the cornfield next door.

Demonstrate on the board that a partial fence around a group looks similar to a division symbol.

Model for the students as they do an example. Ask: How many rows are shown? (4) How many columns? (3) What multiplication fact is shown? (4 groups of 3: 4 × 3 = 12)

How would knowing the multiplication fact help with division? Encourage discussion and remind students of fact families in addition and subtraction.

Ask: What division fact is shown? (12 divided into 4 groups: 12 ÷ 4 = 3)

What if we turned the group of tiles sideways?

Students respond: It would show 3 groups of 4: 3 × 4 = 12; or 12 divided into 3 groups: 12 ÷ 3 = 4.

Students continue discovery exercises.

Review with students how to use tables to find answers to multiplication facts. Can they find division answers on the same matrix?

Students use tiles to set up models of multiplication arrays; they make up stories that require division to solve, write the equations, and check their answers with the multiplication/division tables (matrices).

Procedure 2

To write and use relationships

Use *geoboards and bands, counters, egg cartons, multiplication/division tables,* and *tag board strips.*

Have students put bands around four groups of three, sides touching to make a 4 × 3 rectangle. Then have them put another color band around the whole group.

Write the multiplication fact that this shows. (4 × 3 = 12) Ask: What division fact could this show? (12 ÷ 4 = 3) How are these alike?

Students continue to explore the facts using their geoboards and writing the facts on paper. It is important for students to understand that the written form is just a description of what is happening.

Hand out egg cartons and counters to groups so that they can work with higher facts.

Student groups show 3 groups of 7 and write the fact with its answer. Then they take 21 other counters and "share" them among 7 groups.

Continue with more examples, making up stories to go with the "sharing." Be sure students see the relationship with the multiplication fact.

Students work in pairs to make up problems and solutions to share with the rest of the class. They check their facts with their tables, using tag board strips to read along columns or rows.

Procedure 3 ▢■

To develop the concept of missing factors

Use *counters*.

Put the following illustration on the board, and discuss the relationship of multiplication and division: The number of groups or rows times the number in a group is the total.

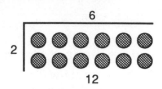

Write 2 × 6 = ? on the board.

Each student makes one row of 6 counters. Underneath that they make another row of 6 counters. Students count and reach the answer of 12.

Now write 2 × ? = 12. Have students make two rows of one counter each on their desks.

Students pick up enough more counters to total 12 and divide these between the two rows. They report 6 are in each row.

Now write ? × 6 = 12. Ask: How you could find the answer with the counters?

Students respond: Take 12 counters, and separate the 12 counters into groups of 6.

Ask: How many groups? (2)

Repeat with other missing factors until students are adept at the skill and begin to realize they can use division to solve these kind of problems.

Students make up word problems to go with missing factor problems. Example: Six students are playing 12 games. How many games can each play?

Continue the procedure until students are aware of all the places for missing numbers in multiplication problems and are comfortable with the process of using division to find what the missing number is.

Procedure 4 ▢

To practice finding missing factors

Use *graph paper, multiplication/division tables,* and *tag board strips.*

Have students draw a rectangle that encloses 12 squares. The top and bottom sides are to be 4 squares long. Write ? × 4 = 12.

Students draw around the space. They tell you the other sides are three squares tall.

Continue with such problems as 3 × ? = 15, ? × 7 = 21, describing walls to be constructed from blocks.

Students work with graph paper or the matrices and find the missing factors. They use the tag board strips to read along columns or rows. As soon as they feel ready, they try solving equations without drawing rectangles.

Tell students that using letters in place of the question mark is the way math equations are written in algebra. Have them create some problems they could pose in algebraic language.

Practice and Extension

Have students use *problems from the textbook* and make up situations to solve that require knowing the related procedure. For example, if the problem is to find how many apples are 8 baskets of 7 apples, they find that answer on the *multiplication/division tables* and reword the problem: I have 56 apples and 8 baskets. How many apples are in each basket?

Have students think of *counters* as cars in a parking lot, or cans to be put into different recycling containers, and so on. Students make up multiplication or division story problems. Their partner shows the fact with counters, writes it, and adds to the story, using the opposite operation.

Have students make up story problems that require finding a missing factor. Students write the problem and solve it on the back of the paper. They exchange with a partner who first estimates a reasonable answer and then tries to solve the problem.

Have students bring in *newspaper advertisements*. Give each student a specific amount of money to spend. If an item is a certain price, how many of each can be bought? Students should write the equations before solving the problems. Encourage them to write the equations in algebraic language.

Multiplication 7

Skill: To understand multiples of ten and how to multiply tens by 1-digit numbers

Time: 3 periods

Materials:

light-colored markers in 2 colors: 1 of each per student

place value (pv) materials to 1000s, use counters as 1000s

file-folder or other pv mats to 1000s

2" × 3" × number cards as shown in Illustration 1a: 1 set ×2 to ×9 per student

See Reproducibles for: hundred boards—1 per student, number lines to 1000, pv mats to 1000s, or directions for file-folder mats, graph paper with 1 cm squares

Anticipatory Set

Use *hundred boards, number lines*, and *markers*.

Have students highlight (or mark) all tens on hundred boards and number lines. Do they see a pattern? Ask: How many are three tens, four tens, and so on.

Count off the students by tens. How does counting by tens help us with our number system? Students should relate to our base ten place value system.

Procedure 1

To recognize and use multiples of 10

Use *pv materials, pv mats, graph paper, markers, and completed hundred boards and number lines from Anticipatory Set.*

Have groups place one ten rod in the tens place and say "one ten, zero ones." Continue adding tens until they have 10 rods in the tens place.

Review regrouping. Continue having students add tens and read chorally until reaching 200.

Dictate some higher multiples of 10 for students to place. Have them read each new number and the resulting total. Continue to 990.

Ask: What would happen if we added 10 more? What earlier activity does this remind you of? Discuss.

Students take graph paper and color in 10 squares.

How many are colored? (10) Color in 10 more squares. How many are colored now? (20) How many are two groups of 10? (20)

Continue until students see the pattern. Discuss patterns and how multiples of 10 are written.

How can knowing multiples of 10 help us in math?

Students discuss rounding numbers to the nearest 10 as a way of estimating answers and of being sure the answer for a problem is reasonable.

Instruct students to look at the marked hundred board and number line. Have them count off 3 tens. What is the total? (30) Continue with 6 tens, 11 tens, 23 tens, and so on.

Students make up problem situations for the class to estimate answers and then solve.

Procedure 2

To multiply 10 by 1-digit numbers

Use *pv mats, materials*, and × *number cards*.

Note: *Do not teach multiplying the digits and annexing the zero.*

Since multiplication problems are solved right to left, the following procedure tends to eliminate some later math confusion for certain students.

In this procedure students work with materials only, while you write on the board, showing partial products.

Have students put a ten rod on their mat. Ask: How many tens? (1) How many ones? (0)

Write 10 on a place value chart on the board.

Tell students they need five tens in all on their mats. Place a ×5 on the board below the 10 as in Illustration 1b on the next page.

What value does each rod represent? (10) How many tens? (5) How many ones? (0) How many in all? (50)

Did they add or count to get the answer? Discuss.

Say: We can also multiply to arrive at an answer.

Have students take 4 of the 10 rods off their mats. Under the remaining rod they should place the ×5 card as in Illustration 1a on the following page.

The "times five" is just the directions.

What you have on your mats now represents the problem 5 × 10.

You already know how to multiply 1-digit numbers by other 1-digit numbers. When we multiply 2-digit numbers, we first multiply the ones as we did before and then we multiply the tens.

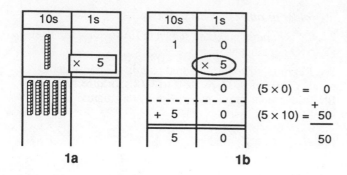

1a   **1b**

$(5 \times 0) = 0$

$(5 \times 10) = \underline{+\ 50}$

50

What are five groups of no ones?

Students respond: Nothing.

So we have no one cubes in our answer. How can I show this on the board?

Students respond: Put a zero in the ones place.

Place a 0 in the ones column, and to the side of the problem write $5 \times 0 = 0$ as shown in Illustration 1b.

How many tens did the directions say we needed? (5)

Now you need to place those five ten rods onto your mats.

Emphasize groups of 10. **How many groups of 10 are below the directions on the mat? (5)**

So we have five ten rods in our answer. What number have you made with your rods?

Students respond: 50.

Write 50 in the board example as shown. Beside that write the partial product: $5 \times 10 = 50$.

First we multiplied the zero ones by five, and then we multiplied the one ten by five. We get a final total by adding the two answers together.

Finish the board example as in Illustration 1b.

Continue with other examples, emphasizing "groups" of tens and the place value. Students should use only materials. You show on the board a written mathematical description of what is happening.

Procedure 3   □■

To multiply multiples of 10 by 1-digit numbers; no regrouping

Use *pv mats, pv materials, × number cards,* and *paper.*

In this procedure students work with materials and write on a pv chart. You write the problem on a board chart with partial products on the side as shown in Illustration 2b.

Have students fold paper in half and label ones and tens. Next have them place a group of two tens on their pv mats.

Say: This is the number of juice boxes in a package. You want to know the number of boxes in three packages. First put directions on your mats.

Under the two ten rods students place the ×3 card. (Illustration 2a)

Instruct students to write 20 on their paper charts, and under that a circled ×3 as the directions. (Illustration 2b)

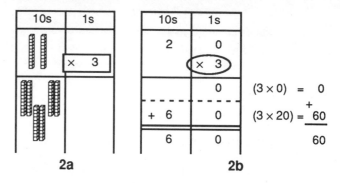

2a   **2b**

$(3 \times 0) = 0$

$(3 \times 20) = \underline{+\ 60}$

60

What does the ×3 mean?

Students respond: It's "just the directions" for how many groups we want of our starting number.

As students respond to questions, show the process on the board with partial products, as in illustration 2b.

How many cubes are in the ones place? (none) How many is three groups of none? (none) Where on our charts would we show that?

Students respond: Put a zero in the ones place because we are multiplying ones.

Now what do the directions tell us about the tens?

Students respond: We need three groups of two tens. They place three groups of two tens on their mats below the directions.

What is the total of three groups of two tens?

Students count and respond: 60.

Where in the answer would we show this?

Students respond: Put a six in the tens place, because we are multiplying tens, and a zero in the ones place.

Review: **First we multiplied the zero ones by three, and then we multiplied the two tens by three.**

How do we get the total number of juice boxes? (add) Complete the example on the board.

Practice the procedure, keeping the products under 100. Have students work with the materials and record their work on the paper charts.

Procedure 4   □■

To multiply multiples of 10 by 1-digit numbers; with regrouping

Use *pv mats, pv materials, × number cards*, and *paper*.

This time have students divide their paper into three columns and label 100s, 10s, and 1s.

Using the same procedure as before, challenge students to show 3 groups of 50 on both mats and paper, circling the ×3 and using their ×3 card.

Students do as instructed and make up a word problem to go with their block problem.

Ask: After you multiply, how many ones in all? (0) How many tens? (15) Do you have a problem?

Students respond: Too many tens are in the tens place. We have to regroup.

Students regroup with materials and on charts as shown:

100s	10s	1s		
	5	0		
		× 3		
		0	(3×0) =	0
				+
1	5	5	(3×50) =	150
1	5	0		150

What do we have once we regroup? (one hundred and five tens) Is this like any other regrouping we have done?

Students should relate this to the previous skills of regrouping in simpler multiplication and addition.

Students complete the problem by adding partial products.

Continue the procedure with problems up to 90 × 9. Ask students whether they can see a pattern. Discuss.

Procedure 5

To develop the traditional algorithm

Use *prepared pv paper to 100s* and *counters*, if needed.

Stress to the students that since the ones answer in these problems is always zero, they can eliminate that line of partial products.

Introduce the form:

100s	10s	1s		
	5	0		
		× 3		
1	5	0	(3×0) =	0
				+
			(3×50) =	150
				150

Still emphasize that they are multiplying ones first and then tens. They can take the shortcut in this type of problem because when we have tens, we have zero digits in the ones place.

Allow students to use counters to help solve the problems.

When students begin working independently, have them use graph paper—one number to a square, or have them turn lined paper sideways. Either aid will help them remember to keep their numbers in the right columns and to place the zeros where needed.

Practice and Extension

Have students look at their marked *hundred board* and count off numbers of tens. Ask for examples of when the mental skill of knowing tens would be useful. Discuss estimating costs, etc., with students.

Students make up problems that use groups of 10 and exchange them with other students. They see whether they can use their knowledge of multiples of 10 to arrive at the answer mentally. They check accuracy with the *hundred board*.

Go around the room, and orally count the number of fingers in the room, with each student taking a turn: "one student—10 fingers, two students—20 fingers . . . ." Continue with toes, giving each student the chance to participate twice in the counting activity.

Now you can teach the following shortcut:

1. Drop zero down into ones place.
2. Multiply the number in the tens place by the number of groups.

Hand out *catalog advertisements* and *bills*. Have students round prices to the nearest $10. Example: Shoes are $37. Round to $40, and then buy 3 pairs. About how much did they spend? How many different ways can they spend $100?

Have students use *bills* and play a shopping game in which every item they buy will cost $10. They throw a *die* to see how many items they can buy. After three turns, the student with the most items bought correctly is the winner.

Have students predict how they would multiply hundreds by 1-digit numbers. Can they also predict how they would multiply thousands by 1-digit numbers?

Multiplication 8

Skill: To multiply with more than two factors

geoboards, or geoboard paper

graph paper: any size

See Reproducibles for: geoboard paper, place value (pv) mats to 100s—1 per group

Time: 2 periods

Materials:

counters: two colors; 6 of each color per student

pattern blocks: several of each kind per group

Anticipatory Set

Use *counters*.

Have students make a rectangle of two groups of three counters. Repeat for another rectangle.

How many in the first rectangle? (6) How many in the second rectangle? (6) How many in all? (12) Both arrays show that $2 \times 3 = 6$, and together they show that two of these arrays equal 12, or $2 \times 2 \times 3 = 12$.

If two students combine their arrays, they have four arrays that equal 24, or $4 \times 2 \times 3 = 24$. This is what we will learn today.

Proceduro 1

To discover the process of multiplying by more than two factors

Use *pattern blocks*.

Have students set out two triangles. Ask: How many sides are on each? (3) How many sides are displayed altogether? (6) What multiplication sentence do the students think this shows?

Students respond: $2 \times 3 = 6$.

Now have students set out two more triangles. How many sides on each? (3) How many sides on this new set? (6) How many sides on both sets together? (12) How do the students think this multiplication sentence should be stated?

If students respond that two groups of six equal 12, relate back to the first sentence of $2 \times 3 = 6$. Since we have two sets of these numbers, we are showing the complete multiplication sentence is $2 \times 2 \times 3 = 12$.

Now continue with various numbers of different shapes. Have students practice with some multiplication sentences that start with the number one as a factor.

Students display blocks, state the multiplication sentence shown, and check with each other for accuracy.

Procedure 2

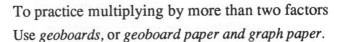

To practice multiplying by more than two factors

Use *geoboards, or geoboard paper and graph paper*.

Have students enclose one group of two squares. Ask: How many squares in all? (2) What multiplication fact is shown? ($1 \times 2 = 2$)

Have students enclose a second group of two squares, not touching the first. Now how many squares in all? (4) What multiplication sentence is shown by the entire geoboard? ($2 \times 1 \times 2 = 4$)

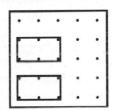

Have them enclose a third group of two squares. Now what multiplication sentence is shown? ($3 \times 1 \times 2 = 6$) If students do not see how it changed, encourage discussion so that they can see that they now have three sets of one times two.

Continue with other number examples that can be completed on the geoboard.

Students work with the lower numbers on the geoboards or geoboard paper until they are comfortable with the process.

Hand out graph paper. Now introduce some larger numbers. Ask students to make a square of two times three. How many squares are enclosed? (6)

Tell them to make three more just like the first. How many total squares have they enclosed? ($4 \times 2 \times 3 = 24$) Use story problems about acres of land or squares of chocolate.

Students complete drawings, compare answers, and check each other for accuracy. At this point students are not writing but are only giving oral answers using the manipulatives. After students are confident with this process, they can move to the next stage.

Procedure 3 □

To write the process of multiplying by more than two factors

Use *pv mats, counters,* and *paper*.

Have students work in groups for the beginning of this exercise, with each student recording after the group uses the manipulatives.

Have students place counters representing two rows of three on the pv mat. Ask: What multiplication sentence is shown by this array? ($2 \times 3 = 6$)

Now have them place a second group of two rows of three. How many in all? (12) What is the complete multiplication sentence shown? ($2 \times 2 \times 3 = 12$) Write the complete multiplication sentence on the board.

Students place counters and write the equation on their paper.

Make sure students understand that the written form they are learning is just a description of what is actually happening with their counters and pv mats.

Now have them place a third group of counters. How many in all? (18) What multiplication sentence is shown now? ($3 \times 2 \times 3 = 18$) If all do not agree, discuss why this is so, and continue the practice.

Students continue placing counters, deciding what the multiplication sentence is, and writing the complete equation on their papers.

Students continue using counters to demonstrate and find products of $2 \times 3 \times 3$, $3 \times 4 \times 3$, $5 \times 2 \times 3$, etc.

After students become confident with the process, they can move to writing the problem first and then checking each step with their counters. At this time give the students some independent practice of the process.

Practice and Extension

Students are to pretend they work in a local bakery and need to make up story problems in which they will have to multiply with more than two factors; for example: 10 packages of 8 rolls in each big box. If a store manager orders 6 boxes, how many rolls will the student have to pack? ($10 \times 8 \times 6$) There are 2 loaves of bread in a package. If 8 of these packages are in each box, how many loaves are in 3 boxes? ($2 \times 8 \times 3$) They can use *any manipulative* to represent the items and draw circles to represent the packages.

After writing the problem on paper, the students solve the problems on the back of the paper and then exchange with a partner. The partner first estimates a reasonable answer, remembering the last lesson of multiplying tens, and then solves the problem. Both students compare answers. Encourage students to diagram their problems, as well.

Have students present other problems to the class where they would need to multiply using more than two factor in order to arrive at an answer.

Multiplication 9

Skill: To multiply 2-digit numbers by 1-digit numbers

Time: 4 periods

Materials:

file-folder or other place value (pv) mats to 100s or 1000s

pv materials to 100s

×*number cards:* as shown in Illustration 1; 1 set ×2 to ×9 per student

counters in 3 colors: 25 of each color per group

See Reproducibles for: pv mats to 100s—1 per student, directions for file-folder pv mats, if needed

Anticipatory Set

Use *pv mats* and *pv materials*.

Have students work in pairs and place three tens and two ones on their mats. Now tell them to place an identical group below the first one. They now have two groups of materials both representing 32 on their mats. How many do they have in all? (64) What process did they use to get that number? (Some will say add, others multiply.)

Now have them add another group of materials representing the number 32 on the mats. How many groups of 32 do they have now? (3) Now it will be better to multiply. Students could still find the total by adding, but when the numbers are higher, multiplication is easier.

Procedure 1

To introduce partial products: assumes students can multiply ten by 1-digit numbers

Use *pv mats*, *pv materials*, and ×*number cards*.

In this procedure students work with materials only, and you write on the board showing partial products.

Have students work in pairs and place materials representing 11 on their mats (Illustration 1). Now have the students place the ×2 card under the 11 on their mats. Explain that these are the directions for the problem.

Students place the card and draw a line to separate the problem from the answer.

Ask: What does the two tell us?

Students respond: To make two groups of 11. Students place two groups of materials representing 11 below the line on their mats:

How much would two groups of 11 be?

Students push materials together and respond: 22.

Say: You added the two 11s together.

Could we have first multiplied the ones by the two, then multiplied the tens by the two, and added the answers? (yes) Let's see whether this is so.

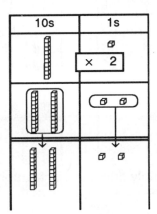

1. Serial addition.

Have students remove the answer materials from their mats. What are two groups of one one? (2)

Students place two one cubes below the directions.

What are two groups of one ten? (20, or 2 tens)

Students place two ten rods as shown in Illustration 2. They push all materials to the bottom for a total.

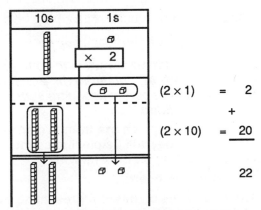

2. Partial products, no regrouping.

On the board, total the partial products as shown.

Continue with other groups of materials on the pv mats and other × number cards. Do not use numbers that require regrouping at this point.

Emphasize multiplying the ones and then the tens, adding them together, and reading the resulting total.

Students place groups of materials, multiply as directed by the cards, and find the products.

Now you can introduce some simple regrouping problems such as 2 × 16 for the students to place, regroup, and arrive at an answer. Students are not writing on paper at this stage. Write problems and partial products on the board while students work with the materials.

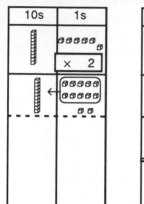
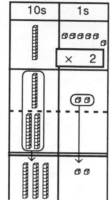

3a. Multiply ones; regroup.   **3b. Multiply tens; add.**

After students are comfortable with making separate groups of materials and arriving at the answers, use some simple problems to see whether they can predict the answer before placing materials. Continue with this procedure until all seem familiar with the process.

Procedure 2

To develop partial products; regrouping ones

Use *counters,* × *number cards,* and *paper.*

In this procedure students work with counters and write on a pv chart. You write the problems on a board chart with partial products at the side as shown in Illustration 7.

Have students make pv charts from two sheets of paper as shown. They will be placing counters on one chart and writing on the other.

Draw a chart on the board.

Have students place counters representing the number 15 on their mats. Under this they should place the ×5 card.

Put the problem on the board chart, and have students copy it onto their second chart, circling the ×5.

Ask: How many is 5 × 5 ones?

Students respond: 25 ones. They place 25 one counters below the line on one chart. They write 25 in the ones column on the other as shown:

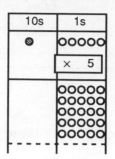

4.   Multiply ones by five.

Write (5 × 5) = 25 on the board.

Do we have too many ones? (yes)

Students regroup.

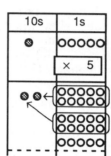

5.   Regroup ones.

We no longer have 25 ones. Any written problem is just a description of what we are actually doing. How should we show this?

Students respond: Cross out the 25. Write a five in the ones column and a two in the tens column.

We've multiplied everything in the *ones* column by five. Now we need to multiply everything in the *tens* column by five.

Ask: How many is 5 times 1 ten?

Students place counters and respond: 5 tens.

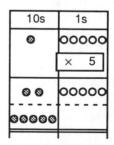

6.   Multiply tens by five.

Let's write down what you did with the counters. How many ones? (0) How many tens? (5)

Write (5 × 10) = 50 on the board below the (5 × 5) = 25.

Students write 50 below the 25.

We followed all the directions. How do we find out how many in all? (add)

Students push down all counters that are below the directions. They add the partial products in the ones and tens columns. They find the final answer is 75.

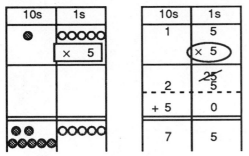

7. Add partial products.

Total the partial products on the board. Do both the materials and the numbers show 75? (yes)

Repeat with other numbers. Have students work with the counters, writing down each step as in the illustrations.

Students need much practice at this stage. They should continue writing the partial products to the side of their problem as they are shown in Illustration 7.

After students become confident about the process, they can move to writing the problem first and then checking each step with the counters.

Procedure 3 □■

To develop a traditional algorithm

Use *counters* and *paper*.

Have students make pv charts and write 15 on one. On the other have them place counters. Under both tell them to put a circled ×5. You write on the board. Students first use counters *and then* write steps as instructed.

Ask: What do we multiply first? (ones)

Students multiply ones:

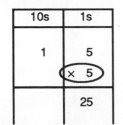

8a. Multiply ones.   8b. Regroup ones.

We have 25 in the ones column. Can we have that many ones? (no, we need to regroup)

Draw a line through the 25, and place a 5 below it.

Where does the two belong? (tens column)

Yes, but we still have a one in the tens column to multiply, so we have to put this two on hold for a while.

Place a circled +2 above the one in the tens column as shown in Illustration 8b.

We've taken care of the ones column. Now what does the one on our chart represent? (1 ten) How many is 5 × 10? (50)

When we worked before, we put the tens product on a separate line. But, when we multiply tens, do we ever have any ones? (no)

So we can put the number for the tens answer in line with the ones number. We don't really need to use a separate line for it:

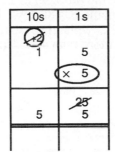 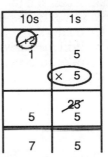

9a. Multiply tens.   9b. Find total.

How do we find our total? (add)

We had two tens on hold from regrouping the ones. In order to get a final answer, we need to remember to add those two tens to the five tens we got from multiplying tens.

Draw a double line, and add to find the final answer.

Students finish the problem. (See Illustration 9b.) They make sure to cross out the circled +2 after adding it, proving that they remembered to take care of the regrouped number.

Review the process for this problem to check for understanding. Have students check their results.

Students check their results with the counters.

Repeat the entire process with many other problems, including some that result in regrouping tens.

It is important for students to understand that the written form is just a description of what is actually happening. Students need much practice at this step.

Students continue to use counters, writing each step as they do it. When they are comfortable with the process, they will see that they can write any regrouping in one step rather than the two steps shown in Illustration 8b.

Call their attention to the similarity to regrouping in addition.

After students become competent in the skill, they can move to writing the problem first and then checking each step with their counters. Remind them to circle the regrouped number and to cross it out after they have taken care of it.

Practice and Extension

Have students use *counters* and *pv mats* to make up games to play in which they have to multiply 2-digit numbers by a 1-digit number in order to "move" or win.

Take *checkerboards* and put problems on the spaces. Play as in regular Checkers except the students have to answer the problems correctly in order to move.

Have students write original problems, solve them on a separate sheet, and then give the problem to a partner to solve. Example: A piano has 88 keys. If 7 pianos are on the stage, how many piano keys are on the stage? Will the answer be more than 400? How do you know? (Students explain their process of estimating.)

Multiplication 10

Skill: To multiply hundreds by 1-digit numbers

counters color-coded to 100s

See Reproducibles for: number lines to 1000—1 per student, graph paper with 1 cm squares—4 sheets per student, pv mats to 1000s, directions for file-folder pv mats

Time: 1 period

Materials:

file-folder or other place value (pv) mats to 1000s

2" × 3" × number cards as shown in Illustration 1a: 1 set ×2 to ×9 per student

Anticipatory Set

Use *number lines, graph paper,* and *plain paper.*

Count by tens to 100. Count by hundreds to 1,000. Review how to write the number 1,100.

Students number by hundreds from 100 to 1,000 on the number line. Discuss patterns. Then they cut graph paper into 10 × 10 squares to represent hundred flats.

Students draw three vertical lines on their paper to make four columns, and label them 1000s, 100s, 10s, and 1s.

Procedure 1

To multiply hundreds by 1-digit numbers; partial products

Use *pv mats, × number cards,* and *prepared graph paper hundred flats from Anticipatory Set.*

Note: *Do not teach multiplying the digits and annexing the zeros.*

Since multiplication problems are solved right to left, the following procedure tends to eliminate some math confusions.

Have students place a hundred flat on their mats. Ask: How many 100s? (1) How many 10s? (none) How many 1s? (none)

Write 100 on the board in a place value chart.

Tell students you want five 100s in all.

Students place four more 100s on their mats.

What value does each flat represent? (100) *Emphasize that we are working with groups of 100.*

How many 100s? (5) How many 10s? (none) How many 1s? (none)

What is the total of the manipulatives? (500) Did they add or count to get the answer?

We know how to multiply 5 × 10; we can also multiply to find the answer to 5 × 100. Do you think the problems will be similar?

Students discuss.

On the chart on the board write a circled ×5 under the 100. Remind students that the directions are circled to help them remember what to do.

Instruct students to take four of the hundred flats off their mats. Under the remaining hundred flat on their mat they should place the ×5 card, as in Illustration 1a. This represents the problem 5 × 100 = ?.

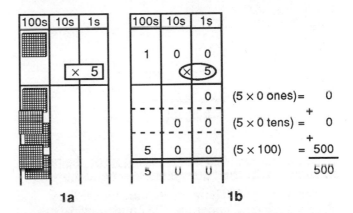

1a   **1b**

You know how to multiply 1-digit numbers by other 1-digit numbers. How many is 5 × 0? (none)

How can I show that on the board?

Students respond: With a zero in the ones column.

You already know how to multiply tens by 1-digit numbers. How many tens are on your mats? (none)

We place that answer on the second line in the tens column. The second zero "holds" the ones column.

Place these numbers on the board with the partial products to the side, as shown in Illustration 1b.

How many hundred flats are on your mat? (1) What did the directions say we needed to do?

Students respond: We need five groups of 100. They place five hundred flats on their mats under the line.

What number do your flats show? (500)

Write 500 in the board example as shown.

Review the process: **First we multiplied the zero ones by five and got zero. Next we multiplied the zero tens by five and got zero.**

Last we multiplied the 100 by five and got 500. We get a total by adding those three answers.

Repeat the procedure, emphasizing groups of hundreds and the place value.

Have students place a hundred flat on their mats. This is the number of pepperoni slices on the giant party-size pizza from Marcella's Magnificent Pizza.

Have them place three more hundreds. Now they show the number of pepperoni slices on four of the pizzas. Have them write the number 400 on their pv papers.

Students place materials on their mats and write 400 on their papers. Students want to buy four more pizzas. This will be a second group just like the first.

Students place the ×2 card under the four hundred flats on their mats.

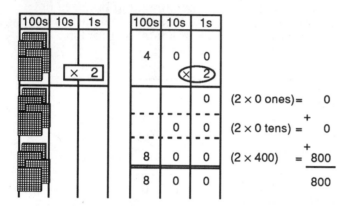

100s	10s	1s	
4	0	0	
	⊗	2	
		0	(2 × 0 ones)= 0
	0	0	+ (2 × 0 tens) = 0
8	0	0	+ (2 × 400) = 800
8	0	0	800

Write the number 400 and a circled ×2 on the board as shown. Why did I draw a circle around the ×2?

Students respond: Those are the directions. They place a circled ×2 under the 400 on their pv paper.

Ask the same kind of questions as before. Finish the problem on the board while students do the same on mats and papers.

Does your answer on paper show the same number as your flats on the place value mat? (yes)

Repeat the procedure.

When students are confident with the procedure, continue with problems up to 9 × 900, with regrouping. Ask students whether they see a pattern. Discuss responses.

After students are competent using the manipulatives and writing the problem, they can begin writing the problem first and then checking with the materials.

Procedure 2 □■

To develop a traditional algorithm

Use *prepared paper* and *counters*, if needed.

Stress to the students that since the ones and tens answers in these problems are always zero, they can "double up" those lines in the problem.

Introduce the form:

100s	10s	1s
4	0	0
		× 2
8	0	0

Still emphasize that they are multiplying ones first, then tens, and then hundreds. They can take the shortcut in this type of problem because when we have hundreds, we have zero digits in the ones and tens places.

Students use counters to help solve the problems until they are no longer necessary.

When students begin working independently, have them use graph paper—one number to a square, or turn lined paper sideways. Either aid will help them remember to place numbers in the correct columns and to place zeros where needed.

Practice and Extension

Now you can teach the shortcut:

1. Drop a zero into the ones place.
2. Drop a zero into the tens place.
3. Multiply the digits.

Have students make up word problems using groups of hundreds and exchange for peers to solve.

Have students use *catalogs*. They round prices to the nearest $100 and purchase several of the same items. About how much did they spend? How many ways can they purchase multiples of items totaling $1,000?

Can students predict how to multiply ten thousands by 1-digit numbers? Can they predict how to multiply millions by 1-digit numbers? What can they generalize about multiplying any number that has zeros in all places except the largest?

Multiplication 11

Skill: To multiply 3-digit numbers by 1-digit numbers

Time: 3 periods

Materials:

file-folder or other place value (pv) mats to 1000s

pv materials to 1000s; use counters as 1000s

2" × 3" × number cards as shown in illustration 1a: 1 set ×2 to ×9 per student

counter-trading materials to 1000s

markers in 3 colors

See Reproducibles for: pv mats to 1000s—1 per pair, directions for file-folder pv mats to 1000s, counter-trading boards, bills to 1000s—in different colors

Anticipatory Set

Use *pv mats* and *pv materials*.

Have student pairs place materials for the number 132 on their mats and then place an identical group below the first one. They now have two 132s on their mats.

Ask: How many do you have in all? (264) What process did you use to get that number? (most say add)

Now have them add another 132 to the mats. How many groups do you have now? (3) You could still find the total by adding, but when the numbers are higher multiplication is easier.

We know how to multiply 2-digit by 1-digit numbers. How we could expand that to this problem? Discuss.

Procedure 1 □■

To use partial products

Use *pv mats, pv materials,* and *× number cards.*

In this procedure students work with materials while you write the problem on the board.

Have student pairs place materials for the number 111 on their mats with the ×2 card underneath.

Ask: What does the ×2 tell us? (to make two groups of 111)

Students draw a line and place two groups of 111 on their mats. (Illustration 1a)

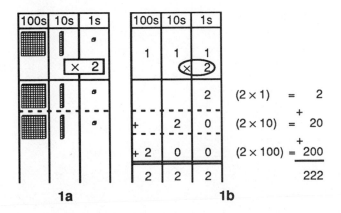

1a   **1b**

How much would two groups of 111 be?

Students push materials together and respond: 222.

Tell students they have added, but they could have multiplied. Have them clear materials from below the line. Tell them to do the problem again, using multiplication, while you write each step on the board as in Illustration 1b.

How many one cubes do you have? (1) How many do the directions say we need? (2) Write 2 × 1 = 2.

Students place two one cubes below the line.

How many ten rods are on your mats? (1) How many are two groups of 10? (20) Write 2 × 10 = 20.

Students place two ten rods.

How many hundreds are on your mats? (1) How many are two groups of 100? (200) Write 2 × 100 = 200.

Students place two hundred flats.

I wrote just what you did on your mats. Remember how we multiplied 2-digit numbers before, and tell me how to finish the problem.

Students respond: Add the three amounts together. They add materials together and tell you to write 222.

Repeat with other numbers. When students seem familiar with the process, have them write each step with you as they do it with materials.

It is important to include the stage of connecting the concrete materials to the writing of the process.

Procedure 2 □■

To develop a traditional algorithm

Use *counter-trading boards, counter-trading materials, markers, × number cards,* and *paper.*

Have students draw vertical lines to separate paper into three columns and label them "Ones," "Tens," and "Hundreds." Have them color-code these charts and place counters for 234 on their counter-trading boards.

Say: There are 234 people at a conference, and each needs four note pads. How many note pads must be provided? How would we show this as a multiplication problem?

Students place a ×4 card under the 234 on their boards and write 234 with a circled ×4 on their chart. They will use materials and then write each step with you as they do it.

Make sure students understand that this is an abbreviation of the process they learned in Procedure 1 and that it is still just describing what is actually happening as they do it.

100$s	10s	1s
□ □ (+1) 2	□ □ □ (1) 3	□ □ □ □ 4 (× 4)
8̸	1̸2̸ 1̸8̸	1̸6̸
9	3	6

Say: Make four groups of four. Where does that answer go? (ones column) (You write the 16 as shown, as students follow your example.) Do we need to do something with them? (regroup)

Students regroup counters and cross out the 16.

How many ones are left? (6) (You write a six in the ones column. Students continue to write as well.)

We haven't multiplied the three in the tens column yet. We need to put the one from regrouping on hold for a while. Put a one with a small plus sign at the top of the tens column. We circle it to remind us to add it in later.

How many are four groups of 30? (120)

Where would the zero go? (ones column) Since adding zero won't change the total of ones, we don't need to show the zero. We don't need to write this product on a separate line anymore.

We place the 12 in the tens column. Do we need to do anything else?

Students respond: Add the +1 to the 12. That makes 13 tens. They do this with materials and in writing.

Now what should we do? (regroup)

Students regroup on their boards, cross out the 13, make it a 3, and place a +1 in the hundreds column.

We still have another number to multiply. What is four groups of 200? (800) As before, the zeros won't change the column totals of tens or ones, so we don't have to use a separate line. Where would the eight go?

Students respond: In the hundreds column.

What happens to the regrouped +1 in the hundreds column? (add to the eight) Show this on the board, and point out that their written problems show just what they did with the materials.

Repeat the procedure with other numbers. Students need much guided practice on these steps.

Procedure 3

To practice multiplication

Use *bills, pv mats,* and *paper.*

Have student groups generate their own problems. They should place the bills and then multiply on the mats as in Procedure 2.

Students do problems with bills and write each step on a group sheet of paper. They share their problems with the rest of the class, along with their solutions.

Have each student now create a problem. Post these for other students to prove with the bills.

Practice and Extension

Students can play Money Madness. Use *bills to 1000s* and *pv mats.* Divide the class into teams, and have each start with $1,000. Use *number cards* or *dice* to generate numbers in turn for a 3-digit number and a multiplier.

Use story problems like the sale of stock, pairs of shoes bought, and so on. Teams predict answers before multiplying, then compare their actual answer with their prediction.

When all team members have the correct answer, flip a *two-sided coin* or *counter* to see whether the answer is to be added or subtracted from a running total for the week.

Extend activities to four or more digits by 1-digit multiplication, a free-ride skill, as they already know the process. Do part of a large number problem each day for a week. Have students predict the final answer. At the end, see how close the estimate was.

Division 1

Skill: To learn division concepts:
sharing and repeated subtraction

Time: 1 week

Materials:

similar objects for sharing: beans, tiles, counters, etc.;
about 20 per student

containers, or 6" ×6" squares of paper: 1 per student

graph paper: ¹/₂" or larger squares

markers

interlocking cubes, or Cuisenaire® rods

geoboards and rubber bands

See Reproducibles for: hundred boards—1 per student

Anticipatory Set

Use *similar objects for sharing.*

Have three students stand up. Say: I have a number
of beans I want to share. How can I do it?

Discuss sharing with students. Reinforce that objects
are to be shared equally among the three.

Procedure 1

To develop the concept of division as sharing

Use *objects for sharing* and *containers or squares of
paper.*

**Give each student about 20 beans. Vary the
amounts. Say: These are magic beans. You have
four friends you want to give them to. Find a way
to give each friend the same amount of beans. If
you have any left over, just put them to the side.**

Students place beans in containers or on paper
squares.

**Ask each student: How many beans did you start
with? How many beans did each friend get? Did
each get the same amount? How many beans did
you have left over?**

**Restate the process for each student: You shared
your beans evenly with four friends. We can say
you *divided* your beans evenly into four piles.
Each friend or pile got five beans (if students
started with 20).**

**Repeat the activity several times, having each
student use a different number of beans.**

**Repeat the questions and the restatement of
sharing as division as before.**

**What did you notice when you used fewer beans
for your dividing? What did you notice when you
used more beans?**

Students respond: More beans meant the friends each
got more. Fewer beans meant they got fewer. Some
numbers of beans had a lot of leftovers, and some
had none.

**Have students look at the last results of their
sharing. For example: We have four piles with five**

beans in each pile. That's 20 beans we shared. Do
the results look like anything we've done before?
How could I write this in math language?

Students respond: It looks like multiplication. We
could write $4 \times 5 = 20$.

**Repeat the procedure with differing amounts of
beans and friends, comparing and discussing
results. Students can make up different stories to
go with each problem.**

Go on to Procedure 2.

Procedure 2

To record division as sharing; to introduce the ÷
symbol

Use *objects for sharing* and *containers or squares of
paper.*

**Have each student start with 20 beans and divide
them evenly among three friends.**

**Say: We'll want to keep a record of our results,
and look for any patterns.**

Draw the following chart headings on the board:

#Beans		#Friends	#For Each Friend	#Left
21	÷	3	7	0
20	÷	3	6	2
19	÷	3	6	1

**Say: We use the division symbol, ÷, to show
sharing evenly. It looks like two beans shared
evenly, one above and one below a line.**

**Vary the number of beans shared among three
friends, and record the results as shown above.
What do students notice?**

Students should notice that a larger starting number
gives a larger amount in each group. They may notice
that three are never left over.

What would happen if you had three left over?

Students respond: Enough would be left for another
sharing.

**Can students find multiplication on the chart?
Discuss the multiplication/division relationship.**

Repeat the procedure with a different number of friends, and have students predict results, chart, and discuss.

Now have students record each division experiment on paper as shown:

20 ÷ 4 = 5	and	0 left over	5 × 4 = 20
19 ÷ 4 = 4	and	3 left over	4 × 4 = 16
18 ÷ 4 = 4	and	2 left over	4 × 4 = 16

Continue until students are comfortable with division as sharing and the relationship to multiplication. Emphasize that the written form shows what is actually happening.

Have students make up stories to go with each experiment: fire extinguishers shared among four dragons, mud puddles shared among five pigs, etc.

Procedure 3

To practice and record division as sharing

Use *graph paper, markers,* and *interlocking cubes or Cuisenaire® rods.*

Follow the same basic procedure as before. When using the interlocking cubes, have students work in pairs. One student divides the cubes, and the other records as shown:

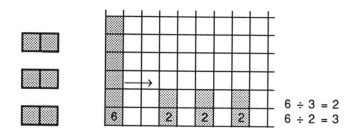

$$6 ÷ 3 = 2$$
$$6 ÷ 2 = 3$$

When the division is completed, have students make cubes into sticks. How many are in each stick? How many are shown in each column on paper?

Students complete the task. They compare results and then write them on paper as shown in Procedure 2.

If using Cuisenaire® rods, students make a starting number and then use an equal number of one rods for the division. After all rods have been shared, they find an equivalent rod for each group, charting as before.

Procedure 4

To develop the concept of division as repeated subtraction; to relate to multiplication

Use *objects for sharing* and *containers or squares of paper.*

Say: You have been sharing magic beans with friends. If you were dividing the beans among three friends, you gave one bean to each of the friends and then started over. Each time, you took three from your total beans so that you could share.

If we have lots of beans and lots of friends, sometimes there's a faster way to divide.

We could take out enough at a time for each person to get one. Let's share among three people. Take out enough beans for each person to have one.

Students do this.

Ask: How many did you take out? (3) Take out another group and put it into another pile for the second sharing.

Students do this.

How many out this time? (3 again) How many piles so far? (2 for 2 sharings) So each friend will get how many so far? (2)

Repeat until no more groups can be removed. Any leftovers?

Students respond, depending on how many beans they started with.

We'll save those left over for another time because there's not enough for each friend to have the same amount.

Now, notice how many piles you took out of your starting number, and then share each pile among your three friends.

Students share each pile.

How many groups did you start with? (answers vary) How many beans did each friend get?

Students respond: Each friend got one bean from each pile.

Repeat with a variety of numbers. How do you know what size group to subtract from your total each time?

Students respond: You need enough for each friend to get one. The size of the group is the same as the number of friends.

Discuss that to divide 20 beans among four friends, we can subtract groups of four. Division is a shortcut for subtracting the same number each time. The answer is how many times we took a group out.

Relate this to multiplication. How could we know how many beans we started with?

Students respond: Add up the beans in each group. Some will say: Multiply the number of beans times the number of groups.

Repeat until students are comfortable with the idea of division as repeated subtraction.

Go on to Procedure 5.

Procedure 5

To record division as repeated subtraction

Use *objects for sharing* and *containers or squares of paper*.

Explain that we need to keep track of our results and look for patterns. Write the following chart headings on the board.

# Beans		# Friends	Group Size	# Groups	# Each Gets	# Left
21	÷	3	3	7	7	0
20	÷	3	3	6	6	2
19	÷	3	3	6	6	1

Students do division as you keep the chart. They discuss all patterns and the relationship of multiplication to division, as in Procedure 4.

When students are comfortable with charting, have them work in pairs. One should do the division and one the recording. Can they predict the results? Have them make up different stories to go with the problems.

Procedure 6

To practice and record division as repeated subtraction

Use *geoboards and rubber bands, interlocking cubes, Cuisenaire® rods, or hundred boards and markers.*

If using geoboards, have students enclose the total number with a rubber band and use other rubber bands to enclose groups.

If using Cuisenaire® rods, have students make a train equal to their starting number; for example, 16. If they are dividing by four, they will lay four-rods alongside until they have as many as possible. One rods are used to make up the difference, the leftovers.

If using interlocking cubes, put out enough cubes to equal the starting number. Have students subtract out enough cubes for each group and snap them together.

If using hundred boards, have students either use a marker to put a line at the end of their starting number or put a counter on it. If the number is 21, students would draw a line after 21. If they are dividing 21 by 3, they should color three spaces and then outline that group of three in another color. Next they should color a second group of three and outline that group.

When they are done making groups of three, have them count the number of outlined groups. Any numbers not colored will be the leftovers.

Students continue charting and writing results.

It is important for students to practice with a variety of materials. This helps build understanding of underlying concepts.

Students complete the assignment and discuss the differing answers that were found.

Procedure 7

To introduce arrays and the ⌐ symbol

Use *cubes, counters, or tiles* and *paper*.

Have students lay out 15 counters as in Illustration 2a.

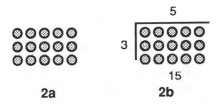

2a   2b

Explain that the lines across are called *rows*, like a row of seats in an auditorium. The lines up and down are called *columns*, like columns holding up a building. Do students have other memory aids?

Students practice building arrays of specified rows and columns.

Now have students put out five columns with three in each column and write a 15 below as shown in Illustration 2b.

These are a farmer's 15 pigs. He has them in three lines. However, he doesn't want them to get away, so he puts a fence around them. Draw a fence as shown.

The farmer walks around to the front of the lines. (Show on the board where the three will go.) How many lines does the farmer see? (3) Write the three in the correct place. The pigs have been divided into three lines, or groups.

The farmer needs to know how many pigs are in each line, so he walks around to see. Indicate on the board where the five will go.

How many pigs in each line? (5) Write the five in place. Five pigs are in each line.

This fence is used as one of our division symbols. It shows 15 pigs divided into three groups with 5 in a group. You could also think of the problem as 15 pigs divided into five columns with 3 in each column.

Have students make arrays using other numbers of counters. Write the array and written division problem on the board as before.

Any remainders can be put to the side as left-overs, or you may write them as remainders.

Have we done anything with rectangles or arrays before?

Students respond: This is like multiplication. So many groups, with so many in each group, tells how many in all.

Provide much practice for students.

When students are comfortable with arrays, they work in pairs. One student works with the counters while the other writes the problem. As each step is done with the counters, the result is put onto paper. They write the related multiplication fact and make up stories to go along with their manipulations.

Procedure 8 ☐

To practice the concept and writing of division, using arrays

Use *graph paper and markers* or *geoboards and rubber bands*.

Have students outline a rectangular array of their starting number on graph paper. For example, if the starting number is 18 and it is to be divided by three, students will make a rectangle three squares high.

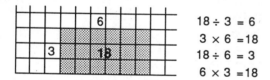

$$18 \div 3 = 6$$
$$3 \times 6 = 18$$
$$18 \div 6 = 3$$
$$6 \times 3 = 18$$

Have students write the resulting number of columns above the rectangle and then write the division and multiplication facts discovered.

Or, have students use geoboards instead of graph paper to make their arrays. Have them use other rubber bands to enclose the columns.

Students continue to use the division symbol and write down each step as they do it.

Practice and Extension

Have students work individually. Give each student 15 *$1 bills*. The mall is having Dollar Days. Each item they find at the mall costs $3, so they will be dividing their money into groups of $3. They are to keep a record on paper of each purchase and the amount left. Have students complete the exercise, continuing to subtract until they have no money left. How many items were they able to buy? (5)

Have students pool their money and work in pairs. They are to take the $30 and divide it into equal groups by spending an equal amount of money at each store. How much do they spend at each store, and how many stores do they visit before all their money is gone? (Answers will vary.)

Have students use *any of the materials* listed or *place value materials* to create story problems for each other to solve. Challenge students to discover ways that repeated subtraction and repeated addition are related activities.

Division 2

Skill: To learn division facts

Time: 5+ periods

Materials:

counters of 2 colors: buttons, cubes, tiles, or 1" × 1" paper squares

markers to match colors of above objects

interlocking cubes

small containers, or 4" × 4" squares of paper

Cuisenaire® rods, or bundled craft sticks

place value (pv) materials to 10s

dice: 1 per student pair

See Reproducibles for: pv mats to 100s, division paper, bills to 10s—in different colors, matrices for facts

Note: Although some students may have had preliminary division work in earlier grades, by working through Division 1 before starting on division facts, you insure greater understanding for all. At least do Procedures 7 and 8. *It is well worth the time.*

Eventually, you want students to be able to divide using a base ten format. Students need to understand how to divide several kinds of groups (tens and ones, for example), how to trade from one kind of group to the other (trade a ten for ten ones), and how to record their actions in a base ten format.

By teaching each of the following procedures, you increase the chances of students' thinking of "facts" in a base ten format. Division of any 2- or 3-digit number by a 1-digit number then becomes a logical extension of what has gone before.

Anticipatory Set

Use *counters* and *plain paper*.

If you have worked through Division 1—Procedures 7 and 8 and students know how to divide using arrays, then have students put out a 3 × 4 array of 12 counters and review. Have students draw the division fence around their array, count the number of lines and number in each line, and put the three and four where they belong.

If you have not had students work with arrays (Division 1—Procedures 7 and 8), spend some time doing this until all students understand the concept.

Procedure 1

To divide with two kinds of objects; no regrouping

Use *two colors of counters* and *plain paper*.

Say: Sam had jelly beans left over from his lunch, which he decided to give to two friends. Take eight red counters for eight red jelly beans.

Sam also had four yellow jelly beans. Put them to the right of the red jelly beans, and draw a line

between them because there are two different kinds of jelly beans. Draw a division fence above them. (Illustration 2a)

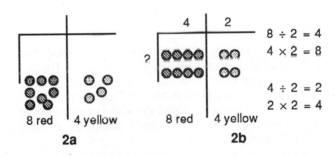

$$8 \div 2 = 4$$
$$4 \times 2 = 8$$
$$4 \div 2 = 2$$
$$2 \times 2 = 4$$

Ask: How many friends do we have? (2) Let's put the two here to show how many groups we will have. (Illustration 2b) Divide the red beans into two lines.

Students do this.

How many red beans are in each group? (4) I'll show the divided beans and put the four up here to show how many red beans each friend got. (Illustration 2b)

Divide the yellow beans to see how many each friend will get.

Students do this.

We still have two friends. How many will each friend get? (2) I'll put the two up above the yellow jelly beans.

Does anyone see a division fact I can list?

Students respond: 8 ÷ 2 = 4, 4 ÷ 2 = 2.

I'll list these on the board to the side.

Could we check our results with math? Who sees something they've seen before?

Students respond: It's like multiplication. $4 \times 2 = 8$ red jelly beans and $2 \times 2 = 4$ yellow jelly beans.

Write these facts next to the division facts.

Say: Take all the jelly beans for the first friend and put them in a pile to the side. Do the same for the second friend. How many jelly beans in all for each friend?

Students respond: They get 4 red beans and 2 yellow beans—6 in all.

Repeat the procedure with other stories and numbers until students understand the concept. Tell students extra beans are called leftovers.

Go on to Procedure 2.

Procedure 2

To practice and record division with two kinds of objects

Use *two colors of counters, markers to match,* and *paper.*

When students are comfortable with dividing two kinds of objects, have them work in pairs. Have one work with the counters and the other record the results, as in Illustration 2b. The recorder is to draw in the counters using markers and place the results on the chart. Leftovers can be written to the side with a +.

Students need much practice at this stage of both manipulating materials and recording results. As they become confident, ask whether they can predict the result before using the materials.

Procedure 3

To divide with two kinds of objects; with regrouping

Use *interlocking cubes* and *small containers or 4" × 4" squares of paper.*

Say: Today we will be handing out gum to friends. The gum comes in packs of five. Take some of your interlocking cubes and make them into packs of five.

Students do this

Let's start with three packs and two pieces. Put them on your paper, and draw a line between them.

Now draw a division fence above because we are going to divide among two friends. (Illustration 4a)

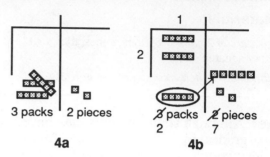

4a   **4b**

Ask: How many friends? (2) I'll write that to the left. Divide your three packs among two friends.

Students do this. They comment that one is left over.

How many packs does each friend get? (1)

On the board draw the divided packs as in Illustration 4b.

Say: Each group has one in it, so I'll write the one in the pack column. What does this show?

Students respond: How many packs each friend gets.

What can we do about the extra pack?

Students respond: Break it into single pieces. They do this.

We only have two packs now. I'll cross out the three and put a two.

Make sure all your pieces are on the "pieces" side of your paper. How many single pieces do you have now? (7)

Divide your seven pieces for your two friends. If any are left over now, just put them to the side and we'll save them for later.

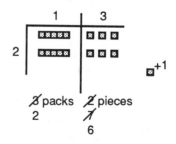

Students divide the pieces and put one piece to the side.

How many pieces does each friend get?

Students respond: Each friend gets three pieces. One is left over.

Where will I show this?

Students respond: Above, where the pieces are.

Finish the problem on the board. List any division and multiplication facts students see.

Repeat the procedure with many different combinations. As students become adept at dividing and trading, change the value of the packs. Have six pieces in a pack, or four pencils in a bundle, or three anteaters for each anthill.

Ask questions: How many packs and pieces did we start with? How many packs and pieces did each friend get? Any left over? What division and multiplication facts did you find?

Procedure 4

To practice division with two kinds of objects; with regrouping

Use *Cuisenaire® rods* and *paper*.

Repeat Procedure 3 with different materials and different values. This time have students record the division after completing the steps with the manipulatives.

Procedure 5

To divide with base ten materials

Use *pv materials, pv mats,* and *division paper*.

Repeat Procedure 3 with ten rods and one cubes. Start with numbers that do not require trading, such as 24 ÷ 2. On the board write the problem as shown in the illustrations below.

Have students place materials for 24.

Say: We are giving out erasers, which are packaged in tens. We'll give them evenly to two friends.

Write the two on the board, and have students divide their rods and cubes into two groups.

Ask: How many groups of tens did you make? (2) How many eraser packages in each group? (1) Where can I record that?

Students respond: Above, in the tens column.

Yes, if you divide tens, you get a certain number of tens and your answer is in tens.

What division fact did you show? (2 pkgs. ÷ 2 = 1) Write this on the board.

How can we check that our division is right?

Students respond: With multiplication. $1 \times 2 = 2$.

How many groups of ones, or single erasers, did you make? (2) How many erasers are in each group? (2) Where can I record that?

Students respond: Above, in the ones column.

Yes, if you divide ones, you get a certain number of ones and your answer is in ones.

What division fact did you show? (4 ÷ 2 = 2) Write this on the board.

How can we check that our division is right?

Students respond: With multiplication. $2 \times 2 = 4$.

Divide 2-digit numbers with and without trades, recording the results on the board after each trade. Ask the same questions for each problem.

Provide practice also for 1-digit numbers. Make sure students understand where to place the answer.

Go on to Procedure 6 when students are comfortable with making divisions and trades.

Procedure 6

To record division with base ten materials

Use *pv materials, pv mats, division paper,* and *dice*.

Have students work in pairs. Have one student use the materials to do the problems and one record each step as shown in Procedure 5. Work through several problems with students before having them work on their own. Students need much practice at this stage of both writing and using concrete materials.

In recording regrouping, make sure students cross out original numbers and write in new amounts for both tens and ones, as in Procedure 3.

Students keep a list of division and multiplication facts they discovered as they work.

Dice may be used to generate problems: The first two numbers are the dividend, and the third is the divisor.

Procedure 7

To practice and record division

Use *pv mats, dice, division paper,* and *bills*.

Repeat Procedure 6 with different materials. Use dice to generate the problems.

Procedure 8

To develop knowledge of facts; to relate division to multiplication using a matrix

Use *pv materials, pv mats,* and *matrices for facts.*

Have students start with two one cubes and divide them by two. Ask: How many in each group? (1) What is the division fact? (2 ÷ 2 = 1) What is the related multiplication fact? (1 × 2 = 2)

Can you find a place on this matrix where you could put the number you started with? Pretend the upper left-hand corner of the blank squares is your division fence.

Students place two in the appropriate place.

	0	1	2	3
0				
1				
2		2	4	
3				

Now have students divide four by two. Repeat the procedure, having students repeat both division and multiplication fact. Place four in the appropriate place.

Continue through the multiples of two. Do students see a pattern?

Some may recognize multiples of two.

Have students recite the multiples of two as they check their materials. How many times did they say a multiple? Does this relate to the answer to their division problem?

Suggest that as they divide by two, they are taking groups of two from their total each time to put in lines. The answer at the top of their division problem tells how many times they removed a group of two.

Continue through the matrix, writing both division and multiplication facts.

Practice and Extension

Have students use any of the materials listed to make up division problems. They can act them out with friends.

Have students build arrays with *interlocking cubes* or *counters* and then write the two related division problems they could prove using the array.

How many problems will give a remainder of 1? Of 2? Which ones will never give a remainder of 3?

Students can make *division flash cards* to use in Concentration (facts on one card and answer on another).

Division 3

Skill: To learn multiplication and division fact families: to relate division to multiplication

Time: 4 periods

Materials:

1" tiles: ceramic, plastic, or 1" × 1" paper squares

1 cm cubes

light-colored markers

scissors

geoboards and colored rubber bands

interlocking cubes

counters

narrow strips of tag board: 2 per student

See Reproducibles for: graph paper with 1 cm squares—1 sheet per student, multiplication/division tables—1 per group

Anticipatory Set

Use *tiles* and *blank sheets of paper.*

Review with students that rows are the across lines and columns are the down lines. Compare them to rows of seats and columns of buildings. Have students make and discuss several arrays. Does every number make an array? (Yes, it at least has 1 × itself.)

What if we turn the group of tiles so that the rectangle is sideways? (Illustration 2b)

Students respond: It would show 3 groups of 4: $4 \times 3 = 12$; or 12 divided into 3 groups: $12 \div 3 = 4$.

Write these on the board, and bracket them as a fact family. Relate this to addition/subtraction fact families.

Have students suggest other groupings and show their groups with the tiles. Write the fact families on the board until the students understand the procedure. They then can see how many families they can discover and record.

Procedure 1

To use arrays to discover fact families

Use *tiles* and *paper.*

Have students make a 3 × 4 array as shown above.

Explain that the tiles are pigs in a pigpen. The farmer has divided them into four lines but needs to keep them from running into the cornfield nearby.

Demonstrate on the board that a partial fence around a group looks similar to a division symbol:

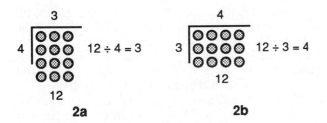

2a   **2b**

Model for the students as they do an example (Illustration 2a). Ask: How many rows are shown? (4) How many columns? (3) What multiplication fact is shown? (3 in each group × 4 groups: $3 \times 4 = 12$)

What division fact? (12 divided into 4 groups: $12 \div 4 = 3$) Write these on the board.

Procedure 2

To draw and write fact families

Use *graph paper with 1 cm squares, 1 cm cubes, markers,* and *scissors.*

Have students work in groups to explore arrays of fact families. Have students start by labeling their paper: "Fact Families for Six." Take six cubes and make a row. Ask: What fact family can I show with this rectangle?

Students respond: $1 \times 6 = 6$, $6 \times 1 = 6$, $6 \div 1 = 6$, $6 \div 6 = 1$. They form the rectangle with cubes, color the graph paper to match, and write the fact family below:

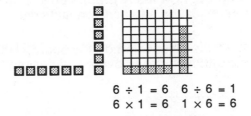

$$6 \div 1 = 6 \quad 6 \div 6 = 1$$
$$6 \times 1 = 6 \quad 1 \times 6 = 6$$

Students explore fact families in this manner, making as many rectangles as possible with each number. Groups can cut out and post their discoveries.

How were they sure they got all the combinations? What do they notice about the shapes of the rectangles? What patterns do they see? Can they tell you how multiplication and division are related?

Procedure 3

To practice and write fact families

Use *geoboards and rubber bands*.

Have students put a band around a 3 × 4 rectangle. Then have them use another color band to make four separate rectangles as shown:

$$12 \div 4 = 3$$
$$3 \times 4 = 12$$

What multiplication fact is shown? (3 × 4 = 12) What division fact could this show? (12 ÷ 4 = 3)

How are these alike? Have students reposition the bands for a 4 × 3 rectangle and write the rest of the fact family. (4 × 3 = 12 and 12 ÷ 3 = 4)

Continue with more examples.

As students do each step with the geoboards, it is important for them to understand that the written form is just a description of what is happening.

Students continue to explore both the multiplication and the division facts they can discover. When they are comfortable, have them predict the fact family for each new dividend before using the geoboard.

Procedure 4

To practice and write fact families

Use *interlocking cubes*.

Write 12 ÷ ? = ? on the board.

Have students build a stick of 12 cubes. Ask: How many ways can you separate the stick into equal groups?

After students have done this, ask how many are in each group. How many groups do you have? What multiplication and division facts did you discover?

Write the facts discovered on the board, and continue until you have covered all desired facts.

Procedure 5

To use the multiplication/division table to find facts

Use *multiplication/division tables, light-colored markers, counters,* and *strips of tag board*.

Have students color in the six and position the strips:

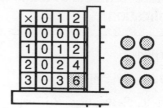

Say: The six you colored tells how many counters to start with. We'll use the far left column as our first directions. The number is three, so divide the six counters into three groups. How many in each group? (2) Do you see that answer anywhere?

Students respond: In the top row above the starting 6.

Ask: What division fact did we show? (6 ÷ 3 = 2) What multiplication fact did we show? (2 × 3 = 6)

Write these on the board.

Say: Now try the *top* directions. They say to divide your six counters into two groups. How many in each group? (3) Do you see that answer anywhere?

Students respond: In the side column, next to the 6 we started with.

What is the division fact? (6 ÷ 2 = 3) And the multiplication fact? (3 × 2 = 6)

Write the complete fact family on the board. Repeat until students understand the procedure.

Students then work in groups to color squares, use the strips, divide the counters, and write the facts.

Do they see any patterns? Will they have to do all the higher numbers to know whether the chart works for them?

Practice and Extension

Have students use *counters* to show three groups of seven and then write the multiplication fact with its answer. Then have students take 21 other counters and "share" them among 7 sections of an *egg carton*. Have students write the division fact this shows and find the other facts that are related. Have them continue with more examples, making up stories to go with the "sharing." Students can work in pairs to make up problems and solutions to share with the rest of the class. They can exchange problems to solve.

Division 4

Skill: To divide a number by itself, divide by one, and divide zero

Time: 2 periods

Materials:

counters: 8 per student pair

paper plates: 1 per student

1 cm cubes

crayons

paper circle

See Reproducibles for: graph paper with 1 cm squares

Anticipatory Set

Use *counters*.

Have students work in pairs, and give each pair eight counters. Tell the students that each counter represents a birdhouse. Ask the students to separate the birdhouses into equal groups for hanging. They may choose as many groups (trees) as they want, as long as each tree has the same number of birdhouses.

After completing, discuss how they divided the groups. Have them state what division sentences you should write on the board.

Procedure 1

☐■

To develop the concept of dividing a number by itself

Use *counters* and *paper plates*.

Tell students that you want to hang an equal number of bird feeders on eight trees. Into how many groups would they divide the eight counters? (8)

How many counters would be in each group? (1)

Write $8 \div 8 = 1$, $8\overline{)8} = 1$.

Have students work in groups of four and divide their counters so that each has four.

Say: I have just enough paper plates for the whole class. How many is that? (e.g., 24)

Hand out the paper plates.

Say: I divided the plates among you evenly. How would I write that?

Students respond: $24 \div 24$, $24\overline{)24}$.

Ask: How many did you each get? (1) Write the answer on the board.

What could be a multiplication fact we made?

Students respond: $24 \times 1 = 24$, $1 \times 24 = 24$.

The counters now will be grapes. Have one person in the group take his or her four counters and divide them among all the students in the group. How many grapes does each of the four have? (1)

What facts have they discovered doing this activity? Do they see any patterns on the board?

Students do as instructed. They discuss that $4 \div 4 = 1$, $1 \times 4 = 4$, $4 \times 1 = 4$.

If students do not realize that a number divided by itself is one, tell them to keep in mind they are looking for a discovery. They may need to do more problems until they discover a general rule.

Continue to give students new sets of numbers in a story format. For example, 6 video games are available at the store, and 6 students want to buy them. How many games can each student buy? (1)

The manager decides to package the games as one set—6 to a set. How many sets can the manager make from the 6 games? (1)

Have students write the problems and solutions as they work them. What rule do they have to follow for today's activity? (a number needs to be divided by itself)

Procedure 2

☐■

To divide a number by itself; to divide by one; to use arrays

Use *1 cm cubes, graph paper with 1 cm squares,* and *crayons*.

Have students place six cubes on their paper. Demonstrate how to show $6 \div 6$:

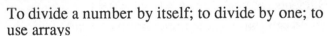

$$6 \div 6 = 1$$
$$1 \times 6 = 6$$

Students arrange their cubes into six rows.

Ask: How many are in each row? (1) Color the rectangle you have made on your graph paper, and write the fact beneath it. What multiplication fact do you find?

Students color rectangles and write: $6 \div 6 = 1$, $1 \times 6 = 6$.

What if you turned your rectangle so that it was lying down? ($6 \div 1 = 6$, $6 \times 1 = 6$)

Repeat with other numbers. Do students see a pattern? Can they state a rule about dividing a number by itself? About dividing by 1?

Procedure 3 □■

To divide zero

Use *paper plates, paper circle,* and *counters or cubes.*

Hold up a paper circle. Say: This represents a cookie. At my birthday party I planned to have enough cookies so that each of you would have one to eat. How many cookies did I have? (e.g., 24)

Unfortunately, the Cookie Monster came by before the party and ate *all* the cookies.

Put the circle away.

Ask: How many did I have to share? (none)

How many cookies would you each get to eat? (none) Write $0 \div 24 = 0$.

Zero cookies for 24 students is how many in all? (0) Write $0 \times 24 = 0$.

Continue with such extravagant ideas as: I *was* going to give each one of you $100 to spend. Unfortunately, the door to the delivery truck flew open, and all the money fell out. How much money did I have to share with all 24 of you? (none)

How much did each of you get when I divided no money? (none) Write $0 \div 24 = 0$.

What's a multiplication fact you could make?

Students respond: $0 \times 24 = 0$. $24 \times 0 = 0$.

Hand out paper plates and small objects.

Continue to make up stories for students to act out: You have 4 cars to share with your partner, but they are all broken. (Students put the four cubes aside.) I have no cars to put on two plates. ($0 \div 2 = 0$)

What can you tell me about dividing the number zero? Do you see any patterns?

Students discuss that dividing zero is trying to divide nothing. The answer has to be nothing. They make up their own stories to act out and write the equations they discover.

Practice and Extension

Have students use *interlocking cubes* or *geoboards* to show a number of division facts. Include other problems besides dividing a number by itself, dividing by one, and dividing zero.

Division 5

Skill: To use multiplication to check division

Time: 2+ periods

Materials:

geoboards and rubber bands: 1 set per group

interlocking cubes or counters: 24 per student pair

12-month calendars (not leap year): 1 per group if possible, if not—1 large teacher calendar

markers: 4 colors per group

file-folder or other place value (pv) mats to 100s or 1000s

pv materials to whatever place you wish

See Reproducibles for: directions for file-folder pv mats, pv mats to 100s—1 per student, division paper—2 sheets per student

Anticipatory Set

Use *geoboards and rubber bands.*

Have student groups enclose a 2 × 3 rectangle. What multiplication and division facts are shown by this figure?

Repeat, having students make shapes and record multiplication and division facts found. Share results with the class, discussing fact families.

Procedure 1

To develop the concept by checking division facts

Use *interlocking cubes or counters* and *paper.*

Have students work in pairs and draw a partial fence on their paper. Tell them to place 24 counters to show 24 cows in a field.

Say: A farmer has three barns and wants to divide these cows evenly so that each barn has the same number of cows. What kind of a math problem will this be? (division) Write 3)‾24 on the board.

Say: Put a three outside the fence. This number gives the directions. Put your 24 cows into three rows.

Ask: How many cows are in each row or barn? (8) Place the answer above the fence, as in a division problem.

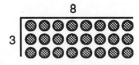

Say: The farmer wants to make sure all cows are taken care of. To check, he sees eight cows in each of three barns.

Ask: What kind of problem is this? (multiplication) Write 8 × 3 = 24 on the board. Ask: Do you notice anything about our two problems?

Students may see the numbers are the same but used differently; the starting and ending numbers are the same.

Relate this to fact families. Repeat the procedure until students understand that multiplication and division are related and can be used to check each other.

Procedure 2

To check division of 2-digit numbers by 1-digit numbers

Use *calendars, markers,* and *paper.*

Give each student group a calendar. *If using only one teacher calendar, adapt this to be a whole-class activity.* Ask: How many days are in a year?

Some students will know the correct number: 365.

How many months are those days divided into? (12)

Do all the months have the same number of days? (no) How many days does February have? (28)

How many days are in a week? (7) How can I find how many *weeks* are in February?

Students respond: Divide 28 days by 7.

Write 7)‾28 on the board. How could I check?

Students respond: Count on a calendar and add up the weeks. Multiply number of days by number of weeks.

How would I write this check the quickest way in math language? (4 × 7 = 28) Write this on the board.

So if a month had 28 days, it would have four weeks. Now look at March.

Students see that March has 31 days.

How do we find the number of weeks in March?

Students respond: Divide the 31 days by 7. Students use the calendar and see that the answer is not even.

Write 7)‾31 on the board.

Have students place a red dot on the first seven numbers, a blue dot on the second seven numbers, a green dot on the third seven numbers, and a black dot on the fourth seven numbers.

Say: We divided the 31 days by 7 and show 4 weeks. How can we check using math language?

Students respond: Multiply 4×7.

Write $4 \times 7 = 28$ on the board.

I've checked and find that March has 28 days. Is that right?

Students respond: No, it has 31; some days have no dots on them. We need to add the extra days that didn't divide into weeks.

Repeat with other months. Show the remainder when doing the division problem on the board.

After developing the concept, you can expand to as many digits as you desire. Emphasize to students that the process and procedures remain the same.

Procedure 3

To divide and write a multiplication check

Use *pv mats, pv materials,* and *division paper.*

Have students place two ten rods and six one cubes on their mats and write 26 on their division paper.

Say: I want to divide this into two groups.

Write $2\overline{)26}$ on the board.

Students write the problem on their division paper. They divide the two ten rods into two lines and then divide the one cubes. After each step with their materials, they write on paper what they did.

Ask: What is $2\overline{)26}$? (13) I want to be able to check that to make sure all the blocks are accounted for. What do your blocks show now? (2 groups of 13)

Write $2 \times 13 =$ on the board.

Did you use all the blocks (yes) So $2 \times 13 = 26$? (yes) Put your blocks together to check that you have what you started with.

Students do this and then write the multiplication check in the proper column on their paper.

I started with 26, divided it into two groups, and then multiplied back to check. What if I make a mistake?

Students respond: The numbers won't match.

Draw a smile line from the number you started with to the product you ended with:

Say: If I see you haven't really *looked* at the match, I will draw a line back. This turns your smile into a banana, which is something you don't want to see!

Repeat the procedure with other problems until students understand the concept.

Now introduce checking with remainders. Have students put two ten rods and seven one cubes on their mats. Write $2\overline{)27}$ on the board.

Students write the problem, divide blocks, and write a check. They notice the materials didn't divide evenly, so it doesn't check.

The reason we check is to make sure all the materials are accounted for. Not all the blocks could be put into the two groups. What could we do with the remainder blocks to get our starting number? (Add them back in.)

Demonstrate how to add the remainder by writing it in under the multiplication problem and adding.

Provide practice with both materials and written work until students understand the concept.

Have students do problems that have regrouping, as well as remainders, such as $3\overline{)47}$.

Practice and Extension

Have students make up word problems to solve with *bills* and to check with multiplication.

Have students use *cards* or *dice* and work in pairs. The first two or three numbers turned over are the dividend for both, the following two are separate divisors. Students do problems and check. The winner is the student with the larger quotient or remainder.

Give students remainders, and have them build problems to fit. What problems can't be built with a given remainder? (ones with a smaller divisor)

Division 6

Skill: To find missing dividends and divisors

Time: 2 periods

Materials:

Use several of the following (about 20 per student):
tiles

1" × 1" construction paper squares
1 cm cubes
counters
See Reproducibles for: bills—1s only

Anticipatory Set

Use *one of the manipulatives in the Materials list.*

Write $3\overline{)15}^{\,5}$. Review with students that this shows 15 divided into three groups with five in a group. Have students construct arrays that show this. Have them draw the division fence around their array and write the division sentence.

Repeat for 12 ÷ 2 and 16 ÷ 4.

Procedure 1

To find missing dividends

Use *one of the manipulatives in the Materials list.*

Write on the board: ? ÷ 2 = 6. Say: We don't know how many we started with, but what does the two mean?

Students respond: Something is divided into 2 groups, or we have groups of 2.

Ask: What does the six mean?

Students respond: The 6 means we have 6 in a group, or 6 groups of 2.

Have students build an array that shows two groups with six in a group.

Students do so and discover they have used 12 tiles:

⬤⬤⬤⬤⬤⬤   12 ÷ 2 = 6
⬤⬤⬤⬤⬤⬤

What if I had written the problem as $2\overline{)??}^{\,6}$? Would this have been easier to solve? (yes) Why?

Students respond: It looks more like what we are doing with tiles.

What does this suggest to you?

Students respond: Rewrite the problem.

Give students several more missing dividend problems. Each time, have them identify the meaning of each number, build the array, and write the complete division sentence as in the illustration above.

Ask them to be able to explain how they went about solving the problems.

Students solve problems.

What ways did you find to solve these problems? For example: ? ÷ 2 = 6.

Students respond: Some laid out groups of 6, some did groups of 2, some noticed they could multiply to find the answer.

Some of you laid out groups and added them. Do you know a shortcut way of adding same-sized groups? (multiplication)

Yes, you are multiplying the number of groups by the number in each group. Do we ever use multiplication in doing a regular division problem?

Students respond: Yes, when we multiply back to find out how many of our total we've been able to put into groups so far.

You could also solve this by thinking of multiples. How would that work?

Students respond: If you used multiples of 6, you find the second multiple of 6, since you have 2 groups.

Often a problem can be solved in many ways. Now try ? ÷ 3 = 13. Use either tiles or paper and pencil, and rewrite the problem first if you wish. That's a lot of tiles. Do you know a faster way?

Students arrive at an answer. They discuss multiplying to find the missing dividend.

Have students construct problems for others to solve. They should make up story problems to go along. For example: I started with a mystery amount of money. I spent it on 2 tapes, each costing $6. How much money did I start with?

Continue the procedure until students demonstrate an understanding of how to find missing dividends.

Procedure 2 □■

To find missing divisors

Use *another of the manipulatives from the Materials list.*

Write on the board 12 ÷ ? = 6. What does the 12 mean?

Students respond: How much we start with.

Ask: What does the question mark stand for?

Students respond: How many groups 12 is divided into, or the size group we'll take out.

What does the six mean?

Students respond: 6 are in each group, or we have 6 groups.

Say: Use 12 tiles to build an array that has 6 in a group. Find how many groups you have.

Students do this. They have two groups.

What if I had written ?)¯1̄2̄ (with 6 above)? Would this have been easier to solve? (yes) Why?

Students respond: It looks more like what we are doing with tiles on the paper. We could rewrite the problem.

Give students several more missing divisor problems. Each time, have them identify the meaning of each number, build the array, and write the complete division sentence, as in the Procedure 1 illustration.

Ask them to be able to explain how they went about solving the problems.

Students solve the problems.

What ways did you find to solve these problems? For example: 12 ÷ ? = 6.

Students respond: Some laid out groups of 6 until they had used up 12 tiles. Some recognized it as a division problem, dividing 12 by 6. Some recognized that they could think of multiples of 6 until they reached 12, a multiplication problem.

Have students build a 6 × 2 array. This shows 12 ÷ 2 = 6. Have them turn their array around. What does this show?

$$6)\overline{12}$$

$$2)\overline{12}$$

What is the total in each case? (12) In one we have groups of six, and in one we have groups of two.

Discuss the relationship of multiplication and division and that a problem often may be solved in many ways.

Give students more difficult problems, and have them use either tiles or paper and pencil. They should rewrite the problem first.

Add estimation questions at this time, such as: What number would be too big? Too small? What two numbers will the answer come between?

Students now construct problems for others to solve. They make up story problems to go along. For example: I started with 18 buttons. I need to sew 6 on each shirt. How many shirts can I put buttons on?

Continue the procedure until students are able to explain the process of how to find missing divisors.

Practice and Extension

Have students take handfuls of *tiles* and construct problems. Have students discuss how to handle remainders.

Have students write division problems and work in pairs to play Missing Numbers. They throw a *die* or use a *two-colored counter:* An even number or a certain color means they cover the *divisor* with a *counter.* An odd number or the other color means they cover the *dividend.* They switch problems and solve them, keeping a total of the missing numbers found. The lowest score at the end of five rounds wins.

Division 7

Skill: To divide 2-digit numbers by 1-digit numbers

Time: 1 week

Materials:

counters: 27 per group

file-folder or other place value (pv) mats to 100s or 1000s

pv materials to 10s

dice: 1 per student pair

See Reproducibles for: directions for file-folder pv mats, pv mats to 100s—1 per group, division paper—4 sheets per student, bills to 10s—run off in different colors

Note: If students are not used to dividing with base ten materials on a place value mat, do Division 2, Procedures 3 and 4. This will reinforce basic division concepts and provide a concrete base for the written division algorithm.

The written format in Procedures 3 to 5 is a change from the standard form. No "bring down" is used because nothing is brought down when dividing objects. DMSB—divide, multiply, subtract, and bring down, becomes DMSR—divide, multiply, subtract, and regroup. Send a note home to parents, explaining that this way of writing the problems more accurately reflects division. Otherwise, you will soon find out who is getting help at home.

Anticipatory Set

Use *counters* and *paper.*

Say to student groups: Imagine that 3 students have up to 27 marbles (counters) between them. Write as many problems and solutions as you can using those facts.

After 5 to 10 minutes, discuss results.

Tens
$2 \div 2 = 1$
$1 \times 2 = 2$

Ones
$4 \div 2 = 2$
$2 \times 2 = 4$

2a   **2b**

Procedure 1

To establish the concept of dividing 2-digit by 1-digit numbers

Use *pv mats, pv materials to 10s,* and *dice.*

Say: Today we'll be dividing yo-yos, which come ten to a package. Your ten rods will be one package. One cubes will be separate yo-yos. You have 24 yo-yos. Show that with blocks on your mats.

On the board write the problem as in Illustration 1b.

1a   **1b**

We'll give the yo-yos evenly to two friends.

Write the two and the division fence on the board as in Illustration 2b. Say: Divide yours into two groups.

Students divide rods and cubes as in Illustration 2a.

Ask: How many groups of tens did you make? (2) How many whole packages are in each group? (1) Where can I record that?

Students respond: Above, in the tens column.

Yes, if you divide tens, your answer is in tens.

Draw in the divided rods and the 1 on the board.

What division fact did you show? (2 ÷ 2 = 1) Write this on the board.

How can we check that our division is right? (with multiplication: $1 \times 2 = 2$)

How many groups of ones, or single yo-yos, did you make? (2) How many yo-yos are in each group? (2) Where can I record that?

Students respond: Above, in the ones column.

Yes, if you divide ones, your answer is in ones. Write the one cubes and the 2 on the board.

What division fact did you show? (4 ÷ 2 = 2)

Write this on the board.

Ask: How can we check? (with multiplication: $2 \times 2 = 4$)

How many yo-yos in all does each friend get?

Students respond: One ten and two ones equals 12 yo-yos.

How could I check the whole problem? (with multiplication)

Write and solve 2 × 12 on the board.

Repeat with other 2-digit numbers *with and without regrouping*, recording only the results on the board after each step.

When students are comfortable with making divisions and trades, have them write results. In pairs, one should do problems with blocks, and one should record each step as in Illustration 2b. Work through several problems with students before having them work on their own.

Students need much practice at this stage of both writing and using concrete materials. They should check all results with multiplication. See Division 5 for checking division with multiplication.

Use dice to generate problems: The first two numbers are the dividend, and the third is the divisor. Discuss what to do with remainders.

Repeat the procedure with different materials.

Procedure 2

To develop a written algorithm; no regrouping

Use *pv materials* and *pv mats*.

Write 36 ÷ 3 on the board in a place value format.

Tell students that 36 bats go evenly into 3 caves. This time when we divide, we will record *all* steps.

Students place three ten rods and six one cubes at the bottom of their mats.

We'll make a chart that will help us when we don't have blocks. Every time we take out enough to put one more bat into *each* cave, how many have we taken out? (3)

The second time, how many total bats are now taken care of? (6) Another time? (9) We're talking about multiples of three. Make a chart:

Number of Groups Out	Bats Divided
1	3
2	6
3	9

We'll start by dividing the ten rods into three groups. Look at the chart of multiples, and predict how many groups of three ten rods we'll be able to take care of.

Students predict 1 group of 3. They divide their rods.

Ask: How many ten rods are in each cave? (1) How many bats so far in each? (10) Where will I write that?

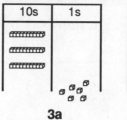

3a   3b

Students respond: Above, in the tens column.

Yes, if you divide tens, you end up with tens. One is in each cave. 3 ÷ 3 = 1. How could I check that? (with multiplication) Yes, I multiply back 1 × 3 = 3 to check that I divided right and to see how many bats I've taken care of.

How do I see on paper whether any tens are left? (subtract those taken out) I'll write it this way (Illustration 3b)—no groups of 10 bats are left.

I wrote exactly what you did to find no more ten rods. Written numbers just show what would be happening if we used blocks all the time.

Now what bats do you have to divide?

Students respond: 6 in the ones column.

Do you see anything on your multiples chart that would help you predict the answer?

Students respond: 2 groups of 3 bats take care of all 6 bats. They divide the one cubes. (Illustration 4a)

4a   4b

Where do I write this? (Above the ones. If we divide ones we get ones.)

How do I check that no bats are left? (multiply) I multiply 2 bats in each cave times 3 caves and find I've taken care of 6 more bats. (Illustration 4b)

How do I see whether any are left? (subtract)

Look at the bat piles. How many total bats do you show in each cave? (12) What have we written at the top of our problem? (12)

Let's check the whole problem. How many caves? (3) How many bats in each cave? (12)

Write 3 × 12 on the board, and have students solve it with you.

Say: Check that the answer equals the number you started with.

Repeat with other problems. Emphasize that you are writing just what they do with the blocks.

Students work in pairs. One works with the blocks, and a partner records each step as in Illustration 4b. They make multiples charts and try to predict the answer to each problem before using the blocks.

Students need much practice at this stage of both using the blocks and writing the process. With practice, they should be able to do the problem first on paper and then check with blocks.

Procedure 3

□■

To divide 2-digit by 1-digit numbers with regrouping; 2-digit quotients

Use *pv mats, division paper,* and *pv materials or bills.*

When we divide 2-digit numbers, sometimes we have to regroup. We're going to figure out how to write this down so that our written problem shows exactly what we do when we divide.

We'll start with 47 socks that we want to put into 3 boxes. They come in packages of 10, and we have 7 extra.

Write 47 ÷ 3 on the board.

Students place blocks for 47 on their mats.

Ask: How should we start? (make a multiples chart)

Number of Groups Out	Socks Divided
1	3
2	6
3	9
4	12

You want to divide four packages of socks. Would anything on your multiples chart help you predict the answer? (1 × 3 = 3)

But we have *four* packages of 10 socks.

Students explain the one package left is not enough to divide evenly. They divide and find one package for each box, with one left over. (Illustration 5b)

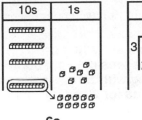

5a   5b

How do I write this? (put a 1 in the tens column) How do I check how many socks are in boxes?

Students respond: Multiply 1 package times 3 boxes.

How can I tell how many are left over? (subtract) I show one left over. That's exactly what you have with your blocks.

What can you do about the leftover package?

Students respond: Trade it for 10 single socks. They do this and find they have 17 ones. (Illustration 6a)

I need to show the regrouping in my problem. How many tens do you have left? (none) I'll cross out the one leftover ten.

Do I still have seven ones? (no) I'll cross that out and write what we have now, 17. (Illustration 6b)

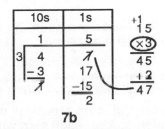

6a   6b

Now divide 17 into three groups. Check the multiples chart, and make a prediction.

Students respond: $5 \times 3 = 15$, some will be left over.

Why can't I use 6×3?

Students respond: That would take 18, and you don't have 18 socks. They divide the blocks and discover there are 5 socks in each box, with 2 left over.

7a   7b

Where will I write the five single socks in each box? (in the ones column) How do I check? (multiply) Finish the problem on the board. (Illustration 7b)

What is left to do? (check the whole problem) Multiply with students: 15 socks in 3 boxes is 45 socks. Is that what we started with?

Students respond: No, 2 were left over. Add those to the socks we did put in boxes.

Repeat with other problems. If the tens digit is only one or two more than the divisor, students will not have to exchange more than two ten rods.

When students are comfortable with the skill, have them begin writing each step on division paper as you write on the board.

When they can write each step accurately, student pairs make multiples charts and try to predict the answer to each step. One student works with the blocks, while the other records each step.

Students need much practice at this stage of both using the blocks and writing the process.

Procedure 4

To divide 2-digit by 1-digit numbers with regrouping; 1-digit quotients

Use *pv mats, division paper,* and *pv materials or bills.*

Write 27 ÷ 3 on the board. Have students place materials and develop a chart of multiples. Now tell students to start by dividing the tens.

Students respond: We don't have enough tens to put into three groups.

Say: You show no tens as having been divided. I could put a zero in the tens column, but we don't write numbers starting with zero. What's the next step? (regroup the tens for 20 ones)

Follow the previous procedure to finish the problem. Remind students that when we divide ones, we get ones and need to put the answer in the *ones* column:

10s	1s		10s	1s
				9
3 ⟍2	⟍7		3 ⟍2	⟍7
	27			27
				−27
				0

What if I put the nine in the *tens* column. What would the nine be worth? (90)

That would mean I divided 27 into 3 groups and got 90 in each group. That would be wonderful if I were dividing money, but it's just not possible.

Do several more problems of this type with students. After each step with the blocks, have them write on their division paper as you work on the board.

When students feel comfortable with the skill, they do each step first on paper and then check with the materials.

Procedure 5

To divide with zeros in the quotient

Use *pv mats, division paper,* and *pv materials or bills.*

Place 30 ÷ 3 on the board, and have students place blocks. Have students make a chart of multiples and divide their ten rods. Record this on the board.

Say: We have zero ones. What's zero divided into three groups? (zero) If I leave the ones column blank and say my answer is 1, what's the problem?

Students respond: We have 1 ten, not just 1.

We need zero as a placeholder. How many blocks total do you show in each group? (10) I have to show the same thing in my answer.

10s	1s
1	0
3 ⎜ 3	0
−3	−0
0	0

Repeat with other problems. Students write on division paper after each step, as you work on the board. When they feel comfortable with the process, have them do each step first on paper and then check with the manipulatives.

Practice and Extension

Use any of the following materials: *two-colored counters, different-colored counters, chip-trading materials, interlocking cubes, bundled craft sticks,* or *bills.* Use *cards* or *dice* to generate numbers for division problems. Students can work in teams, one using the manipulative and one writing on paper.

Play Money Madness. Divide the class into two teams. Have them use *$90 in bills* and *pv mats.* Use *cards* or *dice* to generate divisors. In turn, teams are given a divisor and must divide their money and then write the problem on paper. Remainders are discarded. The team whose money lasts longer is the winner.

Explore problem solving with remainders. Example: Mae needed 13 feet of string, which came 6 feet to a package. How many packages did she need? By having students use manipulatives or draw pictures, it becomes clear that Mae will need to buy an extra package.

Write two identical division problems such as $2\overline{)\underline{}}$ on the board. You will play against the class. Use *cards* or *spinners* to get numbers to fill in. Remainders are allowed.

Other types of problems are $\underline{}\overline{)25}$.

Ask such questions as, If I divide by six, how many numbers will end up with a remainder of one?

Fractions 1

Skill: To understand halves, thirds, and fourths

Time: 3 periods per fraction

Materials:

interlocking cubes in 3 colors: 8 of each color per student

graph paper to match cube size

markers or crayons to match cube colors

scissors

paste

paper squares 4" × 4" and 6" × 6": 1 of each size per student

geoboards and rubber bands

See Reproducibles for: geoboard paper—several sheets per student

Anticipatory Set

Discuss sharing among two friends. How would we divide marbles, cookies, etc., into fair parts?

Procedure 1

To understand equal parts

Use interlocking cubes, graph paper, markers, scissors, and *paste.*

Have students make a one-color stick six cubes long. Next have them make a stick with three cubes of the second color and three cubes of the third color.

Students make the sticks compare to make sure they are the same length.

Now have students separate their two-color stick in half.

Say. When we divide something into same-size parts, we say those parts are equal in size. Are your parts equal?

Students compare halves.

If we have *two* equal parts, we call each part a half.

Write ¹/₂ on the board.

Students hold up first one half then the other.

Ask: Will your halves fit together to make a whole?

Students put the halves together. They compare their two-color stick with the one-color stick to see that the size of the whole has not changed.

Repeat with other lengths of sticks.

Students color the correct numbers of squares on graph paper, cut out, compare, and paste them together on another sheet labeled "¹/₂s."

Now have students make a two-color stick of unequal numbers of cube colors. Have them separate the sticks and compare.

Ask: Why aren't these halves?

Students respond: They aren't the same size; they aren't equal.

Have students color the matching squares on graph paper, cut them out, and paste on a sheet labeled "Not ¹/₂s."

Students work together to make sticks of various lengths, half of one color and half of another. They break the sticks apart, compare lengths, and then color these on graph paper as before.

Discuss that not all the lengths can be divided into halves. What could they do about this?

Can they make sticks with three or four equal parts? Repeat the procedure using sticks of different starting lengths.

Procedure 2

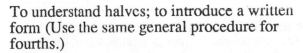

To understand halves; to introduce a written form (Use the same general procedure for fourths.)

Use *paper squares, graph paper,* and *scissors.*

Have students take squares. Explain that each one is a whole square. Write 1 on the board. Have students fold a square in half and cut on the fold. How many same-size parts of the square do you have now? (2)

Say: Each of these rectangles is called one of the two equal parts of our whole. Each one of two parts is called a half. Write ¹/₂ on the board.

Students put the parts together.

Ask: What do you have? (1 whole) Write ²/₂ = 1 on the board. Explain that two of two equal parts makes one whole.

Hold up a square that is cut into two unequal parts. Say: We can't call these parts halves. Why not?

Students respond: They aren't the same size.

Have students put one half away, keeping the other half for a new whole.

Students fold and cut to make two new halves.

Ask: What did you start with? (a whole) What do you have now? (2 halves)

Students put these together again to make one whole.

Write $2/2 = 1$; two halves equals one whole. Say: When we divide something into two same-sized or equal parts, each part is called a half.

Students repeat the procedure with the other size of paper.

Emphasize starting with a whole, dividing into two equal parts, and calling these parts halves. Explain that we write $1/2$ to show one of two parts; two of two parts equals the whole.

Repeat the procedure for fourths. Make sure students refer to one of four equal parts as equal to one fourth.

Have students outline six rectangles on graph paper and cut them out. Have them fold three in half, mark the fold line, and label $1/2$ on the back of each part.

Students fold the other three into *unequal* parts, mark the fold and label the back of each part "Not $1/2$." They switch rectangles with a partner and try to identify which are divided into halves.

Procedure 3

To relate the size of the whole to the size of the fraction; to understand that not all halves are equal (Use the same procedure for thirds and fourths.)

Use *plain paper*.

Have four students stand at the front of the room. Call them one whole group. Divide them into two equal groups.

Ask: How many parts in our whole group? (2) What can we call one part? (one of two equal parts, or $1/2$) What can we call the other part?

Write $1/2$ on two pieces of paper. Give each group one of the pieces of paper to hold up.

Have six more students stand in a separate group at the front. Ask: How can we divide this new group into two equal parts?

Students respond: 3 students in each group. They move into two groups and hold up two more $1/2$ signs.

How many parts of the group do we have? (2) What can we call each of these parts? ($1/2$ or halves)

Point to the original halves and then to the new halves. Ask: Why aren't these the same size if we can call them each halves?

Students respond: One of the wholes was bigger.

Have students go back to their original groups. Ask: How could they be divided so that we *couldn't* call the parts halves?

Give students much practice, and have students make up story problems to go with the parts: What part of the students in this group are girls?

These students wanted to go to the store; what part of the whole group are they? What part of the whole didn't go to the store?

Procedure 4

To practice using halves, thirds, and fourths (Use the same general procedure for all three.)

Use *geoboards, rubber bands, geoboard paper*, and *scissors*.

Have students fit bands around three pegs across and three down.

Say: This is our whole we start with. Can you use two more bands to divide this whole into halves?

Students fit bands to make two equal rectangles.

Ask: How many equal parts do you have now? (2) What do we call each part? ($1/2$) What do the two halves together make? (a whole)

Have students see how many ways they can divide the geoboard into two equal halves.

Students divide a geoboard and copy on geoboard paper. They cut out parts to see whether they are equal. Then they chart and label all successful attempts on a separate sheet of geoboard paper.

Have students experiment to find shapes that can be divided into halves. Then have them copy, cut, check, chart, and label successful attempts as before.

Repeat for other fractions as desired.

Practice and Extension

Students draw pictures of things they can divide into halves, thirds or fourths, and then circle each fractional part. Emphasize that all fractional parts must be of equal size.

Use *colored tiles* or *cubes*. Have students make squares or rectangles that are half blue and half red. Repeat with other numbers or tiles and other fractions.

Use *pattern blocks*. Have students make symmetrical designs that are half one color, half another.

Use *objects* such as beans. Have students divide them into equal parts. Do all numbers of beans divide into halves? Have students color those numbers that do divide evenly on a *hundred board*. Have students look for patterns.

Fractions 2

Skill: To understand and write fractions

Time: 1 period per procedure

Materials:

construction paper cut into 3" × 18" strips—red, blue, orange, green, yellow: 1 of each color per student

scissors

business-size envelopes for storing completed fraction sets: 1 per student

counters in 4 colors: several of each per student

small paper bags: 1 per group

objects: cubes, beans, counters, etc.; 12 per student

pattern blocks

See Reproducibles for: bills to 100s—in different colors

Anticipatory Set

Use *construction paper strips, scissors,* and *envelopes.*

Make paper fraction bars for whatever fractions you wish; the red piece is left as the whole unit. Have students fold the blue strip in half and cut on the fold to make two halves.

The orange strip makes fourths: first fold and cut into halves; then fold and cut each half to make fourths. Continue in the same way, making the green strip into eighths and the yellow into sixteenths.

Discuss relationships as students fold. Have them label each piece and store them in a business-size envelope, folding the red strip to fit.

Save for Procedure 3 and for many future lessons.

Procedure 1

To identify fractions

Have six students stand at the front of the room. Write the headings "Boys" and "Girls" on the board.

Ask: How many are girls? (2) Two out of the group of six are girls. Write $^2/_6$ under Girls. We say this as two sixths.

Repeat for boys: $^4/_6$.

Write $^2/_6 + ^4/_6 = ^6/_6 = 1$ as you explain: two of the six are girls, and four of the six are boys. Together they make all six of the group of six, one whole group.

Repeat with other groups until the class can dictate what you write.

Now use the class as a whole. Choose categories that will not overlap, such as hair color, eye color, ice-cream flavor preferences.

Ask: If you were ordering ice cream for a store, how would knowledge be useful?

Chart each set of results, and have the class dictate the appropriate fractions.

Procedure 2

To identify and write fractions

Use *counters* and *bags.*

Write headings on the board for each of the counter colors. Put a handful of mixed counters into a bag.

Have a student tally each counter under the appropriate heading as you draw them out of the bag:

Blue	Red	Yellow	Green	All
3	3	4	2	12

Three of the 12 are blue. What fraction is blue? ($^3/_{12}$) Write this under Blue. Repeat for the other colors.

Write plus signs between colors: 3 of the 12 are blue, + 3 of the 12 are red, and so on.

We've counted all 12 of 12 and have one whole bagful: $^3/_{12} + ^3/_{12} + ^4/_{12} + ^2/_{12} = ^{12}/_{12} = 1$

Repeat until students understand the process. *Make sure you include some times when not all colors are represented.*

Students repeat the process in their groups. They each place a secret number of counters in the bag. One student tallies as they take turns drawing out the counters and putting them in color groups. Students agree on the total and appropriate fractions and equation to be written down.

Procedure 3

To write different fractions of a whole

Use *construction paper fraction bars from Anticipatory Set.*

Have students lay their red whole at the top of their desk. Have them find the color that has only two pieces and make a bar below the red one.

Students make a blue bar.

Continue until all bars are laid out. Ask: What do you notice about your bars?

1

$\frac{1}{2}$	$\frac{1}{2}$

$\frac{1}{4}$	$\frac{1}{4}$	$\frac{1}{4}$	$\frac{1}{4}$

$\frac{1}{8}$	$\frac{1}{8}$	$\frac{1}{8}$	$\frac{1}{8}$	$\frac{1}{8}$	$\frac{1}{8}$	$\frac{1}{8}$	$\frac{1}{8}$

$\frac{1}{16}$	$\frac{1}{16}$	$\frac{1}{16}$	$\frac{1}{16}$	$\frac{1}{16}$	$\frac{1}{16}$	$\frac{1}{16}$	$\frac{1}{16}$	$\frac{1}{16}$	$\frac{1}{16}$	$\frac{1}{16}$	$\frac{1}{16}$	$\frac{1}{16}$	$\frac{1}{16}$	$\frac{1}{16}$	$\frac{1}{16}$

Students respond: All the same-color bars together make the same size as the red one. All the same-color pieces are the same size.

Look at the halves. The denominator shows how many equal parts in the whole. How do we write one of these two parts? ($\frac{1}{2}$) How about two of these two parts? ($\frac{2}{2}$) The numerator shows how many of the equal parts we have.

Have students pick up one, two, three, then four fourths. Write $\frac{1}{4}$, $\frac{2}{4}$, $\frac{3}{4}$, $\frac{4}{4}$. How many fractions can be made with fourths? (4)

Students should make a list of fractions, beginning with $\frac{1}{1}$ on the first line, and $\frac{1}{2}$, $\frac{2}{2}$ on the second. They continue to explore possible fractions from each color bar, looking for possible patterns.

Ask: What patterns do you see?

Answers might include: All bars are equal to a whole, the numerators increase until they equal the denominator, the number of fractions possible equals the number of parts. Students may notice that some fractions are equivalent to others.

What fraction of the whole bar is three green pieces? ($\frac{3}{8}$) Five yellow pieces? ($\frac{5}{16}$)

Continue practicing in this way. Have students write their answers when they feel comfortable identifying the fractional parts.

Procedure 4

To identify different fractions of a group of objects

Use *objects*.

Have each student make a group of 12 objects. This will be the whole group. Have them make 2 groups of 6.

Ask: How many parts do we have now? (2) Write $\frac{1}{2}$ on the board. Are they equal in size? (yes)

Pull one of the groups toward you. What fraction name can we call this part? ($\frac{1}{2}$) Add the ^{1} to the $\frac{}{2}$ on the board.

Put the objects together into 1 group again. Now divide them into 3 equal groups.

Students divide the objects into 3 groups with 4 in each group. They identify each as a third or $\frac{1}{3}$ of 12. Next they name the possible fractions ($\frac{2}{3}$, $\frac{3}{3}$) as they pull the groups toward them.

Ask: What other fractions are possible with 12 objects? Are some not possible? Why?

Students explore the possibilities and write them down. They should realize that only factors of 12 can be fractional parts of 12.

Repeat with other numbers of objects. Make a large chart for the class results.

Procedure 5

To write fractions of a whole, using fractions equal to 1, 0

Use *pattern blocks* and *paper*.

Say: A yellow hexagon is one whole. Cover one yellow hexagon with red trapezoids. How many does it take? (2)

Students trace around a hexagon on their papers, divide it into two trapezoids and write $\frac{1}{2}$ on each part.

Hold up two trapezoids. Ask: How many of the two equal parts do I have? (2) If we have both equal parts, we can write the two halves as $\frac{2}{2}$.

What do you notice about having both of the trapezoids?

Students answer: They are the same as one hexagon.

We can write $\frac{2}{2} = 1$ to show that both of two equal parts is the same as the whole.

Say: Now take the hexagon and cover it with green triangles.

Students cover the hexagon with six triangles and draw this on their paper.

How many equal parts do the triangles make? (6) We can call each part a sixth and write one part of six as $\frac{1}{6}$.

Students write $\frac{1}{6}$ on each triangle.

Hold up two triangles. How many of the six equal parts do I have? (2) How could I write this as a fraction? ($\frac{2}{6}$) Continue asking about increasing numbers of triangles until reaching $\frac{6}{6} = 1$.

Now hold up *nothing*. How many sixths do I have? (none) How could I write this? ($\frac{0}{6}$)

Students trace the outline of a hexagon. They can mark it with a large × to show no parts and then label it ⁰/₆.

Repeat with other colors until students are comfortable with all possibilities. Have them use same-color blocks to make a chart to show all fractions possible with the blocks. Start each new color with the hexagon outline to represent zero parts of the fraction being explored:

Students continue with their chart and designs to show a variety of fractional parts.

Have students look for patterns. They should see that more parts mean more fractions, all of the parts together equal one whole, and zero parts equal zero no matter what the denominator.

Procedure 6

To find a fraction of a number

Use *objects* and *bills*.

Have students make a row of 12 objects and find ¹/₄ of them:

Ask: If one of the fourths is three objects, how many objects are two of the fourths?

Students find ²/₄ of 12 is 6.

Have students find ³/₄, ¹/₃, ²/₃, ³/₃, and so on, of the row of 12. Emphasize first dividing the 12 into the equal parts called for.

Repeat the procedure with rows of various sizes.

Have each student take $100, which will be shopping money.

Say: New socks will cost ¹/₁₀ of your money. How much will that be? What do I need to do first?

Students respond: Divide the money into 10 groups by exchanging the $100 for 10 $10s. They make the exchange and find ¹/₁₀ of $100 = $10.

You have $90 left. New tapes will cost ²/₉ of that. How much is that?

Students divide their money into 9 groups, add 2 groups together, and find ²/₉ of $90 is $20.

Students work in pairs, using all their bills to create, solve, and write down problems.

Practice and Extension

Have students use *graph paper* and *markers*. Groups decide on categories. They outline a row as long as the number in the class and color in appropriate amounts, for example, ³/₂₅ live in brick buildings, ⁴/₂₅ live in wood buildings, and so on. They label the fractions.

Label *blank dice* with fraction amounts. Students use *fraction bars*. They throw a die and put out that amount. They add additional amounts each turn. If they can trade, for example, ¹/₄ for ²/₈, they do so to get the least number of pieces. The winner is the first to make a whole exactly.

Have students use *markers* or *crayons* and draw six identical pictures of trees, clowns, etc. They draw fruit on the trees or buttons on the clown suits, and then chart fractions: ²/₆ have 2 buttons, ⁴/₆ have 3 buttons; ³/₆ of the trees have red fruit, ¹/₆ of the trees have blue fruit, ²/₆ have green fruit.

Ask students to use a *multiplication chart* to figure out what fractional parts are possible for any number.

Have students bring in *advertisements* for items they are interested in purchasing. Allow them a certain amount of *money,* and have them identify the fractional amount of their money it would take to buy items.

Example: You have $50, and you may spend half of it. If you buy books for $15, how much will you have left? Student use *bills* to solve the problem, writing down each step on *paper*.

Use fractional amounts in daily directions, for example, ¹/₅ of each row, ³/₄ of the boys, ¹/₄ of 12 crayons, and so on.

Fractions 3

Skill: To compare fractions

Time: 3 periods

Materials:

interlocking cubes: 2 colors

graph paper: ½" or larger squares

markers

geoboards and rubber bands

scissors

objects: buttons, beans, counters; 20 per student

See Reproducibles for: geoboard paper, equivalency charts

Anticipatory Set

Use *interlocking cubes* or *graph paper and markers.*

Have students use interlocking cubes or graph paper to show various fraction amounts; e.g., $^3/_4$, $^5/_{12}$. Have them make up fraction word problems to go with the models. For example: Four foxes went hunting, and 3 went home. What fraction of the foxes went home?

Procedure 1

To compare fractions with like denominators; same-size whole

Use *interlocking cubes, graph paper,* and *markers.*

Have each group make a stick of six cubes all the same color. Then have each student use graph paper to outline a horizontal row one square high and six squares wide, as in the illustration. Explain that this is the size of our whole stick.

Ask students to make another stick with five cubes of the original color and one of a different color. What fractional part of our whole is the *different-colored* cube?

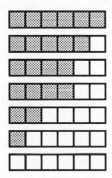

Students respond: $^1/_6$. They color this on their graph paper.

Have students make sticks of two colors to show all possible the fractional parts of the whole.

Ask: What do you notice? Are there any patterns to these fractions? Have students write the fractions.

Students show and write $^0/_6$, $^1/_6$, $^2/_6$, $^3/_6$, $^4/_6$, $^5/_6$, and $^6/_6$.

They may notice the colors make a steplike pattern when lined up and that the numerators increase by one.

What fraction is more of the bar, $^1/_6$ or $^5/_6$?

Students respond: $^5/_6$.

We can say that $^5/_6$ is bigger than $^1/_6$ because it is more of our whole. We can show this: $^5/_6 > ^1/_6$.

Ask: Can you find another pair of fractions with our sixths in which one fraction is larger than another?

How could we make an organized chart that shows which fractions are larger than others?

Students decide as groups how to chart all possible combinations of larger and smaller fractions.

Help students see that organizing their chart makes it easier to read. Example: Start with $^1/_6 > ^0/_6$, and then move on to the $^2/_6$ relationships.

$$\frac{1}{6} > \frac{0}{6}$$

$$\frac{2}{6} > \frac{1}{6} > \frac{0}{6}$$

$$\frac{3}{6} > \frac{2}{6} > \frac{1}{6} > \frac{0}{6}$$

$$\frac{4}{6} > \frac{3}{6} > \frac{2}{6} > \frac{1}{6} > \frac{0}{6}$$

$$\frac{5}{6} > \frac{4}{6} > \frac{3}{6} > \frac{2}{6} > \frac{1}{6} > \frac{0}{6}$$

$$\frac{6}{6} > \frac{5}{6} > \frac{4}{6} > \frac{3}{6} > \frac{2}{6} > \frac{1}{6} > \frac{0}{6}$$

What rule can you find about comparing fraction sizes?

Students respond: Fractions with the same denominators can be compared by comparing their numerators.

Repeat the procedure, using different numbers of cubes in the whole. Have each group choose a different-size whole, make all possible fractions, and chart all possible combinations of larger and smaller fractions. Make a class chart from the group charts. Do they see any patterns?

Procedure 2 ■

To compare fractions with like denominators;
different-size wholes

Use *geoboards*, *rubber bands*, *geoboard paper*,
markers, and *scissors*.

**Have students make a rectangle two squares
wide and two squares long and then divide it into
halves with a rubber band around each half. Ask:
How many squares is the whole we started with?
(4) How many squares is each half? (2)**

Students next make a rectangle two squares by four
squares and divide it into halves.

**Ask: How many squares is our whole now? (8)
How many squares is each half? (4) Which is
bigger?**

Students respond: The half of the larger rectangle.

**Say: You compared fractions using interlocking
cubes and discovered you could put them in
order by their numerators. Can I write 1/2 >1/2 for
our geoboard halves? Why isn't this right?**

Students respond: The numerators are equal, so one
shouldn't be larger than another.

**Can I add any information to make 1/2 > 1/2
possible and to show what's happening with the
rectangles?**

Students discuss. They should realize that they need
to consider the size of the whole. This is shown on
the geoboards: ¹/₂ of 8 > ¹/₂ of 4.

**Have students repeat, dividing the rectangles into
fourths.**

**Emphasize that students need to know the size of
the whole, as well as the size of the fraction,
before they can compare them. Can they think of
any real-life situations in which this might be
important?**

Students find different ways to show ¹/₂, ¹/₃, ¹/₄, etc.
They color and label all combinations on geoboard
paper, cut them out, and make a class chart.

Procedure 3 ■

To compare fractions with unlike denominators

Use *objects* and *equivalency charts*.

**Remind students that in order to compare frac-
tions they need to know the size of the fraction
and the size of the whole.**

**Ask: Which fraction is bigger, ³/₅ or ²/₄? What is
our problem?**

Students respond: The size of the whole is not the
same. The denominators are not the same.

**Give students 40 buttons or beans. Have stu-
dents put them into two groups of 20 each. Ask:
How do we show ³/₅ of the first 20 beans?**

Students divide the beans into fifths and separate
three of the fifths.

Now show ²/₄ of the second group of 20 beans.

Students divide the beans into four groups and
separate two of the fourths.

**How many beans are in ³/₅ of 20? (12) How many
are in ²/₄ of 20? (10)**

**Which is the bigger fraction, ³/₅ or ²/₄? (³/₅) What
did we have to do to compare two fractions with
different denominators?**

Students respond: Make them fractions of the same-
size whole.

**Repeat with other fractions and other-size
wholes, such as ⁵/₆ of 12 aliens had green hair,
and ³/₄ had purple. Which was the more common
color? Use also ³/₈ and ²/₄ (of 8 or 16).**

**Hand out equivalency charts. Point out that the
size of the whole is the same for all fractions on
the chart.**

**Have students start at the left and find the space
taken up by various fraction amounts. They may
use a pencil or ruler lined up top to bottom to find
equivalent fractions.**

Students use the chart to compare. They write the
fractions using < or > to show relationships.

Practice and Extension

Have students use *fraction bars* or *circles cut into
fractions* to compare fractions. Students can check on
an *equivalence chart*.

Write fractions on *wooden cubes* to make fraction
dice. Have students each throw die. The largest
fraction is worth 1 point.

Have students make up fraction questions about the
class; e.g., what fraction is larger, the fraction of
students with brown hair or the fraction of students
with blond hair?

Fractions 4

Skill: To find equivalent fractions

Time: 3 periods

Materials:

fraction bars (directions in Manipulative Information section) or Cuisenaire® rods

pattern blocks

objects: buttons, beans, counters; 48 per student pair

flat toothpicks: 15 per student pair

graph paper: ½" squares

thin, dark markers

See Reproducibles for: equivalency charts

Anticipatory Set

Have students make paper fraction bars, or use Procedure 1 as an Anticipatory Set.

Procedure 1

To learn the concept of *equivalence*

Use *fraction bars or Cuisenaire® rods* and *pattern blocks*.

Have students lay their whole fraction bar at the top of their desk. Below that have them lay the halves, etc. Review that the denominator is the number of equal groups in the whole and that the numerator is the number of those groups we have.

Have students pick up a ½ bar and see whether it is the same size as some other fractions.

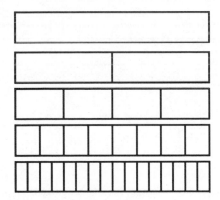

Students discover ½ = ²/₄ = ⁴/₈ = ⁸/₁₆. They write these relationships.

Explain that these are equal-sized, or equivalent, fractions. Have student discover and write all possible equivalencies.

Have the class use pattern blocks to discover other equivalencies. One yellow hexagon equals two red trapezoids, three blue parallelograms, or six green triangles:

Procedure 2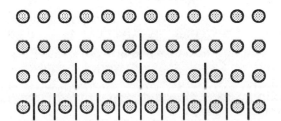

To generate and read an equivalency chart

Use *objects, toothpicks, graph paper, markers,* and *equivalency charts*.

Have student pairs make four rows with 12 beans evenly spaced in each row. Rows should be 3 to 4 inches apart. Each row is a whole of 12.

Have them separate the second row into two parts with a toothpick.

Ask: What do we call each part? (½)

Students use toothpicks to divide the third row into fourths and the fourth row into twelfths.

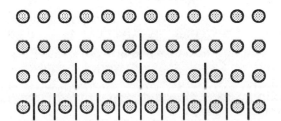

Have them notice whether any of the toothpicks line up. What do the lined-up toothpicks let us see? Have we used anything else that is similar?

Students respond: The toothpicks let us see where the equivalent fractions are. The fraction bars look like the beans and toothpicks.

Have students write all equivalencies discovered. Repeat with the rows divided into thirds and sixths.

Tell the class to leave their beans in place. Have students use graph paper to make an equivalency chart.

Students draw a row 1 square tall and 12 squares wide as their whole and directly below that outline five more identical rows.

Students leave the top row as their whole, divide the second row into halves, the third row into thirds, the fourth into fourths, the fifth into sixths, and the last into twelfths. They use markers to mark divisions.

Relate this graph to the groups of 12 beans and the equivalent fractions they found. Have students

make a list of equivalent fractions to the side of each graph paper bar. For example:

$$1 = {}^2/_2 = {}^3/_3 = {}^4/_4 = {}^6/_6 = {}^{12}/_{12}$$

$$^1/_2 = {}^2/_4 = {}^3/_6 = {}^6/_{12}.$$

Students complete the chart and look for patterns.

Lead students to notice the multiplication relationship of equivalent fractions: Equivalent fractions are multiples of the original fraction; also, if the original denominator is three times the numerator, as in $^1/_3$, all fractions equivalent to $^1/_3$ will have this same relationship.

Hand out the equivalency charts. Show students how to read the fraction amounts on the chart, relating it to the graph paper chart they made and to the fraction bars.

Students use a ruler or pencil to see which fractions line up and thus are equivalent. They duplicate the chart with fraction bars if they wish.

Procedure 3 □■

To use multiplication to find equivalent fractions

Use *student-made chart of equivalent fractions from Procedure 2* or *equivalency charts*.

If students have not made a chart of equivalent fractions, have them use their charts to do so.

Ask whether students see any patterns. They need to find a rule that will work for equivalent fractions in general. Hint: Start with each original fraction, like $^1/_2$. How did we get to $^2/_4$? From $^1/_2$, how did we get to $^3/_6$?

Students notice that if you multiply both numerator and denominator by the same number, you have an equivalent fraction.

Ask: Why does this work? Have students compare $^1/_2$ and $^2/_4$ on their charts. Are there more fourths? (yes) Say: They are smaller, so there are more of them.

Repeat for other fractions. Emphasize the need to multiply the *original* fraction when generating a list of equivalent fractions.

Students find fractions equivalent to $^2/_4$ and $^4/_5$ on their charts. They use multiplication and compare results.

Have students generate charts of equivalent fractions using multiplication. Each fraction should be checked with the equivalency chart.

Practice and Extension

Have students list horizontally all fractions equivalent to $^1/_2$. Have them compare this list to a *multiplication* *matrix*. Repeat for $^2/_3$. Two adjacent horizontal rows on the multiplication chart will list equivalent fractions.

Lead students to recognize that the numerator and denominator can be multiplied by the same number to find equivalent fractions.

Cut the matrices into horizontal rows. Line up different rows to find more equivalent fractions.

Have students rewrite *recipes;* they have lost all measuring cups except the $^1/_3$ or $^1/_8$ cup size, and must adapt.

Fractions 5

Skill: To order fractions

fraction bars (directions in Manipulative Information section) or Cuisenaire® rods

objects: buttons, beans, counters; 36 per student pair

See Reproducibles for: equivalency charts

Time: 3 periods

Materials:

geoboards and rubber bands

interlocking cubes in 2 colors or graph paper with ¹/₂" squares and markers

Anticipatory Set

Use *geoboards and rubber bands.*

Have students enclose a five-pin by five-pin square on their geoboards. How many squares have they enclosed? (16) Have students enclose a single square inside the larger one. What fraction is it of the whole? (¹/₁₆) Write this on the board.

Then have students enclose two squares, identify ²/₁₆, and see which fraction is bigger. Continue increasing area to develop the idea that like fractions can be compared using their numerators.

Procedure 1

To order fractions with like denominators

Use *interlocking cubes,* or *graph paper and markers.*

Work in groups for cubes, individually for graph paper.

Have groups make a stick of six cubes all the same color. (Students using graph paper should outline a horizontal row one square high and six squares wide.) Explain this is the size of our whole stick.

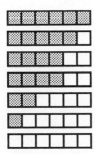

Tell students to make another stick with five cubes of the original color and one of a different color. Ask: What fractional part of our whole is the different-colored cube? (¹/₆)

Students make sticks to show all possible fractional parts of the whole. They write the fractions next to the sticks.

Ask: What do you notice? Are there any patterns?

Students notice the colors make a step pattern when lined up and that the numerators increase by one.

What fraction is more of the stick, ¹/₆ or ⁵/₆?

Students respond: ⁵/₆ is bigger because it is more of our whole.

Write ⁵/₆ > ¹/₆ on the board. Ask: Can you find another pair of fractions with the sixths in which one fraction is larger than another?

Students decide as groups how to chart all possible combinations of larger and smaller fraction pairs.

Help students see that organizing their chart makes it easier to read. Example: Start with ¹/₆ > ⁰/₆, and then move on to the ²/₆ relationships. Ask: What rule can you find about comparing fraction sizes?

Students respond: Like fractions can be compared by comparing their numerators.

Repeat the procedure, using different numbers of cubes in the whole. The class could make a class chart showing a variety of denominators. Students should make up word problems for their fractions.

Procedure 2

To order fractions with unlike denominators

Use *fraction bars* or *Cuisenaire® rods.*

Have students lay their whole bar across the top of their desk; then put the two halves together, below the whole; and then the fourths below the halves.

Ask: Which bar is longer, ¹/₂ or ¹/₄? (¹/₂) The ¹/₂ is a bigger part of the whole and is a bigger fraction.

Write ¹/₂ > ¹/₄ on the board. Have students find all the fractions that are smaller than ¹/₂ and write the relationships.

Students then find all the fractions that are smaller than ³/₄ and list their relationship to ³/₄.

Give students three fractions and see whether they can put them in order, first using the bars and then on paper. Make a class chart of all the relationships possible with the fraction bars.

Procedure 3 ■

To order fractions with unlike denominators; to relate the size of the denominator to fraction size

Use *objects* and *equivalency charts*.

Have student pairs make a row of 12 objects and divide the row into thirds. Ask: How many groups is that? (3)

Have them make a second row of 12 objects and divide it into fourths. How many groups is that? (4)

Students make a third row divided into sixths and respond that there are six groups.

In each case, we started with how many objects? (12) This is the size of our whole. Compare sizes. Which is smaller, the group that is $\frac{1}{4}$ of the 12, or the group that is $\frac{1}{6}$ of 12? Why?

Students respond: The group that is a sixth because fewer objects are in it.

Which is smaller, a group that is $\frac{1}{4}$ of the whole 12, or a group that is $\frac{1}{3}$ of the 12? Why?

Students respond: The fourth because fewer objects are in it.

Have students write $\frac{1}{6} < \frac{1}{4}$. Point out that the six and the four represent how many groups the whole 12 is divided into and that the ones tell how many of these groups we have.

Students compare $\frac{1}{3}$ and $\frac{1}{4}$. They write $\frac{1}{6} < \frac{1}{4} < \frac{1}{3}$.

Do you see a pattern?

Students respond: As the denominators get smaller, the size of each group gets larger.

Have the class predict where $\frac{1}{2}$ will come. (larger)

Change your row of sixths into halves of the 12. How many groups? (2) How many of these will we look at? (1) Does the size of the group fit our prediction? (yes)

If I divided my 12 objects into twelfths, would each twelfth be a large or a small group? Why?

Students respond: A small group. The groups are so many that only one object could be in each group.

Reinforce that as the fraction name—the denominator—gets larger, the size of each group gets smaller.

Repeat this procedure with groups of eight objects, emphasizing the number of groups the whole is divided into and comparing the size of each group.

Have students now compare $\frac{2}{8}$, $\frac{2}{4}$, and $\frac{2}{2}$ of the eight to see whether the relationships hold.

Students pretend their eight objects are silver dollars. They work in pairs to see who would have more money if one student held $\frac{3}{8}$ of their dollars and the other held $\frac{2}{4}$.

Review that they need to divide the whole into the number of groups that the denominator instructs and then to take the number of groups that the numerator instructs.

Hand out equivalency charts. Point out that the size of the whole is the same for all fractions on the chart.

Students start at the left and find the space taken up by various fraction amounts of the whole. They can use a pencil or ruler lined up top to bottom to help compare various fractions.

Have students compare various fractions to $\frac{1}{2}$. Ask them to predict whether the fraction will be larger or smaller than $\frac{1}{2}$. Then have students mentally compare two separate fractions. Explain that relating the fractions to $\frac{1}{2}$ makes it easier to compare them to each other.

Practice and Extension

Have students make *index cards* of fractions on the *equivalency chart*. Each student draws several cards from his or her deck to put in order. Have students make up rules to play a game or to race ordering fractions.

Fractions 6

Time: 3 periods

Materials:

fraction bars (directions in Manipulative Information section) or Cuisenaire® rods

pattern blocks

See Reproducibles for: moon stations

Anticipatory Set

Ask how many students are in the class. Have one student stand. Ask what fraction of the class he or she is. Review: The denominator is the number of equal parts in the whole; the numerator is the number of parts we're interested in.

Ask a second student also to stand. What fraction of the class is he or she alone? What fraction of the class are all the standing students? Continue adding students and emphasizing the adding of single-student fractions.

Procedure 1

To add fractions

Use *fraction bars or Cuisenaire® rods* and *paper*.

Have students lay their eighths in a row below their whole bar. Instruct them to separate $\frac{1}{8}$ and then add another $\frac{1}{8}$ to it. Ask: How many eighths do we have now? ($\frac{2}{8}$)

Write $\frac{1}{8} + \frac{1}{8} = \frac{2}{8}$ on the board.

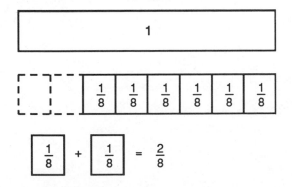

Have students add another $\frac{1}{8}$. How many eighths have we added now? ($\frac{3}{8}$)

Write $\frac{2}{8} + \frac{1}{8} = \frac{3}{8}$. Repeat for one more eighth.

Repeat the process with fourths and sixteenths, writing the process on the board as the students work.

Students separate the amount you call for, add the bars, and find the total.

Ask: Do you see any pattern to what you have written?

Students should see that you have added numerators.

Give students other fractions to add.

Write $\frac{1}{4} + \frac{1}{4} = \frac{2}{8}$ on the board, and challenge students to prove why this is wrong.

Students add $\frac{1}{4}$ and $\frac{1}{4}$ and match this against $\frac{2}{8}$. They see that two fourths are greater in size than two eighths.

Discuss adding the numerators but not denominators. The denominators refer to the number of equal parts of the whole; these don't change. Have students practice with bars only until they are comfortable with the process.

Now you can move to the stage where students write, as well as use manipulatives. As students do each step with the bars, they write the corresponding step on their paper.

It is important for students to understand that the written form is just a description of what is actually happening. Students need much practice at this step.

After students become confident about the process, they can move to writing the problem first and then checking each step with their blocks.

Procedure 2

To subtract fractions

Use *fraction bars* or *Cuisenaire® rods*.

Have students start with a bar of $\frac{8}{8}$. Direct them to pull down $\frac{3}{8}$. Ask: How many eighths do you have left? ($\frac{5}{8}$) Write $\frac{8}{8} - \frac{3}{8} = \frac{5}{8}$ on the board.

Next students pull down $\frac{2}{8}$ from their group of $\frac{3}{8}$. Ask: How many eighths are left? ($\frac{1}{8}$)

Write $\frac{3}{8} - \frac{2}{8} = \frac{1}{8}$ on the board. Repeat several times. Do you see a pattern?

Students respond: Only the numerators change.

Emphasize that the size of their bars didn't change—they are still eighths. Only the number of eighths we had left changed.

Give fractions for students to subtract, using other bars. Write the process on the board as they work.

Students create and solve fraction word problems using their bars. When they are competent in the skill, they also write down the process as they work with the bars.

Procedure 3

To add and subtract fractions

Use *pattern blocks* and *moon stations*.

Give each student pattern blocks and moon stations. Have them review how many of each color block it takes to cover a moon station. (2 yellow hexagons, 4 red trapezoids, 6 blue parallelograms, or 12 green triangles)

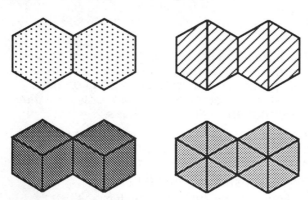

Repeat Procedure 1, using the pattern blocks. For example, have students place one red trapezoid on a moon station.

Ask: What fraction is covered? ($^1/_4$) Have them add another $^1/_4$. How many fourths in all now? ($^2/_4$)

For subtraction, have them cover $^3/_4$ of a moon station and then take away $^1/_4$.

Continue giving fractions to add or subtract on the moon stations. Use halves, fourths, sixths, and twelfths.

Students write equations. When they are comfortable with the skills, they write equations first and then check with the blocks.

Practice and Extension

Give students fractions to add and subtract. Have students divide *moon stations* into fractional parts

and color in the required number on the *moon stations*. For subtraction they can use a light color to color in the first fraction and then a darker color to line through the fraction amount to be subtracted. They should write the problem under the moon station.

Use *place value blocks* with a ten rod as one whole, or *money* with $10 as one whole to work with tenths.

Have students change *recipe* ingredient amounts to all one denominator.

Have students write about a turtle who can't make up its mind. It walks forward $^1/_4$ foot, forward another $^1/_4$, backward $^1/_4$ and then forward $^3/_4$. How far does it go in all? Have students do the intermediate equations as well.

Discuss temperature in tenths of degrees. What is normal body temperature? How much higher is a fever?

Decimals 1

Skill: To relate fractions to decimals: to recognize and order tenths

Time: 2+ periods

Materials:

graph paper: ½" squares

file-folder place value (pv) mats to 1000s

12" × 18" tag board for decimal extensions for pv mats

½" gummed dots: 1 per student

clear tape

rulers

pv blocks to 100s

scissors

counters: 1 per student

envelopes for storing graph paper decimals: 1 per student

See Reproducibles for: directions for file-folder pv mat decimal extensions, decimal bars for tenths—in the same color used for $1 bills, equivalency charts

Anticipatory Set

Use *graph paper*.

Have students outline a 1 × 10 square rectangle. Immediately below, they outline three identical rectangles. Label the top one "One." Divide the second rectangle in half and label "Halves." Divide and label the third as "Fifths." The bottom rectangle is "Tenths."

Have they seen a similar chart? (an equivalency chart) Have students discover all the fractions equivalent to tenths on the chart. Examples: $^2/_5 = {}^4/_{10}$; $^1/_2 = {}^5/_{10}$.

Procedure 1

To relate fraction tenths to decimal tenths and place value

Use *paper chart from Anticipatory Set, pv mats, tag board, directions for decimal extensions, gummed dots, tape, rulers, pv blocks,* and *decimal bars.*

Have students make decimal extensions, tape them to the right-hand side of their pv mats, and place a gummed dot for a decimal point. They should not label yet.

Next have students place one hundred flat, one ten rod, and one one cube on their pv mats. Write 111 on the board.

Ask: How many tens does it take to make 100? (10) What fraction of the hundred is each 10? ($^1/_{10}$)

Repeat for the relationship between 10 and 1.

If something is in the column to the right of the ones, how many of them it take to make a one? (10) What fraction of the one would it be? ($^1/_{10}$ of 1)

Have students replace the cube with a one bar and add a tenth bar in the column to the right.

Say: The whole bar is equal to a one. How many parts does the tenth bar have? (10) We are only interested in the shaded part. One part is shaded.

Ask: What fraction of one is it? ($^1/_{10}$) The shaded part is less than one whole. Find something similar on the graph paper chart.

Students find $^1/_{10}$ on the chart.

How can we write $^1/_{10}$ of one? ($^1/_{10}$)

Have students label "Tenths" on their decimal extensions. Fractions that are tenths are special in our number system because they can go on our place value chart.

We can also call them *decimal fractions* and write them in a special way. You have placed a dot on your pv mat. Everything to the left is one whole or more. Everything to the right is less than one. This dot is a decimal point and goes in all numbers that have tenths in them.

Ask: How would I say the number we have on the mats? (one hundred eleven and one tenth) How would I write it? (111.1)

Have students place two more tenth bars on their mats and identify 111.3 both in words and numbers.

Students place whole numbers with decimal parts on their mats as you write them on the board. They chorally read each place and then write them, as well.

What do we need to do when we have 10 ones on the mat? (trade for a 10) What will we need to do when we have 10 tenths on the mat? (trade for 1 one)

Students place combinations of pv blocks on their mats, which will lead to trading. They chorally read each resulting number, as well as write it.

Procedure 2

To relate decimals and fractions equivalent to tenths

Use *paper chart from Anticipatory Set, equivalency charts, scissors,* and *counters.*

Say: Miles are often measured in tenths. An odometer on your bicycle would be in miles and tenths of miles.

If I bicycled $\frac{1}{2}$ a mile, what would this be in tenths? ($\frac{5}{10}$) How many ways could you write this? ($\frac{5}{10}$, 0.5)

Students write: $\frac{1}{2} = \frac{5}{10} = 0.5$.

Continue until students are comfortable finding and writing decimal equivalents.

Ask: Can some fractions not be written as decimals? Why not?

Students respond: Not all fractions are equivalent to tenths. They use their equivalency charts to check this.

If I biked $2\frac{5}{10}$ miles, how would I see this on the odometer? (2.5) Repeat until students are competent in the skill.

Have students cut their graph paper chart into parts.

Students work in groups of three. One gives a number consisting of 1 and a decimal part, for example, 1.5 ounces of gold. The first student to assemble and write the number gets a point. They use counters for decimal points.

Procedure 3

To order tenths

Use *graph paper, scissors, pv mats with extensions, envelopes,* and *paper.*

Have students cut out four 10 × 10 squares, label two of them "1," and cut the other two into 1 × 10 strips.

Ask: How many equal strips does it takes to equal the whole one? (10) Each strip is what fraction of the whole? ($\frac{1}{10}$) Review writing decimal tenths.

Have students place 1.2 on their mats and then 1.4 below.

Which is more, the 1.2 or 1.4? (1.4) When we have more tenths, the number is bigger. Write 1.4 > 1.2 on the board.

Have students add another seven tenths to the 1.2 to make 1.9 and then chorally read.

Ask: Which amount is more, the 1.4 or 1.9? (1.9) Why?

Students respond: It has more tenths.

Write 1.9 > 1.4 > 1.2 on the board.

Students continue to place numbers as you write them on the board. Use numbers both greater than and less one.

Have students place 1.9 and then add one more tenth strip. How many tenths do we have now? (10)

In our number system, whenever we get to 10 of anything, what do we need to do? (regroup)

Say: Decimals follow the same rule. What is equivalent to $\frac{10}{10}$ that we could trade for?

Students respond: 1 whole. They trade $\frac{10}{10}$ for 1 and chorally read: two ones and zero tenths.

Write 2.0 > 1.9 > 1.4 > 1.2 on the board. Ask: Do you see a pattern to which numbers are bigger?

Repeat, using amounts from 0.1 to 2.9.

Have students work in groups of three. Dictate three decimal amounts and have groups place and compare them. Then have them write the numbers in order of size.

When students are competent in the skill, have them order numbers on paper before checking with the strips.

Procedure 4

To order fractions and decimal tenths

Use *pv mats with extensions, pv blocks, decimal bars,* and *equivalency charts.*

Give story problems using decimals and fractions equivalent to decimals for students to place, solve, and write. Example: Half the class ate hot dogs, $\frac{1}{5}$ ate chicken, and $\frac{3}{10}$ ate tacos. Which food was most popular? Least popular?

Practice and Extension

Have students draw a map that includes several towns. They use a *graph paper 1 × 10 strip* to measure and mark the distances in miles and tenths of miles.

Have students predict and then record a week's mileage on their cars at home. Repeat for a second week and compare the accuracy of the estimates.

Duplicate sheets of *decimal bars for tenths,* and have students color in various amounts from 0.1 to 1.0. Students work in pairs to draw three bars, order them, and write the decimal amounts.

Have students make up word problems with distance and odometer readings. The emphasis should be on which trip covers the greatest or least distance.

Decimals 2

Skill: To add and subtract tenths

Time: 3 periods

Materials:

file-folder place value (pv) mats to 1000s with decimal extensions to tenths

pv blocks to 100s

decimal bars to tenths

coins: dimes, or counters; 20 per student

See Reproducibles for: directions for file-folder pv mats and decimal extensions, decimal bars to tenths—in the same color used for $1 bills, bills to 100s—in different colors

Anticipatory Set

Use *pv mats* and *pv blocks*.

Have students place one hundred, one ten, and one one on their mats. Ask: How many tens make 100? (10) Each ten is $^1/_{10}$ of 100. Repeat for tens and ones. Have students place nine more ones on their mats. Have students add and subtract other amounts to review regrouping.

Procedure 1　□■

To add tenths

Use *pv mats, pv blocks,* and *decimal bars.*

Review with students the relationship between tenths and one whole. Tell students they will be responsible for measuring the progress of a team climbing Mt. Everest. The measurements will be done in meters and tenths of meters.

Have students clear their mats, since the climbing team is starting at ground level. The first day the team climbs 165.6 meters. Write this on the board.

Students place 165.6 on their mats and chorally read: 1 hundred, 6 tens, 5 ones, and 6 tenths of one.

The next day the team climbs 132.3 meters. Write the addition problem on the board, where a running total will be kept.

Students chorally read the amount and place 132.3 on their mats. They chorally read the total: 2 hundreds, 9 tens, 7 ones, and 9 tenths meters.

Add the total on the board. The third day the team climbs 123.0 meters. Write this on the board.

Students chorally read and place 123.0 on their mats. They regroup to get a total of 420.9 meters.

Do the problem on the board, calling attention to the regrouping. Ask: Do you see any pattern to adding with decimals?

Students may see that adding decimals is like adding whole numbers; you have lined up the decimal points. If they do not see this, erase the decimal point in the answer, and have students read the number.

The next day the climbing team went 101.8 meters. Have students place the amount but not total it.

Ask: How many tenths do you have in all? (17) In our number system we regroup when we have how many in any place? (10) Will this be true for decimals as well? (yes)

What are ten tenths equal to? (1) Trade ten tenths for one one and find the total distance climbed.

Students regroup and find the total of their blocks and bars is 522.7 meters.

Call attention to the regrouping in your addition on the board.

The team had a hard next day and only climbed 5 meters. Where should you write the five in the problem?

Students chorally read: 5 ones and 0 tenths. They discuss keeping the numbers lined up in the correct space. They place and total the blocks and bars.

Give more numbers from below, starting with 143.6. Keep a running total on the board.

Amount Added	Total	(Notes)
165.6	165.6	
132.3	297.9	
123.0	420.9	(regroup 1s, 10s)
101.8	522.7	(regroup tenths)
5	527.7	(no decimal part)
143.6	671.3	(regroup tenths, 1s)
100	771.3	(no decimal part)
39.9	811.2	(regroup all places)
80.7	891.9	

Proceed directly to Procedure 2.

Procedure 2　□■

To subtract tenths

Use *pv mats, pv blocks,* and *decimal bars.*

This is a continuation of Procedure 1. Otherwise, have students place 891.9 on their mats, the total meters climbed so far by the team on Mt. Everest.

Explain that a blizzard rages on Mt. Everest and the team has to retreat. Give students numbers of meters retreated each day: 103.2, 31.3, 123.1; *amounts do not include regrouping of decimals.*

Have students continue to chorally read the amount, emphasizing tenths of one.

Students remove blocks and bars as necessary as you do the problem on the board.

Next, introduce an amount to subtract that will include regrouping.

Ask: What do we do when we don't have enough tens on the mat for a subtraction problem? (trade 1 hundred for 10 tens)

What do we do if we don't have enough ones on the mat for a subtraction problem? (trade 1 ten for 10 ones)

What can we do if we don't have enough tenths to subtract? (trade 1 one for 10 tenths)

Students regroup on their mats.

Finish the problem, asking students whether the procedure looks familiar. (It is just like whole number subtraction.)

Dictate more decimal numbers to add and subtract.

Students do problems on their mats and write them on paper when they have understood the concept with blocks and bars.

Dictate several whole numbers to be subtracted from decimal amounts. Emphasize the correspondence of the numbers on the pv mat to the placement in the written problem.

Put the whole number in the decimal position, and challenge students to find your mistake on the board.

Procedure 3

To add and subtract using tenths

Use *bills, pv mats,* and *dimes or counters.*

Ask: How many dimes are in $1? (10) Each dime is what fraction of $1? ($\frac{1}{10}$) Tell students they are traveling in a country that has no pennies, only dimes, or tenths of dollars. One counter equals a dime or 0.1. They will need to keep track of their money.

Repeat the story-type format as in Procedures 1 and 2, with bills and counters. Start with an amount in the hundreds, and either buy items (subtraction) or earn money (addition).

Students take turns suggesting situations.

Continue to emphasize in the choral reading that the counters are $\frac{1}{10}$ of a dollar.

Now have students try problems first and then check their answers with manipulatives and pv mats.

Practice and Extension

Play Bicycle Race. Use four *dice, pv mats, pv blocks and decimal bars or bills and counters,* a *bag or can,* and *counters of different colors.* Divide the class into two parts, each part is to be a bicycle racing team. The distance is measured in kilometers.

The first die drawn from the can will be the hundreds amount, the second die will be the tens amount, the third the ones amount, and the fourth the decimal tenths amount. One color counter will represent addition and the other color subtraction.

Have each team start with the same amount. Draw a counter from the can. The first team will either add or subtract the subsequent number, depending on the color of the counter. Repeat for the second team.

Students place amounts and do the problem on paper. At the end of three rounds the team who has gone farther wins as long as all students on the team have the correct amounts on their mats and papers.

Decimals 3

Skill: To add and subtract money: amounts to $1.00

Time: 1–2 periods per procedure

Materials:

objects: cubes, beans; separate types for each coin value desired

coins: all types, or colored counters to represent them

dice

3" × 3", or 4" × 4" squares of paper: 2 per student

containers: 1 per group of students

symbol cards for =: 1 per student

file-folder place value (pv) mats with decimal extensions, or other pv mats to 100s (adapt with decimal point), or plain paper

See Reproducibles for: bills—1s only, directions for file-folder pv mats and decimal extensions, pv mats to 100s

Anticipatory Set for Procedure 1

Use *objects*.

Introduce objects, such as beans for 1¢, counters for 5¢. Discuss students' previous experiences with money.

Anticipatory Set for Procedures 2 and 3

Use *coins, bills*, and *paper*.

Review with students that ten pennies equal a dime, and ten dimes equal one dollar. Have students chorally count up to ten pennies and then trade for one dime. Next, have them chorally count by dimes (tens) up to 100 and trade for a dollar.

Procedure 1

To recognize coins and values; to make equivalent amounts

Use *coins, objects from Anticipatory Set, dice, paper squares, containers*, and *symbol cards*.

Introduce pennies and the objects worth 1¢ first. Have students draw a handful of pennies from the container, count the pennies, and buy the equivalent number of objects.

Introduce the notation of ¢ to stand for coin amounts. Write 8¢ on the board. Have students count out eight pennies and then exchange for eight objects.

Have students write and draw charts as you dictate amounts. Use the die to generate amounts.

$$3¢ = \text{①①①} = \text{◯◯◯}$$

Students take that many pennies and buy objects or save for a more expensive object.

Introduce nickels next. Have students exchange five pennies for a nickel, chorally counting amounts until they are comfortable with the value.

Write amounts on the board, and have students count out and chart that much in the fewest coins possible. Use a die as before, then both dice.

Students buy objects as before.

Ask: What coins could you use to buy the largest number of objects? The smallest?

Have students place paper squares on their desks with the symbol card between.

Students place a dictated amount such as 15¢ on the left square, and then an equivalent amount on the right with a different configuration of coins. They chart this equation. How many ways can they find to represent each amount?

Follow the same procedure in introducing dimes and quarters. Provide plenty of experience in making trades for equivalent amounts, charting, and buying objects.

Procedure 2

To add money using place value

Use *pv mats, coins, bills, paper*, and *containers*.

Have students set up money mats. If they are not using pv mats with extensions, have them adapt their mats with decimal points. As an alternative, have them place a piece of paper to the right of their mats. It is important for students to realize that money does not go in the regular ones and tens columns.

Students will need a separate paper for writing on, folded and labeled "10¢ or Dimes" and "1¢ or Pennies." Have them complete this as you draw a money place value chart on the board.

Say: Petunia Periwinkle pig is keeping track of her money. She earns 4¢.

Have students chorally count as they place four pennies on their mats and you write it on the board.

Petunia earns a nickel.

Students place a nickel below the pennies and chorally count to the total.

Keep a running addition total on the board. Students are not writing at this point.

Discuss the ways to get 9¢ with coins. Even though the coins may be different, the amount is the same.

Petunia finds a penny.

Students add one more penny and chorally count to ten.

This money mat is just like our regular place value mats. In our number system, what do we do when we have ten of anything in one place? (regroup or trade) We have ten pennies on the mats. Ask: What could we trade for? (a dime)

Students trade ten pennies for a dime and place it on their mats. They chorally read: 1 dime, 0 pennies.

Do addition on the board, calling attention to the regrouping and placement of numbers.

Continue dictating amounts under a dollar for students to place and chorally read until they are comfortable with regrouping money amounts.

Introduce a quarter. Say: This is worth 25¢ but we only use one number in each column of our mats. What can we do?

Students respond: Change it for 2 dimes and 1 nickel.

Say: We can have other combinations, but this is the one we actually write for 25¢.

As students become confident when doing the process, you can move to the stage at which students write, as well as use manipulatives.

It is important for students to understand that the written form is just a description of what is actually happening. Students need much practice at this stage.

Have students clear their mats. Repeat the above procedure, but have students keep a running total on their second sheet of paper. Emphasize correct placement of amounts.

Students place amounts, regroup if necessary to arrive at a total, and write each step on paper. They show all regrouping in their written work, copying what you have done on the board if they need to do so.

As you continue to give problems in a story format, introduce estimation. If Petunia is given 43¢ and 21¢, about how much does she receive? Can you name two money amounts the total will be between?

Discuss strategies. Why won't it be 80¢ or 50¢?

Have the class work in groups. Have students take turns drawing two or more coins from the container and making up a story problem requiring addition. Tell students to place and add them and to do the problem on paper.

As students become comfortable with the process, they do the problems first on paper and then check with the coins.

Procedure 3 □■

To subtract money using place value

Use *coins, bills, paper,* and *containers.*

Have students set up money mats as for addition, one as a money place value mat, and one for writing. Draw a money place value chart on the board.

Have students place 9¢ on their mats as you write 9¢ on the board.

Discuss that 9¢ can be either a nickel and four pennies, or nine pennies, but the amount of money is the same. Students are not writing yet.

Next have students remove, or spend, 2¢. Ask: How much is left? (7¢) Do the subtraction on the board.

When we have nine dogs and lead two away, how many do we have left? (7)

Is this different from subtracting with money? What about the way it is written?

Students respond: The subtraction is the same, but money is written with a ¢ sign.

Dictate several more 1-digit amounts for students to subtract. When they are comfortable with the skill, have them write the problems after they do them with coins, copying what you have written on the board if they need to do so.

Have students clear their coins and place 66¢ on their mats. Call their attention to your placement of the numbers on the board.

Say: We want to take 42¢ away. Have students first subtract the pennies. Do this on the board and discuss starting at the right.

Students finish subtraction and chorally read the answer as you finish the problem on the board.

Continue giving numbers to subtract *without regrouping,* making each one a story problem.

When students are comfortable with the skill, have them begin writing the problem down, doing the subtraction with coins, and then solving the problem on paper.

If you wish to introduce regrouping, have students place 61¢ and subtract 9¢.

Ask: Do we have enough pennies to take nine away? (no) How could we get more pennies? (trade 1 dime for 10 pennies)

Students regroup, subtract, and chorally read the answer.

Do the problem on the board, calling attention to the regrouping.

Dictate several more numbers for students to subtract, using story problems. Some should require regrouping, and some should not.

Remind students that subtracting money is identical to subtracting other numbers but is labeled with ¢.

When students are comfortable with the skill, they begin writing the problem down, doing *each step* first with the coins and then on paper.

Students need much practice doing both to understand that the numbers on paper exactly represent what they are doing with the coins.

As you continue to give problems in a story format, have students *estimate answers first*. Ask: If I start with 90¢ and spend 42¢, about how much will I have left? Will it be as much as 60¢? Why or why not?

Introduce checking with addition. Start with 9¢, and have students spend 5¢ for a pencil, writing the problem down.

Say that they return the pencil, and have them add the 5¢ back on their mats. Do they have what they started with? Where can they find the same process on their written work?

Students see they can "add back up" to reach their original 9¢.

Have students draw a double line below their problem, "add back up," and show the original amount as a check. Will this work for 45¢ – 20¢? Have students test this.

Students work in groups. They take turns drawing four coins from the container and making up a story problem requiring subtraction. They place and add the larger two and write the amount on paper. They add the other two coins together to find how much to subtract.

For each problem, they estimate first and check with addition at the end. As students become comfortable with the skill, they do the problems first on paper and then check with the coins.

Practice and Extension

Play coin games. Student pairs use *coins* to desired values, *counters,* and a pair of *dice*. In turn they generate an amount using the dice and choose which number they will use in the tens place. They make that amount, using the fewest coins possible. For each coin used, they take a counter. The winner is the student with the fewest counters after five turns.

Play Race to $1.00. Students use *coins* and *money mats,* and keep a running total as well. Use *cards* or *dice* to generate amounts. For subtraction, students start with 99¢ and play Race to 0¢. Students can also use long strips of *graph paper* for their calculations, writing one number per square.

Give students 40¢ in *pennies*. Other *coins* will be in the bank. Students throw dice in turn to get an

amount to trade. They try to have the fewest coins at the end. They try first to trade their amount with their opponent for an equivalent amount using fewer coins. If this is not possible, they trade with the bank.

Play Go to the Fair. Students work in pairs and need a *die, coins,* and *paper money mats labeled "Dimes" and "Pennies."* They also need a *two-colored counter* or a *can with two different-colored counters.* They each start with 50¢.

Students take turns to flip a counter or draw one from the can. One color means to subtract, the other to add. The first roll of the die is the dimes amount, and the second roll is the pennies amount. They make up story problems to go with their turn. Example: Win 20¢ at the Baseball Throw, spend 15¢ on a hot dog. First one to spend all the money gets to "go home."

Decimals 4

Skill: To add and subtract money: amounts above $1.00

Time: 2 periods

Materials:

coins: pennies, dimes, or colored counters to represent them

file-folder place value (pv) mats to 1000s with decimal extensions or other pv mats to 100s (adapt with decimal point)

See Reproducibles for: bills to desired value—in different colors, directions for file-folder pv mats and decimal extensions, pv mats to 100s

Anticipatory Set

Use *coins, bills to 10s,* and *paper.*

Review with students that ten pennies equal a dime and that ten dimes equal one dollar. Have students chorally count up to ten pennies and then trade for one dime. Next have them chorally count by dimes (tens) up to 100 and trade for a dollar.

Dictate several amounts over $1, and have students both count out bills and coins and write amounts. Review that $1 can be written as 100¢ or $1.00.

Procedure 1 □ ■

To add money

Use *coins, bills,* and *pv mats with decimal extensions or adapted pv mats.*

If students are using pv mats without extensions, have them adapt their mats with decimal points. As an alternative, have them place a piece of paper to the right of their mats, fold it in half, draw a line on the fold, and label the halves 10¢ and 1¢. Draw a pv chart on the board to correspond.

Say: Ten pennies equal a dime, and ten dimes make a dollar. Ask: How many one dollars make ten dollars? (10) Do you see a pattern?

Students respond: Dollars and cents work just like other numbers.

***Start without regrouping:* Have students place $1.25 on their mats. Write this on the board, calling attention to the placement of numbers. Say: You get $2.20 for your birthday. How much do you have in all?**

Students place $2.20 and add to get total of $3.45. They are not writing at this point.

Write and solve the problem on the board, calling attention to the writing of the zero in the 1¢ place and the need to put in a decimal point.

Ask: What would happen without a decimal point? (The number would be $345.)

Dictate several more amounts for students to place and add without regrouping.

As students become confident when doing the process, you can move to the stage at which students write, as well as use manipulatives. It is important for students to understand that the written form is just a description of what is actually happening.

Students write the problem down, do the addition with coins and bills, and then solve the problem on paper. They do *each step* first with the money and then on paper.

Students need much practice doing both to understand that the numbers on paper exactly represent what they are doing with the money.

Dictate an amount that will require regrouping of pennies. Say: We have too many pennies. In our number system, what do we need to do when we have ten of anything in one place? (regroup) What can we trade for? (dimes)

Students regroup and add money. If they are comfortable in addition with regrouping, they write each step. If not, they need practice with money only first.

When students feel capable of the skill, have them keep a running total. Students need much practice at this stage.

Give problems in a story format. Students can suggest situations.

Introduce estimation. Say: If I buy two books at $1.25 each, about how much will I need? Can you name two dollar amounts the answer will be between?

Students estimate and then check with bills and coins.

Discuss strategies. Why won't the answer be $5.00? Have students suggest situations.

List catalog amounts on the board, and have students estimate and then check how much they will need.

Procedure 2 □ ■

To subtract money

Use *coins, bills,* and *pv mats with decimal extensions or adapted pv mats.*

Repeat Procedure 1 for subtraction. Start with $16.98, and give amounts to subtract that do not require regrouping.

Students pull down the amount to be subtracted and chorally read the answer. When they are comfortable with the skill, they begin writing the steps as they do them.

When introducing regrouping, start with the regrouping of a dollar amount first. Ask whether there are enough $1s to subtract. (no) How can we get more dollars? (Trade 1 $10 for 10 $1s.) Ask: Is this like something you've done before?

Students respond: It's like the subtracting we have done with blocks and regular numbers.

Students do regrouping and then finish subtracting. They will need practice with many examples before writing the problems. When they do write the problems, they do *each step* first with the money and then on paper.

Students need much practice doing both to understand that the numbers on paper exactly represent what they are doing with the money. Eventually they will first solve the problem on paper and then check with the money.

Introduce checking with addition. Start with $5.00, and have students spend (subtract) $1.00 for a goldfish.

Students write the problem, subtract with bills, and then write the process.

The goldfish has to be returned. Have students add the $1.00 back on their mats. Do they have what they started with? Where can they find the same process on the problems they have written?

Students note that they can "add back up" to reach their original $5.00.

Have students draw a double line below their problem, "add back up," and show the original amount as a check.

Provide more story problems of this sort, involving coins as well as bills.

Practice and Extension

Play Go to the Fair. Use a *die* and either a *two-colored counter* or a *can and two different-colored counters*. Students work in pairs and use *bills, coins,* and *pv mats with extensions or adapted pv mats*. They each start with $10.00.

Students take turns to flip a counter or draw one from the can. One color means to subtract, the other to add. The first roll of the die is the dollar amount, the second roll is the dimes amount, and the third is the pennies amount. They make up story problems to go with their turn.

Example: Win 50¢ at the Baseball Throw, spend $1.15 on hot dogs. The first one to spend all the money gets to "go home."

Play Park and Shop. Students draw a map on *paper* or *tag board* of a shopping mall with six different kinds of stores. Each store sells five different objects costing $0.50 to $3.00. Students make lists of objects and costs. Students play in pairs. They go to the mall with $10.00 and must buy one item in each store. The one who gets home with the least amount of money left wins.

Decimals 5

Skill: To round decimals to the nearest whole number

Time: 3 periods

Materials:

clear tape

scissors

file-folder place value (pv) mats to 1000s with decimal extensions

pv blocks to 10s

coins: pennies and dimes, or counters to represent them

See Reproducibles for: Rounding Rhyme, number lines to 1000, directions for file-folder pv mats and decimal extensions, decimal bars to desired place—in the same color used for $1 bills, extra copies of decimal bars for writing on, bills to 100s—in different colors

Anticipatory Set

Use *Rounding Rhyme, number lines, tape,* and *scissors*.

Review Rounding Rhyme. Write 5,937 on the board. Have students round to the nearest ten, hundred, and thousand. Review that we round up when we get halfway to the next number.

Have students cut out and tape together number lines.

Procedure 1

To develop the concept of rounding tenths

Use *pv mats with extensions, pv blocks, decimal bars, extra copies of decimal bars,* and *Rounding Rhyme.*

Have students use extra copies of decimal bars and darken the horizontal line that divides each one in half. Tell them to lightly shade in one half of each one.

Students discuss the relationship of each bar to one. They write 0.5, 0.50, 0.500 (depending on the bars used) on the shaded part of the bars.

Ask: How many tenths does it take to make a one? (10) What is half that amount? (5 tenths) If we had five tenths, we would be halfway to a one.

We consider 0.5 closer to one than to zero, or none. If we were rounding, it would be enough to trade for a one and round up.

Have students place 12.6 on their mats. Have them find 0.6 on the extra decimal bar they shaded in. Ask: Is it more than half the bar? (yes)

Is it closer to one or none? (1) We have 0.5 or more and can trade for a one. Does this follow the Rounding Rhyme?

Students trade the 0.6 for a one and have 13.0 on their mats. They write: 12.6 → 13.0.

Have students add 0.3 to the 13.0.

Say: Find 0.3 on the extra decimal bar you colored. Is it more than half the bar? (no) Is it closer to one or none? (none) We do not have 0.5 or more and cannot trade for a one.

Students pull off the 0.3. They write: 13.3 → 13.0.

We are rounding to the nearest one. Underline the numbers In the ones place in 12.6 and 13.3. Does the rounding follow the rule in the Rounding Rhyme? (yes)

Students continue to place and write numbers as you dictate. They compare the decimal amount with their colored bars and decide whether the amount is closer to one or none.

After manipulating the bars, they underline the ones place in their written number, and round. They check the results with their pv mats.

Repeat the procedure for hundredths and thousandths as desired. Emphasize that 0.5 = 0.50 = 0.500.

Procedure 2

To round money to the nearest $1.00

Use *pv mats with extensions, bills, decimals bars, coins or counters, Rounding Rhyme,* and *extra copies of decimal bars from Procedure 1.*

Follow Procedure 1 with bills and bars. Give students money amounts to place and have them estimate to the nearest dollar. Give amounts with nine and zero in the ones place.

Next substitute coins or counters for the bars and continue; e.g., I only have $10.00, so I need to keep track of purchases at the store. If my items are $2.12, $3.98, and $2.76, do you think I will have enough money?

Students write amounts, estimate with materials, and round amounts on paper. When they are comfortable with the skill, they try rounding first on paper and then checking with materials of their choice.

Procedure 3

To round tenths to the nearest whole number

Use *number lines to 1000* and *Rounding Rhyme.*

Have students start with 0.1 at the first small tick mark and label the numbers to 5.0. Have them draw a light line across at all the 0.5 numbers.

Dictate 1.3, and have students locate it on the line.

Say: Check your light lines. Is the 0.3 part "0.4 or less" or "0.5 and up?" (0.4 or less) Ask: What happens now?

Students respond: It's out of sight.

Ask: Which whole number is the 1.3 closer to? (1)

Students write each new number and then use the Rounding Rhyme and number lines to practice.

Have students think of the number line as a measuring line. Example: About how far did the bee fly from home if it went 1.6 miles straight out? About how far was the round trip?

Ask what numbers round to 2 and are over 1.80. (1.81 to 1.99, 2.01 to 2.49)

When students are competent in the skill, they write and round numbers first and then check with the number line.

Practice and Extension

Give students amounts to round and add in their head.

Give students 2 minutes to look through *catalogs* or *menus*. Have them try to spend as close to $10 as possible without going over. Discuss whether this is easy to do without estimating.

Have students work in pairs. One rounds a list of amounts, while the other adds the list using a calculator. How close were the totals. Which numbers give the least accurate estimates? Why?

Have students use a *centimeter ruler* to measure exact lengths. On paper they round the measurements to the nearest centimeter. They then check with the ruler to see if they were correct.

Play Park and Shop. Students draw a map on *paper* or *tag board* of a shopping mall with six different kinds of stores. Each store sells five different objects costing $0.50 to $3.00. Students make lists of objects and costs.

Students play in pairs. They go to the mall with $10.00 and must buy one item in each store. The winner is the one who spends the amount closest to $10.00 without going over. Have students first estimate amounts and spend the rounded amounts, not the exact amounts.

Geometry 1

Skill: To use patterns in geometric shapes: two and three dimensions

Time: ½–1 period per procedure

Materials:

attribute blocks or paper shapes: 3 shapes, 3 sizes of each shape, 3 colors of each shape and size; 3 of each per group

cubes: regular or interlocking, in several colors, if possible

pattern blocks

graph paper: any size

tiles

Note: Procedures are written from easier to more difficult. After identifying the desired level of difficulty, use a previous procedure as an Anticipatory Set.

Primary skills are in Number Skills 7.

Anticipatory Set

Use *attribute blocks* or *paper shapes.*

Have students work in small groups and sort shapes. They should choose one shape and size and make a single line pattern, varying only the color attribute. Students take turns making patterns for the rest of the group to duplicate.

Procedure 1

To work with attribute patterns

Use *attribute blocks* or *paper shapes.*

Varying two attributes:

Make single line patterns, and have students copy them. Use patterns that vary in two attributes: all squares varying in color and size, all large ones varying in color and shape, etc. Ask: What will come next?

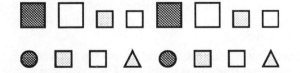

Students copy pattern. They predict the next item and continue the pattern.

Have students work in pairs to devise patterns. Have them copy each other's pattern, predict the next one, and continue the pattern.

Introduce patterns using *combinations,* varying two attributes: all squares—one small blue, a large red and large blue touching, one small blue, a large red and large blue touching, etc.

Students work in pairs as before. When they can do this easily, have them draw patterns and exchange for their partner to continue.

Varying three attributes:

Follow the same sequence as for two attributes.

Procedure 2

To work with positional change patterns

Use *cubes,* or *paper shapes,* or *attribute blocks.*

Positional changes among pairs:

Start by varying only one attribute: Using paired items, reverse which one is above and which is below, or which is left and which is right.

Example: Using small squares, make a pattern of one blue, a red above a blue, one blue, a blue above a red, etc.

When students can copy, predict, and continue the patterns, they work in pairs as before.

Next vary two attributes.

Example: Using all squares, make a pattern of small red paired with large blue, large red paired with small blue, first pair rotated, second pair rotated.

Advanced students can try varying all three attributes.

Positional changes among the items themselves:

Start by varying only the position. Then vary one attribute. Example: Using small squares, make a pattern of one blue, one red, one blue rotated 45°, one red, etc.

The next level is to vary two attributes, then three.

Procedure 3

To work with building-on patterns

Use *paper shapes, tiles, or pattern blocks* and *graph paper.*

Introduce patterns in which each subsequent item builds on the previous one: one small blue square, two small blue squares, three small blue squares, etc. Start by varying only one attribute at a time.

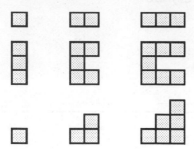

When students are adept at the skill, have them work on graph paper instead of using manipulatives. Challenge them to build and vary with more than one attribute.

Procedure 4

To relate numbers to patterns

Use *tiles or cubes* and *graph paper.*

Work first from the patterns in Procedure 3 and then from these:

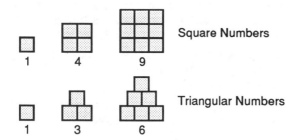

Square Numbers

1   4   9

Triangular Numbers

1   3   6

Have students make charts and look for patterns that will predict the next number in the series. Can they find the 7th? Ask: What rule will work for any number in the series?

	□	⊞	▦	?
Position in series	1	2	3	4
# Blocks	1	4	9	
Possible solutions related to number, position	1 + 0 1 × 1	(1 + 1) + 2 2 × 2 2 + 2	(1 + 1) + (2 + 2) + 3 3 × 3 3 + 3 + 3	

Procedure 5

To work with three-dimensional patterns

Use *cubes.*

Start with repeating patterns that vary in height, and then increase in complexity.

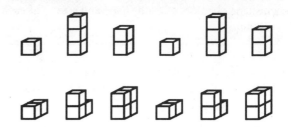

When students can work with repeating patterns, explore three-dimensional patterns in which each subsequent item is built on the previous one.

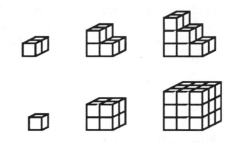

Practice and Extension

As students become adept at the skills, suggest they try the next level of difficulty. Can they show a pattern using a different manipulative? Can they devise patterns using shoes, books, or other students?

Use *treasure boxes* or *object collections,* and have groups create a series, write down the rule on a piece of *paper,* and put the paper face down. Have the groups rotate and try to figure out the rule for the new series.

Have groups explore the relationships between square and triangular numbers. Can they make pentagonal or hexagonal numbers and figure out the series rules?

Have students use *paper shapes, attribute blocks, pattern blocks,* or *graph paper* to explore tiling patterns using two or more shapes, which fit together in a pattern to completely cover a space.

Geometry 2

Skill: To understand and classify angles

Time: 1 period per procedure

Materials:

- *tag board cut in ¹/₂" × 3" pieces:* 2 per student
- *scissors*

rulers or straightedges

paper fasteners: 1 per student

compasses or round objects for making circles

8"–10" string or yarn: 1 piece per pair of students

pattern blocks or tangrams

graph paper: any size

Anticipatory Set

Use *tag board pieces, scissors, rulers, paper fasteners, compasses or round objects,* and *plain paper.*

Make angle arrows: Have students mark the center point of each end of their tag board pieces and connect the points with a line. They should cut corners and fasten as shown with a paper fastener.

Make clock faces: Have students draw large circles, either with compasses or by tracing around objects. They cut these out, fold in quarters, and mark for clock faces: 3, 6, 9, 12.

Procedure 1

To understand angles

Use *pencils, string or yarn, angle arrows and clock faces from Anticipatory Set,* and *pattern blocks or tangrams.*

Have students work in pairs to wrap the center of the yarn around a pencil several times and then place the pencil at the center of the clock face.

Say: Start with both ends of the yarn at 12. Is any space between the lines made of yarn? (no)

Make one end of the yarn point to the three. Use another pencil to trace the space between the two lines, near the center point as shown. This space is called an angle. Ask: Without moving the yarn, can you find another angle?

Students find the 270° angle between 3 and 12.

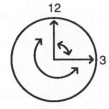

Which angle is bigger? (the one around to the left)

Now move your yarn from the three to the six. Ask: How many angles? (2) Which is bigger? (They are the same.)

Repeat for other combinations of clock times, having students also trace both angles together.

What do you notice about both angles together?

Students respond: They always add up to a circle.

Angles are always thought of as being part of a circle.

Repeat the procedure with angle arrows, and then have students use angle arrows to identify angles in the classroom: corners of desks, where the floor meets the wall, etc.

Have students use angle arrows to find the angles on pattern blocks or tangrams. How many angles does each piece have? Which are bigger? Which are the same?

Students draw pattern block pieces on paper and indicate angles. They make figures with 3, 4, 5, and 6 angles.

Procedure 2

To work with 90° angles

Use *angle arrows and clock faces from Anticipatory Set, pattern blocks or tangrams,* and *graph paper.*

Have students use angle arrows to find and measure several square corners.

Say: Use your angle arrows as clock hands, and show 3 o'clock. What do you notice about the smaller angle you have formed? (It is a square corner.)

We measure the size of an angle in degrees; all around the center point of a circle is 360°. A square corner is 90° and is also called a right angle.

Students find other 90° angles on their clock faces. They identify them as 90°, right angles, and ¹/₄ of a circle.

Move your arrows to show 4 o'clock. Is this a 90° or right angle?

Students identify this as more than a right angle. They find and identify other clock angles as more or less than a right angle.

If I moved 90° and then another 90°, how far would I have moved? (180°) What's a 180 in skateboarding? (a turn from front to back) That's half a circle: 180°.

What's a 360 in skateboarding? (a turn all the way around) That makes a whole circle: 360°.

Students use angle arrows to check angles on pattern blocks or tangrams. They identify them as 90° or smaller or larger than 90°. They use the clock face to check if necessary.

Have students use graph paper to draw angles smaller than, larger than, or equal to 90°. What can they draw with only right angles? No right angles, etc.?

Procedure 3   □■

To work with angles to the nearest 30°, 45°

Use *rulers, clock faces, scissors, angle arrows,* and *pattern blocks or tangrams.*

Have students use the rulers to draw lines on their clock faces from the center to the 12 and the 3.

Ask: How big is the angle between 12 and 3? (90°)

Have students cut out clock faces and fold them so that the 3 is on top of the 12, creasing the fold. Have them then open then up and draw a line on the crease.

Say: You folded the 90° angle in half and marked it; how many degrees are the smaller angles you have made? (half of 90°, or 45°)

Students draw lines from the center to the 6, 9, and 12. They then fold the 90° angles in half and mark the 45° angles. They write 45° in each angle.

Repeat the procedure for 30° and 60°, drawing the lines from the center to each number on the clock.

Ask: What combinations of angles could you use to find 120°? (four 30°s, or 90° and 30°, etc.)

Students repeat with other examples that require them to add angles or to subtract angles from 360°.

Have students use angle arrows to measure the angles of pattern blocks or tangrams. They use their marked clock faces to determine the size of each angle and then chart their results.

Students next use graph paper to construct angles and figures of specified angles. How close can they come? They check with their angle arrows and the clocks.

Practice and Extension

Have students use *art paper, angle arrows,* and *rulers* to draw all-over designs incorporating geometric shapes. They can create designs for buildings or skylines in black and white.

Have students research sundials and how they use angles to tell time.

Have students draw a city plan with streets at various angles.

Have students make patterns with *pattern blocks,* trace the patterns onto paper, and mark all the angles,

Geometry 3

Skill: To understand and find perimeter

Time: 3 periods

Materials:

geoboards and rubber bands or string
scissors

tiles
graph paper: any size
See Reproducibles for: geoboard paper

Anticipatory Set

Have students measure the distance around their desks or tables, using a body part as a unit. Discuss other ways they could measure the distance around.

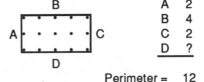

A	2
B	4
C	2
D	?

Perimeter = 12

Procedure 1

To develop the concept of *perimeter*

Use *geoboards, rubber bands, geoboard paper, scissors, tiles,* and *graph paper.*

Have students use the rubber bands to enclose the smallest square possible on their geoboards.

Say: We want to know how far around this square is. We'll call the distance from one peg to the next 1 unit. Start at the bottom left peg and trace the rubber band to the peg at the right.

Ask: How far have we gone?

Students respond: 1 unit.

Write a 1 on the board. Say: Go to the next peg. Now how far have we gone? (2 units)

Write a +1 on the board below the first 1.

Continue until students have gone all the way around. Draw a line under the 1s and write: Perimeter = 4 Units.

$$
\begin{array}{r}
1 \\
+1 \\
+1 \\
\underline{+1} \\
\end{array}
$$

Perimeter = 4 Units

Repeat with a two-peg by three-peg rectangle. Have students identify the length of each of the sides before tracing the perimeter. Write the chart on the board as before. Ask: Can you tell what the word *perimeter* means?

Students respond: It means the distance around.

Repeat with other rectangles, having students chorally count each distance, and continuing to chart perimeter on the board.

Write the following problem on the board.

Discuss with students how to find what's missing.

Ask: What more do we need to add to the distance to get to 12? (4) What is the difference between what we have and what we're supposed to have?

Repeat with other examples.

Students make rectangles with perimeters of 12 units, recording each figure on geoboard paper. They discuss what is the same and different about these.

When students are comfortable with the skill, repeat activities with figures that are not rectangles. *Make sure they do not include slanted lines.*

Students use tiles to make figures with larger perimeters. Each tile must have at least one side touching another tile. They draw and record results on graph paper. They cut out their figures and make a class chart of perimeters.

Procedure 2

To relate perimeter and area

Use *graph paper and tiles* or *geoboards with rubber bands or string.*

Draw the following illustration on the board:

Have students enclose a two-peg by three-peg rectangle on their geoboards, or make a two-tile rectangle.

Ask: How many units around? (6) Each small square covers 1 square unit of space, which is the area. What is the area? (2 square units)

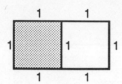

Have students make, and record on graph paper, as many figures as possible with the following perimeters: 4, 6, 8, 10, and 12. For each one, they figure and record the area as well.

Slanted lines are not allowed, and each square must have at least one side adjacent to another square.

Students with geoboards may wish to use string instead of rubber bands.

On the board, set up two perimeter/area charts, one with perimeter first and the other with area.

As students finish, they add their data to both charts, ordering their perimeters and areas from smallest to largest. The class discusses any patterns they see.

Challenge students to discover what figure gives the most area for a given perimeter. (a square) Ask: What is the largest perimeter you can get using a given area? What strategies did you use to figure this out?

Procedure 3   ☐■

To find the formula for the perimeter of rectangles

Use *graph paper and tiles* or *geoboards with rubber bands or string*.

Have students build rectangles, all with a width of 1 unit but of varying lengths. Make a chart on the board, headed "W, L, W, L, Perimeter."

Students make rectangles and add data to the chart. They repeat with rectangles with a width of 2 units.

Ask: What patterns can you find on the chart?

Students respond: Widths are always alike, and lengths are always alike for a given rectangle.

I could write a rectangle's perimeter as w + l + w + l. Is there another way?

Students respond: 2 w's and 2 l's.

We write this as P = 2 × w + 2 × l, or P = 2w + 2l. Does this work for other four-sided figures?

Students explore, using various materials. They discover that this formula works for some but not all four-sided figures.

Practice and Extension

Have students use *tiles or other squares* as pentominoes. How many different shapes can students make with five of them? (12) How many different perimeters are possible? What strategies did students use to find all the shapes?

Have students use *maps* marked with distances to figure out the perimeter of given areas. Can students find a route for a 100-mile bicycle race that begins and ends at the same place?

Have students use *pattern blocks* to explore figures other than quadrilaterals. Can they find formulas for perimeters? How do the perimeters change when the students use more than one block? Have students chart results and look for patterns.

Geometry 4

Skill: To define polygons

Time: 2 periods

Materials:

geoboards and rubber bands

markers: to match pattern block colors

pattern blocks

scissors

See Reproducibles for: *geoboard paper*

Anticipatory Set

Use *geoboards, rubber bands, geoboard paper,* and *markers.*

Have students enclose five different shapes on their geoboards. They should record all shapes on their geoboard paper and color them.

Procedure 1

To develop a definition of *polygon*

Use *geoboards, rubber bands,* and *geoboard paper.*

Tell the students they have been making polygons. Ask: Can anyone can figure out the three rules which define a polygon? Write their possible rules on the board.

Next give them a little more information by drawing a curved, closed figure such as a circle. Say: This is not a polygon.

Students discuss the difference between this figure and their geoboard shapes and decide whether any of their rules are no longer possible.

Draw an open, straight-sided figure on the board, such as a rectangle with one missing side. Ask students whether any of them have made this figure on their geoboards. Explain that this is not a polygon but is called an open figure.

Students discuss which rules now cannot be correct.

Ask: If the last drawing was called an open figure, what do you think a polygon must be? (a closed figure)

Hold up a solid object, such as a cube or book. Explain that this is not a polygon.

Students should now be able to state that a polygon is a flat, closed figure with straight sides.

Ask students whether any of them made a figure on their geoboards like:

Is this a polygon? (yes) Why?

Ask them to figure out which two parts of polygons have names. (sides and vertices) Define the names.

Ask whether any connection exists between sides and vertices. Lead students to discuss ways to gather information about polygons.

Students make a chart showing headings: "Sides," "Vertices," "Name." Using rubber bands and geoboards, they make, draw, and chart information about polygons with different numbers of sides.

Discuss the class's findings. Did some of the figures have more than one name? (square, rectangle) What did they decide to do about that? What patterns did they see?

Procedure 2

To construct polygons

Use *pattern blocks, plain paper, markers,* and *scissors.*

Ask students to see how many different polygons they can make using only two different pattern block shapes.

Tell them to have one side of each touching and then to trace around the whole polygon and then the individual parts.

Discuss what constitutes a "different" polygon, and reach a class consensus.

Ask: How can you keep track so that the whole class can share information? (A chart or table of some kind is a good idea.)

Students work individually to discover and chart polygons.

Some questions to discuss: How many sides did each piece have to start with? How many sides do the new polygons have? Do you see a connection between the number of sides of the original pieces and the number of possible new polygons?

Students color their polygons to match the pattern blocks. They cut them out to add to a large wall chart for the whole class.

Practice and Extension

Have students draw objects. They then use *rulers* to draw polygons over their original drawing, following the lines as closely as possible.

Students can use *geoboards* and *rubber bands or string* to make a polygon with the largest number of sides. Rubber bands can cross over each other; it is the outermost edge that is important.

Challenge students to see how many different polygons they can make using three different *pattern block* shapes.

Geometry 5

Skill: To find lines of symmetry

Time: 2 periods

Materials:

pattern blocks
geoboards and rubber bands

scissors
paste
mirrors: if available
See Reproducibles for: geoboard paper

Anticipatory Set

Use *pattern blocks.*

All grade levels:

Have students put two squares together. These pieces are equal and meet at a centerline. Have students flip one square on the centerline so that it lies on top of the second square. Repeat with other equal and unequal pieces.

Grade three:

Extend the primary activity further, placing shapes other than squares on either side of the original squares. Instruct students to make figures that will flip over to lie exactly on the other half.

Procedure 1

To develop the concept of *symmetry*

Use *geoboards, rubber bands,* and *geoboard paper.*

Have students enclose each of these squares on their geoboards:

Ask: What do you notice about the squares?

Students respond: They are the same size and shape. They share a side.

Say: Put a rubber band around the outside of both squares, making a two-square rectangle. The line the squares share is called a *line of symmetry.* You will have to find out what this means.

Students draw their rectangles on geoboard paper.

Have students place the original squares on the geoboard and then stretch one square to make the figure shown in the next illustration.

Say: Now enclose the whole figure.

Students enclose the figure and draw their geoboard designs on geoboard paper.

This figure has a line, but it is not a line of symmetry. How is this different from the first rectangle?

Students respond: These parts are unequal.

When can you have a line of symmetry? (when both sides are equal) Let's see if this definition is enough.

Have students make and draw the following figure:

Are both sides equal? (yes) This does not have a line of symmetry. What else do you need to add to your definition?

Students discuss their symmetrical and nonsymmetrical figures.

Suggest they fold the drawn figures on the centerline to see what happens.

Students should discover that the halves are not only equal but are positioned so that one side will flip over, on a line of symmetry, to lie exactly on the other.

Repeat with other shapes, and then give students larger and more complex shapes to subdivide with lines of symmetry.

Students construct, draw, and check the symmetry of more complex figures.

Procedure 2

To work with multiple lines of symmetry

Use *pattern blocks, scissors, paste, mirrors* if available, and *paper.*

Make a table headed: "Symmetrical" and "Non-symmetrical."

Using actual pattern blocks on the overhead, or chalk on the board, construct symmetrical and nonsymmetrical figures under the appropriate heading. Include some nonsymmetrical figures composed of the same parts:

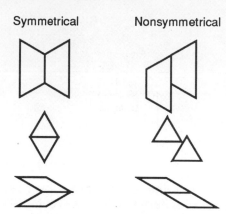

Symmetrical   Nonsymmetrical

Students discuss rules for symmetry: Each half is identical and is positioned so that it can be flipped over the centerline to lie exactly on the other half.

Have students make symmetrical figures with pattern blocks, constructing the figures on paper and then tracing around each part.

Students construct, trace, and fold each figure to check for symmetry. They use mirrors to check, if available.

Have students trace one hexagon. Ask: Is it possible to have more than one line of symmetry?

Students fold hexagons and decide it is possible. They explore multiple lines of symmetry for other pattern block pieces and discuss their findings.

Challenge students to create designs with more than one line of symmetry. What will they have to consider? Is there a pattern to the types of designs that have multiple lines of symmetry?

Students experiment. They trace around, cut out, and paste pattern block shapes to duplicate their design. They mark all lines of symmetry.

Have students explore the relationship between the number of identical parts and the number of lines of symmetry.

Procedure 3

To work further with multiple lines of symmetry

Use *geoboards, rubber bands, geoboard paper,* and *mirrors,* if available.

Repeat Procedure 2 with geoboards. Can students find a large four-sided figure that has four lines of symmetry?

Students construct figures, draw on geoboard paper, and fold to check. They can use mirrors, if available, to check.

Practice and Extension

Challenge students to use *rulers* and *circles* to draw all possible lines of symmetry of a circle. How many can they find? It may take them a while to discover that an infinite number exists.

Have students collect and display *pictures* of examples of symmetry, both in nature and humanmade.

Have students design symmetrical buildings on *graph paper.*

Use *mirrors* and *full-face snapshots* of students. Have students discover that faces are not totally symmetrical.

Geometry 6

Skill: To understand and find area

Time: 4 periods

Materials:

sheets of paper: various sizes

1" tiles or cubes

graph paper: to match tile or cube size

geoboards and rubber bands

pattern blocks or tangrams

See Reproducibles for: geoboard paper

Anticipatory Set

Use *sheets of paper* and *tiles or cubes.*

Have groups of students choose one manipulative and cover their sheet of paper with it. Discuss how many it took to cover each sheet. Can they tell whose sheet was largest? Why not? Discuss the need for all to use the same unit of measurement.

Procedure 1

To establish the concept of *area*

Use *graph paper* and *tiles or cubes (5 per student).*

Tell students they have been measuring area, *a measure of covering.* **Discuss when they would need to know a surface's area; e.g., carpeting, paper wrap, paint, grass seed, etc.**

Say: We are going to say one tile will cover 1 square unit. Cover 1 square unit of your desks by putting a tile somewhere on it.

Students place tiles.

Now place a second tile next to the first one. Ask: How much area have you covered?

Students respond: 2 square units.

Repeat with a third and fourth tile.

Ask: Are all the shapes alike? (no) How can they all cover the same area?

Students discuss.

Hand out graph paper, and have students make shapes with areas of 1 to 5 square units.

Students place tiles, trace shapes, and label with the area.

Now have students make as many different shapes as they can, using five tiles.

Explain that shapes of five squares are pentominoes. Twelve are possible.

Discuss what constitutes a "different" shape. Be sure shapes that only differ in the amount of rotation are recognized as "same shapes."

Students can color, cut, and display shapes.

Procedure 2

To work with area using whole square units

Use *geoboards, rubber bands,* and *geoboard paper.*

Have students enclose the smallest square possible. This will be 1 square unit.

Have students enclose a rectangle with an area of 2 square units, then 3 square units.

Ask: What other shapes can you make with 3 square units?

Students make a chart: "Area" and "Shapes Possible."

They find shapes of given areas and draw them on geoboard paper.

Discuss students' findings. One discovery they should make is that the larger the area, the more shapes possible.

Procedure 3

To further practice the concept of area

Use *pattern blocks* or *tangrams.*

Have students cover shapes in several different ways. Designate a small block or tangram piece as 1 square unit. Ask: How much area do the others cover?

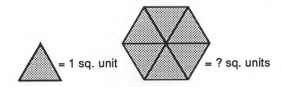

Have students make patterns with the pattern blocks or tangrams.

Students estimate total area and then check with blocks.

Can students make a pattern that covers a specific area? Can they do this without using the unit piece?

It is important for students to use more than one manipulative to establish the concept.

Procedure 4

☐■

To measure area using half square units

Use *geoboards, rubber bands,* and *geoboard paper.*

Have students enclose the smallest square possible. Then have them use another rubber band to enclose a triangle that is ½ the square.

Ask: What is the area of the square? (1 square unit) Then what is the area of the triangle? (½ square unit)

Have students make a rectangle of 2 square units and then use other rubber bands to show the four ½ square units possible. How many whole square units of area? (2)

How many ½ square units? (4)

Do those four ½ square units add to 2 square units?

Students respond: Yes. They discover sometimes with odd-shaped polygons they have to add the ½ square units to get the whole area.

Have students construct shapes with areas of 2½, 3½, and 4 square units on their geoboards. Make sure ½ square units are actually that; all diagonals must be at a 45° angle.

Draw some polygons. Have students duplicate each, and then see whether they can find the area. How did they find the total area?

Students first predict the area and then find and write the separate areas they measured to get a total. They discuss their strategies with the class.

Advanced students can be given drawings and dimensions of odd floor plans that need carpeting. They can duplicate them proportionally with geoboards or geoboard paper and find the amount of carpet needed.

Practice and Extension

Have student draw four polygons on plain paper and estimate their areas. Which is largest? They then cut them out, trace onto *graph paper,* and figure the area. They need to decide whether a partial square should be counted as ½, 1, or 0 square units. How accurate were their estimates? Did they revise estimates after the first polygon was done?

Give students a *polygon shape with an area of 16 square inches.* Then give them a *4" ×4" piece of graph paper.* Students work in groups to decide how to cover the shapes with the graph paper (without actually cutting it). They mark all lines that will be cut, trying for the fewest possible lines.

Geometry 7

Skill: To find area: rectangles

graph paper: any size

scissors

See Reproducibles for: geoboard paper

Time: 3 periods

Materials:

tiles or cubes

geoboards and rubber bands

Anticipatory Set

Use *tiles* or *cubes*.

Review the concept of area by having students make rectangles of different areas. Review that area is a measure of surface either covered or enclosed by boundaries.

Tell students you will be painting a hall. The walls arc cach 8 feet high and 20 feet long. A gallon of paint covers 400 square feet. How much paint will you need?

Go to Procedure 1.

Procedure 1

To find a formula for the area of rectangles

Use *tiles* or *cubes*.

Students discuss possible ways of arriving at the answer to the Anticipatory Set problem.

Say: A quick math way exists to find the area of a rectangle, which is the shape of the walls in the hall to be painted, and today you will discover it.

Students make a chart headed: "Number of Rows," "Squares per Row," and "Area in Square Units."

Write the headings on the board. Review rows and number of squares per row to make sure all are charting the same data.

Students makc ten rectangles and chart results. They look for a pattern.

When students are finished, suggest it would be easier to see a pattern if the data were organized. Discuss with the students ways to do this.

Number of Rows	Squares per Row	Area in Square Units
1	1	1
1	2	2
1	3	3
1	4	4
2	1	2
2	2	4
2	3	6
2	4	8

Explain that one way is to start with a 1×1 rectangle. If nobody made one, what would the area be? (1 square unit) Continue until the chart looks like the illustration.

Again have students look for a pattern.

Students discuss that the first two numbers could be multiplied to find the third.

Ask: When else have we built rectangles from blocks?

Students respond: To show multiplication.

Say: You are adding row after row, with the same number blocks In each row, to make the size rectangle you want.

Ask: What is a shortcut for adding same size groups? (multiplication) When we want to show two groups of three in math language, how do we write it? (2×3)

Math language has a way to write directions for finding the area of any rectangle.

General directions are called *formulas* and have letters or symbols to stand for what is happening. When you have a specific rectangle, you put its numbers into the formula and know what to do.

I want to write a formula for area of a rectangle. I start with A =. A stands for what? (area)

We know we are multiplying two things together for any rectangle. Suppose the rectangle is a football field. What do I call one of the sides? (the length)

And the other side? (the width)

What would I multiply to get the area?

Students respond: Length times width.

Add the words "Length" (squares per row) and "Width" (rows) to the chart on the board.

Students add to their charts.

Write A = length $\times$ width on the board.

Ask: What letters could I use to stand for the words?

Students respond: l and w.

Write A = l $\times$ w.

Suppose I have a rectangle where the length is 5 and the width is 2.

Students build rectangles and find A = 10.

Write on the board to demonstrate form:

A = l × w

A = 5 × 2

A = 10

Explain that math language is just a description of what is really happening. *What we write describes what we can do with manipulatives.*

Give other dimensions, and have students build the rectangles. As students do each step with tiles or cubes, they write the corresponding step on paper. They need much practice at this step.

When students are confident about the process, they can move to doing the problem on paper first and then checking with the manipulatives.

Have students go back and figure the answer to the problem in the Anticipatory Set.

Procedure 2 □■

To find the area of squares

Use *any of the listed materials.*

Have students build squares and chart the dimensions and areas. Discuss patterns: Both factors are the same. These are square numbers.

Procedure 3 □■

To practice finding area

Use *geoboards, rubber bands, graph paper or geoboard paper,* and *scissors.*

Have students make rectangles, make up story problems to go with them, and then find the areas.

Students chart each rectangle, cut them out, and combine them to make a figure of their choice. This helps them see that multiple shapes may be within a larger shape.

Procedure 4 □■

To find the area of shapes made of more than one rectangle

Use *any of the listed materials* and *plain paper.*

Write A = 12 on the board, and have students find all possible rectangle dimensions for this area.

Have students explore areas and trade findings with partners to make a chart.

Draw an L-shaped floor plan on the board.

Students make the shape and then draw it. They devise a way to find the total area.

Students discuss breaking the floor into two rectangles and finding the area of each.

Discuss methods students may have used and situations in which they might need to use these methods.

Give other examples. Can students find the areas first with formulas and prove with a manipulative? Repeat until students are competent in the skill.

Practice and Extension

Have students bring *supermarket containers from home.* They find the surface area of rectangular sides. How many cereal boxes, cut apart and laid flat, would it take to measure their desks?

Have students interview parents or other adults at home to find how they use the concept of area.

Geometry 8

Skill: To classify solid figures

Time: 2 periods

Materials:

solid geometric figures (see Manipulative Information section for ideas)

supermarket containers

cubes

geometric solids: rigid plastic foam or clay

graph paper: to match cube size

Anticipatory Set

Use whatever *solid geometric figures* you plan to teach.

Show students the figures, and have them brainstorm examples of these in real life.

Have students list everything they notice about these figures. Discuss lists.

Procedure 1

To learn the concepts of *face*, *edge*, and *vertex*

Use *geometric figures, supermarket containers,* and *cubes.*

Have students identify and draw the separate sides of each figure or container. Ask: Are they all the same? (not necessarily) Each individual side is called a *face.* How many faces did each figure have?

Students discuss. Did they incude the bottom face?

Have students make a layer of four cubes. On top of these have students build a building three cubes high at its highest point.

Students use various numbers of cubes to build structures.

Discuss the buildings. Some may have made chimneys or smokestacks. How many separate faces does each building have?

Students discuss. Answers will vary.

Have students examine a cube. Tell them to run their fingers over each *edge* and *vertex*. Ask: How many edges does a cube have? (12) Are they straight? (yes)

How many points or vertices? (8) Have students examine their buildings for edges and vertices.

Continue until students have grasped the concepts.

Procedure 2

To practice the concept of face

Use *rigid plastic foam or clay geometric figures.*

Have students predict the shape of the resulting new faces if you cut the figures in half. What clues did they use?

Cut each figure, and discuss which clues worked to help predict correct shapes.

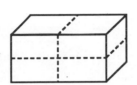

Suggest they label figures with the number of faces and shape of the figure, and set up a display.

Procedure 3

To classify solid figures; prisms, pyramids

Use whatever *solid geometric figures* you plan to teach.

Have students examine each figure to decide where its base would be.

Have students make charts. As you name each figure, have them fill in the data.

Name	Base Shape	Face Shape
square prism (cube)	square (rectangle)	square
triangular prism	triangle	rectangle
rectangular prism	rectangle	rectangle
square pyramid	square	triangle
triangular pyramid	triangle	triangle
rectangular pyramid	rectangle	triangle

Students fill in data and look for patterns that would help them name any new figures.

Discuss the chart with students. If they do not see patterns, ask what is the same about all pyramids.

Students respond: They come to a point, and they have triangular faces.

Ask: What is the same about all prisms?

Students respond: They all have rectangular faces.

Remind students that squares are one kind of rectangle.

Students see that the shape of a face determines whether a figure is a pyramid or a prism.

Say: One way to remember which is which: A prism looks like a building; a prison is a building. *Prism* sounds like *prison*.

Can students discover how to name each *kind* of pyramid or prism?

Students see that the shape of the base determines this.

Have students find geometric solids within the classroom to identify and classify.

Have students hold a *solid figure* behind their back and give a description: faces, edges, vertices, base. Partners must guess the shape.

Draw a pattern on *tag board* of a square, a rectangle with the width of the square, and an equilateral triangle with the base measurement matching the side of the square. Draw tabs along most of each side.

Have students trace those patterns on tag board, cut them out, and construct the figures of their choice. Tabs are folded under and sides are *pasted* or *taped* together. Students may wish to enlarge patterns to make giant geometric solids. By making hexagons, octagons, etc., many solids are possible.

Procedure 4   ☐■

To practice three-dimensional visualization

Use *cubes* and *graph paper*.

Give students a base shape and a silhouette. They use cubes to build buildings. Give advanced students several side views of more complex structures.

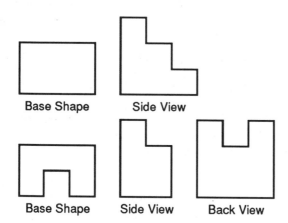

Base Shape   Side View

Base Shape   Side View   Back View

Have students construct their own buildings, draw the base and sides shapes, and give them to partners to construct.

Ask: Are the buildings the same? How many solid figure components can you identify in each building?

Student pairs present their findings to the class.

Practice and Extension

Have students bring in *pictures of their homes* and identify the component solid figure

Students can use *clay* to make and identify different figures.

Geometry 9

Skill: To understand congruence and similarity

Time: 2 periods

Materials:

attribute blocks or paper shapes: triangles, circles, and rectangles of the same and different sizes

pattern blocks

geoboards and rubber bands

scissors

light source: flashlight, overhead projector, slide projector

rulers or straightedges

graph paper: any size

See Reproducibles for: geoboard paper

Anticipatory Set

Use *attribute blocks* or *paper shapes*.

Have students sort first by shape. Then have students sort each shape into groups of the same size.

Procedure 1

To understand *congruence*

Usc *groups of shapes from the Anticipatory Set* and *pattern blocks*.

Say: You have groups of shapes that are exactly the same shape and size. We call shapes *congruent* if they match both shape and size exactly.

Hold up two congruent triangles. Ask: Are these the same shape? (yes) Are these the same size? (yes) Are these congruent? (yes)

Repeat with two triangles different in size from the first.

Have students hold up other congruent figures. Make sure they understand color is not a factor.

Hand out pattern blocks, and instruct students to use three shapes to build a larger shape. Then have them copy their partner's new shapes. Remind them they are trying to make a copy that is congruent.

Next hold up or place on the overhead two congruent shapes. Are these congruent? (yes) Rotate one and ask again.

Students discuss that position isn't a factor for congruence.

Continue until students are responding accurately.

Procedure 2

To practice the concept of congruence

Use *geoboards, rubber bands, geoboard paper,* and *scissors*.

Have students make congruent dot-to-dot shapes on geoboard paper and then cut them out.

Have students set pairs of shapes aside for later to color and display on a class chart.

Have students use different-colored rubber bands to make congruent shapes on the geoboards and then copy a partner's shape.

Ask: How many ways can you find to divide your whole geoboard into two or more congruent parts?

Students chart each on gcoboard paper.

Can they make congruent angles? Can they make triangles with only one, two, or three congruent angles?

Students discuss why they cannot make triangles with only two congruent angles.

Procedure 3

To understand *similarity*

Use a *light source* and *attribute blocks or paper shapes*.

Place a triangle in front of a light source or on the overhead, projecting the shadow onto the wall or a screen. Have students compare the original triangle and the large image.

Ask: Are they the exact same shape? (yes) Are they the same size? (no) We call shapes like this *similar*.

What do we call shapes of exactly the same shape *and* size? (congruent)

Tell students to find all the similar shapes they can with their manipulatives.

Students find similar shapes.

Hold up random pairs of shapes, and have students identify them as similar, congruent, or not alike. Repeat until all students are responding accurately.

Procedure 4

To use the concept of similarity to develop understanding of scale

Use *graph paper and rulers* or *geoboards, rubber bands, and geoboard paper*.

Say: Make a 2 × 2 square on your graph paper. We want to make a similar, not congruent square. We'll make it twice as big.

Ask: How many squares long will it be? (4) How many squares wide? (4)

Students construct similar squares.

Discuss how scale is used in maps and how patterns can be enlarged using scale. Have advanced students draw a picture on small graph paper and transfer it to larger scale graph paper or use a different scale.

Students can also do this exercise using geoboards. They would chart the figures on geoboard paper.

Practice and Extension

Have students make a class chart to display the *congruent figures from Procedure 2*. Have students also make and display a chart of *graph paper similar shapes from Procedure 4*.

Gives students squares of *waxed paper*. Use a square on the overhead. Make two intersecting lines by folding the paper and opening it up. The lines will form angles and will show as dark lines on the screen. Ask students to bisect the angle into two congruent parts. Demonstrate on the overhead after they have experimented. Adapt for triangles and rectangles.

Give students five *tiles or construction paper squares*. Have them find and chart on *graph paper* all possible combinations (pentominoes). Caution students that some congruent shapes may appear to be different if one has been rotated. They are still the same shape. Twelve shapes are possible.

Have students take *maps* and measure distance from one place to another using the scale given.

Have students practice making *scale drawings* using simple pictures from *commercial coloring books*.

Measurement 1

Skill: To learn pre-skills for measurement: length, mass, and capacity

Time: Varies with readiness level

Materials:

Materials for Length:

objects: paper clips or other sets of identical small objects

masking tape

Cuisenaire® rods or interlocking cubes: rods or sticks of 5 or more

Materials for Weight:

scales: a variety of types, including balance scales

objects: heavy and light

treasure box or other objects: beans, rocks, shells

boxes: full and empty of about the same size

objects: paper clips, pencils, or other sets of identical objects that can be used as units of measurement

Materials for Capacity:

materials to measure: beans, rice (see Manipulative Information section for suggestions)

measuring containers: identical, such as paint cups, half-pint milk cartons, plastic cups; some should be glass or easily seen through—1 per group

containers: large and small such as bowls, empty boxes, milk cartons

Note: These skills are presented in a developmental sequence within each category. Each bullet indicates a separate activity that may be used as an ongoing activity or as an Anticipatory Set for other Measurement activities.

Procedure 1

To learn pre-skills for length

Use *materials for length.*

- Have students compare lengths of objects directly. Ask: Which is longer? Which is shorter?

- Have students view two objects and estimate which is longer. Have them make a direct comparison to check.

- Have students view more than two objects and estimate the order of their lengths. Have them make direct comparisons and order them.

- Give groups of students paper clips of identical size. Have students lay paper clips in a line next to one of their books and report how many paper clips long it is.

  Ask such questions as: The book in Jennifer's group is 12 paper clips long, and Jorge's group has a book 10 paper clips long. Which group's book is longer? Which is shorter?

- Stick lengths of masking tape on tables or on the floor. Give each group Cuisenaire® rods or interlocking cubes, one color per group.

  Have each group estimate, measure, and chart how many rods or sticks long the tapes are. "Between four and five rods long" is an acceptable answer. They can write this as 4–5.

- Next have groups put their rods or sticks together to make trains, different lengths for each group. Have them estimate, measure, and chart the lengths of the tapes in train lengths.

As students get more adept at this skill, help them see that a tape may be two trains and a purple rod long. Since trains are different lengths for each group, students should see the need for standard measurements.

Procedure 2

To learn pre-skills for weight

Use *materials for weight.*

- Have students compare the weight of objects directly. Ask: Which is heavier? Which is lighter? Compare the weights on a balance scale. What does it mean when one side goes down? Relate this event to a teeter-totter.

- Have students experiment with objects and a balance scale. How many shells do they estimate will weigh the same as one rock? Have them check and discuss.

- Present students with two boxes of about the same size. Do not tell them one is full and one is empty. Have students estimate which box will be heavier. Have students compare the weights directly. What did they find out about measuring weight?

- Have groups of students all use the same unit of weight, such as a small book. Have them estimate and then weigh other books in "small book units." Have them chart their estimates and actual measurements.

  Ask such questions as: The book in Miguel's group weighs 3 small books; the book in

Latonia's group's weighs 2 small books. Which group's book weighs more? Which weighs less?

- Present students with lightweight and heavy objects to use as units. Which would they use to measure an apple? A large book? Themselves?

- Students can experiment weighing objects of their choice with either of two units. If one group's object weighs 20 paper clips and another group's weighs 5 pencils, whose weighs more? Students should see the need for standard measurements.

- Have students weigh objects on a variety of scales. Are some scales easier to use than others? Have them match varying objects to the appropriate scale. Would they weigh themselves on a big balance scale?

Procedure 3

To learn pre-skills for capacity

Use *materials for capacity*.

- Pour different amounts of beans into identical glass containers. Have students compare amounts directly. Which container is holding more?

- Fill a large and a small container with beans. Have students decide which holds more. Pour beans onto a table to compare which makes the largest pile.

  Repeat with different sizes and shapes of containers. What is a problem with deciding how much something holds? Have students repeat with many sizes. Can they estimate how full the next container will be?

- Give each student group different-sized containers: one as a measuring unit and one to fill. Have them estimate, measure, and chart the capacity of their large container in small container units.

  Which group's large container holds more? Can they put the large containers in order? Students should see the need for a standard measuring unit.

- Present students with various sizes of milk cartons to use as units. Which would they use to measure the capacity of a small bowl? A large bowl? An aquarium or a bathtub?

Measurement 2

Skill: To measure length by inches, feet, and yards

Time: 1 period per procedure

Materials:

graph paper: ¹⁄₂" squares (for older students)—pre-cut if desired into 1" × 11" strips; 1 per student

clear tape

foot rulers: marked to the inch or half-inch as desired

yardsticks

See Reproducibles for: graph paper with 1" squares; pre-cut for younger students into 1" squares—1 per student, and 1" × 11" strips—6 per student

---

Note: Before introducing standard units, make sure students are comfortable with the measuring pre-skills found in Measurement 1.

Anticipatory Set

Have students measure the width of the room in footsteps by placing one foot closely in front of the other and counting the number of steps. Chart the results. Why did we get so many different answers? How wide is the room? Is there a better way to measure things?

Procedure 1

To understand and use inches

Use *1" graph paper and scissors* or *pre-cut 1" squares.*

Hand out or have students cut out six 1" × 1" squares. Identify these as being 1 inch long. Have students draw an arrow from one side of each square to the other, and label each "1."

Have students use only one square and find objects in the classroom to measure. Are the objects more or less than 1 inch?

Students first estimate and then measure by comparing their square with the object.

Younger students need first to be taught to line up the left edge of the square with the left edge of the object.

Have students find a part of their hand that is close to an inch long. This will help establish the idea of an inch and can be used for estimating without a ruler. What else can they find that is an inch long?

Students use their body ruler to estimate, measure objects, and check for accuracy with their paper inches.

They use their paper inches and draw lines that are an inch, more than an inch, and less than an inch.

Procedure 2

To measure inches; to measure to the nearest inch

Use *inch squares from Procedure 1, 1" graph paper strips (for younger students) or ¹⁄₂" graph paper and scissors (for older students), tape,* and *rulers.*

Have groups of students measure a book they all have. How can they find out how many inches long it is? (by using more than one inch-square) All arrows should point to the right.

Younger students can be directed to line up first one, then another, then a third. Each time, ask: How many inches have you measured so far?

Students report the length of the book. If it is not an exact inch measurement, they report which two lengths it is between.

Say: Each arrow point shows us we have measured another inch. Which arrow point is the edge of the book nearer to, the inch square that is not long enough, or the one that is too long? We can say the book is about as long as the nearest inch.

Students estimate and then measure other objects, measuring to the nearest inch. They chart both estimates and measurements.

Did their estimates improve with practice? Discuss strategies students are using.

Can they measure three objects and chart them in order? They may need practice doing this to fully understand that larger measurements mean larger objects.

Next hand out or have students cut out the strips of graph paper. Have them tape squares to the end to make a strip of 12" if necessary.

Have students trace the first arrow with a finger. Ask: How many inches have we gone? (1, two ¹⁄₂s) Mark a one near the arrow point.

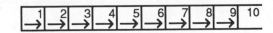

Grade 3 students can mark the half-inch lines as well, with a line that only goes halfway down.

Students continue to trace arrows, count the total inches, and mark the result near the arrow point until the ruler is finished.

They estimate, then measure objects to the nearest inch or half-inch, charting results. They make sure to line up the left edge of their ruler with the left edge of the object and trace along their paper ruler to find the measurement. Additional inch squares can be added. How close were their estimates?

Have students measure with real rulers. They can use their rulers to draw lines or figures to specific lengths.

Procedure 3 ▢■

To understand and use feet

Use *paper rulers from Procedure 2, inch squares,* and *rulers.*

Ask: How many inches long is your paper ruler? (12) Twelve inches is called a foot because one English king's foot was this long.

Have students estimate and then compare objects with the length of their ruler. If the objects are more than a foot, will students need another ruler, or only some extra inch squares?

Students measure and report their findings as more or less than a foot, or a foot and so many inches.

Ask: If you could measure with an inch or a foot, what would you measure with a foot? What would you measure with an inch?

What other lengths of measurement do you know? Would you measure the distance from your house to school in inches? Why or why not?

Have students estimate and then measure objects. Tell them to chart their findings both in feet and in inches. How close were their estimates?

Students read measurements of other groups and predict the biggest and smallest. They check by putting the objects in order.

Have students next practice measuring with real rulers.

Have them construct lines or figures exactly a foot long. When they are adept at this, have them measure or construct objects and lines a foot and a certain number of inches long. Measurements should be reported in feet plus inches, and in inches only.

Ask such questions as: Is 15 inches less than or more than a foot? If 12 inches are in a foot, how many inches are in 2 feet?

Procedure 4 ▢■

To understand and use yards

Use *rulers* and *yardsticks.*

Repeat Procedure 2 with rulers and yardsticks.

Ask such questions as: If a yard is 3 feet long, how many inches is that? Is 4 feet longer or shorter than a yard? Measurements should be reported in feet and inches, as well as yards. Have students do their constructions on chart paper or on the board with chalk.

Practice and Extension

Have students use *rulers* to draw houses for Inch or Foot City. Houses' heights and widths must be 1 inch or foot each. Cut out and display with trees, etc. to match.

Have students design sports events measured in inches and feet. Who runs the 100-inch race? Story problems could be written out with illustrations for a class measurement book.

Have students measure distances around school and post signs; e.g., 100 feet or yards to the office. How many inches would this be?

Compare and chart lengths of students' feet, hands, pencils, etc. This makes a good bar graph activity.

Have a *paper airplane* contest. Students construct airplanes and throw for distance. Measure the flight length.

Measure and mark a sidewalk or playground every 10 feet or yards. Use it for such physical activities as shuttle runs or relay races.

Have students toss *bean bags,* trying to get them exactly 1, 2, or 3 feet or yards away. Measure after they are thrown. Or, have students estimate the distance they have tossed. Give points for close estimates.

Measurement 3

Skill: To change one unit of length to another: inches, feet, and yards

Time: 2 periods

Materials:

clear tape

scissors

rulers

yardsticks

counters: 5 per student

See Reproducibles for: graph paper with 1" squares

Anticipatory Set

Use *graph paper, clear tape, scissors, rulers,* and *yardsticks.*

Have students make 1" × 12" rulers from strips of graph paper, taping extra squares as necessary. Have them mark and number each inch on the graph paper rulers.

Have students practice measuring the same distance in inches, using the graph paper rulers, feet using regular rulers, and yards using yardsticks. Students should make a chart and write in all three measurements.

Procedure 1

To change from larger to smaller units using serial addition or multiplication

Use *graph paper rulers from Anticipatory Set, rulers, and yardsticks.*

On the board draw three columns and label from left to right: "Yards," "Feet," "Inches." Write only three numbers to start: 1, 2, and then 3 vertically in the Feet column.

Yards	Feet	Inches
	1	12
	2	24
1	3	36
	4	48
	5	60
2	6	72
	7	
	8	
3	9	

Have groups of students lay a yardstick on the floor and line up three regular rulers along it.

Say: Each ruler is 1 foot. How many did it take to make a yard? (3) Each yard is a group of 3 feet.

Write a 1 in the Yard column beside the 3 in the Feet column.

Ask: If I have 2 yards, how many groups of 3 feet is that? (2)

Students put two yardsticks together, with the rulers beneath.

Ask: How do I find two groups of 3? (Multiply 2 × 3, or add 2 groups of 3.) Two yards equals how many feet? (6)

Add a 4, 5, and 6 to the Feet column on the board. Write a 2 in the Yards column next to the 6.

Students put three yardsticks together, with the rulers beneath. They find that 3 yards is three groups of 3 feet, or 9 feet. This is added to the chart, continuing the pattern.

Do you see a pattern to the yards and feet on the board?

Students respond: Each time the number of yards increases by one, the feet increase by three.

If I have a certain number of yards, what's the rule for finding how many feet? (Multiply the number of yards by 3 feet, or add groups of 3 feet.)

Students next lay out one regular ruler and place a paper ruler beneath.

Each foot is a group of how many inches? (12)

Add this to the chart.

Students lay another regular ruler beside the first, placing another paper ruler beneath.

Ask: How many feet do we have? (2) How many groups of 12 inches? (2) How do we find how many inches in all?

Students respond: Multiply 2 × 12 inches, or add groups of 12 inches.

Add the 24 to the chart.

Students place another regular and paper ruler, multiply 3 × 12 or add 12 + 12 + 12, and find that 3 feet equals 36 inches. This is added to the chart. They next lay a yardstick above the sets of rulers.

What can you tell me about yards and inches? (1 yard is a group of 36 inches) How many groups of 36 is 2 yards? (2) Two groups of 36 is how many inches? (72)

What is the rule for finding out how many inches are in any number of yards?

Students respond: Multiply the number of yards times 36 inches, or add groups of 36 inches.

Is the yard a big or small measurement? (big) If I measured the door with it, would I have many yards? (no) Is a foot bigger or smaller than a yard? (smaller)

If I measured the door in feet, would I have more or fewer than the number of yards? Why? (It would take more feet because feet are smaller.)

What can you say about measuring the door in inches? (It would be the biggest number because inches are smaller than feet.)

Have students measure out 2 yards 5 inches with their yardsticks and paper rulers.

A yard is a group of 36 inches. Do we have extra inches? (yes, 5) How can we find the total number of inches? (add the extra 5 to the 36) Repeat with other mixed measurements.

Students estimate and then measure the height of the classroom door in yards, feet, and inches. Which estimate was the closest? What strategies did those students use?

As you dictate lengths in yards or feet, students estimate the length and then use rulers and yardsticks to measure and convert to feet and inches. When they feel comfortable with the process, they do the addition or multiplication on paper and then check with the rulers.

See Practice and Extension of this lesson or Measurement 2 for measuring ideas.

Procedure 2

To change from smaller to larger units using division or repeated subtraction

Use *graph paper rulers from Anticipatory Set, rulers,* and *yardsticks.*

Make another chart as in Procedure 1. Write 12 in the Inches column.

Students work in groups. They set out one paper ruler, with a regular ruler above it.

Say: Your paper rulers are 12 inches. How many feet is that? (1) Write 1 in the Feet column next to the 12.

Students add another graph paper and regular ruler. They find that 24 inches equals 2 feet.

Repeat once more.

Students find that 36 inches equals 3 feet. They add each new result to the chart.

Ask: Do you see a pattern? (Inches increase by 12s, and the feet increase one at a time.)

Each time I have a group of 12 inches, what can I do with it? (change it for 1 foot) Does that fit the rest of the chart? (yes)

We are dividing the inches into groups of 12 and calling each group 1 foot. How could I explain this in math language?

Students respond: Subtract 12s from the inches, or divide by 12.

Students continue placing rulers and adding to the chart until they have 72 inches = 6 feet. Each time they convert to feet, they repeat they are dividing the inches into groups of 12 and then subtracting the groups to find the feet.

Have students lay a yardstick above the first three rulers. How many inches measure the same length? (36) Thirty-six inches makes how many groups of 12 to find feet? (3)

Ask: How many feet do we need for each yard? (3)

Add 1 in the Yards column.

Students repeat with a second yardstick and chart 2 in the Yards column by the 72 inches.

Ask: Do you see a pattern for the yards on the chart?

Students again look for patterns, looking this time at feet divided into groups of three and called yards. They see that every 3 feet or 36 inches, the yards increase one at a time.

Each time I have a group of 36 inches, what can I do with it? (change it for 1 yard) Does that fit the rest of the chart? (yes)

We are dividing the inches into groups of 36 and calling each group 1 yard. How could I explain this in math language?

Students respond: Subtract 36s from the inches, or divide by 36.

Is an inch a big or small measurement? (small) If I measured the door with inches, would I have many of them? (yes) Is a foot bigger or smaller than an inch? (bigger)

If I measured the door in feet, would I have more or fewer than the number of inches? Why? (It would take fewer feet because feet take up more distance.)

What can you say about measuring the door in yards? (It would be the smallest number because yards are the biggest measurement.)

Have students measure out 15 inches with their paper rulers.

Ask: How many groups of 12 can we get? (1) How many inches are left over? (3) We call this length 1 foot 3 inches. Repeat with other lengths.

As you dictate lengths in inches, students estimate the length and then use rulers and yardsticks to measure and convert to feet and yards. When they feel comfortable with the skill, they do the subtraction or division on paper and then check with the rulers.

Procedure 3

■□■

To compute using mixed measurements

Use *graph paper rulers from Anticipatory Set, graph paper, scissors, tape,* and *counters.*

Have students cut 20 1" × 1" squares, and three more 1" × 12" rulers, which need not be labeled with inches. Then have them make a place value type chart headed "Yards," "Feet," "Inches." Counters will represent yards.

Say: I need to measure a package to wrap it. One side is 1 foot 8 inches wide.

Students put 1 ruler and 8 inch-squares on their charts.

The next side is 4 inches.

Students place and report they have 1 foot 12 inches.

Ask: How can I make this simpler? (change the 12 inches for 1 foot) What is another word for making this kind of exchange? (regrouping) How is this like or unlike our usual regrouping?

Students discuss. This regrouping is done at 12 instead of 10. They now show 2 feet.

Say: The next side is again 1 foot 8 inches. Place the amount and make your total as simple as possible.

Students place and have 3 feet 8 inches. They exchange the 3 feet for 1 yard-counter and show 1 yard 8 inches. They discuss that the regrouping is at three, different from the exchange at 12.

The last side is 4 inches, but why am I not done?

Students allow another 4 inches for overlap. They place 8 inches and show 1 yard 16 inches, which is regrouped to 1 yard 1 foot 4 inches.

Summary:	Yards	Feet	Inches
Place:		1	8
Place:			4
Show:		1	12
Regroup:		2	0
Place:		1	8
Show:		3	8
Regroup:	1	0	8
Place:			8
Show:	1		16
Regroup:	1	1	4

Repeat with other measurements.

Students place and write each new measurement as an addition problem. They write each step after doing it on their charts.

When they "carry" what will they do? (They will carry 1 to the feet column for every 12 inches regrouped, and 1 to the yard column for every 3 feet regrouped.)

Repeat the procedure for subtraction, starting with a roll of paper 3 yards 2 feet 10 inches long. Subtract 8 inches at a time.

Students write each problem as they are doing it. They discuss the need to show an extra 12 in the inches column when they "borrow" from the feet, and an extra 3 in the feet column when they "borrow" from yards.

Have students make up mixed measurement problems for the class to do.

Practice and Extension

Have students research lengths of sharks, whales, or other animals. They measure and mark these with *tape* along the wall and label the distance in yards, feet, and inches.

Students estimate, measure, and chart each other's heights. They add all the heights together to find the total in yards, feet, and inches. Next they measure this distance down a hall. By lying down in a line, they can check for accuracy. What is the average height of the students in the class?

Students can estimate and then measure the distance between classrooms in yards and then convert. How many yards do they walk each day between classes? How many feet or inches? Post signs with arrows giving the distances to various points in several units.

Measurement 4

Skill: To measure length by centimeters and meters

Time: 1 period per procedure

Materials:

place value (pv) materials to 10s

centimeter rulers

scissors

clear tape

metersticks

See Reproducibles for: graph paper with 1 cm squares; pre-cut for younger students into 1 cm squares and 1 cm × 10 cm strips—5 of each per student

Note: Before introducing standard units, make sure students are comfortable with the measuring pre-skills found in Measurement 1.

Anticipatory Set

Have students work in groups to measure the widths of different, identical-size desks. Each group chooses a body part to use as a unit. Chart the results. Why are there so many different answers? Do we need a better way to measure an item? Students should remember measurement terms of inches and feet. Discuss why people all over the world need to be able to arrive at standard measurement terms.

Procedure 1

To understand and use centimeters

Use *pv blocks, rulers, and precut 1 cm squares and 1 precut strip per student (younger students) or graph paper and scissors (older students).*

Give students one cubes and explain that these are 1 centimeter long. Have students use only one cube and find objects in the classroom to measure. Ask: Are they more or less than 1 centimeter?

Students first estimate and then measure by comparing their cube with the object.

Have students find a part of their hand that is close to a centimeter long. This will help establish the idea of a centimeter and can be used for estimating without a ruler.

What standard objects can they find that are 1 cm long? Example: a raisin.

Students use their body ruler to estimate and measure objects and then check for accuracy with their cubes.

To establish the concept that a ruler is a series of added units, hand out or have students cut out five 1-cm squares.

Have students draw an arrow on each square from the left side to the right and label the squares "1" as shown. All arrows should point to the right.

Have students measure a book they all have. How can they find out how many centimeters long it is? (by using more than one square)

Younger students may need to be taught to line up the left edge of the square with the left edge of the object. Have them add one square at a time and report the measurement so far at each step. If the total is not an exact centimeter measurement, they should report the closest one.

Students estimate and measure other objects, measuring to the nearest centimeter and charting results. When they can do this accurately, they can look for objects a specific length, such as 6 cm or 10 cm.

Next hand out or have students cut out 1 cm × 10 cm strips of graph paper for paper rulers. Have students darken the centimeter division lines and draw the arrows.

Have students trace the first arrow with a finger. How many centimeters have we gone? (1) Mark a 1 as shown.

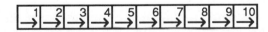

Students continue to trace arrows, count the total centimeters, and mark the results until all 10 centimeters are marked.

They estimate and trace along their paper ruler to measure objects to the nearest centimeter, checking results with partners. How close were their estimates? Are they getting more accurate with practice? Can they use the centimeter hand part to help estimate?

Have students measure with real rulers. See Practice and Extension for ideas.

Have students use their rulers to draw lines or figures to specific lengths. Continue the procedure until all students are competent in the skill.

Procedure 2 ◻◼

To understand and use meters

Use *pv materials to 10s, tape, metersticks,* and *all precut strips and squares (younger students) or 1 cm graph paper, scissors,* and *tape (older students).*

Have students work in groups and place 10 one cubes next to 1 ten rod. Review centimeters if necessary, and have students then place 10 ten rods in a line.

Ask: About how long is this line? (a yard) It is a little longer than a yard and is called a meter.

How many one cubes would it take to equal this? (100) If a meter were a dollar, what would a centimeter be? (cents or pennies)

Students estimate and then measure and chart lengths with their 10 ten rods. At first they only decide whether a length is more or less than a meter. Next they measure to the nearest meter. Are their estimates more accurate with practice?

At a more advanced level, they can report lengths in meters and the number of extra centimeters. Older students can chart or graph how close their estimates were each time.

Discuss with students what they would measure with a meter. A centimeter.

Hand out precut strips and squares, or graph paper, and have students work in pairs to cut 1 cm × 10 cm strips. They will need ten strips per pair.

Have them tape these together to make a meterstick. For the first centimeter on the left, have them draw an arrow from left to right and put a 1 near the arrow point as shown in Procedure 1.

Students repeat until ten squares have been labeled. They only *count* the next ten squares, mark 20, and darken the vertical line. The entire meterstick should be labeled *every 10 cm.*

Have students estimate and then measure distances. See Practice and Extension for suggestions. Findings are charted both in meters and centimeters. Have them compare their measurements with other groups as a check on accuracy.

Have students now practice measuring with real metersticks.

When they are adept at this, have them measure or construct lines a meter and a certain number of centimeters long. Measurements should be reported in meters plus centimeters, and in centimeters only.

Students use paper or real metersticks to answer such questions as: How many centimeters are in 2 meters?

Practice and Extension

Have students bring in lightweight *objects a cm long.* Glue these to tag board for a display.

Have students use *rulers* to draw houses for Centimeter City. Houses' heights and widths must be 1 centimeter each. Cut out and display with trees, etc., to match. Other students can make a Meter City mural with buildings' heights and widths 1 meter each.

Have students design sports events measured in centimeters and meters. Who runs the 100-centimeter race? Story problems could be written out with illustrations for a class measurement book.

Have students measure distances around school and post signs; e.g., 100 meters to the office. How many centimeters would this be?

Compare or chart lengths of students' feet, hands, pencils, etc. This makes a good bar graph activity.

Have a *paper airplane* contest. Students construct airplanes and throw for distance. Flight length is measured in meters and centimeters.

Measure and mark a sidewalk or playground every 10 meters. Use it for such physical activities as shuttle runs.

Have students toss *bean bags,* trying to get them exactly 1, 2, or 3 meters away. Measure after they are thrown. Or, have students estimate the distance they have tossed. Give points for close estimates.

Measurement 5

Skill: To change one unit of length to another: centimeters and meters

Time: 2 periods

Materials:

centimeter rulers

metersticks

place value (pv) materials to 100s

Anticipatory Set

Use *rulers* and *metersticks*.

Have pairs of students measure several distances. One uses a ruler and measures in centimeters. The other uses a meterstick and measures in meters. They compare measurements and look for patterns.

Procedure 1

To change from larger to smaller units

Use *pv blocks* and *metersticks*.

On the board draw three columns and label as shown. Students should copy.

Say: This chart is like a place value chart because metric measurement is base ten. However, we usually use only meters and centimeters. On the board put 1 under Meters.

Meters	Decimeters	Centimeters
1		100
2		200
3		300

Have groups lay a meterstick on the floor and make a line below it of 10 one cubes and 9 ten rods.

Say: Look at the centimeter markings on the ten rods. How many did it take to make a meter? (100) A meter is a group of 100 centimeters.

Students write 1 in the Meters column and 100 in the Centimeters column.

Ask: If I have 2 meters, how many groups of 100 centimeters is that?

Students add another meterstick and 10 ten rods. Two meters = 200 cm. Students add this to the chart.

How could I find two groups of 100?

Students respond: Add together, or multiply 2 × 100.

How many centimeters would 3 meters be? (three groups of 100 = 300) Chart this.

Do you see a pattern on the chart?

Students respond: With every meter we add, the number of centimeters increases by 100.

If I have a certain number of meters, what's the rule for finding how many centimeters?

Students respond: Add 100 centimeters for each meter or multiply the number of meters by 100 centimeters.

Is the meter a big or small measurement? (big) If I measured the door with it, would I have many meters? (no)

Is a centimeter bigger or smaller than a meter? (smaller) If I measured the door in centimeters, would I have more or fewer than the number of meters? (more) Why?

Students discuss that they would need more centimeters.

Students find this pattern on the chart. They practice measuring as you dictate lengths in meters, using rulers or rods, and metersticks to convert measurements. When they feel comfortable with the skill, they do the addition or multiplication on paper and then check with the rulers.

Have students measure out 2 m and 5 cm with their metersticks and rulers.

Say: A meter is a group of 100 centimeters. Do we have extra centimeters? (yes, 5) How can we find the total number of centimeters? (add the extra 5 to the 100) Repeat with other mixed measurements.

Students estimate and then measure the height of the classroom door in meters and then centimeters. Which estimate was the closest? What strategies did those students use?

Continue until students are competent in the skill.

Procedure 2

To change from smaller to larger units

Use *pv materials* and *metersticks*.

Make another chart as in Procedure 1. Write 100 under Centimeters.

Students work in groups. They place 10 one cubes and 9 ten rods in a line. Looking at the centimeter marking on the rods, they find they have 100 cm. Next they place a meterstick above.

Say: Imagine that you have a distance of many centimeters. You have started by measuring a group of 100.

What can you say about centimeters and meters? (It takes a group of 100 cm to make 1 m.) Because we usually use only meters and centimeters, we wait until we have enough centimeters to regroup to meters. Chart this.

Add another 10 ten rods and another meterstick.

Students find that 200 cm equals 2 m. They look for a pattern on the chart and decide 300 cm equals 3 m.

Ask: If all I had were centimeters, how would I know how many meters they would equal? Can you state a rule?

Students respond: Each group of 100 centimeters makes 1 meter. You can subtract 100 centimeters at a time for each meter; you divide the centimeters into groups of 100 to find meters.

Add more numbers to the chart so that students can see whether this pattern holds.

Ask: What can you say about measuring the door in meters? (It would be the smallest number because meters are the biggest measurement.) If I start with centimeters and want to change to meters, will I get a larger or smaller number? (smaller)

Students practice measuring as you dictate lengths in centimeters. They use rulers or rods, and metersticks to convert measurements. When they feel comfortable with the skill, they do the subtraction or division on paper and then check with the rulers.

Have students measure out 115 centimeters. To find out how many meters this is, think: how many groups of 100? (1) Ask: How many centimeters are left over? (15) We call this length 1 meter 15 centimeters.

Repeat with other mixed unit measurements until students are competent in the skill.

Procedure 3   □■

To compute using mixed measurements

Use *metersticks* and *rulers*.

On the board draw the chart below. Do not add numbers yet.

Meters	Decimeters	Centimeters
1		30
2		40

Remind students that this chart is similar to a place value chart. Say: Remember, we usually don't use decimeters, so we wait until we have enough centimeters (ones) to regroup all the way to the meters (hundreds) place.

Students copy the chart. They will lay out measurements on the floor using rulers and metersticks and then write the numbers on their charts.

Say: I love licorice. My first piece is 1 meter 30 centimeters long.

Students measure this on the floor. They write 1 in the Meters (hundreds) place and 30 in the Centimeters (ones) place.

My second piece is 2 meters 40 centimeters long. What is the total?

Students extend the measurement on the floor and find the total length is 3 m 70 cm. They add 2 m 40 cm to their charts and add the measurements.

Say: Add 30 more centimeters. How many centimeters now? (100) What do you have to do? (regroup) Since we are using only centimeters and meters, we wait until we have 100 centimeters to regroup.

Repeat with examples until the class is competent in the skill.

Introduce subtraction as well. This is a good time to assess whether the students know what they are doing when they "borrow" in subtraction. How does computing with measurement units compare with the computing they're used to?

Practice and Extension

Have students research lengths of sharks, whales, or other animals. They measure and mark these with *tape* along the wall, writing the measurements in meters and centimeters.

Students can estimate and then measure and chart each other's heights. They add all the heights together to find the total in meters and centimeters. They measure this distance down a hall. How many students does it take to equal a whale?

Students can measure the distance between classrooms in meters and then convert. How many meters, etc., do they walk each day between classes?

Research lengths in the *Guiness Book of World Records*. Convert as desired.

Measurement 6

Skill: To understand capacity: cups, pints, quarts, and gallons

Time: 1 period per procedure

Materials:

materials to measure: water, unpopped popcorn, rice, or beans

containers: small and large (see Manipulative Information section)

measuring sets to desired capacity (see Manipulative Information section for suggestions)

counters: separate colors for each desired capacity

Note: Before introducing standard units, make sure students are comfortable with the measuring pre-skills found in Measurement 1.

Anticipatory Set

Use *materials to measure* and *two containers of similar but different sizes.*

Pour beans into one container. Have students decide whether this container holds more or less than the second container. How could they tell? (pour the same beans into the second container) Have them predict results with other containers.

Procedure 1 □■

To understand and use cups, pints, quarts, and gallons

Use *measuring sets to desired capacity, materials to measure,* and *containers of different sizes.*

Directions are written for understanding cups. Follow the same procedure for other measures. As students measure, have them work with any previously learned units, as well as the new one.

Have students use cup measures to estimate, measure, and chart the capacity of a few of the containers. Ask: What will you decide to do if a container doesn't hold an exact amount?

After measuring, discuss the problems they had estimating. Does the shape of some containers make estimation more difficult? Did their estimates get better as they practiced?

Identify the unit they have been using as 1 cup. Explain they have been measuring *capacity,* or the amount a container will hold.

Students use their data to arrange containers in order according to capacity.

Students discuss examples of when using estimates would be appropriate. They practice estimating, measuring, and charting amounts to the nearest cup. Are their estimates getting more accurate? They discuss what they could measure using a cup.

Procedure 2 □■

To change from one unit of capacity to another

Use *cup, pint, quart, and gallon measures, materials to measure,* and *counters.*

Designate counter colors for units. On the board draw four columns and label as shown. Do not add numbers yet.

Gallons	Quarts	Pints	Cups
			1
		1	2
			3
	1	2	4
			5
		3	6

Students copy the chart and add to it during the lesson.

Fill one cup with beans and put a 1 under Cups.

Students put one cup-counter on their chart and mark a 1 next to it.

Repeat the process for a second cup. Ask: What can I do with 2 cups? (trade for a pint)

Pour the 2 cups into the pint measure and mark 1 in the Pints column.

Students trade two cup-counters for a pint-counter and mark a 1 in the Pints column.

Continue the procedure until the desired capacity is reached. Discuss the relationships among the measures; e.g., how many cups to make a gallon, what's the smallest number of containers you could use to hold 7 cups.

A cup is a small measurement. If I filled one large container with *cups* of beans, and an equal size container with *quarts* of beans, would I have used a larger number of cups or quarts? (cups)

Students demonstrate with counters.

Repeat for other measures.

If I only know *pints,* how can I find the number of *cups*? (Trade a pint for 2 cups; add together 2 cups for each pint.)

If I am adding the same number each time, what shortcut could I use? (multiplication)

I could multiply the number of pints by the 2 cups I know are in each pint, or I could add 2 cups to the total for each pint I have.

Students practice converting from a large measure to a small measure. They use actual measurements, as well as counters, to check their calculations. They write each step of the process as they do it.

Say: Remember when we go from a large unit like quarts to a small unit like cups, we end up with a larger number of cups.

What if we knew only how many *cups* we had but needed to know the number of *pints* we could fill? Are we going to end up with a larger or smaller amount of pints than cups? (smaller) How could we actually measure?

Students respond: Pour the cups into the pints.

We would put all the cups into groups of two to trade for pints, subtracting groups of two from the total cups we have. What's another way to it?

Students respond: Divide the cups into groups of two; each group means another pint.

Students practice converting from a small measure to a large one. They use actual measurements and counters to check their calculations. They write each step of the process as they do it.

Procedure 3 □■

To compute using mixed capacities

Use *cup, pint, quart, and gallon measures, materials to measure,* and *counters.*

Have students make charts as shown in the illustrations. Designate counter colors for capacity.

Say: I'm collecting rainwater to test for acid rain. I need a gallon, but I only have unusual-sized containers. How can I see how much water I've collected?

Students respond: Pour the water into a measuring container, and add the amounts.

Say: The first one holds 1 pint and 1 cup. Measure out 1 pint and 1 cup.

Students place one pint-counter and one cup-counter. On a separate paper they write: 1 pint 1 cup.

Say: The second holds 1 pint. Measure out 1 pint. Write on the board:

$$\begin{array}{rr} 1 \text{ pint} & 1 \text{ cup} \\ + 1 \text{ pint} & \end{array}$$

Students place pint-counter and copy the problem. They check their counters: 2 pints 1 cup.

Quarts	Pints	Cups
	⊙	⬤
	⊙	

Ask: Can I do anything else?

Students respond: Trade 2 pints for a quart. They trade counters and regroup on paper.

Quarts	Pints	Cups
	1	1
	1	
1	2̸	1

The next holds 2 cups. Repeat the process, discussing the regrouping at 2 cups and adding to the total. How is this similar or different from regular adding?

Students discuss. The cups are regrouped at 2, not 10.

Continue adding and regrouping, discussing and writing.

Repeat for subtraction. This is a good time to assess whether students really understand what they are doing when they "borrow" in subtraction. Do students see patterns? How is this related to other subtraction we've done?

When students are comfortable with the skill, they make up measurement problems with partners and then exchange with other pairs.

Practice and Extension

Have students bring in *containers from home* to measure. Make a class chart, and order the containers by capacity.

Have students find out the gasoline capacity of their families' cars in gallons. How many quarts, pints, or cups is that?

Use *self-sealing plastic bags of different sizes* and *rice* as a display. Have students use these to help estimate the capacity of their *shoes, desks, paper bags,* etc.

Have students research the capacity of nearby lakes, reservoirs, water towers, etc. Have them then figure the equivalent cups, pints, and quarts. How much water is used for a bath? A shower? A bath a day for a week, month, or year? A faucet that leaks a cup an hour?

Have students bring in *recipes* from home and rewrite them, increasing ingredients to serve 3×, 4×, 5× the number of people. Can they change measurements to use the least number of measuring devices possible?

Measurement 7

Skill: To understand capacity: liters and milliliters

Time: 1 period per procedure

Materials:

materials to measure: water, unpopped popcorn, rice, beans

containers: small and large; of different sizes (see Manipulative Information section for suggestions)

liter measures: marked with milliliters

containers: small; of identical size and less than 1 liter, such as paper cups

measures smaller than 1 liter: marked with milliliters, if possible

Anticipatory Set

Use *materials to measure* and *two containers of similar but different sizes.*

Pour beans into one container. Have students decide whether this container holds more or less than the second container. How could they tell? Do the measurement.

Procedure 1

To understand and use liters

Use *liter measures, materials to measure, identical small containers of less than a liter,* and *containers of different sizes.*

Have students use liter measures to estimate, measure, and chart the capacity of a few of the containers. Ask: What if a container doesn't hold an exact amount?

After measuring, discuss the problems they had estimating. Does container shape make estimation more difficult? Did they improve with practice?

Identify the unit they have been using as 1 liter. Explain that they have been measuring *capacity,* or the amount a container will hold.

Students use their data to arrange containers in order according to capacity.

Have students find containers that hold exactly 1 and 2 L. Explain that you have a liter of beans. You need to use the liter to measure something else. Ask: How many of the small containers will you need for the beans?

Students discover how many small cups or containers it takes to total 1 L of capacity.

Reinforce estimation by measuring two containers, one close to 1 liter and one close to 2 liters. Measure the first one. How do the students know it's close to 1 liter? (Few beans are left over.)

Measure the second one. Ask: How do you know it's close to 2 liters?

Students respond: It was almost full with 2 liters of beans in it.

We can call the first capacity about 1 liter. What do you suppose we can call the second capacity? (about 2 liters)

Students discuss instances when it would be appropriate to have only an approximate measurement of capacity.

They practice estimating and then measuring to the nearest liter. See Practice and Extension for suggestions.

Discuss with students what they could measure using a liter. Is a liter the only measure of capacity they will need? What's a better way to measure the amount of water an eyedropper will hold?

Procedure 2

To understand and use milliliters

Use *liter measures, materials to measure, identical small containers of less than a liter, containers of different sizes,* and *measures smaller than a liter.*

Have students examine the liter measures to discover how many milliliters are in 1 L. (1,000) Ask: When would you be more likely to use milliliters than liters? (medicine amounts, cooking, science experiments, small amounts)

Have students fill their small identical containers with beans. How many milliliters of beans do they think they have? Write all amounts on the board.

Students measure the amount in milliliters.

Repeat with other containers, charting all estimates and then having a student do the actual measurement. Are their estimates becoming more accurate?

Set up measuring stations with containers of different sizes at each stations. Have students make a chart: "Container," "Liters and Milliliters," "Milliliters."

Students work in groups to estimate, measure, and chart the results at each station. For each container, they should have both estimates and actual measurements. They compare their results with those from other groups.

Procedure 3   ▢▪

To change from one unit of capacity to another

Use *liter measures* and *materials to measure*.

On the board draw the following chart headings.

Liters	Deciliters	Centiliters	Milliliters
1			1,000

Point out that this is like a place value chart, since metric measurement is base ten. However, since we usually use only liters and milliliters we have to regroup across three places.

Have one group of students measure 1 liter and another measure 1,000 milliliters. Compare.

Write 1 in the Liter column. Ask: How many go in the Milliliter column? (1,000) Repeat for 2 liters.

Students predict the next figures will be 3 liters and 3,000 milliliters. They confirm by measuring.

Every time I added another liter, it was equal to another group of how many milliliters? (1,000) Ask: If I had something that contained 8 liters, how would I find the number of milliliters? (add 8 groups of 1,000)

If I'm adding same-size groups, what's a shortcut? (multiply) I can multiply the number of liters I have by 1,000, or I can add that many 1,000s together. How many milliliters in 8 liters? (8,000)

Repeat with more examples until students are comfortable with the concept.

Next show students 2,000 mL of beans. I only know how many milliliters this is, 2,000. How can I find how many liters?

Students respond: Separate the milliliters into piles of 1,000.

Write 2,000 mL on the board. Pour beans into a liter measure. Write –1,000 under the 2,000. Ask: How many liters do I have so far? (1)

Repeat for the second liter.

I can subtract 1,000 milliliters at a time. I'm separating them into groups of the same size—1,000. Ask: What's a shorter way of doing this? (dividing)

I can divide by 1,000 to find the number of groups or liters that size, or I can subtract 1,000 at a time to make liters. Relate to the chart on the board.

Is liter a large or small measure? (large) If I measure an amount in both liters and milliliters, which will I measure more of, liters or milliliters?

Students respond: Milliliters. They are smaller; it takes more of them.

Repeat with examples until students are comfortable with the concept.

Procedure 4   ▢

To compute using mixed capacities

Use *paper*.

On the board draw the chart headings shown in Procedure 3. Remind students that it is similar to a place value chart but that we usually use only liters (thousands) and milliliters (ones).

Students copy the chart. They write 1 in the thousands place and 550 in the ones place.

I have something containing 1 liters 550 milliliters. I add 2 more liters and 400 more milliliters. What's the total?

Students write and find: 3 liters 950 milliliters.

Add 50 more milliliters. How many milliliters now? (1,000) What do you have to do? (regroup) Since we are using only milliliters and liters, we wait until we have 1,000 milliliters to regroup.

Repeat with examples until the class is comfortable with the concept. Introduce subtraction as well, starting with 3 liters of ice cream and dipping out various amounts. How much is left each time?

Practice and Extension

Have students bring in *containers from home*. They estimate and then measure the capacity. Make a class chart and order the containers by capacity.

Have students find out the gasoline capacity of their families' cars in liters. How many milliliters is that?

Fill *self-sealing plastic bags* with 1 L, 500 mL, and 250 mL of *rice*. Mark amounts on the bags with marker. Students use the bags to help estimate the capacity of their *shoes, small containers,* etc. They then fill the objects with rice and measure the capacities accurately.

Have students add capacities of *snack drink containers*. How much would they drink if they finished an apple drink and an orange drink? Which add up to a liter?

Have students bring in *recipes* from home and measure the amounts in liters and milliliters. Are any amounts similar to standard measurement?

Measurement 8

Skill: To measure temperature and read thermometers

Time: $2\frac{1}{2}$ periods

Materials:

containers of hot and cold water: 2 per group

thermometers: Fahrenheit or Celsius; 1 per container

large demonstration thermometer: made from tag board with ribbon loop running through it to represent the alcohol—mark half of ribbon red with marker

scissors

clear tape

red crayons or markers: 1 per student

See Reproducibles for: number lines to 1000

Anticipatory Set

Use *containers of hot and cold water.*

Work in small groups. Give each group two containers of water, one cold and one warm or hot. Have students decide which water is warmer. Explain that *temperature* means how hot or cold something is.

Ask each group to describe the temperature of their warm or hot water. Then ask which group has the warmest water. How could they tell? (feel each one and compare)

Have groups try to order the warm water containers from least warm to most warm. Is this difficult? (Some are very close.) Do they need a way of measuring temperature more accurately? (yes)

Procedure 1

To measure temperature

Use *containers of hot and cold water, thermometers, number lines, tag board thermometer, scissors, tape, and crayons or markers.*

Have students work in small groups. Hand out number lines. Ask: Which number is larger, 10 or 30? (30) Have students turn their number lines vertically. Have the numbers changed? (no) Is 30 still larger than 10? (yes)

Say: When we measured weight and capacity, we used numbers to tell how many pounds or quarts we had. We measure temperature with numbers, too. The more heat we have, the higher the temperature numbers.

For temperature our unit is degrees instead of pounds or quarts. Which would be the higher or warmer temperature, 30° or 10°? (30°)

Students put thermometers in their containers of water.

Move the ribbon on the tag board thermometer to demonstrate a variety of temperatures. Have students practice reading temperatures until they can read them accurately.

Relate warm and cool temperatures to the bowls of water and to air temperature. Heat makes the

alcohol inside the thermometer expand, or take up more space.

Students draw thermometer bulbs and a thermometer around each vertical number line. They cut these out and tape them together. They label 10°, 20°, etc. As they measure temperatures, they will fill in the exact degrees.

Have groups decide on the thermometer reading of their bowls.

Students use red crayons or markers to duplicate the readings on both their thermometers. They mark one "Cool" and one "Warm" or "Hot."

Before, we couldn't tell for sure which group had the warmest water. Can we tell now? (Yes, check the temperature.) Ask each group their temperatures, and discuss which groups have the coldest and warmest water.

Students decide which of their thermometers shows the colder temperature and which is the warmer.

Holding their number line thermometers, students order themselves from coldest to warmest. They check the order by calling off their temperatures in degrees.

Procedure 2

To estimate and measure temperature

Use *containers of hot and cold water, thermometers, and number line thermometers from Procedure 1.*

Replace the water in the bowls, and put thermometers into the water. Turn the thermometers so they cannot be read.

Have each group make a chart headed "Guess" and "Temperature." If you wish, they can also make a column headed "Degrees Off." Down the left have them list the station numbers as they come to them.

Students go from station to station. They first decide on and chart an estimate for the warm temperature. Then they read and record the actual temperature, both on their number line and on their chart. Next they subtract to find how many degrees off they were. They repeat for the cold water.

Discuss with groups how close they were able to come with their estimates. Ask: Did you get more accurate as you practiced? How can you tell?

Students respond: They weren't so many degrees off.

Ask: Was it easier to estimate cold or warm water? How could they figure this out using their data?

Students respond: Compare the degrees off for the cold versus the warm.

Have students compare first and last readings for several containers. Why might they not agree? Was the water getting cooler or warmer? Why?

First a student throws the dice and chooses which 2-digit temperature to make from the numbers. The temperature is marked with a paper clip on the thermometer and is written in the Degrees column.

For the second round, the second temperature thrown is marked with a paper clip and in the Degrees column. The difference between the two temperatures is added to or subtracted from the 100 in the Total column, depending on the rise or fall in temperature. The winner is the student with the highest total. If the winner is then changed to be the student with the lowest total, the students will need to change their strategy.

Procedure 3   □■

To find changes in temperature

Use *number line thermometers from Procedure 1* and *tag board thermometer*.

Use a tag board thermometer or a thermometer drawn on the board to review the reading of temperatures with students. Then set the temperature at 40° and explain that this was a morning temperature. As the day warmed, the temperature rose to 50°.

Students count the number of degrees as you change the reading to 50°.

Ask: How many degrees difference between 40° and 50°? (10°) How do we find the difference between two numbers? (subtract) Does this work with temperature? (yes)

Repeat with several other temperature changes, using such examples as temperature in the shade, in the sun, a sudden rain shower dropping the temperature, etc.

Students practice with their thermometers and on paper as you give temperature changes and different degree readings.

Practice and Extension

Have students leave *thermometers* in various places around the room, school, and outdoors. Record temperatures at various times of the day and discuss.

Have students experiment with *thermometers* left in the sun on white versus black paper, in and out of boxes, etc.

Provide *ice cubes*, and have students design experiments using *thermometers*.

Use two *dice, number line thermometers,* and two *paper clips* per student to play Degree Derby. Students make two columns on paper: "Degrees," "Total." They start with 100 in the Total column.

Measurement 9

Skill: To understand pounds and ounces

Time: 1 period per procedure

Materials:

objects: weighing a pound, such as a loaf of bread, boxes of sugar

measurement sets: pounds and ounces

scales: balance, kitchen, bathroom

collections of objects: weighing under and over a pound, such as pencils, boxes of crayons

objects: weighing an ounce, such as several pencils held with a rubber band, small bags of paper clips, buttons

collections of objects: weighing under an ounce, such as paper clips, beans

counters: 32 per group

Note: Before introducing standard units, make sure students are comfortable with the measuring pre-skills found in Measurement 1.

Mass is a measure of the amount of material an object contains. *Weight* is the force with which an object, or mass, is attracted toward the earth (or other body) by gravitation. Balance scales measure mass; kitchen scales measure weight. However, when a kitchen scale's unit of measurement is kilograms, it is commonly accepted that, at sea level, the reading is interchangeable with that of the mass of the object. For everyday purposes, the distinction between mass and weight is not critical. Scientists and engineers, however, appreciate the difference.

Anticipatory Set

Use *1-pound objects or weights, balance scales,* and *collections of objects weighing over and under a pound.*

Set up balance scales several days ahead, and ask students to find objects and groups of items that weigh the same as the weights or objects weighing 1 pound. Let students experiment with the equipment without introducing pounds as a label.

Procedure 1

To understand and use pounds

Use *1-pound objects or weights, collections of objects weighing under and over a pound,* and *scales.*

Identify objects as weighing 1 pound. Have students lift each one and compare two at the same time. Objects in their dominant hand often will feel lighter; have them switch hands several times.

Weigh the 1-pound object on a kitchen scale. Identify the pound markings, and add objects to make 2 and 3 pounds of weight.

Ask: Do you see a pattern? (The heavier an object is, the higher the number on the scale.)

Ask students to compare the weight of a pencil to a pound. Does the pencil weigh more or less than a pound? (less)

Have them use a balance scale to check. Then have them use a kitchen scale. Was the reading closer to 0 or to 1 pound? (0)

Students make a chart labeled: "Object," "Estimate," "Result," and then measure a variety of classroom objects. They estimate the objects as more or less than a pound and then check with the balance scale. They check with the kitchen scale. Were their estimates more accurate as they practiced?

Next have the class find several different objects that together will weigh 1 pound. Encourage them to use their findings from before to predict the results.

Ask: How many pencils weighed 1 pound? How many crayon boxes? Can you find a mix of pencils and crayon boxes that will weigh 1 pound?

Students weigh and chart their estimated and actual results. They can add any combinations that weigh 1 pound to a large class chart. They repeat with weight of 2 pounds.

Next have student volunteers weigh themselves on a bathroom scale.

Ask: How many 1-pound weights do you equal? How much will two students weigh? How much will they weigh holding two 1-pound weights?

Introduce estimation by measuring an object on the balance scale that is obviously closer to 1 pound than 2 pounds. What do the students observe?

Students respond: The scales almost balanced with the 1-pound weight but were not balanced at all with the 2-pound weight.

Students practice estimating and then measuring to the nearest pound. They note the position of the pointer on the kitchen scale to help them decide the nearest pound.

Procedure 2 ☐◼

To understand and use ounces

Use *1-ounce objects or weights, collections of objects weighing over an ounce, balance scales,* and *kitchen scales.*

Use activities from Procedure 1 with ounce weights instead of pounds. Have students discover how many 1-ounce objects are needed for 1 pound.

After charting an activity for 1 ounce, students repeat for groups weighing 8 ounces, or half a pound.

Introduce approximation by weighing an object on the kitchen scale that is closer to 1 ounce than 2 ounces. Ask: Where is the pointer? (closer to the 1) We can call this about 1 ounce.

Continue to add objects, having the class name both the nearest ounce and the nearest pound.

If students have mastered the rounding skill, introduce the following part of concept.

Say: In our number system, what number is halfway between one place and another on a place value chart? (5) We've learned to round up at the halfway mark. What is the halfway number for ounces and pounds? (8 ounces—half a pound)

Students practice estimating and weighing as they complete a class chart: What weighs 1 ounce, 2 ounces, 3 ounces, etc., up to several pounds.

Procedure 3 ☐◼

To change from one unit of weight to another

Use *counters* and *larger objects such as pencils.*

Have student groups make a chart labeled "Pounds" on the left and "Ounces" on the right. Draw the same chart on the board; in the Ounces column, write the numbers vertically 1 through 16.

Students add counters representing 1 ounce each to their charts as you write.

Say: When I have 16 ounces of anything, can I call that amount something else? (1 pound)

I can exchange, or regroup, 16 ounces for a pound. Ask: What is this like in our number system? (regrouping)

On the chart write 1 in the Pounds column next to the 16 Ounces.

Students exchange 16 ounce-counters for 1 object to represent 1 pound.

Repeat to 2 pounds. Ask: Do you see a pattern? (For every 16 ounces, there is another 1 pound.)

What if we had 64 ounces and needed to know the number of pounds?

Students respond: Change groups of 16 for pounds.

We could subtract out groups of 16 to find the number of pounds.

Repeat with other examples until students are competent with the concept.

Ask: What if we start with pounds? Clear your charts and place 2 pound-objects.

Regroup to find how many groups of 16 would be in 2 pounds. (2) How else could I find how many ounces that would be? (add 2 groups of 16)

Repeat with other examples. Have students write conversions on paper as they do them with objects until students are competent in the skill.

Procedure 4 ☐

To compute using mixed weights

Use *counters* and *larger objects such as pencils.*

Counters will be ounces, larger objects will be pounds. Have students make a place value type chart labeled "Pounds" and "Ounces."

Say: I raise pigeons and can only carry 10 pounds of pigeons at once. I'll have to add up their weights to know which pigeons to take.

The first pigeon weighs 1 pound 5 ounces. The second one weighs 2 pounds 10 ounces.

Students place counters and objects. They report the total so far is 3 pounds 15 ounces.

Does this look familiar? (It is like adding on a regular place value chart.) The next pigeon weighs 1 pound 1 ounce.

Students place additional objects and counters. They regroup the ounces and have a total of 5 pounds.

Continue adding and then subtracting weights until students are comfortable with the concept. Then have students do the addition and subtraction on paper as they move the counters and objects. This is a good time to assess whether students understand what they are doing when they "borrow" in subtraction.

Practice and Extension

Have students weigh and chart their *snacks or lunches* for a week. Compile a class chart. How could they sort these data: by day of the week, sex, type of snack, etc. What was the average snack weight?

Have students research the weights of various animals and make a bar chart showing relative weight.

Have students estimate and weigh various *articles of clothing.* How much would a whole outfit weigh? Do winter outfits weigh more or less than spring outfits?

Measurement 10

Skill: To understand kilograms and grams

Time: 1 period per procedure

Materials:

measurement set: grams, kilograms

objects: with a mass of 1 kilogram (2.2 pounds)
collections of objects: under and over 1 kilogram
scales: balance, metric kitchen
objects: with a mass of 1 gram, such as raisins
collections of objects: under and over 1 gram

Note: *Mass* is a measure of the amount of material an object contains. *Weight* is the force with which an object, or mass, is attracted toward the earth (or other body) by gravitation. Balance scales measure mass; kitchen scales measure weight. However, when a kitchen scale's unit of measurement is kilograms, it is commonly accepted that, at sea level, the reading is interchangeable with that of the mass of the object. For everyday purposes, the distinction between mass and weight is not critical. Scientists and engineers, however, appreciate the difference.

Anticipatory Set

Use *1-kilogram objects or weights, collections of objects under and over 1 kilogram,* and *scales.*

Do this the day before. Refer to the exercises in measuring pounds and ounces. Then let students explore measuring the mass of the objects in kilograms and grams.

Procedure 1

To understand and use kilograms

Use *1-kilogram objects or masses, collections of objects under and over 1 kilogram, and scales.*

Identify objects as having a mass of 1 kilogram. Have students lift each one and compare two at the same time. Objects in their dominant hand often will feel lighter; have them switch hands several times.

Weigh the 1-kilogram object using a kitchen scale. Identify the kilogram markings, and add objects to make 2 and 3 kilograms. Have students predict the scale readings as you add objects.

Ask students to compare the mass of a pencil to a kilogram. Does the pencil have more or less mass than a kilogram? (less) Have them first use a balance scale to check, then a kitchen scale.

Students make a chart labeled: "Object," "Estimate," "Result." They estimate the mass of classroom objects as more or less than 1 kilogram and then check with the balance scale and kitchen scale. Were their estimates more accurate as they practiced?

Next have the class find several different objects that together will have a mass of 1 kilogram. Encourage them to use their findings from before to predict the results. How many shoes together

had a mass of 1 kilogram? Can they find a mix that will measure exactly 1 kilogram?

Students use scales to measure and chart their estimated and actual results. They can add any combinations that have a mass of 1 kilogram to a large class chart. Repeat with mass of 2 kilograms.

Introduce approximation by finding the mass of an object that is obviously closer to 1 kilogram than 2 kilograms. Is the mass closer to 1 or 2 kilograms? (1 kilogram) We call this measuring to the nearest kilogram.

Students practice estimating and then measuring to the nearest kilogram.

Procedure 2

To understand and use grams

Use *1-gram objects or masses, collections of objects under and over 1 gram, and scales.*

Identify objects as having a mass of 1 gram. Have students lift each one and compare two at the same time. Weigh the 1-gram object using a kitchen scale. Identify the gram markings, and add objects to make several grams.

Have students predict the scale readings as you add objects. How many grams to a kilogram? (1,000)

Ask students to compare the mass of a paper clip or pencil to a gram. Ask: Is the pencil's mass more or less than 1 gram? Have them use a balance scale and then a kitchen scale to check. Which is the better scale to use? Why? Repeat with 10 grams. Why is this more accurate?

Students make a chart labeled "Object," "Estimate," "Result." They estimate and find the mass of objects. Were their estimates more accurate as they practiced?

Next have students find objects that have a mass of exactly I gram, 5 grams, 10 grams, and 500 grams. How many pencils? How many paper clips? Make a class collection of objects or groups of objects that have a mass of exactly these amounts.

Introduce approximation by weighing an object that is closer to I kilogram than 2 kilograms using the kitchen scale. How many grams over 1 kilogram? Where is the pointer? (closer to the 1) We can call this about 1 kilogram.

Continue to add objects, having the class name both the nearest gram and the nearest kilogram. In our number system, what number is halfway between one place and another on a place value chart? (5) We've learned to round up at the halfway mark. What is the halfway number for grams and kilograms? (500 grams or 0.5 kilogram)

Have students practice estimating, weighing, and rounding to the nearest kilogram or 0.5 kilogram.

Procedure 3

To change from one unit of mass to another

Use *1 kilogram objects or masses, 3,000 grams of objects or masses,* and *balance scales.*

On the board draw the chart shown below. Point out that it is similar to a place value chart, as metric measurement is base ten.

1000s kilograms	100s hectograms	10s decagrams	1s grams
1			1000

Say: Since we usually use only grams and kilograms, we commonly wait until we have enough grams (ones) to regroup all the way to the kilograms (thousands) place.

Have students balance 1 kilogram against 1,000 grams. Write 1 in the Kilogram column and 1,000 in the Gram column. Repeat for 2 kilograms = 2,000 grams.

Students predict the next figures will be 3 kilograms and 3,000 grams. They confirm this with the scale.

Every time I added another kilogram, it was equal to another group of how many grams? (1,000) If I had something that had a mass of 8 *kilograms,* how would I find the number of *grams?* (add 8 groups of 1,000)

Repeat until students are competent in the skill.

Students make up and solve problems. They write the process as they are measuring. Later they can do the problem on paper first and then check by measuring.

If I only knew how many *grams* I had, how could I find how many *kilograms?* (separate the grams

into piles of 1,000) I can subtract out 1,000 grams at a time. I'm separating them into same-size groups of 1,000.

Repeat with examples until students are competent with the concept.

Students make up and solve problems. They write the process as they are measuring. Later they can do the problem on paper first and then check with the objects and scales.

Procedure 4

To compute using mixed masses

Use *1-kilogram objects or masses, 3,000 grams of objects or masses,* and *balance scales.*

On the board draw the chart shown in Procedure 3. Remind students that the chart is like a place value chart, but we only use grams and kilograms.

Students copy the chart and write 1 in the thousands place and 550 in the ones place.

I have something with a mass of 1 kilogram 550 grams. I add 2 more kilograms and 400 grams. What is the total?

Students write and find the total is 3 kilograms 950 grams.

Use the objects and scales to demonstrate.

Add 50 more grams. How many grams now? (1,000) What do you have to do? (regroup) If we are using only grams and kilograms, we wait until we have 1,000 grams to regroup.

Repeat with examples until the class is competent with the concept. Introduce subtraction as well. This is a good time to assess whether the students know what they are doing when they "borrow" in subtraction. How does computing with weight units compare with the computing they're used to?

Practice and Extension

Have students find the mass in grams of their *snacks* for a week and chart the results. Compile a class chart. How could they sort these data: by day of the week, sex, type of snack, etc. What mass did the average snack have in grams? The total mass in both grams and kilograms? Are there patterns? How would these results be helpful to a grocer?

Have student bring in *food packages with nutritional information marked in grams.* How many grams of protein in each one? Have students choose a food and figure out how much they would need to eat a kilogram of protein. Repeat for other nutrients.

Measurement 11

Skill: To measure volume

Time: 2–3 periods

Materials:

boxes: of different small sizes, such as pencil boxes, milk containers, jewelry gift boxes; 1 per group

cubes: small, enough to fill one of the boxes; 30 or more per group

graph paper: any size; several sheets per student

Anticipatory Set

Use *boxes* and *cubes.*

Have students work in groups to find how many cubes their box holds. What will they do if they have space left over too small to measure with a block? Is this an accurate way of finding out how many cubes a container will hold?

Procedure 1

To understand volume

Use *cubes* and *graph paper.*

Tell students they have been finding *cubic volume,* the number of real or imaginary cubes that will fit into a space. We measure volume in cubic units because it is the number of same-size cubes it takes to fill a space. Ask: When might they want to find the volume of something? (classroom air, desks, cars)

Have each group hold up its box and report their findings. Ask: Were any the same volume? Were they the same shape? Which had the larger volumes? (the bigger boxes) Did you discover any shortcuts to finding the total?

Have groups use 30 cubes to build a building of 30 cubic units. Building shapes will vary.

Discuss the variety of shapes. How could they all have the same volume?

Students respond: They hold the same number of cubes.

Have pairs of students make rectangular prism buildings of different numbers of cubes. Have them exchange positions with another pair and estimate the volume of the new buildings.

Have pairs then show their building to the whole class for an estimate.

Did anyone find ways to make a close estimate?

Have students look for patterns. Some may begin to see that layers repeat themselves.

If students are capable, have them draw side, top, and back views of their building. They should mark the volume on the back. Have them switch drawings with other groups and try to construct buildings from the drawings. Have them use the measurement on the back as a check.

Procedure 2

To measure volume

Use *cubes* and *graph paper.*

Have students build a 2×3 rectangle, the first layer of a building. What's the volume so far? (6 cubic units) Write a chart on the board headed:

Layers	Cubes in Each Layer	Volume
1	6	6

Say: Add another 2×3 layer on top of the first. Now what is the volume?

Students respond: 12 cubic units. Chart: 2, 6, 12.

Repeat with another layer. The chart now reads 3, 6, 18. Ask: Do you see any patterns?

Students who can multiply may see that they can multiply the number of layers by the number of cubes in each layer. Others may see it as serial addition.

Repeat with another layer. Can students predict the next result before building it?

Give students dimensions of buildings to build, and have them chart the volume after each layer. Can they predict the total before finishing?

If students start with 36 or 48 cubes, can they chart several different buildings *before* they build them?

Relate this to state requirements of a certain number of cubic feet of air per classroom. If they built for ants some classrooms that conform to the regulations, should they consider other things as well? Have students list these and sketch several views of their classrooms on graph paper.

Have students write a rule for finding the volume of a rectangular solid.

Explore volume and numbers. See Practice and Extension for suggestions.

Procedure 3 ☐ ■

To develop the concept of volume; to find the formula for the volume of a rectangular prism

Use *cubes*.

Review the concept of volume. Before, they filled the space and then counted all the cubes. Ask: What's the problem with this technique?

Students respond: You can't always fill a space with cubes; it takes a lot of time.

We'll build a building with a volume of 30 cubes. On the board write and have students copy the following chart, headings only:

l Length of Row	w # Rows Wide	# Blocks per Layer	h Height	V Volume
3	2	6	1	6
3	2	6	2	12

Have students make a row of three cubes. Say: Our first row is a group of three cubes. Now make another identical row next to the first one. What shall we put on our charts?

Students respond: Length is 3; width or number of rows is 2.

This is our first layer. How many cubes?

Students respond: 6. They add this to their charts. They write 1 as the height and 6 as the volume so far.

How could you get that total without actually using cubes? (Add two rows together; multiply the number in each row by the number of rows.) We can call this length times width, and write it: l × w.

Students build a second layer on top of the first.

How many cubes have we used so far? (12) How did you get that number? (added six and six) Since we're adding same-size groups, what is a shortcut? (multiply 2 groups × 6 in each group)

What is the height so far? (2) The volume is the number of cubes used in all. Add these numbers to your chart.

Student groups finish the buildings, using 30 cubes. They add the data from each layer to their charts.

We are looking for a way to find V, or volume. Do you see any patterns?

Students respond: You can multiply the number of cubes in each layer by the number of layers.

We could add each layer, but multiplication is faster. We multiplied the length times the width and then we multiplied by the height to get volume. I've used letters on the chart.

Can you come up with a description of the math we did, *using only letters*?

Students respond: Multiply l × w × h.

Yes, V = l × w × h. Now predict what the volume in cubic blocks will be of a building 10 blocks long, 1 block wide, and 3 layers high. (30 cubic blocks) Can you find another shape building that has a volume of 30 cubic blocks?

Students build more buildings. They add each set of data to the chart and check that the formula would work.

Repeat the building activities. Give dimensions or volumes. Have students use the formula to predict results and then check with the cubes.

Say: In the real world, we can't measure with real cubes, so we use imaginary ones. If we measure a small volume, we could use cubes 1 centimeter long, wide, and high. Our volume would be in cubic centimeters or cm³. Your place value one cubes have a volume of 1 cubic centimeter each.

What size cubes would we use to measure the volume of your desks? (cubic inches or feet) What about the volume of air in the classroom? (cubic feet, yards, meters)

Students discuss possible volumes and appropriate choices of measurements. They imagine cubes of those sizes.

Practice and Extension

Use *tag board or construction paper, rulers, yardsticks or metersticks,* and *tape.* Have students build cubes for each different unit of measurement in which you are interested.

On one side of the cubes have them write (for example) Volume = 1" × 1" × 1" = 1 cu. in. On another side of the cube have them list instances in which their unit of volume would be used.

Have students put several cubes together to make a building. How will they find the volume? (find the volume of separate sections and add together) What should they do if one section is in feet and one is in inches? (change one unit to the other)

Explore cubic numbers. Have students construct shapes using *place value blocks.* How can they quickly make a building of 48 cu. cm? If they have 27 one cubes, can they build a building that has equal dimensions? (3 × 3 × 3) What other numbers make cubes?

Addition/Subtraction Table

	0	1	2	3	4	5	6	7	8	9	10
0	0	1	2	3	4	5	6	7	8	9	10
1	1	2	3	4	5	6	7	8	9	10	11
2	2	3	4	5	6	7	8	9	0	11	12
3	3	4	5	6	7	8	9	10	11	12	13
4	4	5	6	7	8	9	10	11	12	13	14
5	5	6	7	8	9	10	11	12	13	14	15
6	6	7	8	9	10	11	12	13	14	15	16
7	7	8	9	10	11	12	13	14	15	16	17
8	8	9	10	11	12	13	14	15	16	17	18
9	9	10	11	12	13	14	15	16	17	18	19
10	10	11	12	13	14	15	16	17	18	19	20

Blank Matrix: 10 × 10

Ones Bills

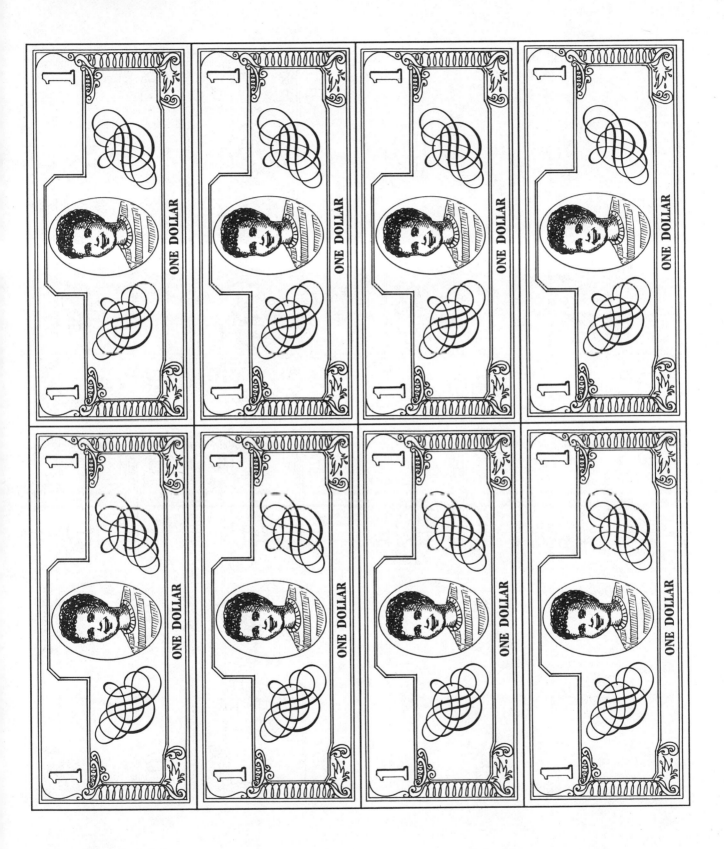

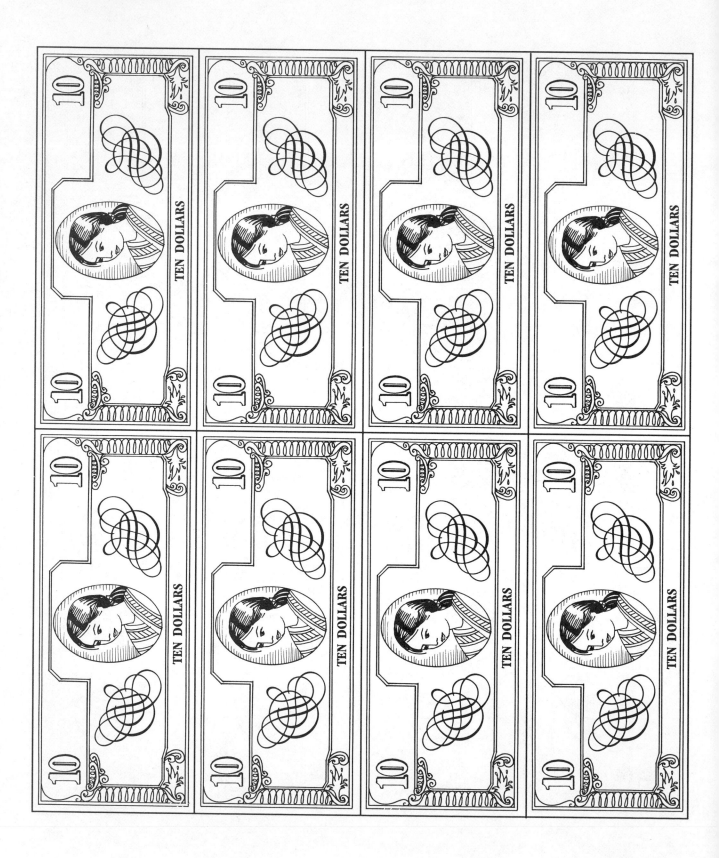

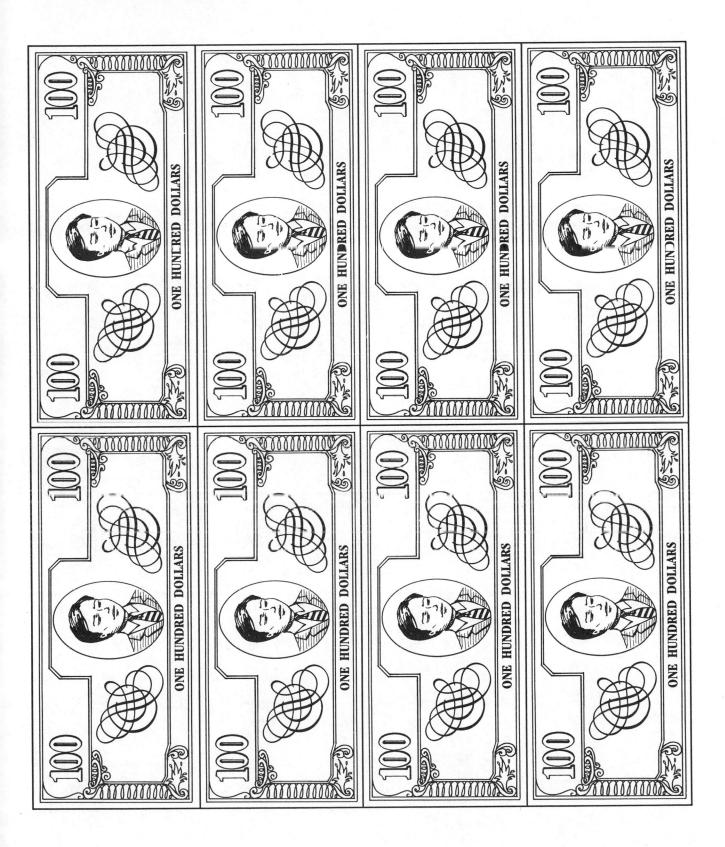

Thousands Bills

Hundred-Thousands Bills

Counter-Trading Board

Counter-Trading Board

One	One	One	One
One	One	One	One

Decimal Bars—Tenths

Division Paper

Hundreds	Tens	Ones	Check	Hundreds	Tens	Ones	Check
5 ⌐ 1	3	5					

Equivalency Chart

1 Unit											

$\frac{1}{2}$	$\frac{1}{2}$

$\frac{1}{3}$	$\frac{1}{3}$	$\frac{1}{3}$

$\frac{1}{4}$	$\frac{1}{4}$	$\frac{1}{4}$	$\frac{1}{4}$

$\frac{1}{5}$	$\frac{1}{5}$	$\frac{1}{5}$	$\frac{1}{5}$	$\frac{1}{5}$

$\frac{1}{6}$	$\frac{1}{6}$	$\frac{1}{6}$	$\frac{1}{6}$	$\frac{1}{6}$	$\frac{1}{6}$

$\frac{1}{7}$	$\frac{1}{7}$	$\frac{1}{7}$	$\frac{1}{7}$	$\frac{1}{7}$	$\frac{1}{7}$	$\frac{1}{7}$

$\frac{1}{8}$	$\frac{1}{8}$	$\frac{1}{8}$	$\frac{1}{8}$	$\frac{1}{8}$	$\frac{1}{8}$	$\frac{1}{8}$	$\frac{1}{8}$

$\frac{1}{9}$	$\frac{1}{9}$	$\frac{1}{9}$	$\frac{1}{9}$	$\frac{1}{9}$	$\frac{1}{9}$	$\frac{1}{9}$	$\frac{1}{9}$	$\frac{1}{9}$

$\frac{1}{10}$	$\frac{1}{10}$	$\frac{1}{10}$	$\frac{1}{10}$	$\frac{1}{10}$	$\frac{1}{10}$	$\frac{1}{10}$	$\frac{1}{10}$	$\frac{1}{10}$	$\frac{1}{10}$

$\frac{1}{11}$	$\frac{1}{11}$	$\frac{1}{11}$	$\frac{1}{11}$	$\frac{1}{11}$	$\frac{1}{11}$	$\frac{1}{11}$	$\frac{1}{11}$	$\frac{1}{11}$	$\frac{1}{11}$	$\frac{1}{11}$

$\frac{1}{12}$	$\frac{1}{12}$	$\frac{1}{12}$	$\frac{1}{12}$	$\frac{1}{12}$	$\frac{1}{12}$	$\frac{1}{12}$	$\frac{1}{12}$	$\frac{1}{12}$	$\frac{1}{12}$	$\frac{1}{12}$	$\frac{1}{12}$

File-Folder Place Value Mat to Thousands

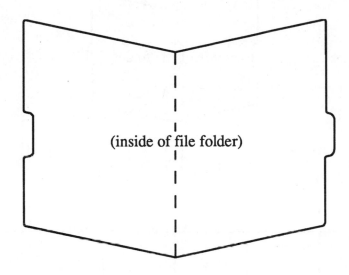

(inside of file folder)

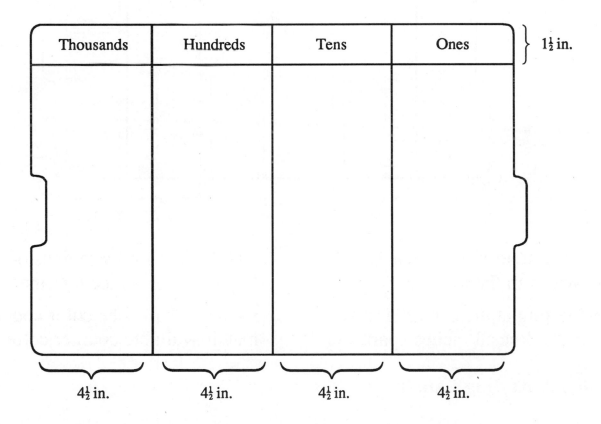

Thousands	Hundreds	Tens	Ones

} $1\frac{1}{2}$ in.

$4\frac{1}{2}$ in. $4\frac{1}{2}$ in. $4\frac{1}{2}$ in. $4\frac{1}{2}$ in.

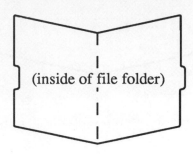

(inside of file folder)

Step 1. Setting up File Folder

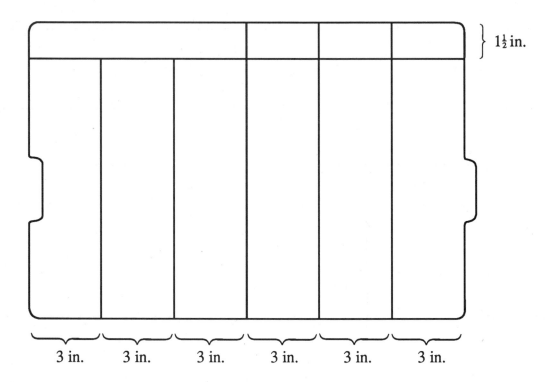

$1\frac{1}{2}$ in.

3 in. 3 in. 3 in. 3 in. 3 in. 3 in.

• Draw a horizontal line $1\frac{1}{2}$ inches down from the long edge.

• Starting at the center, draw five vertical lines 3 inches apart.

• Note: The first two lines on the left *do not* cross the top line.

• Columns may be color coded to match available counter colors.

Step 2. Adding Labels

Thousands					
Hundreds	Tens	Ones	Hundreds	Tens	Ones

Geoboard Paper

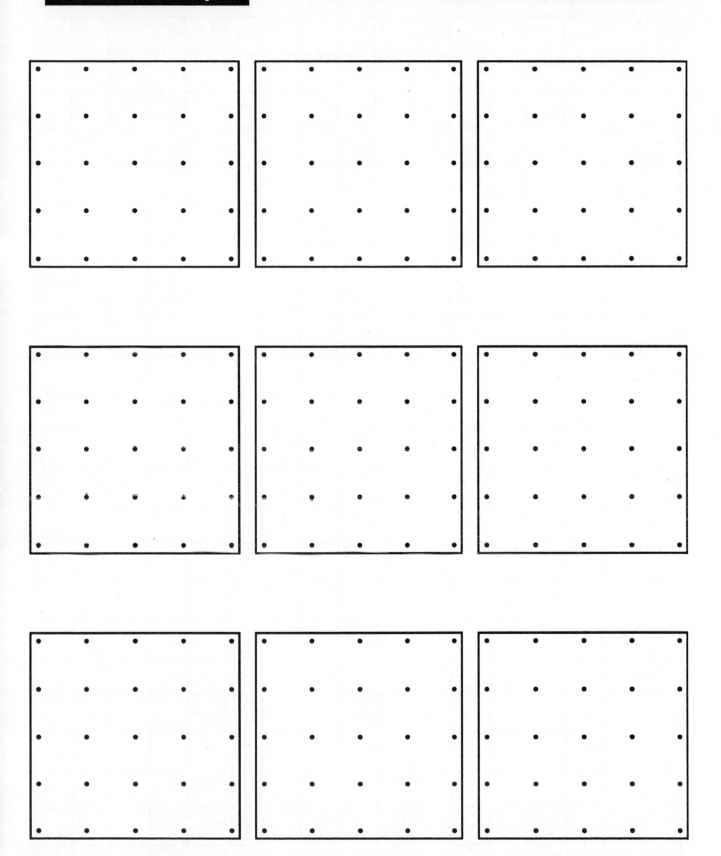

Graph Paper: 1 in.

Hundred Board

1	2	3	4	5	6	7	8	9	10
11	12	13	14	15	16	17	18	19	20
21	22	23	24	25	26	27	28	29	30
31	32	33	34	35	36	37	38	39	40
41	42	43	44	45	46	47	48	49	50
51	52	53	54	55	56	57	58	59	60
61	62	63	64	65	66	67	68	69	70
71	72	73	74	75	76	77	78	79	80
81	82	83	84	85	86	87	88	89	90
91	92	93	94	95	96	97	98	99	100

Matrix for Facts

	0	1	2	3	4	5	6	7	8	9	10
0											
1											
2											
3											
4											
5											
6											
7											
8											
9											
10											

Moon Stations

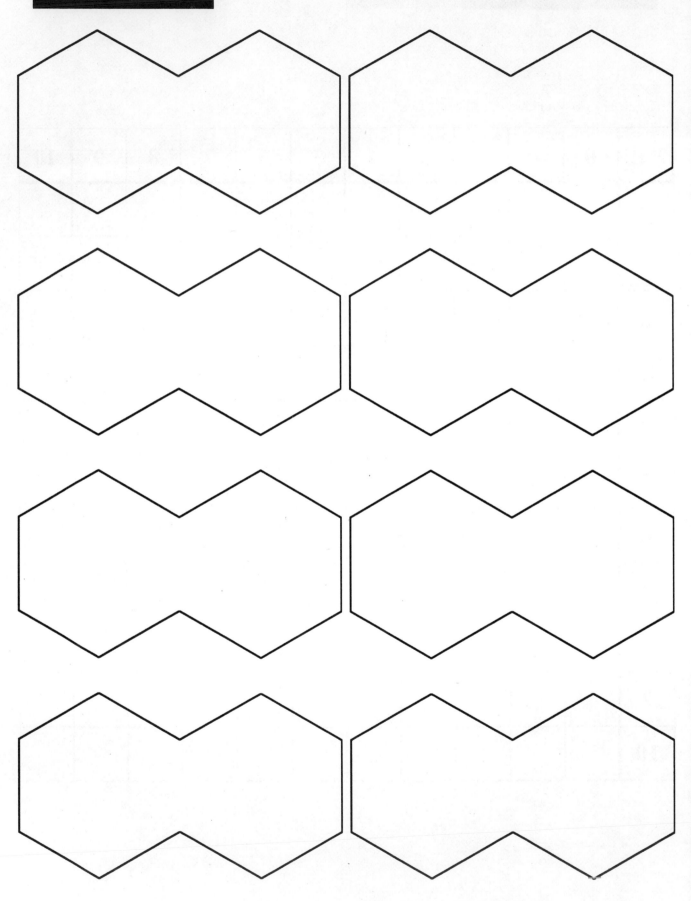

Materials:

permanent markers

old or new garden gloves: 1 pair per student

For Help with Facts

This activity can be done without gloves by writing the numbers on the finger tips with washable markers. It can also be copied and sent home for parents to use to help students after they master the process.

Anticipatory Set

Review, saying answers to facts with products up to 16. We will be doing garden glove multiplication today. Have students wear the gloves and put the numbers 6 to 10 on their fingertips, as shown in the illustration. (Numbers go on the palm side of fingertips.)

Ask: How can we use these to do multiplication facts? Let the students work in pairs to make some guesses about how this could work.

Procedure

With the numbers facing them and their thumbs pointed up, instruct the students to touch a 7 to an 8. Count the touching fingers and all fingers of lower numerical value, counting by tens. Students may find it easier to remember to count the touching numbers and all other fingers closer to the floor. All count chorally: 10, 20, 30, 40, 50.

Then, multiply the number of fingers remaining on each hand, rather than counting by tens. In this case there are 2 fingers left on one hand and 3 left on the other; $2 \times 3 = 6$. Add this product to the sum of the tens $(50 + 6 = 56)$.

Do the same activity with 6 and 7. (This is slightly harder, as the students must add 30 plus 12.) Give the students about 5 to 10 minutes to experiment with other pairs and to write down their results.

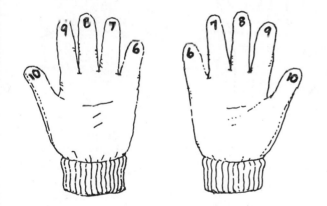

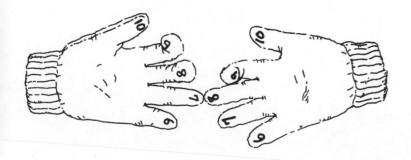

Multiplication Aids 2

Finger Nines

This is a hands-on way to multiply by nine.

Procedure

Have students place their hands on their desks with the backs of the hands up. To do 3×9, each student tucks under the third finger from the left, starting as they do when they read. See illustration below.

The answer is displayed with their fingers. The tens are to the left of the tucked finger, and the ones are to the right of the tucked finger. The number is read, as usual, from left to right.

Repeat with 4×9. This time the students tuck under the fourth finger from the left before reading the untucked fingers to the left and the right.

Have the students practice other nines facts, writing down the results and checking with each other to make sure they understand the procedure.

Practice and Extension

Use garden glove multiplication to discover and write down lists of $\times 6$, $\times 7$, and $\times 8$ facts. Use finger nines to write down $\times 9$ facts. Have the students work in small groups and check each other.

Have students look for patterns in their lists of $\times 9$ products. For each product, the tens digit is always one less than the number which was multiplied by nine, and the sum of the tens digit and the ones digit is always nine. Example: $7 \times 9 = 63$. Six is one less than the seven; $6 + 3 = 9$.

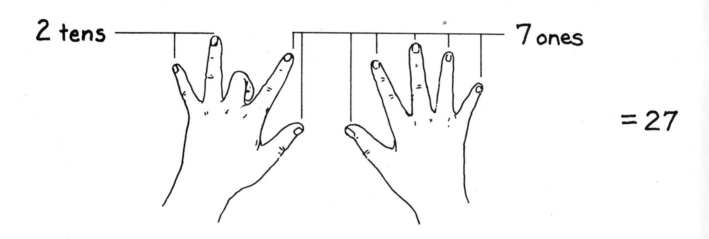

2 tens   7 ones   = 27

Multiplication Clue Rhymes

3 and 7 played cards;
Lenny won.
They played the game of 21.

3 and 6 are legal teens;
See them now,
They are 18.

3 and 8; 4 and 6; 2 and 12;
All stand at Denny's door,
Let them in . . . all 24.

4 and 7 stand at the gate,
Plenty old to make a date;
They are 28.

4 and 8 lost dirty shoe(s),
Help them find all 32.

Multiplication Clue Rhymes

6 and 7 are sort of blue,
What an age to be—
It's 42!

6 and 6 play
Pick up sticks,
They pick up all 36.

6 and 8 hurry
So they won't be late;
They equal 48.

Clue for 7 and 8—COUNT
1 2 3 4 5 6 7 8
Strike out 1 to 4 and
$56 = 7 \times 8$.

7 and 7 stand in a football line;
See them play;
They're the 49(ers).

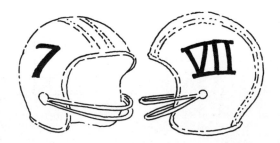

8 and 8 fell on the floor,
Pick them up;
They're 64.

Multiplication/Division Table

	0	1	2	3	4	5	6	7	8	9	10
0	0	0	0	0	0	0	0	0	0	0	0
1	0	1	2	3	4	5	6	7	8	9	10
2	0	2	4	6	8	10	12	14	16	18	20
3	0	3	6	9	12	15	18	21	24	27	30
4	0	4	8	12	16	20	24	28	32	36	40
5	0	5	10	15	20	25	30	35	40	45	50
6	0	6	12	18	24	30	36	42	48	54	60
7	0	7	14	21	28	35	42	49	56	63	70
8	0	8	16	24	32	40	48	56	64	72	80
9	0	9	18	27	36	45	54	63	72	81	90
10	0	10	20	30	40	50	60	70	80	90	100

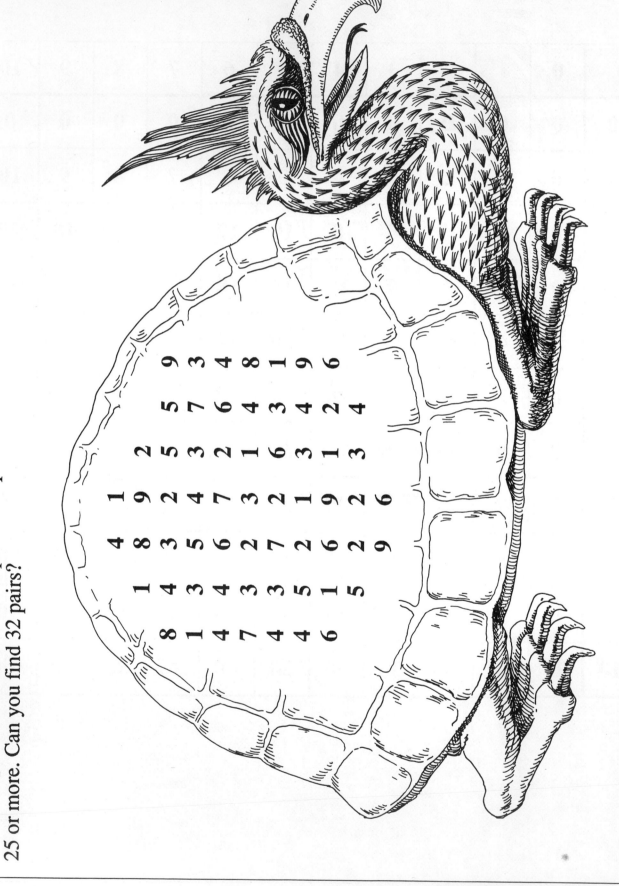

Circle all pairs of numbers whose product equals 25 or more. Can you find 32 pairs?

This animal is a _____

Number Find—Sample 2

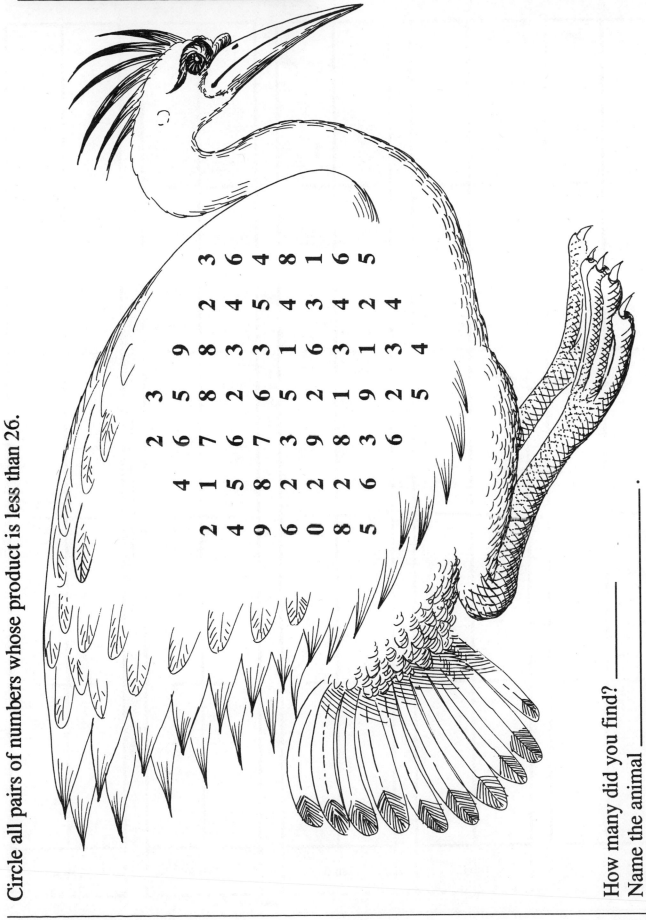

Circle all pairs of numbers whose product is less than 26.

How many did you find? _____

Name the animal _____.

Write a story about it on the back of this sheet.

Number Line 0 to 25

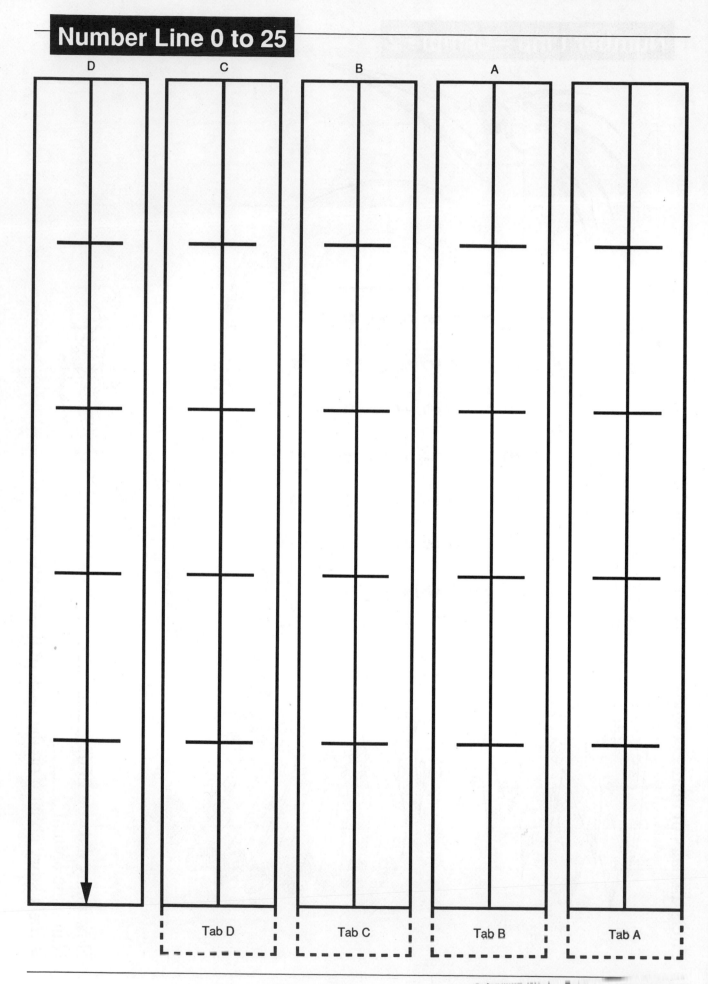

D   C   B   A

Tab D   Tab C   Tab B   Tab A

Number Line 0 to 100

D   C   B   A

Tab D   Tab C   Tab B   Tab A

Number Line 0 to 1000

C   B   A

Tab C   Tab B   Tab A

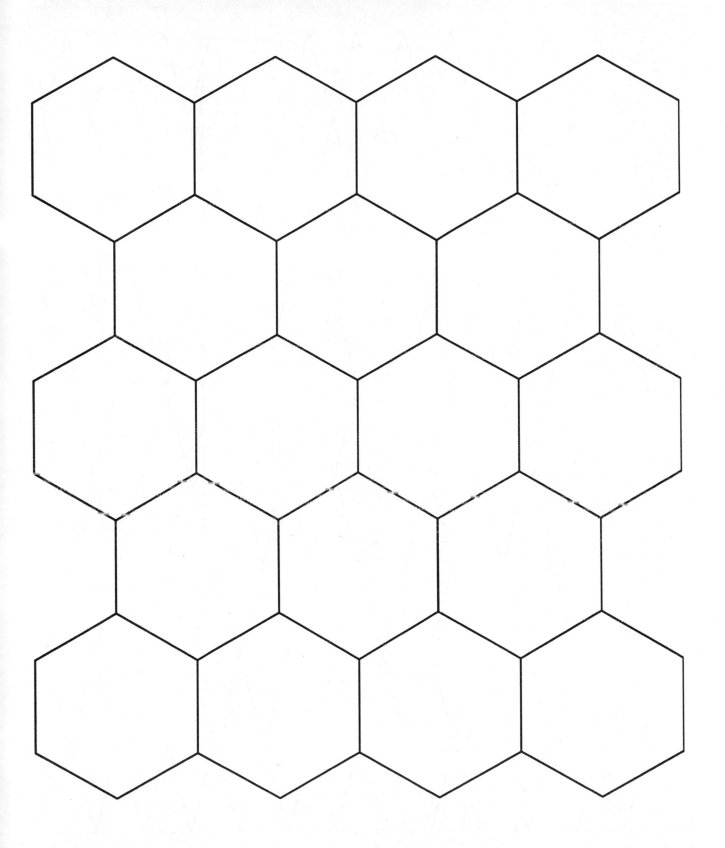

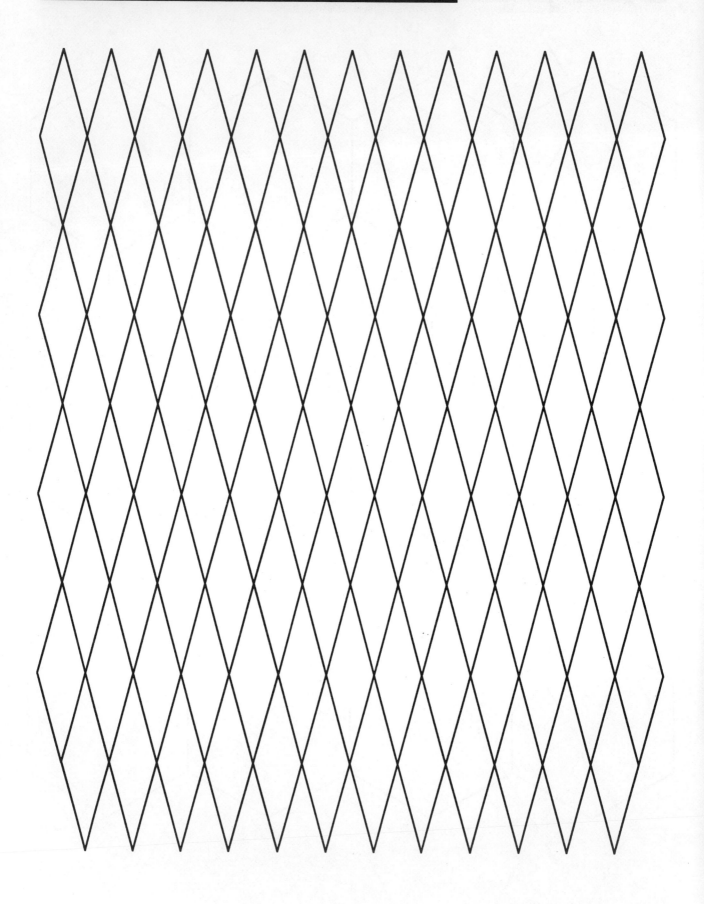

Pattern Blocks: Orange Squares

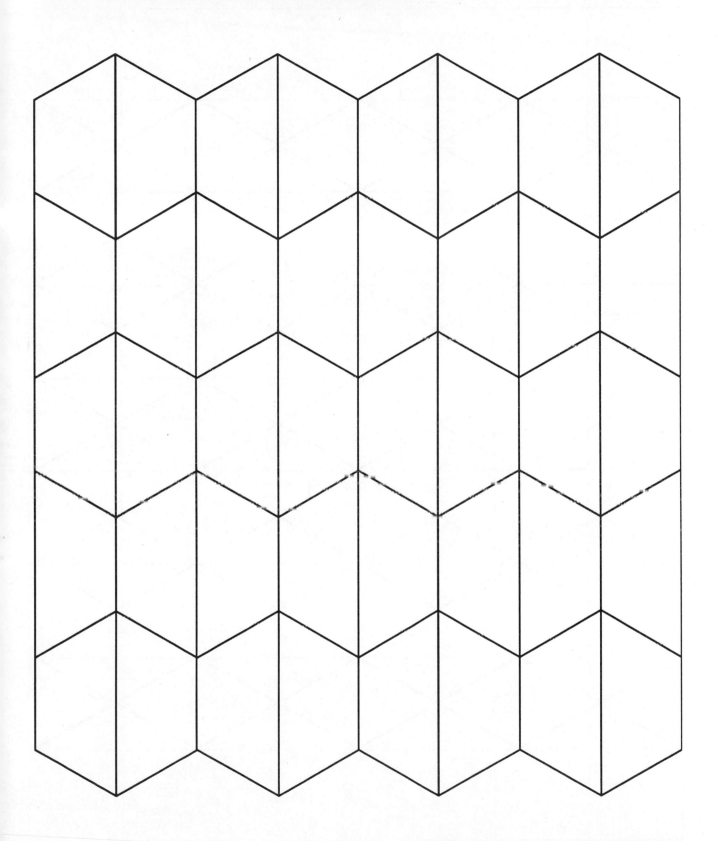

Pattern Blocks: Green Triangles

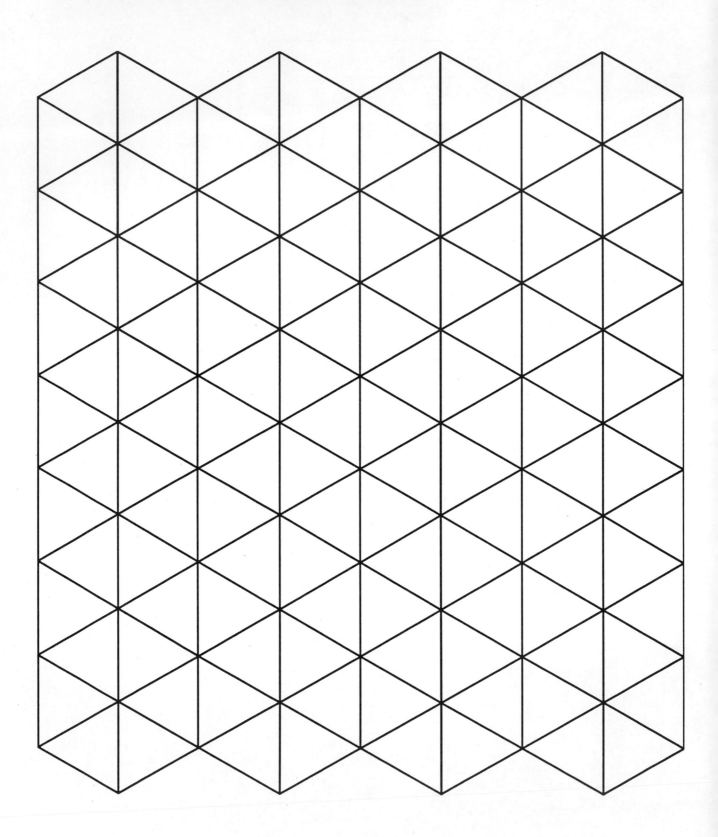

Place Value Mat Decimal Extension

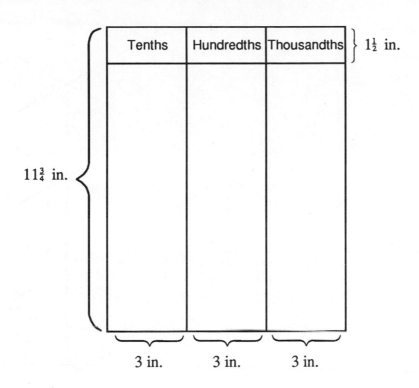

Use 12" × 18" tag board, cut to $11\frac{3}{4}$" × 18".

Adjust directions according to need:

Decimals to tenths:
3" × $11\frac{3}{4}$" per student

Decimals to hundredths:
6" × $11\frac{3}{4}$" per student

Decimals to thousandths:
9" × $11\frac{3}{4}$" per student

- Draw a line $11\frac{1}{2}$" down from the long edge.

- Starting at the left, draw two vertical lines 3" apart.

- Tape to right side of file-folder place value mat. Extension will fold inside mat.

- Place a large adhesive dot on label line between ones and tenths as a decimal point.

Place Value Mat to Hundreds

Ones

Tens

Hundreds

Place Value Mat to Thousands

Thousands	Hundreds	Tens	Ones

Rounding Rhyme

(Read using a RAP rhythm)

Mark the place,	**<u>3</u>** 4 2
Look to the right.	
Four or less are out of sight.	**<u>3</u>** 4↗ 2↗

Five and up	+1 **<u>3</u>** 6 2
Will buy one more	
Before they, too, are out the door.	**<u>4</u>** 6↗ 2↗

In those empty	**<u>3</u>** 0 0
Right-hand spaces,	
Zeros keep the proper places.	**<u>4</u>** 0 0

Rounding Rhyme

(Read using a RAP rhythm)

Mark the place,	**<u>3</u>** 4 2
Look to the right.	
Four or less are out of sight.	**<u>3</u>** 4↗ 2↗

Five and up	+1 **<u>3</u>** 6 2
Will buy one more	
Before they, too, are out the door.	**<u>4</u>** 6↗ 2↗

In those empty	**<u>3</u>** 0 0
Right-hand spaces,	
Zeros keep the proper places.	**<u>4</u>** 0 0